Beginning
Literacy
with
Language

This book is printed on recycled paper. ♻

Young Children
Learning at
Home and School

Beginning
Literacy
with
Language

edited by

David K. Dickinson, Ed.D.

Center for Children and Families, Education Development Center
Newton, Massachusetts
and
Center for the Improvement of Early Reading Achievement
Ann Arbor, Michigan

and

Patton O. Tabors, Ed.D.

Harvard Graduate School of Education
Cambridge, Massachusetts

·P·A·U·L·H·
BROOKES
PUBLISHING C°

Baltimore • London • Toronto • Sydney

Paul H. Brookes Publishing Co.
Post Office Box 10624
Baltimore, Maryland 21285-0624

www.brookespublishing.com

Typeset by A.W. Bennett, Inc., Hartland, Vermont.
Manufactured in the United States of America by
The Maple Press Co., York, Pennsylvania.

All of the individuals in this book have been given pseudonyms to protect
their privacy, and some identifying details have been changed.

Storybook excerpts in Chapters 2 and 5 are reprinted by permission from the
following sources:

The Very Hungry Caterpillar by Eric Carle, copyright © 1969 by Eric Carle. Used
by permission of Philomel Books, an imprint of Penguin Putnam Books for
Young Readers, a division of Penguin Putnam, Inc.

Animals in the Wild: Elephant by Mary Hoffman. Copyright © Belitha Press Ltd
1983, 1988. Text copyright © Mary Hoffman 1983, 1988.

What Next, Baby Bear! by Jill Murphy, copyright © 1983 by Jill Murphy. Used
by permission of Dial Books for Young Readers, an imprint of Penguin Putnam Books for Young Readers, a division of Penguin Putnam, Inc.

Library of Congress Cataloging-in-Publication Data
Beginning literacy with language : young children learning at
   home and school / edited by David K. Dickinson and
   Patton O. Tabors
      p. cm.
   Includes bibliographical references and index.
   ISBN 1-55766-479-X
    1. Language arts (Preschool).   2. Home and school.
  I. Dickinson, David K.   II. Tabors, Patton O.

  LB1140.5.L3 B44   2001
  372.6—dc21   00-051887

British Library Cataloguing in Publication data are available
from the British Library.

Contents

About the Editors

David K. Dickinson, Ed.D., Senior Research Scientist, Center for Children and Families, Education Development Center, Inc., 55 Chapel Street, Newton, Massachusetts 02458, and Affiliated Researcher, Center for the Improvement of Early Reading Achievement, University of Michigan School of Education, 610 E. University Avenue, Ann Arbor, Michigan 48109; DDickinson@edc.org.

After 5 years of experience teaching in elementary schools in the Philadelphia area, Dr. Dickinson attended the Harvard Graduate School of Education and then served as Director of Teacher Education at the Child Study Department at Tufts University and joined the Education Department at Clark University in Worcester, Massachusetts, where he received tenure. He moved to the Education Development Center (EDC) in 1994 to join the team that developed the Early Childhood Generalist certificate for the National Board for Professional Teaching Standards. In 1995 he established the New England Research Center on Head Start Quality, which examined the impact of Head Start on children's language and literacy development and on families, with special attention to the development of children whose first language is Spanish. He and Catherine Snow received the initial funding that launched the Home–School Study of Language and Literacy Development in 1987, and he directed the school portion of the study during the preschool years.

Drawing on early results from this study, he and colleagues at EDC developed the Literacy Environment Enrichment Project, an approach to helping preschool teachers and their supervisors adopt more effective practices to support children's language and literacy. He and others at EDC are developing and researching a version of this program that will be delivered using the Internet in combination with interactive television. His work has been published in numerous articles, and he has edited two other books, *Bridges to Literacy: Children, Families and Schools* (Blackwell, 1994) and *Handbook of Early Literacy Research* (co-edited with Susan Neuman, Guilford Press, 2001). He also is co-author (with Miriam W. Smith, Angela Sangeorge, and Louisa Anastasopoulos) of a set of tools for evaluating the quality of literacy support in early childhood classrooms.

Patton O. Tabors, Ed.D., Research Associate and Instructor, Human Development Department, Harvard Graduate School of Education, 306 Larsen Hall, 14 Appian Way, Cambridge, Massachusetts 02138; patton _tabors@harvard.edu.

Prior to beginning her doctoral studies at the Harvard Graduate School of Education in 1981, Dr. Tabors was an elementary school teacher and a childbirth educator. During her doctoral studies she focused on first and second language acquisition in young children. Her qualifying paper and dissertation research, based on 2 years of ethnographic investigation in a nursery school classroom, described the developmental pathway of a group of young children learning English as a second language. She was able to use this information as the basis for the material in *One Child, Two Languages: A Guide for Preschool Educators of Children Learning English as a Second Language* (Paul H. Brookes Publishing Co., 1997).

Since 1987, Dr. Tabors has been the research coordinator of the Home–School Study of Language and Literacy Development in collaboration with Catherine Snow and David Dickinson. During this time she has also directed research related to low-education and low-income mothers reading to their preschool-age children as part of the Manpower Development Research Corporation evaluations of two welfare-to-work projects—New Chance and JOBS—and for the Harvard Language Diversity Project, a subproject of the New England Research Center on Head Start Quality, directed by David Dickinson. Dr. Tabors's latest research—a longitudinal project that is following the language and literacy development of Spanish-speaking children from preschool to second grade—combines her interests in early language and literacy development and second language acquisition in young children.

About the Contributors

Diane E. Beals, Ed.D., Assistant Professor of Education, University of Tulsa, 600 South College Avenue, Tulsa, OK 74104; diane-beals@utulsa.edu.

Dr. Beals has been a member of the Home–School Study of Language and Literacy Development research team since 1989, beginning with her doctoral studies in the Human Development and Psychology Department at the Harvard Graduate School of Education. Her research on the project has focused largely on the use of narrative and explanation in family mealtime conversations, beginning with her dissertation, completed in 1991, *"I Know Who Makes Ice Cream": Explanations in Mealtime Conversations of Low-Income Families of Preschoolers.* From 1991 to 1999, she was an assistant professor at Washington University in St. Louis. At the University of Tulsa, she has continued her research on the development of children's ability to use different genres of discourse. In collaboration with Patton Tabors, she has expanded this work to examine the informativeness of the use of rare vocabulary within these discourse genres and situations.

Linda R. Cote, Ph.D., Assistant Professor, Department of Psychology, Marymount University, 2807 North Glebe Road, Arlington, VA 22207; LRCote3@aol.com.

Dr. Cote is Assistant Professor of Psychology at Marymount University and has recently completed a postdoctoral fellowship at the National Institute of Child Health and Human Development. Her research examines the influence of adult–child interaction on infants' and young children's development. She worked on the Home–School Study of Language and Literacy Development while a doctoral student in developmental psychology at Clark University in Worcester, Massachusetts, assisting with data transcription and coding and overseeing data management and analysis efforts connected to the preschool data.

Jeanne M. DeTemple, Ed.D., Private Consultant, Harvard Graduate School of Education, Larsen Hall, Third Floor, 14 Appian Way, Cambridge, MA 02138; detemple@post.harvard.edu.

Dr. DeTemple was a preschool and kindergarten teacher for 11 years before she began graduate studies in Human Development and Psychology at the Harvard Graduate School of Education. She began work with the Home–School Study of Language and Literacy Development during its first year, working on all aspects of the project but particularly focusing on book reading and literacy in the home. Her dissertation, *Book Reading Styles of Low-Income Mothers with Preschoolers and Children's Later Literacy Skills*, was based on data from the study. As coordinator of the Harvard Observational Studies of Mother–Child Interaction, Dr. DeTemple examined book reading and other language tasks in large-scale, national studies of teen mothers and welfare families. Her research interests include language development of internationally adopted children.

Jane R. Katz, M.Ed., Harvard Graduate School of Education, Larsen Hall, Third Floor, 14 Appian Way, Cambridge, MA 02138; jane_katz@ gse.harvard.edu.

Ms. Katz is a doctoral student in the Human Development and Psychology Department at the Harvard Graduate School of Education. She is interested in young children's social understanding, their language use in peer relationships, and cultural factors that help to shape their play. She is working on a dissertation investigating possible relationships between day care teachers' attitudes and practices and young children's social behavior and language use. Before beginning her graduate studies, she was a day care teacher for 12 years, teaching primarily 2- to 3-year-olds.

Michelle V. Porche, Ed.D., Research Analyst, Harvard Graduate School of Education, 303 Larsen Hall, 14 Appian Way, Cambridge, MA 02138; michelle_porche@gse.harvard.edu.

Dr. Porche first became involved with the Home–School Study of Language and Literacy Development as a doctoral student in the Human Development and Psychology Department at the Harvard Graduate School of Education, participating in many phases of data collection and analysis. For her dissertation, she tested the long-term effects of maternal involvement at school and at home on young children's academic achievement, using longitudinal data collected from the low-income families participating in the study. She continues to consult on this project, analyzing links between parent involvement and children's language and literacy development, as well as exploring motivation and achievement outcomes for these children as they move through adolescence. Currently, Dr. Porche also is a Research Scientist at Wellesley College Center for Research on Women, working on several projects related to adolescent development and gender.

Kevin A. Roach, Ed.M., Harvard Graduate School of Education, Larsen Hall, Third Floor, 14 Appian Way, Cambridge, Massachusetts 02138; kevin_roach@gse.harvard.edu.

Mr. Roach is a doctoral student in the Human Development and Psychology Department at the Harvard Graduate School of Education. He joined the Home–School Study of Language and Literacy Development in 1994. He is interested in literacy development over time and how longitudinal methods can be used to better describe and explain children's literacy development. His dissertation examines how children's preschool-age language and literacy experiences relate to the shift from narrative literacy to information-text literacy in middle school. In addition to doing graduate work, he is a seventh- and eighth-grade science teacher in Cambridge, Massachusetts.

Miriam W. Smith, Ed.D., Private Consultant

Dr. Smith began work on the Home–School Study of Language and Literacy Development in 1987 as a data collector during the preschool visits and continued working with the study for 12 years. Those early visits (and their resulting data) were instrumental to her dissertation, which she completed in 1996 at Clark University in Worcester, Massachusetts. Since then, Dr. Smith has continued her research and professional development work in preschool classrooms through work with the Center for Children and Families at the Education Development Center in Newton, Massachusetts, as well as in other settings.

Catherine E. Snow, Ph.D., Henry Lee Shattuck Professor of Education, Harvard Graduate School of Education, 313 Larsen Hall, 14 Appian Way, Cambridge, Massachusetts 02138; catherine_snow@harvard.edu.

Dr. Snow received her doctorate in psychology from McGill University and worked for several years in the linguistics department of the University of Amsterdam studying first and second language acquisition. After Dr. Snow joined the faculty of the Harvard Graduate School of Education, her research interests expanded to include the relation of language to literacy development, social and familial influences on literacy development, and the acquisition of literacy and school success in bilingual and language minority children. She has co-authored books on language development (*Pragmatic Development,* with Anat Ninio, Westview Press, 1996) and on literacy development (*Unfulfilled Expectations: Home and School Influences on Literacy,* with Wendy S. Barnes, Jean Chandler, Irene F. Goodman, & Lowry Hemphill, Harvard University Press, 1991). From 1997 to 1998, she chaired the National Research

Council Committee on the Prevention of Reading Difficulties in Young Children, which produced a report that has been widely adopted as a basis for reform of reading instruction and professional development throughout the United States. From 2000 to 2001, she served as the president of the American Educational Research Association. She has been the principal investigator of the Home–School Study of Language and Literacy Development since 1987.

Zehava O. Weizman, Ed.D., Research Assistant Professor, Department of Speech and Hearing Sciences, Faculty of Education, The University of Hong Kong, Prince Philip Dental Hospital, Fifth Floor, 34 Hospital Road, Hong Kong, Hong Kong, SAR CHINA; zweizman@hkucc.hku.hk.

Dr. Weizman received her doctor of education degree in Human Development and Psychology in 1996 from the Harvard Graduate School of Education. Her dissertation, *Sophistication in Maternal Vocabulary Input at Home: Does It Affect Low-Income Children's Vocabulary, Literacy, and Language Success in School?* was based on data from the Home–School Study of Language and Literacy Development. Her primary research interest is the role of vocabulary acquisition in facilitating language and literacy development. She is currently involved in cross-linguistic projects investigating early vocabulary and grammatical development in Cantonese- and English-speaking preschoolers in Hong Kong and in the construction of a Cantonese/Mandarin communicative development inventory.

Foreword

The early years of life are a time of making connections. Young children connect first with their families and then with others beyond that closely knit circle. The cycle continues as children repeatedly connect what they already know to new learning. So it is fitting that a book such as this one deepens and strengthens our understanding of some of the most important connections that occur during early childhood.

Across the different chapters, various authors thoroughly document and clearly describe three critical connections that occur for preschool-age children. The first is the reciprocal relationship between language development and early literacy. Of course, we have known for some time that these two critical learning areas are interrelated. But over the years our understanding of that relationship has been transformed. In the past it was assumed that the primary task of children in the preschool years was exclusively language development. It was thought that children first developed language well during the years prior to schooling and then learned reading and writing when formal education began in kindergarten or first grade.

With the increased availability of early literacy research on younger children in naturalistic settings, we have come to recognize that children acquire important early literacy skills beginning at birth and that success in reading at first grade is largely dependent on how much children have learned before they get there. Unfortunately, this knowledge has led some to overemphasize early literacy skill acquisition and neglect language development. So we have the potential for another of those inevitable pendulum swings that characterizes education, from an overemphasis on language to an overemphasis on literacy.

Fortunately, the work of Drs. Dickinson and Tabors and their colleagues should prevent such a mistake. Their research demonstrates the indelible connection and reciprocal relationship between language development and literacy. Moreover, they illustrate the complexity of language development and the nature of the adult's role in supporting it. Different kinds of experiences contribute to different aspects of children's language learning. All are important, whether conversation during mealtime, reading, or pretend play.

This book draws a second connection that is essential for the healthy development of preschool children—the link between home and school. Indeed, the name of the major study which frames this book is the Home–School Study of Language and Literacy Development. By studying young children's development in both contexts, the authors have made a significant contribution to the literature, most of which tends to look at child development either at home or in a group program. With this research we gain a fuller picture of how children's experiences influence and are influenced by each context, as well as the relationship between them. The complex tasks of language and literacy development occur over time and are the result of many cumulative experiences both in the home and beyond. This book reveals both the similarities and differences and identifies ways that home and school, parents and teachers, can complement each other to support children's optimal development and learning.

The third connection made in this book is perhaps the strongest—the almost seamless blend of research and real life. The research presented here comes at a most opportune time for early childhood education. The field is experiencing intense political pressure to demonstrate positive learning outcomes for children served. Likewise, more and more educators are expected to adhere to practices that are "research based," those that have been found to result in educational benefits. The Home–School Study provides powerful evidence in support of certain, specific early childhood classroom teaching practices, as well as excellent guidance for parents and other adults who work with children at home or in the community. This kind of research-based guidance is exactly what early childhood teachers, parents, and community members need to improve their work with children. Perhaps most important, the study's researchers find that these practices, although present to some extent in these homes and schools, are not as common as we would like to see, especially for the children who are most in need.

But what gives this research and this book life are the real children and families we come to know and care about in its pages. Astra, Casey, Mariana, and Todd, as well as the other children described here, are what motivate the reader to move from experience to experience, from setting to setting, to find out what happens to them and what kinds of teaching and parenting practices are the most effective for them. We really want them to have the very best and to succeed. In so many ways they are typical preschool children—eager to learn, curious, full of wonder, wanting to please. In other ways, they are each so unique with their own strengths, interests, and needs. By the end, we have been given such well-drawn pictures of them that we want to know them in person, to reach out and be able to clutch a hand, share a laugh or a lap for a story. The authors create these intimate connections at least in part by introducing them as members of families so that we also know their parents and siblings and by continuing to study their development within the family context.

The other real life we come to know in this book is the life of typ-ical preschool classrooms and teachers. Here we see much that is famil-iar—routines, materials, and experiences that are repeated daily in preschools throughout the country. Unfortunately, we also see many missed opportunities for learning, especially for enriching language or supporting early literacy. We see teachers who tend to dichotomize their approach, emphasizing either social development or academic instruc-tion almost exclusively. This research clearly teaches us that neither set of practices alone is good enough. Children need teachers who engage in extended conversation throughout the preschool day, who introduce rare words through book reading or other experiences, and who pro-vide content-rich curriculum to support vocabulary development and a broad range of language and literacy skills. Many teachers are doing a good job under difficult circumstances, but few of the classrooms observed in this book provide all of the good things necessary for opti-mal language and literacy development. Early childhood teachers and teacher educators have much to learn from the research-based practices and the children and families described in this book.

The strength of this book is its foundation in a well-designed, well-implemented longitudinal study of young children's language and lit-eracy development at home and in school. This book is only the beginning of the story, just as early childhood is only the beginning of the life experience. Much that is of great significance will follow. But the results reported here clearly demonstrate the relationship between early experiences and later success in school. The complete study has followed these children into high school, providing a wealth of data to inform parents and teachers.

But we need not wait until the final conclusions are drawn. The connection is well established for the long-term effects of early experi-ence. This book strengthens that connection by giving specific guidance about what types of early language and literacy experience have the most positive and lasting consequences. Given the difficulties that many children experience in school, especially children from low-income families, early childhood educators have a responsibility to heed the real-life lessons pointed out by this important research. And our coun-try has a responsibility to provide the necessary resources to ensure that well-qualified teachers and well-equipped early childhood programs are available for all children.

Sue Bredekamp, Ph.D.
Director of Research
Council for Professional Recognition
Washington, D.C.

Acknowledgments

Our first and greatest debt of gratitude is to the families who have been participants in the Home–School Study of Language and Literacy Development. They welcomed us into their homes for repeated and extended visits, they granted permission for us to observe and record their children in their classrooms, and they allowed us to assess their children on language and literacy tasks year after year. We also owe a great debt of gratitude to the preschool and kindergarten teachers who were willing to have researchers spend time in their classrooms, audiotaping and videotaping them and the children, and to speak with us about their practice. Without such cooperation this study would not have been possible.

We also are eternally grateful to the graduate and undergraduate students and the research assistants who have worked on the project. The work reported in this book reflects Herculean efforts by many, as each step of the process presented its own challenges, drudgery, and rewards. To all who helped with data collection, transcribing, coding, data cleaning, and data analyses we simply say thank you. We hope the good company, the joy of glimpsing delightful children and families, and the satisfaction of contributing to an important effort are what you recall most vividly.

While we cannot individually acknowledge many who contributed to this effort in important ways, a few played such critical roles that they must be mentioned individually. Stephanie Ross and Petra Nicholson took leadership roles in data collection in the homes and in the preschool and kindergarten classrooms attended by the children in the Home–School Study. We are particularly in their debt for their determination and sensitivity in staying in touch with the families and the teachers, as well as for their ability to win the cooperation of the children in the study. Furthermore, we would like to thank Brenda Kurland for her efforts as watchdog of transcript and data quality, as indefatigable analyst "on call," and as queen of definitions and magnets.

In addition, David Dickinson wants to thank Kathi Holmes, for her endless analytical efforts on the classroom data, and Margo Sweet, for her willingness to create and recreate tables, review manuscript, and handle a myriad of details. He also thanks Ann B. Morse for her patience and good humor as this book took form. He also acknowledges his daughters Liza and Jessa, who learned language and became literate in parallel with the children in this book, providing vivid examples of the processes we explored, and he thanks Mary Fischer for her support during the long years of data collection and analysis.

And finally we wish to acknowledge the many funders of this study, including the Ford Foundation (Grant No. 880-0381) for its willingness to launch this effort, the Spencer Foundation (Grant No. 9501083), which funded us during the primary school grades, the Head Start Bureau, which supported this work with Grant No. 90CD0827, and the W.T. Grant Foundation (Grant Nos. 95-1703-95 and 99-1703-95) for its support as we continued the study into the middle and high school grades. For support during the final writing phase, we thank the Head Start Bureau (Grant No. 90YD0017) and the Center for the Improvement of Early Reading Achievement for its support of David Dickinson.

Beginning
Literacy
with
Language

Chapter 1

Language Development in the Preschool Years

Catherine E. Snow,
Patton O. Tabors, and David K. Dickinson

Parents and early childhood educators want children to become good readers and writers. They are fully aware of how crucial reading and writing skills are to school success. But parents and early childhood educators may not know how important language development is in preparing preschool-age children for later literacy development. The purpose of this book is to provide information to parents and early childhood educators about the connections between young children's early language development and later literacy development so that they can support and facilitate young children's language skills both at home and in early care and education.

The material in this book is based on the findings of a research project, the Home–School Study of Language and Literacy Development, carried out since 1987 by a collaborative research team composed of members from the Harvard Graduate School of Education; Tufts University; Clark University; and the Education Development Center in Newton, Massachusetts. Researchers in this study have collected data in the homes and preschool, elementary school, and high school classrooms of a group of children from low-income families, starting when the children were 3 years old. This book reports on the information from the preschool and kindergarten period—a period that we have found makes crucial contributions in preparing children for their later literacy achievement.

In this book we not only present the findings from this research study but also make the findings come alive by presenting examples of the types of language that were audiotaped during visits to the homes and classrooms of these children, as well as quotes from teacher and mother interviews. Furthermore, to personalize the findings of the study, we have chosen four children and their families as examples of the overall group of children being studied. These children and their families are introduced later in this chapter, and further information about their lives—at home and in preschool—appears throughout the chapters that follow.

IMPORTANCE OF LANGUAGE DEVELOPMENT IN THE PRESCHOOL YEARS

As mentioned, the focus of the Home–School Study is on young children's literacy development—how children become readers and writers. When we started this study, there was considerable interest in class differences with regard to children's literacy achievement. These socioeconomic differences led many researchers to focus on children's access to information about literacy as a determinant of their success in school. It was argued that before ever getting to school, some children have lots of opportunities at home to learn letters and sounds and to learn about handling books, making lists, writing notes, and other uses of literacy. These opportunities, which are generally available to children in more middle-class homes, might explain their literacy success.

Yet other researchers noted the robust relationship between reading achievement and vocabulary and suggested that individual and social class differences in children's vocabulary development would explain their reading outcomes. Although little work had been done on precisely how children developed larger vocabularies, it was clear that, in general, children from families with higher incomes and children of more highly educated mothers did have larger vocabularies at school entry than children from low-income families. This, too, might explain differences in reading outcomes.

Though we were not rejecting either of the previous explanations, we started this study with an interest in another aspect of language skill as well. We were particularly interested in children's experience with language that replicates some of the demands of literacy—that is, talk that requires participants to develop understandings beyond the here and now and that requires the use of several utterances or turns to build a linguistic structure, such as in explanations, narratives, or pretend. We call this type of talk *extended discourse,* and looking for differential opportunities to develop extended discourse skill was one of the goals of this project.

Why would anyone seek the sources of success at literacy in the domains of vocabulary or extended discourse skills? Ultimately, reading is a linguistic activity. Of course, there are specifically literate facts and procedures having to do with letters and with the sounds they represent that readers need to master. Increasingly, though, evidence suggests that learning about letters and sounds presupposes knowing a lot about the internal structure of words—knowledge that is hard to acquire without first knowing a lot of words. Furthermore, even the fairly straightforward system of how letters represent sounds is simplified if children can learn and practice it by reading words that they know. This is why beginning reading texts include only simple and highly frequent words.

All too soon, however, children, including many who have a reasonable grasp of letter–sound correspondences, encounter difficulties in reading if the texts they are reading in third or fourth grade use words they are not familiar with. Furthermore, such texts may deal with topics the children know little about, making comprehension a chore. And such texts are likely to include complex grammar and to use specific linguistic cues to indicate how the information presented is organized. If children have not learned these grammatical and organizational constructions orally, they will have difficulty using them while reading. We started this project, then, with the hypothesis that young children's language learning constitutes one important early step toward success in literacy.

In 1987, when we began the data collection process, the conviction that language was a crucial precursor to literacy was based more on intuition than on evidence. More recently, though, this conviction has come to be widely shared. Whereas we have long known that children's word knowledge is closely linked to reading accomplishments (Anderson & Freebody, 1981), more recent work has shown strong relationships between children's early language skills and later reading abilities (Hart & Risley, 1995; Purcell-Gates, 1988; Walker, Greenwood, Hart, & Carta, 1994). Other studies have shown that the levels of language and literacy skills that children have in kindergarten and first grade are strong predictors of achievement many years later (Cunningham & Stanovich, 1997).

Understanding the role of language in fostering children's later literacy skills has important implications for all children, but it is of special significance for those who work with low-income families. Children growing up in these families are more likely to have difficulties with learning to read than children from middle-class families, and these gaps in performance begin to appear as early as kindergarten (Brizius & Foster, 1993; Dickinson & Snow, 1987). These early disadvantages can have serious long-term effects because children who experience reading difficulties in the middle grades are more likely than children without reading difficulties to drop out of school later in their academic careers (Barrington & Hendricks, 1989; Lloyd, 1978).

Differences in early achievement linked to parental income levels suggest that families vary in how effectively they support children's early language growth. One factor seems to be that children in families with limited incomes typically have fewer conversations with adults and are exposed to far fewer words than more advantaged children are. As a result, they tend to have smaller vocabularies than children from families with higher incomes (Hart & Risley, 1995). Also, these children tend to have fewer opportunities to hear books read aloud on a regular basis, thereby losing out on an experience known to support language growth (Zill, Collins, West, & Hauskin, 1995). Though many studies have confirmed the existence of quantitative differences in the language experiences of children from low- and higher-income families, the Home–School Study presents an in-depth view of how parents and children in low-income families actually talk together in a variety of settings and the ways that this talk can support children's language growth.

The fact that children from low-income homes need additional support during the preschool years has long been recognized, as evidenced by the establishment of Head Start in the 1960s. Research conducted over two decades has given some evidence that Head Start and preschool programs similar to Head Start are benefiting low-income children (Barnett, 1995). Also, several major studies that have evaluated overall program quality have found that strong programs are more likely than programs of lesser quality to benefit preschool-age children (Bryant, Lau, Burchinal, & Sparling, 1994; Layzer, Goodson, & Moss, 1993; McCartney, Scarr, Phillips, & Grajek, 1985). Studies such as these look across many programs, identifying fairly general features of programs that are indicators of high quality, such as qualifications of staff and the adult–child ratio. Our research complements these studies by taking a more fine-grained look at the nature of what goes on in preschool classrooms. As a result, the findings of the Home–School Study can provide some concrete guidance regarding areas of preschool classroom life that are most likely to have beneficial effects on children's language and literacy development.

Educational Implications

The importance of early childhood experiences with rich language input and appropriate exposure to the uses and functions of print was emphasized by a series of national organizations in the late 1990s. The International Reading Association and the National Association for the Education of Young Children jointly issued a position statement in 1998 emphasizing the appropriateness of providing rich language and literacy experiences in preschool classrooms. A report from the National Academy of Sciences entitled *Preventing Reading Difficulties in Young Children* (Snow, Burns, & Griffin, 1998) argued that attention to children's language and literacy environment during the preschool years constitutes a crucial prevention effort and concluded, furthermore, that preschool classrooms serving young children at risk are often somewhat impoverished language and literacy environments. Federal legislators further endorsed this perspective when writing the Head Start Amendments of 1998 (PL 105-285) by setting specific goals for the knowledge about literacy and language that 4-year-olds in Head Start would be expected to achieve.

In other words, there seems to be a consensus that the environments of young children should be language-rich, with lots of words used during interesting conversations, and should be enriched by stories and explanations. The study presented in this book shows what such an environment looks like at home and at preschool, under which conditions it is likely to emerge, and precisely how it relates to children's learning.

In this book, we present descriptions of the language and literacy environments of 74 young children from low-income families. We relate our descriptions of the crucial features of those environments—at home and at preschool—to the children's accomplishments at the end of kindergarten. Of course, children at the end of kindergarten are typically not yet reading, so they can hardly yet have started to display reading difficulties, either. But we do know from a wide array of research carried out by others and from our own ongoing studies of the children in the Home–School Study that some aspects of children's skills at the end of kindergarten predict later literacy accomplishments quite well. Thus, even though the topic of this book is limited to the very beginnings of reading development, we have a basis for saying that the features of homes and preschool classrooms that support children's literacy in kindergarten help to pave the way for children's later reading success.

Although the analyses in this book are focused on the preschool to kindergarten period of the Home–School Study, the research team has continued to visit the homes and classrooms of the children in the study. Home visits were made to the families when the children were 7, 9, and 12 years old, and school visits have been made each year up to sophomore year in high school except for fifth and eighth grade. During these visits we have continued to collect data on language interactions at home, on family support for literacy skills, on types of reading instruction in classrooms, and on the children's accomplishments in the domains of language and literacy. The final chapter provides some updates concerning the participants of the study when they were in fourth and seventh grade.

So, why does the information in this book stop at kindergarten? We have found that knowing how well these children did on language and literacy tasks as kindergartners tells us a lot about how they went on to succeed or to struggle in their later schooling. Furthermore, we have found that the foundation of the children's kindergarten abilities can be found in their home and preschool classroom language and literacy environments. What the Home–School Study tells us is that the preschool years are critical.

ANATOMY OF A RESEARCH STUDY

The original plan of the Home–School Study was to identify and collect data on the language and literacy environments of a group of children from low-income homes beginning when the children were 3 years old. To compose a complete picture of the children's language and literacy environments, we chose to visit both their homes and their preschool classrooms. We were not sure whether the best situation would be for children to have a maximum amount of the experiences we expected would be crucial in promoting development—an additive model—or whether some absolute level of exposure would be sufficient. But we did want to be in a position to integrate information about the types of experiences that the children were having both at home and in preschool.

Focus on Low-Income Families

In designing the study presented here, we decided early on to focus our attention on children who were growing up in low-income families. The focus on low-income families was in part a response to our limited funding and our desire to learn a lot about every family involved in the study. More important, though, it reflected our sense that researchers had developed good descriptions of the language and literacy environments of middle-class children but had little sense of the range of variation within families of more limited economic and educational means. Given the high risk of reading difficulties among children from low-income families and the large variability in home and school support for language and literacy development within this group, we believed that concentrating our efforts on this population was the practical research strategy.

Finding the Children for the Study

With initial funding in hand, the first job was to find the children and families we would study. We contacted a wide variety of child care programs and health centers serving low-income families in eastern Massachusetts. Many of the programs were willing to help us by distributing letters of introduction to the parents in their programs. These same programs invited us to visit their classrooms if the parents agreed to become part of the study.

Families were included in the study if they spoke English at home and were eligible for Head Start or subsidized child care or health care. In the spring of the first year, we were able to locate 40 three-year-old children whose families agreed to join the study; the following spring, we were able to add 43 children to the project, for a total of 83. Of these 83 children, 74 were still part of the study when we did our kindergarten assessments 3 years later. (Of the families that no longer wished to participate, some told us that they had only agreed to be part of the study while their children were in preschool and did not wish to continue their children's participation in the study in kindergarten.) These 74 children and their families, which we named the *kindergarten sample,* are the children and families we report on in this book.

The group of children who make up the kindergarten sample is split almost evenly between boys and girls (36 male and 38 female). They come from a variety of racial/ethnic backgrounds: 47 of the children are Caucasian, 16 are African American, 6 are Latino, and 5 are biracial. At the time of the first home visit, when the children were 3 years old, 28 of them lived in one-parent households (all mothers), 40 of them lived with two adults (not always a mother and father), and 6 children lived in households with three to five adults. Eighteen of the children were single children at the time of the first home visit, thirty had one sibling, nineteen had two siblings, and seven had four or five siblings.

The mothers in the kindergarten sample were asked a series of questions about their own backgrounds and about family circumstances. Twenty-three of the mothers reported that they had less than a high school education, thirty mothers reported that they had a high school diploma or a general equivalency diploma (GED), and twenty-one of the mothers said that they had some education or training beyond high school, although none of the mothers had a bachelor's degree at the beginning of the project. Thirty-two of the mothers reported that their family had an annual income of less than $10,000; nine reported $10,000–$15,000 per year, thirteen reported $15,000–$20,000 per year, eight reported $20,000–$25,000 per year, and twelve reported more than $25,000 per year. Thirty-one of the mothers reported that the family income came from Aid to Families with Dependent Children (AFDC; since renamed Temporary Assistance for Needy Families), and the remainder reported a variety of other income sources, including their or their spouse's or partner's income, disability payments, or child support. Not surprisingly, 18 of the 28 mothers who were single parents were in the lowest income category and were receiving public assistance.

One of the important aspects of this group of children and their families is the variety of family configurations and family circumstances. The kindergarten sample is, in fact, a group of children whose situations varied a great deal from the beginning and continued to change as the project continued. Because we would be looking at some of these family background factors as possible influences on the children's language and literacy development, we viewed this group's variety as one of the strengths of the sample.

Collecting Information at Home and at Preschool

From the beginning of the project, we knew that we wanted to collect information both at home and at preschool, but we needed to decide what information to collect and how to collect it. We made two different sets of plans: one for home visits and the other for preschool visits.

Home Visits   We decided that home visits would be made once each year to the families in the Home–School Study during the first 3 years, when the children were 3, 4, and 5 years old. We believed that it was important to go to the children's homes rather than ask the mothers and children to come to a laboratory setting. In spite of the fact that we knew that home visits could well present the challenges of crowd management, interruptions, and recording quality, we believed that dealing with these distractions would be well worth it. We believed that preschool-age children and their mothers would respond more readily in the comfortable surroundings of their homes than they would in an unfamiliar and perhaps intimidating laboratory setting.

The home visitors contacted the individual families and set up the appointments for the home visits. Occasionally, it was necessary to make two visits to a family to get through the entire interview and the language activities, but for most of the families, the home data were collected during a single visit of 1–3 hours.

Two types of information were collected during the home visits:

1. *Language data:* The home visitors audiotape-recorded the mothers and children while they read books, told a story about a recent event, and played with toys, and the visitors asked the mothers to audiotape-record a family mealtime after the completion of the home visit.

2. *Mother interview data:* The home visitors, who were trained in interview techniques, asked the mothers to talk about their life circumstances and about the types of activities that the family participated in. These interviews were audiotape-recorded.

Preschool Visits   The children in the study were visited once each year in their preschool classrooms (64 were visited as 3 year olds; 74 were visited as 4 year olds). Visits began as the children arrived in the morning and usually extended through lunchtime. The school visitors sometimes returned for a second day to complete data collection.

Life in preschool classrooms is complex, with children moving frequently and activities changing often. Along with changes in activities come changes in the kinds of conversations that occur. For example, during group times, children spend time listening to and responding to teachers, whereas during free play they talk to other children or may even play silently. Because we expected that the activity settings would have an important impact on conversations, we decided to audiotape during all major activity periods, with the exception of gross motor and outdoor time. Thus, we have data from group meeting times, large-group book reading, small teacher-led groups, free play, mealtimes, and transition times.

An added challenge was that we were interested in the child's as well as the teacher's conversations during the day. We knew that a particular child whom we were observing might spend relatively little time talking with the teacher during our visit; therefore, we decided to audiotape both the teacher and the child throughout the day. Finally, because we were especially interested in book reading, we videotaped a full-group book-reading session in each classroom.

We collected three types of data in each classroom:

1. *Language data:* The child who was participating in the Home–School Study and the lead teacher in the classroom each wore a small backpack with an audiotape recorder that had a small lapel microphone that could be attached to a shirt collar. The child and the teacher were taped individually in as many of the activity settings of inter-

est as possible. While making these recordings, an observer made notes about what the child was doing and to whom he or she was talking. We collected more than 1½ hours of talk for each child and comparable amounts for teachers at each visit. We also obtained language data from the videotapes we made of book-reading sessions.

2. *Classroom curriculum data:* The preschool visitors examined displays and materials in various areas (for example, book reading, writing, science) in order to learn about the nature of the curriculum in the child's classroom. The visitors also completed items from the Early Childhood Environment Rating Scale (ECERS; Harms & Clifford, 1980) that related to language, furnishings, and general classroom climate.

3. *Teacher interview data:* The school visitors interviewed the teachers about the makeup of their classroom groups (numbers of children, children's ages). The teachers were also interviewed about how they planned to use time during the day and responded to questions designed to reveal their beliefs about pedagogy.

Kindergarten Measures

When the children in the project were 5 years old, we had them complete a series of language and literacy tasks that we call the *SHELL–K* (the School-Home Early Language and Literacy Battery–Kindergarten; Snow, Tabors, Nicholson, & Kurland, 1995). These tasks were designed to capture the spectrum of skills that young children are known to need when they begin the process of literacy acquisition. Although these tasks were administered at home, the children completed them without support from their mothers. A brief description of each of these tasks follows. More detailed information about the SHELL–K, including scoring and descriptive statistics of the kindergarten sample's performance on these measures, can be found in the appendix (see Table A1.1).[1]

Narrative Production   The Narrative Production task, also called the Bear Story, involved having the children look at a sequence of three slides that depict a family of teddy bears in an adventure involving a flyaway kite and a baby bear falling from a tree. The children were allowed to look at the three slides in sequence as often as they wished,

---

[1]The SHELL–K was described previously in Snow, Tabors, Nicholson, and Kurland (1995). The statistics reported for this test in the appendix are slightly different from the previously published data because the sample reported on here is slightly different from that in the 1995 article.

but they were asked to put down the slide viewer before telling the story. Here is a sample Bear Story:

> One's rolling around in their little wagon and then one of the bears got up the tree and got the kite and then he fell down and they said, "Speak to me," and he didn't answer 'cause he fell off the tree.

Picture Description   For the Picture Description task, the children were handed a slide viewer with a slide in it depicting a brightly colored scene outside a circus tent. The administrator asked the children to look carefully at the picture and then, while looking at it, describe the picture as completely as possible because "I have a whole lot of slides here, and I need to know which one this is." A sample picture description follows:

> A girl with her father and all the balloons. And a girl with her mother. And a clown with an umbrella. And a guy who's selling tickets. And a flag on the top of it. And a clown with red shoes is standing on a board.

Definitions   For the Definitions task, the children were asked to define 14 familiar nouns (*alphabet, bicycle, bird, clock, diamond, donkey, flower, foot, hat, knife, nail, stool, thief,* and *umbrella*) using the prompt, "What's a/an _____?" Sample responses for *bird* were "It's a flying animal with wings" and "It flies and lives outside." Sample answers for *thief* included "Is a person who sneaks around and gets things that doesn't belong to them" and "A thief is for stealing stuff."

Superordinates   In the Superordinates task, we asked the children to supply a superordinate term. The request took a form such as "What are tables and chairs?" After the child answered, he or she was asked, "Can you tell me another kind of furniture?"

Story Comprehension   In the Story Comprehension task, the children and the assessor looked at the book *The Snowy Day* by Ezra Jack Keats (1962). As the assessor read the book aloud, she inserted various scripted comprehension questions such as the following:

- What did Peter use to make another track in the snow?
- Where did the snow come from?
- Why didn't Peter join the big boys?
- What does it mean to "pretend"?
- Where is the snowball? Where did it go? What happened to it?

Emergent Literacy   To assess the children's level of emergent literacy, we chose five subtasks from the Emergent Literacy strand of the Early Childhood Diagnostic Instrument: The Comprehensive Assessment Program (CAP; Mason & Stewart, 1989). These subtests were Writing Concepts, Letter Recognition, Story and Print Concepts, Sounds in Words, and Environmental Print.

Receptive Vocabulary   The children's receptive vocabulary skill was measured with the Peabody Picture Vocabulary Test–Revised (PPVT–R; Dunn & Dunn, 1981). For this task, the children were shown panels of four pictures, the assessor named one of the pictures, and the children were asked to point to the picture that matched the word said by the assessor.

Processing the Information from the Home and Preschool Visits and the SHELL–K Tasks

As the home and preschool visits and the SHELL–K tasks were completed, the research team began the process of turning the information that was collected into data that would be useful in our analyses. The information from the mothers' and teachers' interviews and the observations from the preschool visits were entered into databases in preparation for statistical analyses. The audiotapes of the conversations between the children and their mothers during the activities at home, the family mealtime conversations, and the teachers' audiotapes were all transcribed using a transcription system called *CHAT* [2] that made it possible to use computer coding and analysis. Audiotapes of the children's conversations at preschool were coded directly from the audiotapes, bypassing the time-consuming step of transcribing. All of the SHELL–K tasks were scored or transcribed and coded according to established guidelines.

During this part of the process, steps were taken to ensure that the data that were developed from the visits represented, as closely as possible, the variety and depth of information that had been collected. For the audiotape transcripts this required a verification process during which the audiotapes were initially transcribed by one researcher—often the person who had made the visit—and then verified by a second researcher. All of the interview and testing data were also double

---

[2]Codes for the Human Analysis of Transcripts (CHAT) is an integral part of the Child Language Data Exchange System (CHILDES) project (MacWhinney, 2000), which makes it possible for child language researchers to use software called *Child Language Analysis* (CLAN) to perform analyses. For more information about this transcription system, see MacWhinney (2000).

entered to be sure that mistakes were not made in that part of the process. Furthermore, during the course of coding the material, the research team always computed reliability statistics on the coding schemes. This meant that two individual coders had to code a proportion of the material and reach sufficient agreement (greater than .85) in order to ascertain that the coding scheme was being used reliably. No coding scheme was used until this level of reliability was reached. By using these techniques we ensured the quality of the data that we would be using in the analyses that resulted in the findings that we are reporting in this book.

Statistical Analyses on the Home–School Study Data

There were three main types of analyses used on the data from the study: descriptive analyses, correlational analyses, and regression analyses. In each of the chapters, the authors mention the types of analyses that they are reporting on, but much of the technical information about the statistical analyses is available in the appendix at the end of the book. Following is a short description of each of the three main types of analyses we used on the data.

Descriptive Analyses   Once we had all of the data from a particular transcript, interview, or task ready for analysis, the first step was to look at the basic statistics on the data. One of the basic statistics that we knew would be important was the *range* or overall spread of the values on the variables. We wanted to know, for example, whether the children scored differently, and how differently, on the tasks on the SHELL–K. Researchers refer to this as *variability* or *variation*. Obviously, if all of the children had the same scores there would not be any reason to pursue the question, "Are there factors that are related to and can help explain the differences in children's scores?" Fortunately we found that we had a considerable range of values on all of the data that we have used in this book, making the possibility of significant findings more likely.

Another basic statistic used often in the book is in reference to the *mean,* or *average.* The mean, or average, is a measure of central tendency, computed by adding all values and then dividing by the total number of values. So, for example, if we wanted to know how tall the *average* girl was in a fourth-grade classroom, we would measure the height of all of the girls, total those results, and divide by the number of girls in the classroom, giving us the average on that variable for the sample. Although we know that there are shorter girls or taller girls in the group, the average gives us a way to compare this group with, for example, a group of girls in tenth grade, whom we would expect, *on average*, to be taller than the fourth graders. For the Home–School Study, we often wanted to know how certain kinds of talk were used, *on average*, so that we could compare that type of talk over time or between groups.

Correlational Analyses   In a correlational analysis, values from two variables are compared with each other to see what the relationship might be between them. For example, if we were to record the height and age of a group of students in an elementary school and graph the results, we would find that younger children tend to be shorter than older children, as can be seen in Figure 1.1.

Even though not all children grow at the same rate and not all children achieve the same height, there is still a relationship between age and height. In this case, we would say that there is a *positive* relationship between age and height because high values on one are related to high values on the other. A *negative* relationship is one in which low values on a variable are related to high values on another variable, such as amount of television watching and school achievement as measured by grade point average, as shown in Figure 1.2.

As well as wanting to know whether there is a positive or negative correlation between two variables, it is also important to know how strong the relationship is. The strength of the relationship is expressed as a correlation coefficient, or *r value*, from -1.0 (for a perfect negative relationship) to $+1.0$ (for a perfect positive relationship). Looking at Figure 1.1, it is clear that the two variables are strongly related because they tend to cluster tightly along the diagonal. This figure represents a positive correlation of .78. On the other hand, in Figure 1.2, the relationship is not as strong because the two variables are more loosely clustered along the diagonal. This figure represents a negative correlation of $-.30$.

In addition to wanting to know how strong a relationship is, we also want to know what the probability is that the result is likely to have occurred by chance. Researchers report the probability of a result having occurred by chance as a *p* value. In this book, we have reported, on occasion, results that are likely to have occurred by chance less than 10 times in 100 ($p < .10$), but more frequently we have reported results that are likely to have occurred by chance less than 5 times in 100 ($p < .05$) or better ($p < .01$, less than 1 time in 100; $p < .001$, less than 1 time in 1,000; or $p < .0001$, less than 1 time in 10,000). By combining the information about the *r* value (representing the *magnitude* of the relationship between two variables) and the *p* value (representing the *likelihood of that result having occurred by chance*), researchers can express how strong and how significant the relationship is between two variables.

In the Home–School Study, correlational analyses were used to

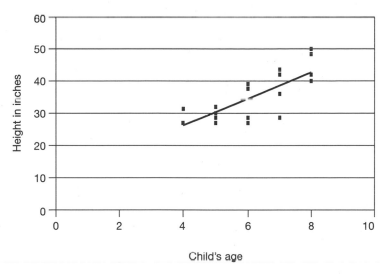

Figure 1.1.   Height of children 4–8 years old (showing positive relationship between age and height).

show how various aspects of the children's home and preschool environments were *related* to each other and how they were *related* to the results on the SHELL–K. Although correlation procedures are extremely valuable to our understanding of *relationships* between variables, they do not provide evidence of *causation*.

Regression Analyses   The final type of analysis that was used in the Home–School Study was regression analysis. Researchers often describe regression equations as a tool to predict an *outcome* based on *predictor* variables. In the Home–School Study we used regression analysis to look at how the various aspects of the children's home and preschool environments (the *predictors* for the study) were related to the results on the SHELL–K (the outcome measures for the study) when they were *combined* in the same analysis.

Regression results are expressed in terms of an r^2 *value*, which is a value between 0 and 1 that tells the researcher what percent of the variation in the *outcome* variable is explained by the combination of *predictor* variables in the model. The closer the r^2 value is to 1, the better job the researchers can be said to have done in identifying *predictors* for that *outcome*. Typically, in social sciences research, the r^2 value tends to be small, and many research studies describe significant findings with an r^2 of less than .20.

Variable Names   The names of the variables used in these analyses have been represented in two ways. Variable names that indicate a

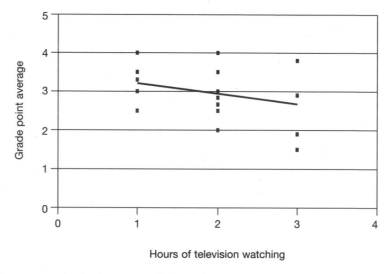

Figure 1.2. School achievement of television viewers (showing negative relationship between achievement and hours of viewing).

score from a particular task, transcript, or data source collected at a particular time (for example, *narrative talk* or *ratio of teacher talk to child talk*) are italicized. Variable names that represent a composite of variables (see Chapter 6; for example, Home Support for Literacy or Quality of Teacher Talk) are capitalized. Background control variables (see Chapter 6; for example, Mother's Education or Family Income) and variables from the kindergarten measures (for example, Narrative Production) are also capitalized.

THE PORTRAIT CHILDREN

As we began to write this book, we decided to spotlight a few of the children in the study whose stories could illustrate the results for the whole kindergarten sample. Obviously, each of the sets of background characteristics of the sample mentioned previously—such as family income and income source, mother's education, number of children in the family—refers to real children and their families. But it is difficult to remember this fact when the discussion is about the whole group and includes a lot of numbers. For this reason, we chose some children for whom we would present more detailed and qualitative information. We hope that by the end of this book, these four portrait children and their families will be familiar to readers and that their experiences—at home and at preschool—will have helped explain the influences that shaped the children's language and literacy skills.

Selection of the Portrait Children

A number of criteria were used in selecting the portrait children. We wanted them to represent some of the diversity of the overall sample in terms of ethnicity, family circumstances, and configurations, and, of course, we wanted to have complete information from their home and preschool environments. We were not looking for children who did particularly well or particularly poorly on our language and literacy assessments. We reviewed our home and preschool information, the information from the mother and teacher interviews, and the results of the kindergarten assessments and then chose four children and their families.

Introducing the Children and Their Families

The four children who were selected were Mariana, Casey, Astra, and Todd. Each of these children and their families are introduced next.

Mariana   During the first 3 years of the study, Mariana lived with her mother and her older brother, Manny, on the second floor of a two-story building in a residential section of the city of Boston. The neighborhood in which Mariana's family lived was quiet and was located some distance from any main thoroughfares, which could have been inconvenient for them because they did not have a car. However, this did not deter Mariana's mother, Elena, from getting out with her children and taking advantage of a wide variety of activities, such as skating, ballet, and karate. She told a home visitor, "It's boring staying in the house. . . . Even if I don't have a car, I'll take them, because I want them to have the things I never did."

After the visit when Mariana was 3 years old, the home visitor described the apartment:

> [It] was very clean and tidy, with hardwood floors and big rooms. The living room was to the left, off the hallway, part of a large, open room that had shelves and a plastic-covered table at one end and couches at the other. There were big windows and plenty of light. The shelves did not have a lot of books on them; children's books were kept in a lower drawer. The table with the plastic cloth looked like it was used for painting and coloring activities and probably not for eating. At the opposite end of the room from the table and shelves, three couches were arranged in a U shape with their backs to the front windows. The couches were probably old and in disrepair, since they were covered with sheets of fabric and [were] very uncomfortable to sit on. I saw a Bible (I think in Span-

ish or in Spanish and English) down near the children's book
drawer, but no other adult literacy materials, i.e., no newspapers
or magazines. . . . It looked like Mariana and Manny shared a
large bedroom at the back of the apartment (with two twin beds
in it). The bathroom and kitchen were both large, homey, and
clean. The kitchen had a table in it and appeared to be used for
meals (as opposed to the crafts table in the living room).

Mariana was described by one home visitor as "a very pretty and
quiet little girl, shy at first" and by another as "very sweet, agreeable,
and thoughtful." Her brother, less than a year older than Mariana, was
described by his mother as hyperactive: "So active!" Her mother said
about Mariana, "She likes to play with dolls. She loves coloring, playing. She doesn't read, but you know I do that for her. Watching TV, she
does that. I have to supervise her. . . . She likes looking at the books
and pretend she's reading."

The main source of income for the family throughout this period
was AFDC. Mariana's mother, Elena, rented the family's apartment
with help from a housing subsidy. Although she had had jobs in the
past—working in a convenience store and a dentist's office—Elena had
not worked or gone to school since the birth of her two children. When
asked about her family's income, Elena remarked, "We are poor, you
know, below the poverty level, believe it or not." She concluded, "See,
that's my job, staying with my kids. . . . Yeah, I devote myself to them,
you know. I don't have anything else other than my kids."

Elena was born and raised in Mexico, and her native language is
Spanish. She finished "something that is considered high school in Mexico" before moving to Texas. Once in Texas, she attended high school
in an intensive English as a Second Language program, completing a
high school diploma in a year and a half. She mentioned that she would
like her children to speak Spanish, but English was used almost exclusively in her home. In later interviews, she said that she speaks English
with an accent and that she thought that this was a source of prejudice
against herself and her children.

Mariana did not attend any type of group program as a 3-year-old
and was in a 4-year-old and then a 5-year-old kindergarten in a Boston
public school. Elena remarked about Mariana's 4-year-old kindergarten
experience, "The teacher says she's very proud of Mariana." When
asked whether she had been to visit the school during Mariana's 5-year-
old kindergarten year, Elena replied that she had been to the open house
and that she also had visited the classroom to observe and had been in
contact with the school by letter and by telephone. She remarked, "I
show up if I have to. Unexpectedly. They don't like it, you know, but

sometimes you have to. There are occasions that I really have to talk to them." When asked about making future decisions about Mariana's school placement, Elena said it would be hard for her to decide because "She's gonna be full-time. I need to know who she's gonna be with. . . . Who's her teacher, who the kids are, everything, you know? I'm a mother. . . . I need to know everything, and I'm concerned."

Casey   During the first 3 years of the study, Casey lived in a two-bedroom unit in a housing cooperative with his mother and father and his older brother, Mack. The housing cooperative was located in a town on the border of the city of Boston that was described by a home visitor as "having a distinctly urban feel to the place." Outside, there was a small play space that was in constant use by the children from the co-op. The home visitor described the apartment as "compact" but "very comfortably decorated with wall-to-wall carpeting, a big dining room table, matching furniture, and pictures of the children on the walls."

A home visitor described Casey as a "wunderkind" who "does well in school and sports, . . . is extremely responsible, and good-looking to boot." His mother even called him a "Bread and Circus kid" who ate his vegetables and everything else.

Casey's mother, Stacy, had grown up in this town and had completed her high school education at the local high school. She was 18 when Mack was born. She reported that the family frequently visited with her sister, who lived only a few minutes away, and also spent time with her grandmother in a nursing home nearby. Stacy reported that her sister as well as a sister-in-law and some friends provided lots of babysitting help for the family. She also occasionally used a babysitter who lived nearby, but she preferred having the children spend time with her relatives because "I just can't afford a sitter." During this time, Stacy was working 5 mornings a week at an answering service and 3 nights a week at a local department store. Casey's father, Gary, drove a delivery van from 8:00 A.M. to 4:00 P.M., then he took care of the boys in the evenings while Stacy worked. The reported combined annual family income at the first home visit was more than $25,000.

Casey's father's involvement with the family was extensive. Stacy reported that Gary prepared breakfast for the boys every morning, played a lot of different types of sports with Casey and Mack, and read books with them every evening. The only activity that Gary was not involved in was Stacy's and the boys' weekly attendance at church and Sunday school.

Casey attended preschool at his neighborhood school every morning and then was enrolled in the extended-day kindergarten until

2:00 P.M. every day. Stacy reported that she had started Casey at the extended-day kindergarten for only 2 days per week but that she had "ended up putting him in for 5 days 'cause he liked it so much he didn't want to come home, and [the] days he didn't go to extended day he was upset, so I just paid the money to send him and he went 5 days, and I used to pick him up at 2:00 instead of picking him up at 11:15." When asked what Casey's teachers had told her about him, she replied, "All of the teachers that he's had so far I've gotten along with, and I think they're good, and Casey's had, I think, a nice experience with them all. They all pretty much say the same thing about him: that he does fine in school and he's an easy kid."

Astra   During the first 2 years of the study, Astra lived with her mother, Solange, and her father, Truman, in a small apartment in a predominantly minority neighborhood of Boston. By the third year of the study, Astra's little brother, Shandi, had joined the family. Originally from Jamaica, Astra's parents had been living in Boston since Astra was little and had a large group of relatives, including Solange's mother, sister, sister's son, and several brothers, who lived nearby or were temporarily living with them.

The home visitor for the first visit wrote:

> The neighborhood was rundown, with several open lots and boarded-up buildings nearby. . . . Inside the building there was very little light. After undoing a series of deadbolts on the front door, Astra's mother, Solange, let us into the apartment. . . . The living room had two couches facing each other with a coffee table in between. There were several pictures on the wall, a mixture of Caribbean and religious themes. . . . There were also family photographs. A grandfather clock stood in one corner and a guitar in another. . . . Next to one of the couches, there were bookshelves that contained full sets of the *Encyclopedia Britannica* and the *Young Children's Encyclopedia.*

The same home visitor described Astra as "one of the most charming children I've ever met . . . and socially very sophisticated." A later visitor described Astra as "an incredibly friendly, open, and chatty child." Her mother told an interviewer that Astra had a "vivid imagination, I mean vivid, vivid, vivid" and that "she chatters . . . she's always talking." Although Astra said she wanted to be a ballerina, her mother thought she might become a teacher or a lawyer because of her love of talking.

Astra's mother was a teacher at the child care center that Astra attended full-time when she was 3, 4, and 5 years old. Solange had originally trained as a teacher in a college in Jamaica, but she was continuing to take courses in education at the college level in Boston. Her husband, Truman, was a house painter. He was also an avid soccer player and often took Astra with him to the park for soccer matches. They also enjoyed watching cartoons together.

Between the two salaries she and her husband earned, Solange reported that their annual income was more than $25,000. Their living circumstances, however, seemed to indicate that their income may have been supporting quite a number of people beyond the nuclear family. During the interviews, Solange mentioned wanting to move to the suburbs or back to Jamaica, but they remained in the same neighborhood throughout this period. Solange commented in a later interview, "You know, we're living in the city, where we have to be streetwise and savvy."

Solange mentioned that it was very easy for her to check on Astra's progress at school, because she was a teacher at the same child care center that Astra attended. "But even if I wasn't working there, . . . I will stop and talk to the teacher because, when I was home on maternity leave, I went to speak to her [to] see what Astra was doing in school." When she was asked to reflect on Astra's first 2 years at the center, Solange replied, "I was quite satisfied because I think she was not pushed. You know, she learned; it was a gradual process. She wasn't pushed." When asked what she might have done during this time to help Astra learn, she answered, "I guess I just reinforced what her teachers over the years taught her. I didn't really do anything specific or special. I just did what they did over." But then she added, "I bought all kinds of books for her. She was into all kinds of book clubs, you know, because I think reading is important."

Todd   During the first 3 years of the study, Todd lived with his mother, Mary, and two older sisters, Darcy and Elaine, in a suburban town about half an hour from Boston. They lived in a five-room apartment in a two-family house that a home visitor described as "quite cramped and dilapidated," although "the outside of the house [was] well kept and there [was] a large yard for the children to play in."

A home visitor described Todd as a "very friendly, easygoing, agreeable kid . . . actually kind of goofy." Mary, however, mentioned during the home visit when Todd was 5 years old that he had had some problems with fighting on the bus to school and that he was not getting along with Elaine, the sister who is 2 years older than Todd. She also reported that his kindergarten teacher thought that he might not be going on to first grade, because "she said he's not mature enough."

Todd's abiding interest throughout this period was in dinosaurs. Mary mentioned that he liked to pretend he was a dinosaur, and, at the home visit when Todd was 5, he showed the home visitor a book and declared proudly, "This dinosaur book's my favorite book in the world." When asked how she would spend a special day with Todd, Mary replied that she would take him to the Museum of Science in Boston.

Mary, like Stacy, grew up in the area where she was living, and several close relatives were available to help her with the children on occasion. Mary had left school at age 15—"I moved out of the house, and I had to work"—but had received her GED at age 17. Her first child was born when she was 18. During the first three visits, Mary was receiving AFDC, which she supplemented by babysitting. She reported her income to be between $10,000 and $15,000. Todd's father apparently paid child support to the state so that it would be included as part of the AFDC payments.

Todd spent every weekend with his father during this period. His mother reported that his father did not do "anything active" with Todd but watched a lot of videotapes and television with him. When she asked Todd, "Does Daddy play with you?" he answered, "No, he never does." Mary had a steady boyfriend during this time, however, who sometimes watched television, read books, or played ball with Todd.

Todd was in a home-based Head Start program when he was 3 and at a center-based Head Start program at 4 years of age. At age 5, he attended a neighborhood school kindergarten class. All three of Mary's children had attended Head Start, and Mary was very enthusiastic about the program. "Oh, I really like the program a lot. I like the teachers. I think it's better than . . . like, I have friends, most—I don't know anybody who's on welfare—so most of their kids go to . . . preschools. And I just don't—that's not even close to what Head Start is." When Mary was asked if the program had made a difference to her, she replied, "I don't know whether it made any difference for me, because I didn't grow up in a welfare family . . . so I know a difference, and talking about people who don't know a difference and don't have anything to work with, and I think it really shows them a lot." When asked to think back over Todd's Head Start experience and whether she was happy with what he had gotten from it, she replied, "Oh, yeah . . . the confidence that they gave him and . . . socializing with other kids. Learning, too."

PURPOSE OF THIS BOOK

This book introduces the types of language and literacy environments that families like Mariana's, Casey's, Todd's, and Astra's provide for them at home, and the types of language and literacy experiences that children like Mariana, Casey, Todd, and Astra are exposed to in their preschool classrooms. Furthermore, it examines how the differences in these language and literacy environments make a difference in how well the children in the sample performed on language and literacy tasks in kindergarten. We believe that this information can be helpful to both parents and early childhood educators as they think about ways to encourage the language and literacy development of young children. Furthermore, we hope it is read by family visitors, parent educators, pediatricians, and all others interested in ensuring that every child has success in literacy.

Of course, the study described here is limited in a number of ways. The families we visited volunteered to be in the study, and, because we wished to focus on a low-income sample, all had limited economic and educational resources. We collected certain kinds of data in great depth and other kinds not at all. We describe these children and their families at a particular point in history and in a particular geographic region. We do not intend to use these data as a basis for prescribing how parents should raise their children nor which preschool parents should choose for their children. We do hope, however, that the descriptions of children's experiences are sufficiently rich that the reader understands how they might be replicated or avoided and—for this group of children— how aspects of their environments related to their own accomplishments. Such information is a starting point for developing strategies to ensure that every child has the best possible start in the acquisition of reading and writing skills.

How the Book Works

This book is divided into three sections. The first section presents the data and analyses from the home environments of the children in the Home–School Study, the second focuses on data about the preschool classrooms attended by the children when they were 4 years old, and the concluding section examines relationships between homes and schools.

The first section of the book includes information from the home visits that were made to the project participants when the children were 3, 4, and 5 years old. In Chapter 2, Jeanne DeTemple discusses language use and literacy practices related to book reading; in Chapter 3, Jane Katz discusses language used during toy play; and in Chapter 4, Diane Beals discusses two different types of talk—explanatory and narrative—found at mealtimes. In Chapter 5, Patton Tabors, Diane Beals, and Zehava Weizman present an analysis of the types of vocabulary that were used in all three of these conversational settings. In each of these chapters, transcript material from the four portrait children and other children from the study is presented. Each of these chapters also includes information about how home environment language and literacy practices are related to the language and literacy achievement of the children in the Home–School Study as demonstrated on the SHELL–K in their kindergarten year. At the end of each chapter, there are suggestions for parents about how to encourage language and literacy development at home with their children.

In Chapter 6, Patton Tabors, Kevin Roach, and Catherine Snow conclude the first section by introducing a final type of talk—science process talk—and by developing composite variables from the home environment data and reporting on models predicting achievement on three of the kindergarten assessments.

The second section of the book includes information about the preschool environments experienced by the children in the Home–School Study. In Chapter 7, Miriam Smith introduces several teachers and uses two case studies to describe patterns of classroom life seen in many of the classrooms of the children who participated in the study. She examines teachers' stated beliefs about instruction and relates them to the instructional practices that were observed. She also discusses the curriculum in the classrooms and examines some of the complex relationships between teachers' professional and ethnic backgrounds and their approach to working with young children. The chapter concludes with information about how the features of the classrooms discussed are related to the language and literacy achievement of the children in the Home–School Study as demonstrated on the SHELL–K in their kindergarten year.

In Chapter 8, David Dickinson examines book reading in the preschool classrooms, paying special attention to the conversations that occurred while books were being read aloud. This chapter uses examples from Mariana and Todd's classrooms when they were 4 years old to illustrate general patterns in how books were used in the study classrooms. The chapter concludes by reporting how teachers' book-reading styles and what they talked about during book reading were related to the language and literacy achievement of the children in the study as demonstrated on the SHELL–K in their kindergarten year.

In Chapter 9, Linda Cote focuses on mealtimes in the classrooms and describes how the role of teachers influences what occurs during mealtimes, using the contrasting mealtime experiences of Casey and Todd when they were 4 years old to illustrate her findings. The chapter concludes by reporting on how mealtime conversations were related to the language and literacy achievement of the children in the study as demonstrated on the SHELL–K in their kindergarten year.

In Chapter 10, David Dickinson looks at large-group and free-play times, using Astra's and Casey's classrooms to illustrate the variability in teachers' orientations to using varied vocabulary and engaging children in extended conversations. The chapter also identifies aspects of children's conversational experiences that are related to their subsequent language and literacy development and examines factors that might help account for variation in how teachers converse with children.

In Chapter 11, David Dickinson examines all facets of data collected when the children in the study were 4 years old and draws together the many dimensions discussed in earlier chapters of the second section of the book, including patterns of talk throughout the day, teachers' beliefs and approaches to planning their curriculum, and the nature of the curriculum that we observed in the classroom. He reports analyses that examine the overall impact of the children's preschool classroom experiences on their kindergarten language and literacy skills, after taking important aspects of the children's homes into account.

In the concluding section of the book, information about the home and school environments of the children in the Home–School Study is combined in different ways in the final two chapters. In Chapter 12, Michelle Porche focuses on the mother and teacher interviews when the children were in preschool and in kindergarten to see what the level of parent involvement in school activities was and how that involvement was perceived by the mothers and the teachers. The chapter concludes with analyses of the relationships between the mothers' and teachers' descriptions of parent involvement and the language and literacy skills of the children in the study when they were in kindergarten. In Chapter 13, Patton Tabors, Catherine Snow, and David Dickinson present the final analyses, looking at the combined role of home and preschool environments on three of the language and literacy assessments from the SHELL–K. Chapter 13 concludes with educational policy recommendations based on the findings of the Home–School Study from the preschool to kindergarten period.

Section I

Supporting Language and Literacy Development in the Home

Patton O. Tabors

As mentioned in Chapter 1, the research team for the Home–School Study of Language and Literacy Development was committed to visiting the families and children in their homes in order to sample language use in the home environment. There were a number of reasons that we thought that a home visit would be the best situation for collecting the type of language and interview data in which we were interested. First, by going to participants' homes, we eliminated the need for the mothers and children to come to a laboratory setting away from their home and neighborhood, which would have required transportation over considerable distances for many of the families. We knew that some families did not have their own cars and that public transportation often would have involved lengthy time in transit. Second, we felt that the mothers and young children might well have been intimidated by coming to a university laboratory setting. We did not believe we could set up a laboratory situation that would provide the necessary level of comfort to ensure that their interactions would be as natural as possible. Finally, we felt that we would be able to gain valuable extra information from the home visits, including observations of the types of neighborhoods and housing where the families were living.

Having decided that we would have interviewers travel to the homes of the families in the study, we next needed to make plans about what they would do during the home visits. One option would have been to ask the mothers to continue their regular daily activities during the visits and record what went on during that time. The concern about this approach was that it would get extremely variable data that would be very difficult to compare across families. Therefore, we decided to have the home visitors ask all of the mothers and children to do the same activities so that the variability would be in how the mothers and children went about doing the same task, not in which activities they chose to do during the visits.

A second decision was involved in planning the home visits. We decided very early in the planning of the project that audiotape recorders rather than videotape cameras would be used for recording interactions. We believed that videotape cameras, although in common use at the time for informal entertainment purposes, would add an intimidation factor to the visits. In fact, the one time that a home visitor asked permission to videotape-record—when visiting twins and needing to identify which twin was talking—the mother agreed with reluctance. Fortunately, the twins' voices were different enough that we were able to tell them apart on audiotape, and the home visitor did not need to videotape again. This experience did, however, reinforce our decision to use audiotape recorders for data collection in the home situation.

How did we go about doing the home visits? When a round of home visits needed to be scheduled, home visitors were hired or identified from among the students already working on the study, and specific families were assigned to them. Occasionally, home visitors went alone to the home, but more often, particularly if there were other children in the family who might need to be entertained, the primary home visitor would recruit a second visitor to go along.

The home visitors arranged the time for the visits by telephone, collecting as much information as possible about how to find the home. (Detailed maps were an important early purchase of the study.) All visits were done during the day at the convenience of the mother and child. Efforts were made to assign the same visitor to a family in subsequent years, but many families saw a different set of home visitors each year. At each home visit, information was collected about names and telephone numbers of people who would know where the families were from one year to the next. This information often turned out to be important because there were times when families in the study moved, changed telephone numbers, or had their telephones disconnected. By having auxiliary contacts, we were able to find families with whom we would otherwise not have been able to keep in touch.

Each home visit consisted of a prescribed set of tasks that the mothers and children were asked to carry out (see Figure I.1 for the home visit data collection schedule and Figure AI.1 in the appendix for a set of instructions to home visitors about the tasks for the 5-year-old home

Home visit	Book reading	Toy play	Magnets	Mealtime	Maternal interview
3-year-old home visit	*The Very Hungry Caterpillar*	X		X	X
4-year-old home visit	*The Very Hungry Caterpillar What Next, Baby Bear!*	X		X	X
5-year-old home visit	*The Very Hungry Caterpillar What Next, Baby Bear! Elephant*	X	X	X	X

Figure I.1. Home visit data collection schedule.

visit) as well as an interview with the mother (see Figure AI.2 in the appendix for the interview schedule for the 5-year-old home visit). At each home visit, the mothers and children read books aloud (see Chapter 2) and played with toys (see Chapter 3). At the end of each home visit, an audiotape and a tape recorder were left with the family to record a mealtime (see Chapter 4).

There also were some modifications in these tasks over the years. Although the mothers and children were asked to read *The Very Hungry Caterpillar* (Carle, 1979) together at each of the three home visits during the preschool period, a second book was added at the 4-year-old visit (*What Next, Baby Bear!;* Murphy, 1983) and a third was added at the 5-year-old visit (*Elephant;* Hoffman, 1945/1984). For the toy play, we had a consistent set of toys, but we also added items to the set as the children got older to reflect the types of toys we thought the children would be most interested in. For the 5-year-old visit, we added a completely new task—the magnet task (see Chapter 6). In this task, the mothers and children were given a magnet and a set of metallic and nonmetallic objects to play with during the visit.

In all of the interviews, the mothers were asked questions about the children's daily activities and literacy skills, but at the 4-year-old home visit, the mothers were asked about their own upbringing and schooling experiences, and at the 5-year-old visit they were asked to reflect on their children's preschool experiences and what they thought their children had learned. In this way, we hoped to get as extensive and as relevant information as possible within a reasonable time frame for the visit.

Not surprisingly, there were many adventures related to doing the home visits. Although interviewers always asked whether it would be possible for the mother and child to be alone with the interviewer during the visit, it was the rare visit that did not involve more people. Home visitors' notes are filled with comments about keeping interested siblings and friends occupied while the tasks were being completed by the mother and child. Being sat upon by large, shaggy dogs; coping with loud television sets and stereos; working through interruptions from telephone calls; trying to stay cool in blistering summertime heat; and conversing with fathers on state and local politics were all challenges met and conquered by the home visitors. The quality of the data presented in Chapters 2–6 relies heavily on the persistence, flexibility, and dedication of this intrepid band of data collectors.

Chapter 2

Parents and Children Reading Books Together

Jeanne M. DeTemple

Casey and his mother, Stacy, had the following conversation when they were about to read *The Very Hungry Caterpillar* (Carle, 1979), a book that the home visitors had brought to the 3-year-old visit:

Mother: Tell Molly [the home visitor] about your caterpillar at school.
Casey: Um, they growed.
Mother: They growed, and what happened to them? They grew; what happened?
Casey: First, they were butterflies and then they growed, and then we let them away.
Mother: Yeah, they were caterpillars. They turned into butterflies.
Casey: We still keep them for uh . . .
Mother: Five days?
Casey: A long time, and then when we let go of them.
Mother: They let him go.
Molly: Oh, nice. Did they turn into pretty butterflies, or were they sort of plain butterflies?
Casey: Plain butterflies. Then they ate. They were little, then they ate.
Mother: They were little, and they ate. You fed them, right?
Casey: Yeah.
Mother: What did you feed them?
Casey: Don't know the name!
Mother: Butterfly food? [Laughs]

After this conversation, Casey's mother read the book straight through with no additional comments or questions while Casey listened attentively.

When Astra and her mother, Solange, read the same book at the 3-year-old visit, Astra's mother, unlike Casey's, paused frequently to ask questions about the book, particularly focusing on using the illustrations to teach Astra to count:

Mother: "On Tuesday he ate through" how many pears?
Astra: One, two.
Mother: "He ate through two pears, but he was still hungry. On Wednesday he ate through . . . "
Astra: One, two, three.
Mother: "On Wednesday he ate through three plums, but he was still hungry. On Thursday he ate through four strawberries, but he was still hungry."
Astra: One, two, three.
Mother: Count the strawberries again.
Astra: One, two, three! One, two, four.
Mother: Three.
Astra: Three, six.
Mother: Four.
Astra: Four.
Mother: So, on Thursday he ate through four strawberries. Let's count them again. One, two, three, four.
Astra: One, two, three, four.
Mother: Okay. He ate through four strawberries. "On Friday he ate through five oranges, but he was still hungry." Let's count the oranges.
Astra: One, two, three, four.
Mother: Four. . .
Astra: Five!
Mother: Let's count them again.
Astra: One, two, three, four.
Mother: Four. . .
Astra: Five.
Mother: Okay.

When Todd and his mother, Mary, read *What Next, Baby Bear!* (Murphy, 1983), one of the books the home visitors brought to the 4-year-old visit, they frequently stopped to talk about what was going on in the story:

Mother: "'Can I go on the moon?' asked Baby Bear. 'No you can't,' said
          Mrs. Bear. 'It's bathtime. Anyway, you'd have to find a rocket
          first.' Baby Bear found a rocket in the closet under the stairs. He
          found a space helmet on the drainboard in the kitchen and a
          pair of space boots on the mat by the front door."

Todd: Is he gonna go on the rocket?

Mother: Look what he's doing.

Todd: Is the rocket gonna be bigger?

Mother: What do you think? Look at what he's doing. He says that's a
          space helmet and that's a pair of space boots. He's pretend-
          ing. Like you do all the time. "He packed his teddy bear and
          some food for the journey and took off up the chimney. . . .
          WHOOSH! Out into the night. An owl flew past. 'What a great
          rocket,' he said. 'Where are you going?' 'To the moon,' said
          Baby Bear. 'Would you like to come too?' 'Yes, please,' said
          [the] owl. An airplane roared out of the clouds. Baby Bear
          waved and some of the passengers waved back." Do you think
          he's really doing that?

Todd: Are they scared?

Mother: Nah. He likes that. He's pretending.

Todd: How did he fly without no wings for the rocket?

Mother: He's just pretending. You know how you, when at night you play
          with the alligator in your room? You're just pretending, right?
          "On and on they flew, up and up, above the clouds, past mil-
          lions of stars, until at last they landed on the moon." That's where
          they wanted to go.

As can be seen from these examples of three of the portrait children and their mothers from the Home–School Study of Language and
Literacy Development reading a book together, there are many different approaches to book reading with young children. While reading a
book with a preschooler, a parent's approach may range from a straight
reading of the text, to talking about the illustrations or telling a story
with no reading, to reading with extensive interaction. If a parent uses
an interactive style, the interaction may range from focusing on information that is immediately available from the illustrations or text, as
Astra's mother did; to encouraging the child to reach beyond the information given to make inferences, provide explanations, and explore interpretations of motives and characters' behavior, as Todd's
mother did; or to making connections between the make-believe world
of the book and the real world of the child's own experience, as Casey's
mother did.

In this chapter, the interesting features of different book-reading styles and the impact they may have on children's later language and literacy skills are explored. In addition to examining how mothers and children go about book reading, the chapter looks also at the Home–School Study children's broader experiences with books and reading at home.

IMPORTANCE OF BOOK READING IN CHILDREN'S DEVELOPMENT OF LANGUAGE AND LITERACY SKILLS

Reading books to children at home has been linked to early literacy and to school success in the writings of researchers and in the minds and talk of educators and the general public for many years (Bus, van IJzendoorn, & Pellegrini, 1995; Scarborough & Dobrich, 1994). It has generally been agreed, at least since the late 19th century, that book reading to young children is important and is related to children's later success in school (Teale, 1984).

Yet, it is not clear just what the term *book reading* refers to. The activity of an adult's reading to a young child or looking at a picture book with a young child may entail far more than simply reading aloud the words printed on the pages. Book reading may be used as an opportunity for quiet laptime for the child. It may be used as an opportunity to teach the skills and facts that the parent believes will be used in kindergarten or as a setting for intentionally teaching reading. Book reading may also be used as an opportunity to explore imaginary worlds. The stories can be springboards to create elaborate fantasies.

Several hypotheses have been proposed to explain why this activity, carried out in so many different ways, may be associated with the development of strong language and literacy skills. It may be simply that the exposure to print and the experience with books prepare the child for literacy. Through the activity of book reading, the child becomes familiar with print and how books work. Another explanation focuses on the warm, affectionate time between parent and child and the associated development of a love of books. Yet another explanation focuses on what the parent and child *add* to the text: the conversations, comments, and questions that occur during book reading. The research described in this chapter focuses on this final explanation, looking at the type of talk that mothers use beyond the text of the book while reading to their children.

The kinds of talk that occur during book reading may be particularly well suited to the development of language skills that children need to draw on to do well in school. When a child and an adult look at a picture book together, an important, and possibly unique, opportunity presents itself. The reader and the child are jointly focused on a self-contained illustration and text. This joint attention provides support for extending the child's language. In providing the joint topic and focus, the book affords an opportunity for complex, explicit language such as explanations, definitions, and descriptions. The book is also a starting point for facilitating talk about what is not immediately present: past experiences, predictions, and inferences. Furthermore, the reader and the child can return to a book again and again, elaborating on their shared experience from one time to the next. Because reading books provides opportunities for a range of types of talk and the possibility of repeated conversations about the same text, the book-reading situation may provide more opportunities for complex talk with preschoolers than afforded by many other situations.

TALK DURING BOOK READING
IN THE HOME–SCHOOL STUDY

In the Home–School Study, mothers and children read several books together. They were asked to read *The Very Hungry Caterpillar* at all three annual visits during the preschool period; *What Next, Baby Bear!* on the second and third visits; and *Elephant* (Hoffman, 1945/1984) only on the third visit.

    The Very Hungry Caterpillar is a simple, colorfully illustrated narrative following the life cycle of a butterfly. It was unfamiliar to most of the mothers and children in the study at the 3-year-old visit. This is a very popular children's book, however, and it is likely that the children had many exposures to it over the course of the next 2 years in their preschool classrooms or at home.

    What Next, Baby Bear! is a narrative about a little bear's imaginary trip to the moon. It is more complex than *The Very Hungry Caterpillar* in terms of the text and illustrations. This was a new book for everyone when it was introduced during the 4-year-old visit. It is not a widely known book, and few mothers recognized it even when it was reintroduced at the 5-year-old visit. *What Next, Baby Bear!* was included in the second and third visits because we hoped it would elicit more complex talk, such as predictions, inferences, explanations, definitions, and connections to real-world experiences.

    Elephant is a nonfiction children's book with color photographs and text providing factual information about different kinds of elephants, their behavior, and their habitats. This book was included in the 5-year-old visits to prompt interesting conversations about the real world. It was an unfamiliar book for all of the families.

Description of Mother and Child Talk During Book Reading

In the Home–School Study, it was very clearly the mothers, as the readers of the books, who directed the activity, providing both comments and questions throughout the reading of the text. Children responded to their mothers' questions and provided fewer comments and questions spontaneously. Mothers who paused frequently during the reading of a book to make comments or to ask questions had children who tended to talk during the activity, and mothers who read the book with few interruptions for talk tended to have children who talked very little during the activity.

A great deal of variation in the total amount of talk occurred during the reading of each of the books (see Table A2.1 in the appendix for descriptive statistics of each book-reading session for the full sample). One mother read the text of *What Next, Baby Bear!* straight through, without even reading the title. Another mother added only "The end" after reading the text. Although the child said nothing at all, she was very attentive to her mother's reading. It was extremely rare, however, for a mother simply to read the text to her child without adding anything on her own. Most mothers in the Home–School Study, in fact, used an interactive approach that elicited talk from their children.

Analyses of book reading in this chapter were carried out on a subset of the Home–School Study participants. Only the 54 children for whom we had all book readings from all three home visits, as well as kindergarten measures of the child's language and literacy skills, were included. In addition, three children—one boy with severe hearing loss and two sisters with special needs—were excluded from this analysis because their interactions related to book reading and their performances on the kindergarten measures were not at all representative of those of the larger group.

Immediate Talk

When reviewing the transcripts of the book-reading sessions, we found that most of the comments and questions that occurred during book reading focused on the here and now. The topic of the talk was most often closely tied to the illustrations or words in the text that had just been read. The mother drew the child's attention to an illustration (for example, "See the caterpillar?"), pointed out or asked the child to label an object mentioned in the text (for example, "There's the apple"), asked for a demonstration of skills (for example, "Count the plums"), or requested the child's participation through a fill-in-the-blank routine (for example, "He ate through three . . . ?" while pointing to the object to be named). In the following transcript, for example, Rochelle's mother requested labels, counting, and a fill-in-the-blank response:

Mother:	"On Thursday, he ate through . . . ?" What are those?
Rochelle:	Strawberries!
Mother:	How many strawberries?
Rochelle:	One, two, three, four!
Mother:	Very good. "He ate through four strawberries, but he was . . . ?"
Rochelle:	Still hungry!
Mother:	Very good.

We call this type of talk *immediate talk*. On average, 43%–60% (depending on the book-reading session) of the mothers' talk during the book-reading sessions was of this type.

Nonimmediate Talk

Another type of talk during book reading used the text or the illustrations as a springboard for recollections of personal experiences, comments, or questions about general knowledge or for drawing inferences and making predictions. We call this type of talk *nonimmediate talk*. This type of talk was rare for some mothers and children and, on average, accounted for only 11%–18% of the talk in the different book-reading sessions. Here are some examples of nonimmediate talk (in boldface type) from the portrait children's book readings.

During their reading of *The Very Hungry Caterpillar*, Astra's mother asked for an explanation requiring an inference at an important point in the story:

Mother:	"That night he had a stomachache." **Why you think he had a stomachache, Astra?**
Astra:	**I don't know.**
Mother:	**Because he ate too much.**

When Mariana and her mother read *What Next, Baby Bear!*, Mariana's mother drew inferences about the mother bear's thinking and then requested an evaluation:

Mother:	"'Oh, my,' said Mrs. Bear, laughing. 'What will you think of next!'" **She thought he made up whole story, huh, Mariana?**

She didn't know he actually did it. Then she gave him a bath, and that's it. The end. **Mariana, do you like it?**

Todd's mother interrupted the reading of *Elephant* to draw Todd's attention to an interesting vocabulary word and to focus on general knowledge. Todd readily shared his own knowledge and enjoyed playing with a little rhyme. A simple statement in the book prompted a rich exchange that moved well beyond the immediate text and illustration:

Mother: "A baby elephant is called a calf." That's what that's called, a calf. **Just like . . . ?**
Todd: **I know, I know, I know!**
Mother: **What else is called a calf?**
Todd: **Cow.**
Mother: **Right.** "A mother elephant usually gives birth . . . "
Todd: **A tiger is called a calf, a baby one.**
Mother: **No, it's a cub.**
Todd: **Cub the bub.**

A small number of mothers used no nonimmediate talk at all during a particular book reading. Only two mothers used none at all in any of the book readings. So, although nonimmediate talk was relatively rare, it was used to varying degrees by most mothers who did more than straight readings of a book.

It is possible that the total amount of talk and the amount of each type of talk, immediate and nonimmediate, used by the mothers in the study are associated with some aspects of the books we asked them to read. Previous research has demonstrated that different types of picture books promote particular styles of talk and amounts of interaction (Brobst et al., 1993; Pellegrini, Perlmutter, Galda, & Brody, 1990). In general, mothers in this study used more nonimmediate talk while reading *What Next, Baby Bear!* than they did while reading *The Very Hungry Caterpillar*. While reading the nonfiction book *Elephant*, mothers and children talked more than they did while reading the other two books. Also, mothers used more nonimmediate utterances while reading *Elephant*, a factual book, than they did while reading the other two books at the same visit. For example, when Casey and his mother read *Elephant*, they frequently used the text to make connections to Casey's world and world knowledge:

Mother: "African elephants have a dip in their backs. They also have ridges on their trunks, which end in two points. Asian elephants have smoother trunks that end in just one point." See the dip in his back?

Casey: **I know why he's different. He has them [points to tusks], and he doesn't.**

Mother: **He has tusks. Well, this is a female.** "Asian elephants often live in forests and swamps. This Asian cow elephant lives in Nepal, a small country north of India."

Casey: Ma! In India?

Mother: **Yeah, do you know somebody from there? Deepak? Your friend? Yeah!** "African elephants live in the plains as well as forests. This African elephant lives in the open grassland. It flaps its huge ears to help keep cool in the hot African sunshine." **Because it's very hot in Africa.**

Although there were notable differences in terms of the amount and type of talk used while reading the different books on the same visit, there was some consistency in the relative amount and type of talk used across books. Mothers who talked a lot during the reading of one book tended to talk a lot while reading another book; mothers who said little in addition to reading the text of one book said little beyond reading the text of another. This consistency in style was not maintained, however, with the nonnarrative book *Elephant*. The total amount of talk during *Elephant* was not related to the total amount of talk during the other books.

Change Over Time in Talk During Book Reading

Because *nonimmediate talk* refers to information that is not immediately visible in the illustrations or the text, it typically involves longer utterances and more explicit, complex language than does the labeling or the yes-no questioning that constitutes much of immediate talk. This is why nonimmediate talk is considered a form of extended discourse. It is reasonable to predict that the use of nonimmediate talk—talk that both matches the child's increased linguistic capabilities through length and complexity and challenges the child's cognitive skills through more abstract content—will increase as the child gets older and that the use of immediate talk will decrease.

In fact, there was an overall change over time in mothers' talk during book reading (see Tables A2.2, A2.3, and A2.4 in the appendix). Mothers talked less with the older children than with the younger children. The amount of immediate talk used by the mothers did decrease as the children got older. In addition, immediate talk made up a smaller proportion of the mothers' talk over time. Yet, there was no change over time in the number of nonimmediate utterances that the mothers used. They did not use more nonimmediate talk with their children as their children got older. However, because the overall amount of talk during book reading decreased and the number of nonimmediate utterances remained quite stable, the mothers used *relatively* more nonimmediate talk with the older children than they had while reading to younger children, so a larger percentage of their talk was of the nonimmediate type.

Two complementary explanations can be offered for the decrease in the amount of talk by the mothers over time. In general, when a mother and child initially read a book, much of the task involves making sense of the story. The mother checks the child's understanding frequently. This is not necessary as the child gets older and the mother can be confident that the information provided by the text and the illustrations can stand on their own. She does not need to draw the older child's attention to key points or paraphrase each sentence of the text to make sure the child understands the information.

The second explanation is that when a mother uses questions to draw the child's attention to basic information, an older child responds correctly more often; therefore, the mother does not need to repeat or rephrase the questions as often. Because much of the mothers' talk in the Home–School Study, particularly during the reading of *The Very Hungry Caterpillar,* consisted of requests for labels and factual information, the mothers were less likely to need to use more than one request to help their children produce the right answer as time went on. It also is very possible that the changes in the amount and type of talk from one book reading to the next are associated not only with the change in the child's age but also with the child's increased familiarity with the book due to repeated readings.

Immediate and Nonimmediate Talk During Book Reading and Children's Language and Literacy Skills

One purpose of this research was to investigate the relationship between the type of talk mothers used while reading to their children (immediate and nonimmediate talk) and the children's later language and literacy skills as measured by the School-Home Early Language and Literacy Battery–Kindergarten (SHELL–K; Snow, Tabors, Nicholson, & Kurland, 1995). There are reasons to consider both the number of each type of utterance (that is, how often the child gets to hear this type of talk) and the relative amount of each type (that is, the message that the mother is communicating about what to focus on while book reading). Although we predicted that nonimmediate talk would enhance language development overall, there is reason to believe that some immediate talk might enhance a child's ability to carry out particular literacy tasks. One explanation for the later benefits of book reading to preschoolers has concentrated on the value of exposure to print and characteristics of books. Immediate talk, which includes comments drawing children's attention to the story (for example, "See that!") and to the handling of books (for example, "Oh, it's upside down"), may be associated with measures of emergent literacy. Furthermore, attention to labeling, counting, and color naming might help a child with the Picture Description task, and mothers' paraphrasing, repetition of the text, and attention to labeling objects in the illustrations might be associated with a child's performance on the Receptive Vocabulary measure.

An examination of the correlations between the mother's use of immediate talk during book reading and the child's performance on measures of language and literacy during kindergarten revealed surprising associations that contradicted the imagined benefits of immediate talk described previously. There were no associations between the *number* of immediate utterances during any of the five book readings and any of the early literacy measures. The *percentage* of the mother's utterances that were immediate, however, was consistently *negatively* associated with the early literacy measures (see Table A2.5 in the appendix). The three measures of language that one might predict to be positively associated with the use of immediate talk—Picture Description, Emergent Literacy, and Receptive Vocabulary—either were not at all associated with the mother's immediate talk (as in the case of Picture Description) or were associated negatively with the percentage of talk that was immediate. In other words, mothers who used a high percentage of immediate talk while reading to their preschoolers and kindergartners had children who had low scores on kindergarten measures of early literacy. Mothers who used a low percentage of immediate talk while reading these books tended to have children who had high scores on these measures.

The mothers' use of nonimmediate talk while reading *The Very Hungry Caterpillar* with their 3-year-olds was the characteristic of book reading most strongly and positively associated with the children's performances on several SHELL–K measures. The mothers' percentages of nonimmediate talk and the number of nonimmediate utterances during this book-reading session were associated with the children's scores on the Superordinates, Story Comprehension, Emergent Literacy, and Receptive Vocabulary tasks (see Table A2.6 in the appendix). Mothers who engaged their preschool-age children during book reading with talk that went beyond the here and now had children who later scored higher than other children on measures of language and early literacy.

Book Reading as a Unique Setting for the Development of Language Skills

Picture book reading is a unique opportunity for language development in that the mother and child can return to the same story time after time. They not only can focus on the same story and illustrations that they may have discussed previously but also can deal with the same words or concepts that they had attended to in earlier sessions. Most key elements of the context remain unchanged; what varies are the linguistic skill and experience of the child. In one study of a child being read to by his mother from the same book many times, the child clearly incorporated his mother's contributions from previous book-reading sessions, and the interaction provided scaffolding for the child's language acquisition (Snow & Goldfield, 1983).

Repeated readings allow for modifications in the content of the types of comments and questions added by the mother and child. Whereas additions to the text during initial readings may need to focus on basic clarification of meaning and illustrations (typically achieved through immediate talk), later readings can incorporate speculation and interpretation, requiring lengthier, more complex interjections, which are characteristic of nonimmediate talk. A study (Phillips & McNaughton, 1990) of repeated book readings in 10 families from the dominant culture in New Zealand, for example, concluded that contributions during initial readings focused on clarifying the meaning of the text, but that in later readings the talk involved inferences and anticipatory comments. In addition, children initiated comments and participated more fully in the later readings. Repeated readings and discussions of the same page in a book are rich settings for language acquisition. It may be that a certain level of talk occurs with unfamiliar books and that repeated, shared readings are necessary for more complex, elaborate language, typically seen in nonimmediate talk, to emerge.

HOME SUPPORT FOR LITERACY

Book reading is, of course, only one of the many settings in which children have the opportunity to develop language skills. A child's performance on any of the early literacy measures described previously must have been influenced by exposure to and interaction in a variety of contexts. It may be, however, that the language used during book reading is representative of the types of interactions that occur in other settings.

In the following interaction between 4-year-old Mariana, her mother, and Mariana's older brother, there are many evaluations, comments on vocabulary, and interpretations. This seems to be a familiar way of talking for both of them.

Mother:	Look at all the things that caterpillar has been eating. He probably got a stomachache, huh? [Laughs] That's for sure, huh, Mariana?
Mariana:	Yeah.
Mother:	He's gonna get very sick. "One lollipop." Oh, wow! He continue eating. "One piece of cherry pie." Look! "One sausage, one cupcake, and one slice of watermelon. That night he had a stomachache!" You were right! I wouldn't like to be on that caterpillar's plate, huh? He eat so much! "The next day was Sunday again. The caterpillar ate through one nice green leaf and after that he felt much better." Oh. Maybe he had the leaf as a medicine, huh, Mariana?
Mariana:	Fat [laughs].
Mother:	Look at him. He grew so much! Now he needs to exercise. So fat! "Now he wasn't hungry any more—and he wasn't a little caterpillar any more. He was a big, fat caterpillar." Look at him! "He built a small house, called a cocoon, around himself."
Manny:	Cocoon?
Mother:	I don't know what that is! [Laughs] "He stayed inside for more than two weeks. Then he nibbled a hole in the cocoon."
Manny:	What's a cocoon?
Mother:	I don't know. It looks like his home. Some kind of a little nest . . . hive, maybe.

In her interview, Mariana's mother revealed that she did not read to her children often. This book reading, with a high amount of nonimmediate talk, apparently was not a typical activity for the family, but Mariana was apparently exposed to this style of language in other settings (see examples in other chapters). Mariana's mother commented, "Sometimes I have a feeling that with my accent, they don't understand much [of] what I read them, and that's why I don't read books, you know, very often to them." After reading the book twice at Mariana's request and then paging through a third time, helping Mariana tell the story,

Mariana's mother laughingly told the home visitor, "We've had enough, huh? Don't you think I do it very often. I don't have the patience. But they do learn a lot from reading and looking at pictures. Things like that."

Mariana's mother's comments raise a second group of questions about book reading. How often does it occur? Who is involved in book reading at home? Where do the books come from?

We wanted to find out whether the book reading we observed at the home visits was typical for most families. During the first two visits, the home visitors asked mothers several questions about reading in their homes (see Table 2.1). Almost all of the mothers said they read to their children, and more than half reported reading to their children daily. Most of the children in this study were also read to by someone else, although this was less common when the children got older. Most families owned more than 25 children's books at the time of the first visit. Although a small percentage of the mothers said they used the library as a source of children's books with their 3-year-olds, almost one third of the mothers said they used the library a year later. These responses indicate that book reading was a familiar activity for most families in this study but that there was variability in how often and under what circumstances book reading occurred. We named this cluster of questions concerning reading activities, book ownership, and source of books *home support for literacy.*

Let's look at the role of literacy in the home life of one child more closely. One child in the kindergarten sample, Brian, was a rather shy and quiet boy living with his divorced mother and older brother in an urban subsidized housing project. He attended a high-quality Head Start program. The home visitors interviewed Brian's mother about home literacy practices, and she provided us with the following information. She worked outside the home as a secretary and had completed 14 years of formal education. She grew up in the immediate area and gave birth to Brian when she was 28 years old. Brian and his brother were cared for by his grandmother after school until about 5:00 P.M. each day, when his mother returned from work. The family owned more than 25 children's books, which they had bought at bookstores and through book clubs. Brian pretended to read to his mother and when playing alone. He had a favorite book and had memorized the words of the book. Brian's mother read to him at bedtime and said she enjoyed reading all kinds of books to him. They also read toy catalogs together. His brother and grandmother read to him daily, and occasionally an aunt who was a frequent visitor read to him. Brian's mother described herself as an avid reader, preferring biographies and romances, and listed five authors when we asked her if she could name a favorite author. She did not

Table 2.1.   Mothers' reports of home support for literacy

Question	3-year-old visit ($n = 79$)	4-year-old visit ($n = 68$)
Do you read to your child?	96%	97%
Daily?	66	70
Does anyone else read to your child?	83	77
One to two times per week	17	25
Three or more times per week	41	25
How many children's books do you own?		
1–10	11	8
11–25	27	11
More than 25	62	82
Do you get books from the library?	18	30
Do you get books from a bookstore?	42	42
Do you read anything else with your child?		
Funnies	32	28
Catalogs	61	34
Children's magazines	45	40
Newspapers	22	17

Figures represent percentage of mothers answering in the affirmative.

remember being read to by her own parents as a child, but she did remember that her parents read the newspaper and magazines.

Brian's mother used quite a lot of nonimmediate talk during book reading, including explanations and talk about the past and the future, and very little immediate talk. During the 3-year-old visit, Brian's comments after the book reading revealed his enjoyment of repeated readings and his mother's acceptance of and participation in this approach to reading books with her child. She asked the experimenter's permission to reread *The Very Hungry Caterpillar* with Brian before proceeding with the other tasks.

Brian: You read it all?
Mother: I read the whole book!
Brian: Read it again?
Mother: You like to read the same story again and again? [Laughs]

During the 4-year-old visit book-reading session, Brian's mother drew parallels between the fictional world of *What Next, Baby Bear!* and Brian's world. Other comments and questions provided explanations of the character's behavior and of vocabulary.

Mother: He puts on his boots. You saw that picture. They look like your boots. Don't they look like your yellow boots?

Brian: Mine aren't yellow.

Mother: Yellow and blue and red. Right? "'Can I go to the moon?' asked
           Baby Bear. 'No, you can't,' said Mrs. Bear. 'It's bathtime. Any-
           way, you'd have to find a rocket first.' Baby Bear found a rocket
           in the closet under the stairs. He found a space helmet on the
           drainboard in the kitchen and a pair of space boots on the mat
           by the front door."

Brian: That's not a space helmet.

Mother: What is it?

Brian: A bowl.

Mother: Right. It's a strainer. I think it's got another word for it too, uh.
           . . . I don't remember, though. "He packed his teddy bear and
           some food for the journey and he took off up the chimney. . . . "
           Look at all the stuff in that box! "WHOOSH! Out into the night."
           He's flying up the chimney.

Brian: What is that?

Mother: Well, actually, it looks like fire under there, but that's his rocket.
           He's thinking he's in a rocket, remember? See?

Brian: That's not really a rocket. [Laughs]

It is easy to see from these transcripts and from the answers that
Brian's mother gave during the interview that enriching literacy activities focusing on picture books occurred frequently in Brian's home.
Brian was a child whose mother got a high score in *home support for literacy* on both visits.

Each mother was scored twice on *home support for literacy:* once
based on responses from the interview when the children were 3 years
old and once from the interview when the children were 4 years old.
There was, of course, variation in the responses to the interview questions. Some mothers reported much more extensive use of books than
others. We wondered whether the use of books in the home was associated with talk during book reading, given that mothers and children
who have more access to books and read more often might interact differently during book reading from those who do not have many books
at home and rarely read together. Indeed, mothers who scored higher
on *home support for literacy* used more nonimmediate talk while reading
with their preschoolers, whereas those who scored lower used less
nonimmediate talk. In addition, mothers who scored higher on *home
support for literacy* used less immediate talk while reading to their children at the 4- and 5-year-old visits. Also, mothers with high *home support for literacy* scores talked more and used more nonimmediate talk
during the reading of *Elephant.*

One question in the interview focused on the families' source of children's books. Mothers who said at the 3-year-old visit that they used the library used, on average, twice as much nonimmediate talk while reading to their 3-year-olds as those who did not. Mothers who said they got children's books from a bookstore talked less while reading with their 3-year-olds and used less immediate talk. They also talked more while reading *Elephant* and used more nonimmediate talk and a higher percentage of nonimmediate talk than those who did not say they used a bookstore.

Book ownership also was associated with mothers' reading. In families owning more children's books, mothers used more nonimmediate talk while reading *The Very Hungry Caterpillar* when the children were 3 years old and again while reading *Elephant* when they were 5. These mothers also used a smaller percentage of immediate utterances while reading *Elephant*. Children who owned more books at both visits scored higher on kindergarten measures of Story Comprehension and Receptive Vocabulary than those who owned fewer books. Those who reported owning more books at the 4-year-old visit scored higher on all of the early literacy measures in kindergarten.

Finally, we wondered whether the overall measure, *home support for literacy*, was associated with children's later literacy skills. In fact, this measure was quite strongly associated with measures of early literacy in kindergarten (see Table A2.7 in the appendix). The association between *home support for literacy* and kindergarten performance was stronger when the information was gathered from the 3-year-old visit than when the information was gathered from the 4-year-old visit. Children who at 3 were being read to daily (often by more than one person), who owned more books, and who used the library and bookstores demonstrated greater language and literacy skills at age 5 than those who did not have these experiences at this early age.

DISCUSSION

The Home–School Study researchers carried out repeated observations of mothers and preschool-age children reading books together in an effort to shed light on the relationship between reading at home with young children and the children's later language and literacy skills. Home visitors also conducted interviews with the mothers about book-reading practices in their homes. This combination of the mothers' reports and in-depth analyses of the observed interactions during book reading provided data to reveal more specifically which aspects of book reading are linked to better language and literacy skills.

Based on the premise that *any* reading or interaction around books must have beneficial effects, some intervention studies have been carried out in which books were sent home from school (Gallimore & Goldenberg, 1991) or handed out by the pediatrician at the baby's 6-month visit (Needleman & Zuckerman, 1992). Indeed, we found that *home support for literacy*, a measure of quantity of books owned, frequency of reading, and variety of reading activities, was predictive of children's early literacy skills.

Other intervention programs (Home Instruction Program for Preschool Youngsters [HIPPY; Lombard, 1994], Teen Demonstration Project, Parent Readers Program, Self-Help) emphasize reading to young children at home and specifically encourage verbal interaction about the book, based on the belief that *talk* during book reading is conducive to better preparation for later success in school. To varying degrees, these programs specify the types of interaction that should occur during book reading. Our findings suggest that not *all* types of interaction around book reading are associated with the development of early literacy. In fact, for the mothers and children in the Home–School Study, it is only *nonimmediate talk* that is associated positively with later measures of early literacy.

There is evidence that both the quantity and quality of book reading that occur are associated with language performance. In another longitudinal study, the amount of time spent reading books at home between the ages of 1 and 3 was positively correlated with teachers' ratings of children's language and literacy at age 5 (Wells, 1985). Wells made the distinction between 1) simply looking at picture books that depict objects and talking about the illustration in isolation (which would be coded as *immediate talk*) and 2) reading picture books that have a story. Looking at picture books was not associated with later literacy skills, but reading stories (or telling the stories while looking through books) during the preschool years was predictive of the child's knowledge of literacy and the teacher's rating of the child's language at age 5, as well as of the child's reading comprehension at age 7.

We have learned in the Home–School Study that children who had greater *home support for literacy*, particularly those who had higher scores during the 3-year-old visit, demonstrated greater skill on the early literacy measures. In addition, however, the type of talk that mothers used during book reading was also predictive of the children's later skills. The children who had the highest scores on the kindergarten measures of language and literacy skill were the children whose environments provided the highest home support for literacy and whose mothers used a smaller percentage of immediate talk and more nonimmediate talk.

Interestingly, these findings, developed on the basis of a sample of only 54 mothers and children from the Home–School Study, mirror the results of a survey of a much larger, nationally representative sample: the National Household Education Survey (Nord, Lennon, Liu, & Chandler, 1999). This telephone survey, which reported on data collected by interviewing parents of children ages 3–5 years who had not yet started kindergarten, asked questions about home literacy activities, such as frequency of book reading and storytelling, trips to the library, teaching about letters and numbers, teaching songs and music, and arts and crafts activities, and about children's emerging literacy, such as recognizing all letters of the alphabet, counting to 20 or higher, the children's writing their own names, and reading or pretending to read books. In 1999, the survey found that children who were read to three or more times per week were twice as likely to show three or more of the emerging literacy skills than children who were read to less frequently. Furthermore, there were also significant findings with regard to trips to the library, teaching about letters and numbers, and arts and crafts. Only frequency of teaching songs and music did not yield significant results, perhaps because these activities occurred more frequently with the younger children only. When home literacy activities were considered together, 43% of the children whose families had engaged in three or more home literacy activities in the previous week were reported to show three or more signs of emerging literacy, compared with 30% of children whose families reported doing home literacy activities less often. One of the report's conclusions was that "families are helping their children prepare for school by engaging in literacy activities with them at home" (p. 8).

SUGGESTIONS FOR PARENTS

Book reading is a rich opportunity for the use of complex language that goes beyond the here and now. These verbal interactions during book reading promote the development of a cluster of language skills that children will be expected to use in school. Furthermore, the more often this type of talk is used, with a wide variety of books, the more likely it is that children will be prepared for some of the challenges of early literacy. In summary, here are some suggestions for parents to enhance book reading with young children:

- *Choose a variety of types of books to read, and include stories with long text, stories with rhyme, picture books, chapter books, and factual and scientific books.* It is clear that different types of children's books are associated with different amounts and types of talk. Comments by readers differ during rhyming narratives (for example, Dr. Seuss's books), ABC books, factual books, and classic children's story books. *What Next, Baby Bear!* is a good example of a little-known narrative picture book that provides many opportunities for nonimmediate talk. Many factual picture books, such as *Elephant,* may also elicit explanatory talk, opportunities to hear a variety of vocabulary, and chances to make connections to the child's experiences. So, try to select a variety of types of children's books to read with your child from as many sources as possible, including the library, anticipating that different types of interactions will occur more easily with some books than with others.

- *Read books over and over again. Increased familiarity with the story and content of the book opens doors for more complex discussion.* Intervention programs that give books to children so that they have them at home and can return to them again and again provide an opportunity not only for increased familiarity with the story but also for an increase in the level of sophistication in the interaction between the reader and child. Library loans are often longer for children's books (for example, 6 weeks or more) than for adults'. This amount of time conveniently allows for repeated readings and changes in the type of talk that occurs during book reading. It may be that one of the key facilitative features of book-reading interaction requires adequate exposure to the specific book being read. The type of talk and the complexity of the talk may be more affected by the degree of familiarity that you and your child have with the text and illustrations, and by the opportunities that you have created to build on shared experiences, than by the age and developmental level of your child.

- *Discuss some aspect of the book before and after reading.* Some books (for example, rhyming books) lose a lot of the intent of the language with interruptions. You can explain unfamiliar ideas, unusual vocabulary, and concepts before reading. It is always a good idea for you to be familiar with the book before starting to read it to your child.

- *Vary intonation.* You can engage your child in the story and enhance his or her comprehension during book reading by carefully modifying your intonation and using different voices. The focus in this chapter is on the content of the language used during book reading. Yet, effective use of intonation, pauses, or characters' voices provides information that is unexamined in this analysis.

- *Use gestures and point to aspects of the illustrations to add to your child's comprehension without interrupting the flow of the text.* Some readers provide gestural cues to assist the child in comprehension (for example, by pointing to the appropriate illustration while reading an unfamiliar word). These nonverbal "explanations" and supports of a child's understanding can be very important features of picture book reading. They may be especially effective while reading a text that would lose too much through interruptions, such as a rhyming text.

- *Make the book-reading experiences overflow into other areas of life.* Hold conversations with your child about the characters and their personalities, as well as the characters' problems and how they solve them, at other times such as on walks, while driving, or during mealtimes. Also make the connections between what took place in the book and in your child's real world when the opportunity comes up. During book reading, make comments and ask questions that help connect the story with your child's own life. Similarly, in everyday experiences—for example, dealing with friends, feelings, food, observations in nature, or playing with toys—you can recall a story that you have read with your child.

- *Be a reader yourself.* Your own reading for pleasure not only provides a model for your child but also may help you think about what makes stories interesting and compelling and thereby enhance the conversations you and your child have about books.

Chapter 3

Playing at Home
The Talk of Pretend Play

Jane R. Katz

Astra and her mother are playing together in their living room with the toys that the home visitor has provided. Most of the time, they have been using the toy telephones to talk about family, friends, and activities. Then Astra declares:

Astra:	Now I'm makin' tea or something. Some tea for you and me.
Mother:	Oh.
Astra:	And we're gonta have, we're gonta have a little pie. Okay?
Mother:	A little what?
Astra:	Pie.
Mother:	Pie. What kind of pie?
Astra:	Hmm. Strawberry pie.
Mother:	Strawberry pie.
Astra:	Okay. You like strawberry pie?
Mother:	Yeah.
Astra:	Or chocolate pie?
Mother:	I like chocolate.
Astra:	Okay. But—Okay.

Later, Astra calls her mother on the toy telephone again:

The coding and analysis of the toy-play data have been a group effort. Thanks to Cornelia Heise Baigorria, Linda Caswell, Ann Robyns, and Patton Tabors, and for their contributions to the material for this chapter.

Astra: 4, 2, 7, 7. Hello? Hello?
Mother: Hello.
 Astra: You 'posed to say, "Who's this."
Mother: Hello, who's this?
 Astra: Ummm. . . . Astra.
Mother: Yeah?
 Astra: Umm. I want you to. . . . Why can't you come over to my house
            and see what I'm makin'?
Mother: Okay.
 Astra: You know what I'm makin'? Strawberry pie and chocolate pie.
Mother: Mmmmmmm. Save some for me.
 Astra: I'm making a whole pot.
Mother: Okay.
 Astra: Okay. Bye-bye. No. Ummm. I will leave them where you are. I
            will leave it in the oven.
Mother: Okay.
 Astra: And when it is ready, I want it hot. That's why I leave it in the
            oven. Okay? Bye-bye.
Mother: Bye.

This conversation was part of a play session that Astra and her mother shared during the home visit when Astra was 4 years old. Clearly, this conversation is part of a game of pretending: The roles that Astra and her mother are assuming (host and invited guest), the plans they are laying (dropping by the house), and the objects they are referring to (for instance, *my house, a whole pot, strawberry and chocolate pies, the oven*) are all part of a fantasy creation. In this chapter, we present information about preschoolers' early at-home social pretend play with adults. In particular, we suggest that young children develop ease and skill in pretending from early, enjoyable experiences engaging in pretend play with adults. We explore the difference between the kind of play talk that labels and describes objects and activities, and the talk of pretend play, which is based on symbolic transformations of the real world and the communication of novel information. Finally, we present analyses that show that children's early exposure to and participation in pretend play talk in the preschool years is related to their emergent literacy skills when they reach kindergarten.

DEFINING SOCIAL PRETEND PLAY

To define *social pretend play,* we first need to identify the larger spheres of activity to which it is related: *interpersonal engagement, language,* and *play.* The diagram on this page (see Figure 3.1) shows the separate but overlapping activities that these terms represent. The sphere of *interpersonal engagement* in Figure 3.1 refers to all kinds of interactions, with and without talk, that occur between two or more people. The *language* sphere includes all efforts at intentional communication, either verbal or gestural, that are part of a meaningful, organized system. The sphere of *play* embraces a wide variety of children's activities, including skipping down the street, playing tag, inventing funny words, building a huge tower with blocks, and pretending to be a firefighter with a friend while the living room sofa serves as a fire truck. *Play* can be both physical and mental, both wildly extroverted and quietly introverted, both imitative and inventive. Although it often appears to be random, it actually is quite organized. To encompass all this variety, we define *play* broadly as activities that the participants find enjoyable and that they engage in voluntarily to have fun.

Casual observations of young children tell us that their play does not always require social interaction and does not always require language. Very young children often play alone, drawing, digging, building, stacking, or sorting, using toys or everyday objects. Even social play may not require language, such as when two small children play side by side with sand, exchanging looks but not conversing. Furthermore, young children's social play need not be pretend (for instance, when children run races, look at books, paint, or tell jokes together), and their

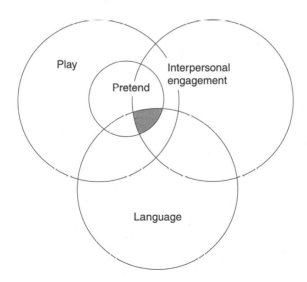

Figure 3.1. Language, interpersonal engagement, and play are distinct yet overlapping activities.

pretend play need not be social (for example, when a solitary child uses a toy backhoe to dig a hole for a house or creates a solo fantasy of traveling in outer space).

In this chapter, then, we look at a very special subset of young children's play activities. The diagram (see Figure 3.1) shows how social pretend play is related to the larger spheres of play, language, and interpersonal engagement. It shows first, not surprisingly, that pretend play is part of the larger category of play. Second, it shows that the spheres of play (including, in part, pretend play), language, and interpersonal engagement intersect. The shaded area that is contained in all three large domains and within the small domain of pretend play represents the social pretend play that is the subject of this chapter: play that is interactive and interpersonal, based on fantasy, and enacted through talk.

To describe social pretend play further, here (based on Garvey, 1990) are some of its other characteristics:

- *In social pretend play, participants explicitly or implicitly make objects, people, places, or other aspects of the here and now represent something other than what they are. That is, they make symbolic transformations.* A child engaged in pretend play constructs an alternate reality based on mental images or inventions. He or she dismisses the real name and function of features in the immediate setting (including, perhaps, the setting itself) and transforms these real-world features in accordance with his or her mental images (Vygotsky, 1978). By such everyday but deeply creative symbolic transformations, an orange shovel becomes a carrot, three toy giraffes become a family of two parents and a baby who argue about bedtime, a television becomes a food dispenser in a cafeteria, and a child can talk to a dolphin on a toy telephone. As a player's skill develops, he or she may label the play explicitly, saying metacognitively, "Pretend that . . . ," or declaring, "This is the castle." In the example of Astra and her mother, Astra's statement "Now I'm makin' tea" labels the play; she uses available props (that is, toy telephones, spoons, cups, and bowls) and engages in other symbolic transformations (designating a space for the oven, objects for sugar and flour, and a toy plate for a baking pan) to play out her scenario.

- *In social pretend play, participants share this nonliteral approach and their transformations.* Pretend play can, of course, be solitary. For there to be a partner in play, however, the pretend transformations must be articulated, shared, and sometimes negotiated. Part of what makes Astra's pretend play so engaging is her ability to share her make-believe agenda in clear and direct language, which brings her play-mate into the center of her fantasy world.

- *In social pretend play, the motivation and the reward for engaging in the activity lie in the experience itself.* What sustains Astra and her mother during their tea party play—and they sustained it through many minutes of repeated telephoning and planning—is the interest and pleasure inherent in the shared fantasy.

Social pretend play can vary according to the setting in which it occurs (for example, home or preschool), the activities involved (for example, gross motor play on a playground or fine motor play with manip-ulatives), and whether the child is playing with an older or younger peer or with an adult caregiver. In this analysis, we focus on the pre-tend play of parents, particularly mothers, and their preschool-age chil-dren in the home.

THEORETICAL VIEWS ON THE DEVELOPMENT OF SOCIAL PRETEND PLAY

Young children's social pretend play has attracted the interest of evolu-tionary biologists and ethologists, anthropologists, sociologists, folk-lorists, musicologists, psychiatrists, and clinical psychologists who have tried to understand its origins and the functions it serves in children's development. Developmental psychologists, too, have offered different explanations for the source and purpose of young children's social pre-tending. We present here two major perspectives on social pretend play.

Swiss developmental psychologist Jean Piaget interpreted young children's pretend play as an activity in which they make the external, real world adapt to their wishes. He saw such play as an advancement over the sensorimotor play (that is, the physical manipulation of the environment) that infants engage in. His observations led him to believe that pretend play begins around the age of 2, when young children develop the ability to make symbolic substitutions, to string together isolated symbolic gestures into whole scenes, and, at least in a rudi-mentary way, to articulate these scenes in language.

Piaget, however, considered pretend play to be nonsocial. Accord-ing to his views of childhood egocentricity, preschool-age children are not capable of understanding the different perspective of another and so of establishing shared meaning. Piaget, therefore, viewed pretend play as an activity that demonstrates the cognitive and social limita-tions of the young child's thought. Furthermore, he believed that pre-tend play does not contribute to children's cognitive development; it merely reflects the child's stage of growth (Piaget, 1945/1962).

Russian psychologist Lev Vygotsky took a different view of the origins and function of pretend play. For Vygotsky, all pretend play, even in its earliest forms, is essentially social. Diverging sharply from Piaget, he held that social interaction is crucial to pretending. It is through social interaction that young children are exposed to the various elements of culture, ranging from specific skills (putting together a puzzle, for instance), to customs and rituals (for example, playing host to a guest), to emotional and moral choices (for example, meting out discipline) that become the content of play. It is also through social interaction, particularly with partners possessing a higher level of skill, that children develop a real understanding of and the ability to use these cultural elements. Furthermore, Vygotsky maintained that pretend play does not simply reflect young children's development but also contributes to it by providing a cognitive space in which children can use functions and skills that are in the process of maturing. And through play with a more skilled partner, a child can attain a level of performance that is beyond his or her actual developmental level. Social interaction within a shared cultural context is thus fundamental to Vygotsky's (1978) conception of pretend play.

In our analysis of pretend play, we subscribe to this social interactionist perspective and take what some researchers have called *a communicative view of pretending* (Haight & Miller, 1993). We hold that young children develop the habit of pretending by hearing and taking part, from their first year on, in pretend interactions with the significant people in their lives. As researchers such as psychologist Judy Dunn (Dunn & Wooding, 1977) have noted, it is difficult to determine whether children *must* be exposed to adult models of pretend to develop pretend play, but it does seem clear that mothers' participation is important to young children's development of interest and skill in pretend. Research findings looking at children from the ages of 12 to 30 months suggest that children incorporate pretend elements from their joint play with their mothers into their own play (El'konin, 1966; Haight & Miller, 1993). When mothers play with their young children, they essentially "teach" role playing by modeling the behavior and talk that is typical of particular activities, such as when a mother tends a baby or when workers construct a building (Garvey, 1990; Miller, 1982). Also, research suggests that children pretend more (Bornstein, Haynes, O'Reilly, & Painter, 1996; Fiese, 1990) and that their play sequences are longer (Dunn & Wooding, 1977; Haight & Miller, 1993; Slade, 1987a), more diverse (O'Connell & Bretherton, 1984), and more complex (Fiese, 1990; Slade, 1987a, 1987b) when they engage in pretend play with adult caregivers, usually their mothers, than when they pretend alone. Moreover, children as young as 18 months can continue pretend play, either gesturally or verbally, that their mothers have started; by the age of 2, children can respond to their mother's pretend talk with pretend talk of their own (Haight & Miller, 1993).

These studies also highlight a reciprocal influence—a kind of feedback loop—between mothers and their young children when they play together. Mothers' talk and play do not merely have an effect on children's talk and play; when children understand language better, talk more, and engage in more pretend play, their mothers respond with more connected (that is, *contingent*) talk, more extending questions about the play, and more pretend talk and play, which in turn encourage the children's pretend talk and play (Kavanaugh, Whittington, & Cerbone, 1983; Tamis-LeMonda & Bornstein, 1994).

The longitudinal research of Wendy Haight and Peggy Miller (1993) gives a detailed picture of how the pretend play skills of a small group of young children from middle-income families developed in the home. Studying the pretend play of nine children from the time the children were a year old until they were 4 years old, Haight and Miller noted that "pretend was not only overwhelmingly social, but mothers served as the primary play partners from one to three years" (1993, p. 6). They found that, on average, when the children were 2 and 3 years old, their episodes of pretend play with their mothers were considerably longer than their episodes of pretend play alone. By the time the children were 4 years old, however, their pretend play with peers and their pretend play alone were more sustained than their pretend play with their mothers. Over the same period, the amount of pretend talk that children produced also increased dramatically. And, the percentage of children's pretend talk that was merely an imitation of their mothers' preceding talk decreased in a similarly dramatic way. Haight and Miller's findings suggest that, in their sample, children developed the skills of pretend in early childhood by playing with their mothers; by the age of 4, these skills had consolidated and children were creating pretend play alone and with their peers. Their findings also support the idea that caregivers of very young children can enhance the children's development of pretend skills by sensitively initiating pretend play when the children are very young and by following up on children's pretend themes with topic-sustaining talk and extending questions.

Language is fundamental to the process of learning and engaging in social pretend play. It is the primary medium in which pretend is invented, conducted, and communicated. It is also the primary medium through which parents socialize their children to pretend play (El'konin, 1966). We hold that the language of social pretend play has distinctive characteristics that set it apart from the language used for communicating literal information; this analysis asks whether such language, with its distinctive features, might help to prepare young children for literacy. To explore this question, we turn back to the Home–School Study of Language and Literacy Development.

ANALYZING THE PLAY SESSIONS

To analyze the talk of pretend play, we looked at the play interactions of the 52 children and their mothers from the play sessions of the home visits when the children were 3, 4, and 5 years old. This group consisted of all of the children who had participated in a toy-play session at each visit and who had completed all of the kindergarten assessment tasks.

During the visits, the home visitors simply asked each mother to play with her child for a short while, using a selection of toys brought by the visitors. Sometimes other family members or friends participated as well. The play sessions had artificial boundaries because they were started and ended by the researchers; however, within the play sessions, each mother–child pair did as they chose, without guidance from the researcher. The bag of toys changed somewhat from year to year to reflect the children's development. When the children were 3, the toy selection included painted blocks; differently colored small toy cars; a small tea set with differently colored cups, spoons, and saucers; a school bus with little people; a parrot puzzle; a toy baby bottle with disappearing milk; toy telephones; and an optiscope that multiplies an image seen through a lens. When the children were 4, we substituted a different puzzle and brought dress-up hats and beads and firefighter hats. At age 5, we again changed the puzzle and included realistic animal toys (giraffes, elephants, lions, zebras, and various dinosaurs) and a toy dinosaur egg. The play sessions varied in length from a few minutes to 40 minutes but were mainly 10–15 minutes long.

Each of our four portrait children and their mothers showed distinctive ways of engaging with the toys and with each other across the three play sessions. Astra was very verbal in her play, regardless of what she was doing. Her mother was an active play partner in all three play sessions, but Astra initiated the play and chose the toys and play themes for them both. As shown in the transcript at the beginning of this chapter, they had an easy give-and-take, which suggested that they played together often. At age 3, Astra was especially interested in the puzzle and spent considerable effort in putting it together with her mother's guidance and encouragement (see the excerpt later in this chapter). At all three home visits, however, pretending was Astra's favorite form of play. In fact, during the second home visit, Astra and her mother had the highest percentage of pretend play of all of the 52 mother–child pairs. Astra focused on the tea set and the telephones, creating pretend scenarios about tea parties and dinners that highlighted social, and espe-cially family, relationships.

Todd, in contrast, showed little interest in the telephones and the tea set. When, at age 5, he used these toys in pretend scenarios, he inter-rupted the pretend by hanging up on his own telephone call and slam-ming down his teacup. He focused instead on the cars and the building blocks, building roads, ramps, bridges, and skyscrapers in all three play sessions. At 4, he integrated the cars into his building play; at 5, he brought in the dinosaurs, which he would pretend were destroying his buildings in a loud brawl. His mother frequently shared in his pretend play (except when the dinosaurs were "rampaging") and was a sup-portive play partner, making suggestions, talking about building, and easing his transitions from one toy to another. Increasingly over the three sessions, Todd initiated more of this joint play with her and man-aged his own transitions from one pretend theme to another.

Like Todd, Casey played primarily with blocks and cars: He built houses, ramps, and racetracks, and raced cars. Casey also showed an interest in the telephones: He played with them by himself when he was 3; at age 4, he played with them with his mother, who used this as an opportunity to teach him telephone manners. Casey's mother tended to talk to Casey about his play rather than to join him in it. Much of their shared talk consisted of labeling and descriptive talk about the toys, with many references to movies, television, and nonpresent family members. Casey's mother tended to direct their interactions with her questions and comments; she asked about his buildings ("Who's gonna live in that house?"), tested his knowledge ("You have some type of pet. What is it?"), and commented on his toy choices ("That's girl stuff").

Mariana used a variety of toys—blocks, the puzzle, cars, telephones, and the tea set. Although she seemed interested in blocks when she was 3, more and more of her play over time focused on the telephones and the tea set. Her pretend play with these toys featured cooking and role playing in which her most frequent scenario involved her mother play-ing "a mother" and herself playing "a girl." Although she played actively, Mariana talked little; when her older brother joined in the play sessions, his talk overshadowed hers. Mariana's mother was an engaged and sup-portive play partner who structured her daughter's play with sugges-tions and directions.

Types of Talk During Toy Play

Because we were particularly interested in the talk that accompanies pretend play, we devised a system for evaluating the "pretend" content of the mothers' and children's talk in each play session. In this system, the three major categories were as follows:

1. *Pretend talk*—talk with pretend elements and a nonliteral approach to features in the immediate environment

2. *Non-pretend talk*—talk that maintained a literal approach to actions and toys

3. *Non–toy play talk*—talk about events or concerns that were unrelated to the immediate play setting

We then assessed the talk of the mother and child in each play session, utterance by utterance, according to this system. To illustrate the categories further, following are some examples from the four portrait mother–child pairs and from other mother–child pairs.

Non–toy play talk includes talk about shared experience or knowledge outside the play setting. Here, for example, Casey (age 4) and his mother have a non–toy play exchange about a relative prompted by the beads in the toy collection:

Mother: What do you think about when you think about beads?
Casey: They're diamonds.
Mother: Diamonds? Who used to wear beads all the time?
Casey: You.
Mother: And who else?
Casey: Kimmy.
Mother: No—who wears beads, all different colored ones that would go [unintelligible]. That used to wear beads.
Casey: Kimmy wear them!
Mother: No! Nana?
Casey: Yeah.
Mother: Remember, she had all the different colored beads?
Casey: Yeah. Where are they?
Mother: We gave them away.
Casey: To who?
Mother: To a church.

As this example indicates, personal information about the lives, the relationships, and the concerns and preferences of the mothers and children is embedded in non–toy play talk. We found, however, that, on average, the percentage of non–toy play talk across the 52 mother–child pairs was fairly low—just more than 10% of the total talk in the play sessions. We also found that non–toy play talk contributed little to children's early literacy. For these reasons, we do not consider non–toy play talk further.

Non-pretend talk is a part of play that is grounded in the here and now and reflects the speaker's literal approach to the toys. Examples in this category are naming, counting, and labeling; descriptions of the toys; and process talk, or negotiations and discussions about the mechanics of play, including the mother's instructions to the child about using the toys. The following is an example of non-pretend talk between Casey (age 3) and his mother:

Casey: We have cars. One there. One there and one there.
Mother: Cars? Oh, wow, I didn't see the cars. Want to play with the cars?
Casey: Yes.
Mother: Here. You like cars, too, huh.
Casey: Yeah. Blue one.
Mother: Blue one. Four cars.
Casey: Green and blue are my favorite colors.
Mother: They are? So you want to have the green and the blue one, and I'll have these two. What colors are these?
Casey: Red and gray.
Mother: Red and what else?
Casey: Yellow. It is . . .
Mother: Gray?
Casey: Gray.

In the following excerpt, Rashida's mother tests her counting. Rashida is 3 years old.

Mother: How many? How many cups?
Rashida: Four.
Mother: How many spoons?
Rashida: Four.
Mother: How many plates?
Rashida: Four!
Mother: No. How many plates?
Rashida: Umm . . .
Mother: How many you see?
Rashida: One, two, three—no. Four.
Mother: Right.

In the following exchange, Anna (age 3) and her mother negotiate what they need for building:

Mother: Do you want me to hand you the blocks?
Anna: Yeah.
Mother: All right. Push these out of the way.
Anna: Gimme, uh, one more blue.
Mother: [Unintelligible] the yellow one. I'll give you all the yellow ones.
Anna: I don't need all the yellow ones! I need, um, [pauses] one big long blue.
Mother: What else?
Anna: Mm [pauses], two red blocks.
Mother: I'll put three green ones [unintelligible] too. Okay. There's all my blocks.

Here is a sample of instructional talk, with Astra's mother helping Astra to put a puzzle together; in this excerpt, Astra is also 3:

Mother: Come on, do the puzzle. I'll give you a hand if you cannot do it.
Astra: Okay.
Mother: Put all the pieces here together. Come and put them here.
Astra: I hope I can get it.
Mother: Yeah, just try. You'll get it if you try.
Astra: This goes. . . . I don't know!
Mother: You have to put these three squares. Look where the piece goes. Look around.
Astra: [Tries the piece somewhere] Nope.
Mother: Okay. [Astra tries it again] Yup.
Astra: Yup. [Tries another one] No. No.
Mother: Okay now?
Astra: Yup. [Tries another] Whoa! [Laughs]
Mother: Take your time, take your time.
Astra: Got it?
Mother: Mm-hm.
Astra: Okay.
Mother: Stop. Put it on the table here. [Pauses] We put this piece back.
Astra: I can't find the—
Mother: Look for the spot where that goes. This fits good, so look and see where that go in. [Pauses] Look and see how that's shaped. All right. [Pauses while Astra works on it] So, you see, you found it?
Astra: Mm-hm, it goes here?
Mother: Hun-hunh.
Astra: Nope. [Sings]
Mother: Mmm, turn it so you can see.

Astra: Yeah.
Mother: Okay.
Astra: Give me another piece. [Speaks under her breath] Come on,
         you. You do it. Get over, get over here, oh, here. [Pauses, then
         speaks at regular volume] Here goes another piece. Uh-oh. I got
         it, Ma!

Clearly, cognitive skills and significant pieces of knowledge are embedded in this *non-pretend talk*. The children develop their perceptual
abilities as their mothers guide them to label and describe, they develop
procedural abilities as the mothers guide them to think of a task as a
series of sequential steps, and they practice interactive skills through
conversation and negotiation. The language used for communicating
this content can be quite challenging. Notice, however, how much support the context provides for these activities and skills. When Astra and
her mother use language such as *that, this, these, here, it,* and *put back*,
they do not need to explain what they are referring to, so firmly is their
talk rooted in the present setting. Astra and her mother are relying on
their shared physical context to establish meaningful communication
about the activity they are involved in. As a result, their talk is less
elaborated and explicit.

Pretend talk, by contrast, is less dependent on the immediate setting. Examples of pretend talk include making an object represent another; attributing actions, thoughts, or feelings to inanimate objects;
assuming or assigning a role or a persona; enacting typical scripts or
routines of everyday events; and creating a narrative about a person or
an object. In the following passage, for instance, Casey (here at age 4)
and his mother, who are building a house with blocks, talk about using
blocks for the chimney and doors:

Casey: Where am I going to put the chimney?
Mother: The chimney?
Casey: Yup.
Mother: Why does it have to have a chimney?
Casey: Yeah, a chimney. Where smoke comes out and Santa comes in.
Mother: Oh, yeah!
Casey: That could be the front door, and this could be the back door.
         [Whispers] Yeah.
Mother: Is that the back door or the front door?
Casey: Yeah. That could be the back door, and that could be the front
         door.

In the next exchange, Melanie (age 3), playing with little people dolls and a school bus, attributes action to a doll:

Melanie: That boy [indicates a doll] is looking out the window.
 Mother: Who's looking out the window?
Melanie: A boy.
 Mother: A boy?
Melanie: His name is Andrew.
 Mother: Andrew? Does he go to your school?
Melanie: Yeah. Wait a minute—I put him in, and he fell.

Astra (again at age 3) takes on the roles of both mother and child in the following excerpt:

  Astra: Baby, your bottle's in the fridge.
 Mother: All right.
  Astra: I'm calling Dora. I'm calling Teresa. What's her number, baby?
 Mother: I don't know. What's her number? I can't remember.
  Astra: 1, 1, 2, 3, 2, 4. [She dials the telephone.]
 Mother: Isn't her number 1, 1, 2, 3, 2, 4?
  Astra: Yeah. Hello, Teresa. How you doing? [In a high-pitched voice] Fine, Mommy. [In a low-pitched voice] I'm not your mommy! [In a high-pitched voice] Yes you are, and your mommy said when we're playing house! [In a low-pitched voice] Yeah! I'm your mommy. Come on over.

In the following excerpt, 4-year-old Todd and his mother, who are playing with toy cars, begin to construct a narrative about getting to school:

  Todd: You better watch out for that guy.
 Mother: I know, he's gonna pass him; oh, he's gonna pass on this side. [Makes engine sounds] Whoops, now he's gonna make a U-turn. [Makes more engine sounds] Whoops, now he has to go slow. He's in back of a bus. [Makes more engine sounds]
  Todd: How did he come back over that side?
 Mother: I don't know; he's just driving around. He likes to drive.
  Todd: You—he has to drive. He's the teacher, right? He's the . . .
 Mother: Yeah, now he's gonna follow. Yeah, he's gonna go to school now, but he'll be ready [unintelligible]. [They're both laughing.]

Todd:	Okay, here's the school.
Mother:	Oh, okay. You gonna all get them out of the bus? You gonna call somebody?
Todd:	How—Where's the, where's the door?
Mother:	Well, you'll just have to pretend the door.
Todd:	[Sings] Da da da
Mother:	Mm-hm. He's getting out of here. He's getting out of his car. Okay, where's the school? Right here?
Todd:	[Laughs]
Mother:	No, that's his desk.
Todd:	This is the school.
Mother:	Okay.
Todd:	I go in.
Mother:	Your teacher's in there now.
Todd:	[Sings and then barks like a dog] Doo doo doo doo. Ruff ruff ruff ruff.
Mother:	Oh no, a dog got in. [They're both laughing.]

Real-world knowledge is often incorporated into fantasy creations. This final excerpt shows how new information (here, knowledge about baby care) is included in play with a doll and a baby bottle. In this exchange, Tina (age 3) and her mother also confront the boundary between real and pretend:

Mother:	That's three bottles of milk she drank, Tina. She must be very hungry. Look at that. She drinks more than you drink, and you drink an awful lot.
Tina:	Yeah, she's probably also . . .
Mother:	You should probably burp her now, before she gets a tummy-ache. You gonta burp her?
Tina:	There's a little bit more left.
Mother:	Okay. I think you should burp her, and then you let her have the rest.
Tina:	Now what can she do?
Mother:	She's gonta burp.
Tina:	No, she, she, she's not real.
Mother:	But she's pretend, so you can have a pretend burp.
Tina:	No, you do it.
Mother:	Okay—you pat her back, and I'll pretend burp. [Tina pats, and her mother burps.]
Tina:	Yuck. Yucky. [Her mother laughs.]

These examples demonstrate that the talk of pretend play, when compared with non-pretend talk, relies less on a shared physical context, on shared background knowledge, and on feedback from words and gestures. The examples also show that the play partners' exchanges extend over several turns as they build a shared understanding of the fantasy. These extended exchanges may be explanations (as in the example from Tina), role plays (as in the example from Astra), or stories (as in the example from Todd). But the quality they all have in common is conveying meaning beyond the here and now through linguistic material and structures. It is this ability to build and understand larger language structures that contributes to children's later literacy. Therefore, we can consider pretend talk during toy play to be another form of extended discourse.

The previous examples also show that the subjects of pretend play do not have to be exotic or unfamiliar. Pretend is built on the features of everyday life and on familiar relationships. Similarly, the talk of pretend play need not be esoteric or sophisticated or bookish. Rather, we are focusing here on a specialized use of language to convey meaning—inventions, wishes, and memories—that is removed from immediate reality. Props such as toy teacups, blocks, animals, and toy telephones can help by serving as both springboard and support for the fantasy. But by themselves, the props do not create the fantasy and cannot communicate it to others. That must be done with language.

Relationships Between Mothers' and Children's Use of Pretend Talk

How much did the mothers and children in the 52 families use pretend and non-pretend talk? To answer that, we calculated the percentages of pretend and non-pretend talk from the mothers and children in each of the 52 mother–child pairs and the average percentages for mothers and children across all of the mother–child pairs.[1] Looking at all of the 52 mother–child pairs in all three play sessions, we found that the mothers' and children's use of pretend and non-pretend talk averaged between 40% and 50% of their total play talk (see Tables A3.1–A3.3 in the appendix for means and ranges for the three toy-play sessions). But, the different pairs were very different from each other in the amount of both kinds of talk that they used.

---

[1]The percentage of pretend (or non-pretend) talk at each play session was calculated as the ratio of pretend (or non-pretend) utterances to the total number of utterances produced by a speaker. The total number of utterances is defined as the sum of a speaker's pretend, non-pretend, non–toy play, and unintelligible utterances.

Focusing on pretend talk, for example, each of the portrait children and their mothers used different amounts of pretend talk in comparison with the average for the sample in each session and across the years. However, the portrait child and mother in each pair tended to produce similar percentages of pretend talk during a given play session (see Table A3.4 in the appendix). In the play session during the 3-year-old visit (when the mothers' pretend talk in the whole sample ranged from 7% to 96% of the total play talk), Casey and his mother had a fairly low percentage of pretend talk (22% and 30%, respectively, of their total play talk). By contrast, Todd and his mother had a much higher percentage of pretend talk (73% and 55%, respectively, of their total play talk). In the play session at the 4-year-old home visit (when mother's pretend talk ranged from 10% to 98% of their total play talk), fully 98% of Astra and her mother's play talk was pretend, the highest in the entire sample. Mariana and her mother also had greater than average percentages of pretend talk (60% and 59%, respectively). In fact, all of the portrait children and their mothers used more pretend talk at the 4-year-old home visit. At the 5-year-old home visit, however (when mothers' pretend talk ranged from 0% to 89%), all of the portrait children and their mothers used less pretend talk; at this play session the amount of pretend talk produced by Astra and her mother dropped to 48% and 61%, respectively. This pattern of rising then decreasing use of pretend talk between the 3- and 5-year-old home visits was also reflected in the sample overall (see Table A3.5 in the appendix).

These first descriptive analyses show us then that these 52 mother–child pairs used talk in different ways while they played with toys. Some mothers and children primarily used non-pretend talk, naming, counting, and describing the toys or discussing how they were using them. Other pairs engaged more in pretending and used their talk to develop play scenarios. No matter what type of talk the mothers and children used, or in what proportion, the mothers and children within each pair seemed overall to be well attuned to each other, producing similar amounts of pretend or non-pretend talk.

Interestingly, these descriptive analyses also show that, on average, mothers and children used less pretend talk when the children were 3 years old, used more pretend talk when the children were 4, and less again when the children were 5. This may indicate that pretend talk was a challenge for the children at age 3; that they were more competent and involved in pretending with their mothers at age 4; but that, as in the Haight and Miller (1993) study, the children became less interested in pretending with their mothers by the time they were 5.

We wondered next whether mothers and children produced relatively the same amounts of pretend play talk in the play session from year to year. Using a correlational analysis, we found moderate stability in the amounts of mothers' and children's talk between the 3- and 4-year-old home visits; stability in the use of pretend talk was even stronger between the 4- and 5-year-old home visits (see Table A3.6 in the appendix). We found no relationship, however, between the amount of pretend talk that the children and mothers produced when the children were 3 years old and when they were 5. So, the mothers and children in the Home–School Study were moderately stable in their production of pretend talk, but only from one year to the next.

Is there a relationship between mothers' and children's use of pretend talk in the same play session and in future play sessions? (See Table A3.7 in the appendix.) The data from each visit show that, overall, there is a very strong association between the amounts of pretend talk used by mothers and children within the same year. As noted previously, higher percentages of pretend talk from the mothers correlated positively and strongly with higher percentages of pretend talk from the children at the same point in time. We also found an association across time between mothers' pretend talk and the children's pretend talk, but only in adjacent years. Use of pretend talk by the mothers when the children were 3 years old shows a weak correlation with the children's use of pretend talk when they were 4 but shows no relationship to the children's use of pretend talk when they were 5. And, mothers' use of pretend talk when the children were 4 shows a similar moderate positive correlation with the children's use of pretend talk at age 5. Similarly, children's pretend talk at ages 3 and 4 had a moderate positive association with mothers' pretend talk at the 4- and 5-year-old home visits. There was, however, no association between children's pretend talk when they were 3 and mothers' pretend talk 2 years later. These findings are consistent with the research literature, which reports strong concurrent associations between mothers' and children's talk but is less clear on the association across time (Tamis-LeMonda & Bornstein, 1994).

From Pretend Talk to Early Literacy

Having examined the relationship between mothers' and children's pretend play talk at the three home visits, we wondered if there was a relationship between the amount of mothers' and children's pretend talk when the children were preschoolers and the children's performance on the language and literacy assessments when they were in kindergarten. Through a correlational analysis, we found first that children's and the mothers' use of pretend talk when the children were 3 had a moderate positive relationship with the children's definitional skill in kindergarten. That is, a greater percentage of pretend talk from both mothers and children when the children were 3 was associated with higher scores on the Formal Definitions task in kindergarten (see Table A3.8 in the appendix). Second, higher percentages of mothers' pretend talk when the children were 3 also had a weak positive association with higher scores on the kindergarten Receptive Vocabulary test. Third, greater amounts of pretend talk from both the mothers and the children when the children were 4 had a moderate positive association with higher scores on the Emergent Literacy tasks. Finally, mothers' pretend talk when the children were 4 had a weak but significant positive relationship with the children's ability in kindergarten to create a narrative. This pattern of relationships establishes that skill with the extended discourse of pretend talk in the preschool years is related to the language and literacy skills that are important for children in kindergarten.

SUGGESTIONS FOR PARENTS

By focusing on the extended discourse of pretend talk, we may seem to be ignoring other aspects of the experience of pretend play. We recognize that children and mothers engage in pretend play for the personal meaning and enjoyment inherent in the activity; the link between pretend talk and literacy is rarely in the mix. We recognize, too, that pretend play carries other important emotional and social benefits: Children can learn communicative strategies in playing out pretend scenarios, can develop social perspective by taking on characters, and can manage inner conflicts by acting them out in the safety of pretending. Other cognitive skills that are both basic to and developed in pretend are also important to understanding and managing the language environment of school. These skills include the ability to plan, to use language to reflect upon language, to "repair" breakdowns in communication (Garvey, 1990, 1993), and to maneuver among different modes of reality (Kane & Furth, 1993).

We also recognize that different cultural beliefs regarding language, pretending, and play may lead to different parenting practices in these areas (Göncü, 1999). In some cultures, for instance, the inventiveness of pretend talk may seem to be an affront to truthfulness rather than a confirmation of imagination (Heath, 1983). In addition, although playing with children is a valued activity among many European American middle-income families, some cultural groups in the United States may not agree. Even in the sample of 52 mother–child pairs, only about 25% of the mothers indicated that they routinely played with their young children. They named siblings, cousins, and neighborhood friends as their children's more frequent playmates, even when the children were 3 years old. While acknowledging these different beliefs, we offer the following suggestions that parents may want to consider:

- *Introduce pretend early in both gestural and verbal play:* Wendy Haight and Peggy Miller's (1993) study, among others, indicated that when parents introduce pretend as a mode of talk and play while their children are still infants, their children develop the habit of pretending by their third year and skill in creating and articulating pretend autonomously by their fourth or fifth year. Be aware of children's early symbolic transformations that may be preverbal and gestural. An 18-month-old, for example, may take a sip from a toy teacup, push a toy car while making humming "motor" sounds, or move his or her spoon in the air in imitation of an airplane. Acknowledge this early make-believe. As psychologist Catherine Garvey wrote, "The meaningfulness of even fleeting symbolic behaviors must be recognized and validated by caregivers if it is to enter into processes of systematic growth" (1990, p. 126).

- *Engage toddlers in play and talk about play:* For younger children, parents' suggestions of and enactment of play themes can model how pretend is done socially; narrating or describing the play can strengthen a child's ability to put actions into words. Follow the child's lead, indicate interest by repeating the child's own comments, and help the child to sustain and enlarge on his or her play by asking projective and open-ended questions that elaborate on the play themes. Reviewing studies of young children's pretending, developmental psychologists Greta Fein and Mary Fryer (1995) found in particular that in the context of child-centered play, specific rather than indirect suggestions (for example, "Would the animals like an airplane ride?" rather than "Those animals look bored") and active engagement from adults rather than passive commentary support young children's early pretending. Fein and Fryer reported also that intrusiveness and a tutorial style in mothers' talk seemed to have a negative effect on children's pretend play development.

- *Introduce knowledge about the world into play scenarios with toddlers and preschoolers:* Bring new and interesting information into play and initiate talk that explores the motivations of, the reasons for, the emotional responses to, or the results of pretend events. Pretend play is more compelling to adults and children and language use is richer and more varied when real-world information, novel information, and open inquiry are part of the play.

Finally, a word about toys: Wendy Haight and Peggy Miller (1993), who authored the longitudinal study on very young children's development of play at home, suggested that children's play is shaped both by the social ecology (that is, who is available and willing to play) and the physical ecology (that is, the space and the kind of toys available) of a child's home. Although different toys encourage different kinds of play, the relationship between particular kinds of toys and the kinds of play that they promote may be complex. For instance, developmental psychologist Vonnie McLoyd (1983) studied a group of low-income, predominantly African American preschoolers' play with low-structure toys (such as pipe cleaners, Styrofoam cups, paper bags, blocks) and high-structure and replica toys (that is, trucks, male and female dolls, a toy medical kit, a tea set, dress-up clothes). She found that use of the high-structure toys led to more non-interactive and social pretend play. The low-structure toys, however, led to more symbolic transformations. In the Home–School Study, the tea set, the telephones, the blocks, the toy cars, and the school bus seemed to elicit the most social pretend play among the mother–child pairs. We also noted, however, that nearly all of the toys were used both in a literal mode and a pretend mode. Elaborate pretend play and talk sometimes emerged with use of the toy animals, while literal talk sometimes accompanied use of the tea set. More important than the playthings was the orientation that a mother and child brought to the activity: An interest in exploring inventive, imaginative play through talk was the key to creating a pretend world.

Chapter 4

Eating and Reading

*Links Between Family Conversations
with Preschoolers and Later Language and Literacy*

Diane E. Beals

Family mealtimes seem to hold special power in American families. In the 1980s and 1990s, the popular media decried the decline in the frequency of families' eating dinner together as portending a bleak future for the child, the family, and the nation. The Roper Center of Storrs, Connecticut, polled families in 1976 and 1986 and found that the number of families sitting down to a meal together had dropped by 10% in 10 years (Bennett, 1995). In 1993, *Family Circle* magazine reported the results of its own survey that nearly one fourth of American families did not regularly eat a meal together (as cited in Bennett, 1995). Oprah Winfrey produced a prime-time television special in which she interviewed several families that had pledged to sit down together at the dinner table for 6 weeks. These families reported some successes and some failures; some pledged to continue eating dinner together forever, whereas others gave up trying to organize their dinnertime together.

Why all the worry? What makes mealtimes so important to Americans? American culture has historically seen mealtimes as events in which family members work out their relationships, pass on family values and lore, and acquaint children with social and cultural norms. Even President Clinton and his family protected their schedules so that they could have dinner together at 7:30 most evenings (Walsh, 1997). Because many families believe that mealtimes have this sort of power, the conversations that take place during mealtimes are a valuable source of insight into families' inner workings. When families sit down together for their evening meal, they are not just consuming protein, fat, and carbohydrates but also are engaging in a social interaction in the form of oral language that passes on to the children the values and norms of speech and behavior of the individual parents and of the larger culture.

In the following piece of a mealtime conversation, 3-year-old Tommy is talking with his mother about a topic that a child his age has great concerns about: monsters and the fears associated with them.

Mother: There aren't a real lot of wild animals here.
Tommy: No, but if we see a whole bunch, um, I would waked up. And when I waked up, they will still be there.
Mother: Think so?
Tommy: Mm-hm. Because I see them when I'm asleep, when I was asleep, I, my dreams [unintelligible].
Mother: Yeah. When you're asleep, sometimes your dreams are very real. But it's just your imagination working while the rest of you sleeps.
Tommy: Mommy, mommy?
Mother: What?
Tommy: My dreams did come true.
Mother: No?
Tommy: It did.
Mother: It did? What was your dream about?
Tommy: It was a monster, and I was [unintelligible] with his tongue, it, Mom, his, his whole [unintelligible], and he dropped me on my neck.
Mother: The monster grabbed you on your head, but that didn't come true. No monster really grabbed you on your neck.
Tommy: It did come true.
Mother: It did? When?
Tommy: A long time ago.
Mother: Yeah?
Tommy: And it jabbed me in the eye.
Mother: It did?
Tommy: Mm-hm.
Mother: No, honey, it didn't come true.
Tommy: Mm-hm.
Mother: You know I would never let any monsters get you. Besides, what did I tell you about monsters?
Tommy: What?
Mother: They're only make-believe, and they only live in movies because somebody with a wonderful imagination makes up monsters. And all other sort of special effects to make the really scary mon-

sters, you know, like how you watch Michael Jackson? And they show him putting his makeup on for "Thriller"? That's just because somebody had a great imagination.

Tommy: Mm-hm.

Mother: But no, there's no such things as monsters.

In attempting to ease Tommy's fears about monsters, his mother uses the word *imagination* to help him understand where monsters come from and that he need not fear them because they are "only make-believe." Her explicit connection to another experience they had shared, viewing a videotape about how Michael Jackson's "Thriller" music video was made, seems to be intended to show how monsters are made up by people with "wonderful" and "great" imaginations. So, neither imaginations nor their products (in this case, monsters) need be feared. Tommy's mother helps him talk about a meaningful topic by giving him an explanation using words that are intended to comfort him and assure him that she "would never let any monsters get" him. Here, Tommy is being initiated into the world of words that passes on to him a belief that monsters are only figments of people's imaginations. During this mealtime, Tommy learned about make-believe and about his mother's determination to keep him safe.

Children can and do learn a lot from listening, watching, and participating in these kinds of conversations with their families. Such talk allows children to think and acquire information about a wide variety of topics and to learn the forms in which people talk about these topics. During mealtimes, children hear and participate in stories and explanations about everyday life. Often, talk about events, either past or future, is in the form of a narrative or story. Talk about objects, words, actions, and motives often comes in the form of an explanation, such as a description of a person or an object; in a cause-and-effect explanation of a chain of events; or in a definition of a word. Hence, mealtime conversations constitute an important place to study the connections between a family's ways of talking during the preschool years and children's developing oral language abilities. In this chapter, specific kinds of talk that have been observed in mealtime conversations in the Home–School Study of Language and Literacy Development are described and the literacy benefits of such talk for young children are outlined.

Let's examine a brief example of talk from another family's mealtime. In this mealtime interaction, several possibilities can be envisioned for Rosalyn, who is 5 years old, to participate in a discussion about events years into the future, planning for when she and her older sister, Cheryl, both hold driver's licenses:

Father: Pretty soon, you'll be big enough to drive to the store and buy the groceries for us.

Rosalyn: I will?

Mother: [Laughs]

Father: Well, about 13 or 14 years.

Rosalyn: I will?

Father: Sure. In 14 years.

Rosalyn: That's fun.

Father: In 14 years, you'll be 17. And you'll have your driver's license and go grocery shopping.

Mother: In 14 years, she'll be 19.

Father: Oh, right, I'm sorry. Gee! Only 12 years and you'll be 17. Suppose Cheryl will go grocery shopping for us when she gets her license?

Rosalyn: Hmm [laughs].

Father: Maybe she'll offer to do it just so she can drive the car [laughing].

Mother: I don't know.

Father: That would be the only reason she'd offer.

Mother: Mm-hm.

Rosalyn: That would be real good. [Giggles] I hope she doesn't crash.

Father: Well, we hope she doesn't crash either.

In this brief segment of a longer mealtime conversation, Rosalyn is getting practice in making future plans and describing those plans to others. This is a form of narrative talk that children need to learn in order to be successful in school tasks such as recognizing sequences of events and planning for getting homework home, completed, and returned to school. Rosalyn hears numbers discussed in terms of calculating her age until she can drive legally, an implied explanation that one must be 17 or some advanced age to drive (5 + 12 = 17). In addition, she is exposed to a new vocabulary word in this conversation, a word that many 5-year-olds do not know: *license*. Her father does not stop to define the word, describe what a license might look like, or show Rosalyn his own driver's license. But there seems to be information in the conversation for Rosalyn to learn at least some sense of the word's meaning. She can infer that it has something to do with driving and that one can get it only when one is older, so she is receiving an indirect explanation of *license*.

On audiotape, this sounds like a very natural conversation for a family to engage in. It appears that Rosalyn's father is teaching her about driver's licenses. Sometimes one assumes that this kind of teaching sounds stilted and bossy; but, in fact, it tends to be comfortable, natural, unplanned, and perhaps even unconscious. Such conversations are important teachable moments that occur all day long in conversation with young children.

So, what exactly are some helpful ways of talking to children at mealtimes that aid their language and literacy development? First, let's look at how the mealtime conversations of the families in the Home–School Study were collected and analyzed.

MEALTIME DATA COLLECTION

At the end of each of the home visits, when the children involved in the Home–School Study were 3, 4, and 5 years old, an audiotape recorder and a blank audiotape were left behind for the families to record what they considered to be a typical mealtime conversation. This means that the mealtime was recorded without the home visitor present. The tape and recorder were collected at a later date.

A total of 160 audiotapes of mealtime conversations were collected (see Table 4.1). A total of 68 different families (with 70 different focus children; two families had twins) returned at least one audiotape. Twenty families returned two of the mealtime tapes. Thirty-six of the families returned all three audiotapes, including the families of the portrait children: Casey, Mariana, Astra, and Todd.

The participants in mealtime conversations varied widely across the families. Some families consisted of only the mother and her child, and other families had siblings or other children present. Fathers were present at only 52 of the mealtimes. Some families included other adults; for example, two families consisted of the mother, the child, and the child's maternal grandparents. Among the portrait children, Astra's and Casey's families had fathers present at the mealtimes, but Mariana's and Todd's families did not. Casey's father participated more frequently in conversations than did Astra's father. Casey, Mariana, and Astra each had one brother and Todd had two sisters present at the three mealtimes that were recorded.

What the mothers thought we expected from the recording of a mealtime is important to take into consideration. The mothers were aware of the fact that we were studying their children's language, and because they were asked to place the tape recorder near the child who was being studied, the implicit message to them was that we wanted them to record the talk of that child. Therefore, most mothers tended to make a concerted effort to draw that child into the conversation. In the 3-year-old home visit, some mothers took the mealtime conversation to be some kind of performance, and, in a few cases, the children

Table 4.1. Number of audiotapes returned

Age 3 mealtime	64
Age 4 mealtime	45
Age 5 mealtime	51
Total	160

were asked to perform their ABCs, to count, or to sing a favorite song. This kind of performance was much less frequent in the 4- and 5-year-old home visits, most likely because of the children's ability to initiate and join in the family's conversations.

Because of the differences in family makeup and in the mothers' varied conceptions of the request to tape the mealtime, mealtime conversations were very different in character from family to family. The mealtime conversations ranged in length from approximately 2 to 47 minutes, averaging around 20 minutes. Most mealtimes consisted of family members' meeting in one place at the same time, although one mealtime consisted of two children eating cereal in front of the television. Another "mealtime" was in fact a conversation that took place while a mother and child made cornbread; the mother reported that because she and her son live alone, there is no formal mealtime. Most other families' mealtimes were an evening meal or a more formal Sunday afternoon family meal. In most families, interaction among family members was clearly a priority, but in a few, the television was a focus of attention. For Casey, Mariana, Astra, and Todd, the mealtimes were conversations among family members with the television off.

The children and parents varied in their contributions to the mealtimes (see Table A4.1 in the appendix for average proportions of the talk by mothers, children involved in the study, and fathers [if present], on the basis of the number of utterances of each speaker). Overall, mothers and children in the study together accounted for approximately three quarters of the talk at mealtimes, on average. Fathers, on average, provided relatively little input into the overall conversations. In Astra's ages 3 and 4 mealtimes, mealtime talk was about the food itself, such as, "You gonna give me a big, big, big, big chicken, Mommy," and "You want bread, Shandi?" During the age 5 mealtime excerpted here, Astra and her mother talk at length about her day at school, including discussing a child who had done naughty things:

Mother: What Miss Connie say today?
  Astra: Uh . . .
Mother: Freddie was good in the class?
  Astra: He say no to Miss Connie when she, when she put, um, when he, when she told him to do his homework.

Mother: Really?
 Astra: Yeah.
Mother: So, what she said to him?
 Astra: He went down to the principal's office.

Also at this mealtime, while the family ate alphabet soup, Astra and her parents tried to spell words with the letters they found—a direct connection between mealtime and literacy! Although the age 3 mealtime for this family was 23 minutes long—slightly longer than average—the other two mealtimes for this family were 2 minutes and 13 minutes long, respectively.

Mariana's mealtimes were of average length: around 20 minutes each. The mealtimes began with her mother attempting to settle down Mariana and her older brother, Manny, in order to read a verse from the Bible to them and then to say grace. Manny assumed dinner to be a time to act up and generally received reprimands from his mother or was dismissed from the table. Mariana seemed to enjoy his antics and joined in. In the following example, Manny complains about some food his mother has put on his plate:

Manny: I don't want this. I don't want this.
Mariana: [Laughs]
Mother: That's not too funny, Mariana. You know better.
Mariana: [Laughs]
Mother: Manny, please.
Manny: [Whines]

Besides Mariana's mother's wrestling for control of her children's behavior at mealtimes, she also attempted to tell the children about her day, as shown in the next example:

Mother: Know who wrote me a letter, Manny?
Manny: Who?
Mother: Carmen. Remember Carmen?
Manny: Why?
Mother: Well, she wanted to come back to Puerto Rico, and she sent me this letter yesterday.
Manny: You told [unintelligible] he went away?
Mother: Yeah. I need her.
Manny: Why you need, why you want [unintelligible]?
Mother: Oh, because I enjoyed her coming here. She was a nice lady, wasn't she?

Mariana: [unintelligible].
Mother: She told me to say hi to you and Mariana. In the letter.

Occasionally, mealtime conversations also included the children's telling about their days at school and planning for the next day.

Todd's family's mealtimes, with his mother and older sisters, Darcy
and Elaine, tended to be more varied in content than the mealtime
conversations of Astra and Mariana. With four people all actively and
positively involved in the conversation, Todd's family tended to have
longer-than-average mealtime conversations. Darcy's more advanced
language skills seemed to "up the ante" for the two younger children,
allowing them to raise the level of their own talk to compete with Darcy.
They told a few exciting stories, as in the following example from the
mealtime when Todd was 3 years old:

Elaine: Darcy, know what? They made me look in Scott's yard. Know
          what they saw under the table?
Darcy: What?
Elaine: A dead mouse.
 Todd: And we saw the blood!
Elaine: And the heart.
Mother: Okay, okay, we're eating.
Elaine: No! We only saw the heart.
Mother: Yeah, Elaine.
Darcy: Oh.
Elaine: I hated it.

Besides telling stories, Todd's family also discussed a lot of people, places,
things, and ideas not present at the dinner table, with topics ranging
from decorating Easter eggs to Madonna's latest song. Besides these
types of talk, there was much commentary about the distribution and
consumption of food.

In Casey's mealtimes, there was a lot of talk about food, but his
family also engaged in rather long stretches of talk about some interesting topics, such as the next one about a visit to his school by firefighters, from the mealtime when Casey was 4 years old:

Casey: The fire guys, the firefighters, um, they have walkie-talkies so
          they can tell where they are.
Mother: In case they need to call for help?
Casey: Yep.

Father: That's right. Tell them how big the fire is. How bad it is. If they need more trucks.

Casey: Yep. We have a lot of firepoles.

Mother: Yeah.

At mealtimes, Casey's family also discussed the oxygen tanks that fire-fighters wear (see Chapter 5), going to the circus with his class, and shooting off fireworks on a past Fourth of July. His father and older brother, Mack, were often leaders of these conversations, and Casey joined in with them. Mealtimes in Casey's family were briefer than the average for the study, but they were full of interesting discussions.

Key Aspects of Mealtime Conversations

Because the purpose of the Home–School Study is to investigate how children acquire literacy skills, I focused my analysis of mealtime conversations on two types of talk that I believe support a child's ability to speak, listen, read, and write in school later on: *narrative talk* and *explanatory talk*. Both of these types of talk are commonly used by children and teachers and in texts in classrooms.

Narratives In my analysis (Beals & DeTemple, 1993; Beals & Snow, 1994), I searched the mealtimes for the presence of narrative talk by all family members. Narratives are one type of extended discourse that tell about an event that has happened in the past or that will happen in the future and that usually take shape over several turns in a conversation. Much of children's first exposure to print in school (both reading and writing) is in the form of narratives or stories. Oral narratives during mealtimes can help children learn what kind of information goes into a good story and how to organize a set of events in a specific sequence to get the narrative told clearly. Narrative talk also gives them practice in comprehending others' narratives and in negotiating the point of telling the story.

Talk during mealtimes was marked as *narrative* when the topic was a past or future event (that is, an event taking place at another time and/or place). Sometimes narratives were constructed entirely by the adults at the dinner table while talking to each other. Although these narratives did not include the children in the telling, they were available for the children as models. More often, however, the narratives during mealtimes involved both adults' and children's *co-constructing* the narrative. For example, in the following narrative, 3-year-old Greg, his mother, and his older brother are telling the story of losing a school project and planning how to recover and display the project. In this narrative, Greg's mother takes the lead in the conversation, but both Greg and his brother contribute to the narrative:

Mother: What did you do?

Greg: And then we made a funky monkey.

Mother: You made a funky monkey? Oh, the monkey that you made, huh? That's a cute monkey. Where is it, anyway? I think we left it in Johnny's by accident when we were there.

Greg: Hmm, Mommy, it's under your coat.

Mother: I know, but I think I left it at the store. We'll have to get it tomorrow, because Johnny's is closed now. I think I left it on the counter by accident.

Brother: Maybe they already threw it away.

Mother: No, I don't think so. I'm sure they'll save it and give it to us tomorrow. Okay? Greg, that was a beautiful monkey. I want to hang him up on the wall.

Greg: Mommy, you had to have it stapled.

Mother: Okay, well, I'll get it stapled. We can hang it up with tape. Put it on the bathroom door. Okay?

Greg: No, on the ceiling.

Mother: On the ceiling?

Greg: Yeah!

Some of the narratives, however, particularly as the children in the study got older, were constructed entirely by the children themselves. For example, the following narrative is initiated and told by 5-year-old Brad about an event that had occurred that day at school. Notice how Brad uses *rhetorical questions* (such as "Guess what?") to initiate and to extend the narrative. He also uses *conversational fillers* (such as "um") and *retracings* (such as "after-school pro-, um, after-school program") as he struggles to compose the narrative. Also notice that Brad uses storytelling intonation that rises at the end of each statement. His grandmother's *backchannel* (such as "mm-hm") in response to the intonation contour gives Brad some time to construct his next utterance and signals that she is involved by listening carefully to his story.

Brad: Guess what?

Grandmother: What?

Brad: Um, um, Roy?

Grandmother: Mm-hm.

Brad: Roy in the after-school pro-, um, after-school program?

Grandmother: Yeah?

Brad:	He made, um, something with blocks?
Grandmother:	Mm-hm?
Brad:	It was a dinosaur down the bottom?
Grandmother:	Hmm.
Brad:	And a hole to make the, um, superball go out?
Grandmother:	Mm-hm.
Brad:	And, um, um, the end, the end [unintelligible] as the ball went out that means you should win?
Grandmother:	Brad, that sounds like so much fun.
Brad:	And, um, and um, Roy and the other kids didn't win?
Grandmother:	Hmm.
Brad:	Only I won.
Grandmother:	Oh! Wonderful.
Brad:	And, and guess what Patrick said?
Grandmother:	What?
Brad:	Patrick said I broke his record.
Grandmother:	Wow!

Narrative Results   Talk around narratives accounted for an average of 17% of all mealtime talk (with a range of 0%–65%) when the children in the study were age 3 (see Table A4.2 in the appendix). Narrative talk made up 11% of the mealtime talk, on average (with a range of 0%–36%), when the children were age 4. When the children were 5 years old, the proportion of narrative rebounded to 17% (with a range of 0%–54%).

This drop in amount of narrative talk at age 4 and rebound again at age 5 is a mysterious one (see Figure 4.1). Prominent researchers of children's narratives Peterson and McCabe (1983) have reported a similar trend. The age 3 mealtime narratives generally consisted of mothers' or fathers' trying to get their children involved in recalling events of the day or of some other day. Perhaps, when the children were 4 years old, mothers seemed less inclined to elicit such talk, and perhaps the children were less inclined to play that game anymore. At age 5, children were initiating their own narratives to tell and were more involved in contributing to others' narratives.

The average mealtime contained slightly fewer than 4 narratives, so the average across all three mealtimes was approximately 12 narratives. Astra's family produced only two narratives in all three of her mealtimes, well below the average. Todd's family produced seven narratives all together, and Mariana's family told nine narratives all together, still somewhat below average. Casey's family told a total of 13 narratives across all three mealtimes, right around the average. Figure

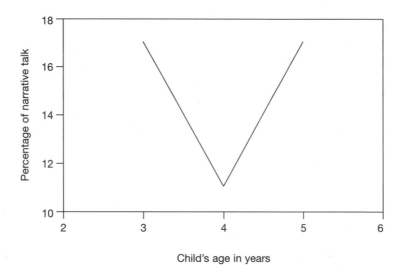

Figure 4.1.   Average percentage of narrative talk during mealtimes for all children.

4.2 presents the frequency of each of the portrait family's narratives over time.

The mothers and children involved in the study contributed most of the talk in narratives, about 45% and 30% at each mealtime, respectively. This is roughly equivalent to the proportions that mothers and children participated in the full conversation.

Explanations   *Explanatory talk* was defined as talk that requested and/or made some logical connection between objects, events, concepts, or conclusions (Beals, 1993). In particular, I searched for explanations of people's actions or speech. In the next example, from the mealtime when Astra was 3 years old, her mother gives a very common type of explanation, one in which she issues a command or a request to the child and then gives a reason for making that request:

Mother: Don't eat too fast, Astra. You'll choke yourself.
  Astra: Okay. Not too fast.

Family members also asked for explanations of actions. In the next example, Mariana's older brother, Manny, notices that his mother has taken the Popsicles out of the box, returned the Popsicles to the freezer, and discarded the box:

Manny: Why you took them out from the . . . out of the box?
Mother: What do you want the box for? Are you going to eat the box?

Manny: No, but there were Popsicles in the box.
Mother: There were only three left, Manny. We don't need the whole
         box in the freezer.

In addition, I looked for cause-and-effect explanations. In the following example, 5-year-old Todd, his mother, and his older sister, Elaine,
discuss the causes of allergies and asthma. Todd, who has allergies,
seems to be much better informed than Elaine, who seems to be trying
to claim that she also has allergy trouble:

    Todd: Do you be borned allergic to stuff?
  Mother: Do.
   Elaine: Do I be born allergic, Mom?
  Mother: There's no such thing "Do I be born."
    Todd: Do you have to? Are you have, do you?
  Mother: It's, "Are you born allergic."
    Todd: Are we?
  Mother: Some people are, some people . . .
   Elaine: Catch it from others.
  Mother: No, you don't catch it, but you just, when you get older you start
            getting allergic to certain things.
   Elaine: I'm . . .
  Mother: Like when you're older
   Elaine: I was [unintelligible].
    Todd: I was the older, I was 4 when [unintelligible]. No one knows if
            I'm not allergic to them anymore, right?

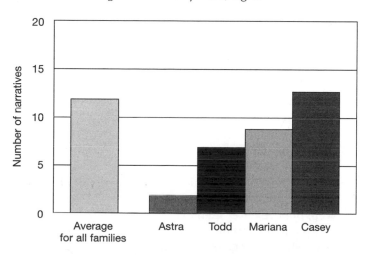

Figure 4.2. Number of portrait families' narratives during mealtimes.

Mother: Right.
Elaine: I was born to asthma. I was born . . .
Todd: I know you . . .
Mother: Not, Elaine! You're not born with asthma, that's right.
Todd: Everybody'd have to be born with asthma.
Elaine: No, sir. You could get it while you get old.
Mother: No, you weren't born with asthma, actually. You didn't get it until you were 2. You had bronchitis.
Elaine: I was born with bronchitis?

I also searched for definitions or descriptions of words and objects as another type of explanatory talk. In the next example, part of a longer discussion about sea animals, 3-year-old Remo's father defines and describes seahorses in great detail:

Mother: I haven't seen a seahorse, Remo, since I was a little girl.
Father: They used to sell them in . . . what store was that? Woolworth's or Kresge's or something, or Sparks'.
Remo: Yeah, they used to make . . .
Father: Little tiny seahorses. They were about the size of a half a dollar.
Remo: Yeah.
Father: When Daddy was a little boy, we used to go buy them. Little goldfish, little seahorses, little turtles.
Remo: Yeah. A seahorse is long with a tail. The . . . that seahorse had a . . .
Father: They had a little tail that curls up.
Remo: That little seahorse had a [unintelligible] that you can eat. . . .
Father: That's right.
Remo: A lot, because they call that shrimp.
Father: Do you know what a seahorse eats?
Remo: Yeah.
Father: What does a seahorse eat?
Remo: I don't know.
Father: A seahorse eats plankton and microbacteria that float around in the ocean.
Remo: Yeah.
Father: Now, you need a special lens or a special pair of glasses to see this microbacteria, but it's food for the seahorses.
Remo: Well, but I've never seen them.
Father: And plankton and microbacteria are just about the same. And that's where they get all of their nourishment from. See?

Explanation Results Explanations also were relatively frequent in mealtime conversations, accounting for an average of 15% of the talk (ranging from 0% to 43%) when the children involved in the study were age 3, an average of 16% of the talk (ranging from 0% to 52%) when they were age 4, and an average of 14% of the conversation (ranging from 0% to 30%) when they were age 5 (see Table A4.3 in the appendix). Unlike narrative talk the percentage of explanatory talk remained stable over the 3 years.

There were about 13 or 14 explanations in the average transcript, compared with three to four narratives found in the average transcript. Although explanations were more frequent than narratives at all three ages, they tended to be shorter (fewer turns by the speakers) than narratives.

There were a total of 80 explanations in the mealtimes in Todd's family, about twice the average amount. Mariana's family produced 53 explanations, also greater than average, and Casey's family gave 37 explanations, right about average, across the three mealtimes. Astra's family again produced fewer than average explanations, giving only 14 explanations in the three mealtimes. In Figure 4.3, each portrait family's use of explanations is graphed across mealtimes and compared with the average.

Mothers and children in the study accounted for approximately three fourths of explanatory and narrative talk at all three mealtimes. Children, even as early as age 3, were very involved in explanatory talk, contributing approximately 30% of the utterances in segments of explanatory talk, whereas mothers contributed roughly 45%. Again, others present at mealtimes, including fathers, siblings, grandparents, and visitors, were relatively infrequent contributors, on average, to both explanatory and narrative talk.

LITERACY OUTCOMES

In a correlational analysis, the amounts of *narrative talk* and *explanatory talk* were both positively associated with a number of the language and literacy measures from the School-Home Early Language and Literacy Battery–Kindergarten (SHELL–K; Snow, Tablors, Nicholson, & Kurland, 1995).

Specifically, the results indicated that the more exposure to explanatory talk that 4- and 5-year-olds in the study received, the greater was the child's ability to connect a word with the correct picture as measured on the Peabody Picture Vocabulary Test–Revised (PPVT–R; Dunn & Dunn, 1981) at age 5. Furthermore, a greater amount of narrative talk at mealtimes at age 5 was associated with higher PPVT–R scores at

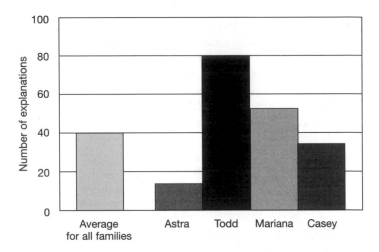

Figure 4.3. Number of portrait families' explanations during mealtimes.

age 5. Also, exposure to more explanatory talk at all three home visits and narrative talk at age 5 had strong relationships with a child's ability to give definitions of words at age 5. Furthermore, the greater the amount of narrative talk that occurred during mealtimes when the children in the study were 4 years old, the higher their score was on the Story Comprehension task. These findings suggest that children do not necessarily need to be giving explanations and narratives in order to benefit from exposure. They can benefit from hearing discussions, requesting explanations or narratives, and adding their contributions to the discussion whenever appropriate.

CONCLUSIONS

The examination of mealtime conversations in the Home–School Study found that there were strong positive relationships between *narrative* and *explanatory talk* at mealtimes during the preschool years and children's scores on literacy-related measures when the children were 5 years old. More extended discourse—in the form of narrative or explanatory talk—was related to higher scores on the vocabulary, definitions, and listening comprehension measures. These skills are drawn on heavily in school, and teachers expect children to bring these skills with them to school. So, a child who has been exposed to a lot of discussions around a variety of topics, including both narrative talk and explanatory talk, is being prepared for the demands of schooling.

SUGGESTIONS FOR PARENTS

Explanatory talk at home offers children the opportunity to make connections between ideas, events, and actions. As the examples in this chapter illustrate, the greater proportion of explanatory talk at family mealtimes appears to support vocabulary development. The amount of explanatory talk is a family measure, not a measure of the child's ability. Thus, this relationship suggests that family environment, not simply the child's language sophistication, sets the stage for later literacy development. The following are some suggestions for how parents can enhance their children's experience with explanatory language:

- Take time each day to have extended discussions with children.

- Allow the children to choose their own topics.

- Answer children's questions, particularly those about causes and effects. You do not have to be an authority on the topic to give children a better idea about how the world works than they had when they asked the question.

- Discuss people's intentions or motivations for what they say or do, including your own.

- Describe objects and events together interactively. Raise questions that extend the descriptions.

- Expose children to new words. Give a definition or a synonym for the words. Use them in that conversation and in future ones.

Narrative talk within family mealtime conversations during the preschool years, another measure of the children's linguistic environment, also appears to be a strong predictor of literacy development. Conversations among family members about past and future events afforded the children in the Home–School Study the opportunity to improve their vocabulary and to learn and practice the structure of event narratives. Such experiences could well be laying a foundation for reading, comprehending, telling, and writing one's own stories. The following are some suggestions for increasing children's exposure to narrative talk:

- Tell about an interesting event in your day or evening, varying your intonation to highlight the interesting portions.

- Encourage children to tell about their day or evening. Ask them questions to support their storytelling.

- When they initiate a story, allow children to tell it on their own. Wait until they stop talking before asking any questions or making comments.

- Discuss future events and plans, real or imagined.

Chapter 5

"You Know What Oxygen Is?"
Learning New Words at Home

Patton O. Tabors, Diane E. Beals, and Zehava O. Weizman

In the previous chapters on the home environments of the children in the Home–School Study of Language and Literacy Development, we have demonstrated the kinds of language-enriching talk that children are exposed to in three different contexts: book reading, toy play, and mealtimes. In all of the examples presented, the reader may have noticed the range of words that are used to discuss different topics within the various contexts. This is no coincidence. It takes lots of different words in order to have an in-depth, extended discussion around a particular topic.

In a large body of research on children's reading, the size of children's vocabularies has been shown to be related to their ability to comprehend what they are reading (Anderson & Freebody, 1981). It seems reasonable to assume, then, that helping a child build an extensive vocabulary during the preschool years will help with reading comprehension during the school years. The purpose of this chapter is to investigate the vocabulary that the children in the Home–School Study were exposed to in the different conversational settings that we recorded in their homes and to look for relationships between that exposure and children's receptive vocabulary in kindergarten.

Let's begin by examining a sample of talk during Casey's mealtime when he was 4 years old. His family has been discussing a visit by some firefighters to his preschool classroom that day. For the visit, the firefighters had brought along some of their specialized equipment, including hoses, axes, and an oxygen tank.

Father: You know what oxygen is? That's . . .

Casey: Yeah, you put that, and you get air from it [unintelligible].

Father: That's the air because when you go in the fires, you're in the fire-house, smoke gets in, and [coughs] you cough and you can't breathe. You can use that oxygen and get some fresh air in you.

Casey: Does it go behind your back?

Father: Yeah, like a scuba diver.

Casey: Oh, yeah, we get them at, uh, wait, um, Ann [his teacher] told us [unintelligible].

Father: Like the guy in the bathtub? Like, you know, that black guy, that plastic thing there?

Casey: Why?

Father: You know the guy in the bathtub there?

Casey: Yeah.

Father: He's got one, doesn't he?

Casey: Yep. He only has two. If you have two, you can have [unintelligible] oxygen tanks. You can stay in the water for 2 minutes, and 1, you can stay underwater 1.

Mother: That's right! Only it's hours. If you have two you can stay under 2 hours. One, 1 hour. Very good! How did you know that?

Casey: Mack [his brother] taught me that.

Mother: Did he? Oh, he teaches you a lot of things, huh?

Here, Casey and his parents are engaged in a discussion that should help Casey gain at least a beginning understanding of the word *oxygen*. He demonstrates knowledge of oxygen tanks as things that "you get air from." His father refers to getting air as *breathing*, so Casey can recognize the everyday function of oxygen or air and why you need it in a smoky house fire. His father notes the similarity between firefighters' oxygen tanks and scuba divers' oxygen tanks. Casey seems to know something about scuba diving because he has a toy diver in the bathtub, and he knows that the number of tanks is related to how long a diver can stay underwater. Though this conversation takes place during an ordinary, comfortable family mealtime, Casey's father and mother appear to be using a variety of techniques, intentionally or not, to teach him a new vocabulary word.

In looking at vocabulary acquisition in the Home–School Study, we wanted to answer three questions:

1. What new vocabulary words were being introduced during conversations that the children in the study were involved in?

2. How were these words used in different conversational settings, such as toy play, book reading, and mealtimes, and how did the

conversational contexts help the children to learn at least some sense of a new word?

3. Are there relationships between vocabulary use by family members and children's later vocabulary skill?

LEARNING NEW WORDS

As can be see in the excerpt from Casey's family's mealtime, when adults and children engage in conversation, they are creating a situation in which children can be exposed to new words. Knowing that vocabulary development would be an important aspect of language development for the children in the study, we decided to see whether it would be possible to look at the words that the mothers and, in the case of mealtimes other members of the family, were using with the children and identify the words that might be new. If we could do that, then we would be able to see whether the use of these words made a difference in the children's vocabulary skill when they reached kindergarten.

In order to get an idea of the kinds of vocabulary words that the children in the study might be learning from their conversations with family members, we developed a technique for identifying and then counting words that might be new words for a preschool-age child. We call these words *rare words.*

The first step in the process of finding the rare words was to take all of the words in the transcript material from a particular conversational context during a home visit and have a computer program[1] combine all of the words spoken by the mothers or, in the case of mealtimes, by all of the family members. So, for example, we combined all of the words that the mothers used during the toy-play session at the 5-year-old home visit and found that there were 36,217 words in all.

Next we checked to see how often these words were used. Not surprisingly, in a large collection of words such as this, some words were used much more frequently than others. In the 5-year-old home visit toy-play sessions, the word *you,* for example, was used the most—1,767 times—whereas *okay* was used 525 times; *go,* 208 times; *think,* 168 times; and *play,* 134 times. Other words were used only once—such as *wicked, volcano, stegosaurus,* and *senile.* The words used most often would be considered *common* or *high-frequency words;* the words used less often, *uncommon* or *low-frequency words.*

In order to begin to sort out which of the words in the conversational settings might be new words for the preschool-age children in the

---

[1]This process of identifying rare words depended upon computer software called *Child Language Analysis* (CLAN) from the Child Language Data Exchange System (CHILDES) project (MacWhinney, 2000).

study, we removed all of the common words from the electronic versions of the transcripts. We did this by comparing our list of all the words used by the mothers or family members with a list of 7,881 common words derived from Jeanne Chall and Edgar Dale's (1995) research and then deleting any matching words. This left us with a list of uncommon words. Not all of these uncommon words were rare words, however, because they included proper names (*Stoneham*), exclamations (*Wow!*), forms of address (*sweetie*), slang, dialect, incorrect forms (*pickinic*), and child culture words (*Ninja Turtles*). These words were also edited out of the word lists so that all of the remaining words were rare words. For the 5-year-old home visit toy-play transcripts, this process left us with 200 rare words (see Table A5.1 in the appendix for the rare-words list).

We were then able to identify the mothers or other family members who used the words on the rare-words list for each of the conversational settings and count how many times they used the words. Because the transcripts were of different lengths, we then calculated a density measure for each speaker. This involved dividing the number of rare words used by that speaker by the number of all words used by that speaker, then multiplying by 1,000. We calculated density measures for the mothers for four of the book readings (using only the mothers' talk, not the text of the book), all of the toy-play sessions, and all of the mealtimes, as well as the *density of rare words* for all of the speakers, except the child, at the mealtimes.

As with most of the analyses in the project, we found a lot of variation in the *rare-word density* measures. In the 3-year-old toy play, for example, the average *density of rare words* used by the mothers was 9 per 1,000, but six mothers did not use any rare words, and one mother had a density measure of 48. For the 4-year-old toy play, the average *density of rare words* used by the mothers rose to 14 per 1,000. Seven mothers, however, did not use any rare words during the 4-year-old toy play (including Astra's mother), and the highest density was 66. For the 5-year-old toy play, the average *density of rare words* used by the mothers was 12 per 1,000, with four mothers who did not use any rare words (again including Astra's mother), and the highest score was 46. We found similar variation for the other *rare-word density* measures for all of the conversational contexts (see Table A5.2 in the appendix for information on rare-word densities for all of the conversational settings).

We also found that there were some associations between mothers' *rare-word density* measures at each home visit and those at the other home visits. This means that though mothers did not use exactly the same level of rare words year after year, there was a tendency for mothers who used fewer or more rare words to maintain something like that level from one home visit to the next for some of the conversational settings. There was a moderate association between mothers' rare-word densities during the 3-year-old and 4-year-old readings of *The Very Hungry Caterpillar* (Carle, 1979), a moderate-to-strong relationship between the mothers' use of rare words during all three toy plays, and a strong relationship between mothers' and all speakers' rare-word densities between the 3-year-old and 4-year-old mealtimes (see Tables A5.3–A5.6 in the appendix).

SUPPORT FOR RARE-WORD USE IN THE DIFFERENT CONVERSATIONAL CONTEXTS

The three conversational settings discussed in this section—toy play, book reading, and mealtimes—present distinctive types of opportunities for the introduction of rare words. Toy play is the least complicated conversational setting because it involves just the mother and the child and there are objects in the immediate context to refer to and few intervening distractions. Book reading, in contrast, is a more complex vocabulary situation because there are two sources of words: the words in the book and the words spoken by the mother. Mealtimes are also complex, but for another reason: They often provide a variety of conversational partners. Though some families' mealtimes consisted of only the mother and child eating and talking together, others had participants ranging from babies to next-door neighbors. In the following discussion, each of the conversational settings is examined to find out how new vocabulary was used by the families and how it was possible for children to begin to acquire that vocabulary.

Toy Play

How did mothers get rare words into the conversations during toy play? Sometimes mothers consciously introduced rare words (underlined) in the course of identifying the toys, as in the following example involving Tricia and her mother at the 3-year-old home visit:

Mother: What's this [holds up stuffed dinosaur]?
 Tricia: It's a dinosaur.
Mother: Yeah. I'm not sure, but this might be a stegosaurus. A stegosaurus. Can you say that?
 Tricia: Stegosaurus?
Mother: Mm-hm. That's the type of dinosaur he is. I think they call him that or, actually, know how you identify him, Tricia? See these things on his back? And see the little spikies on his tail?
 Tricia: Yeah.

In the preceding example, Tricia's mother not only connects the name of the dinosaur with the actual object but also has Tricia pronounce the word and gives her a series of defining features that make this dinosaur a *particular* kind of dinosaur, namely a stegosaurus.

During block play, mothers used rare words that described what was being built, thereby giving the children a chance to understand the meaning of the word from the immediate context of the play. In the following sequence, Mariana and her mother are building with the blocks during the 3-year-old home visit:

Mother: One, two, three, four extra blocks.
Mariana: Extra blocks . . . [knocks block off]. Uh-oh!
Mother: Uh-oh. You can use this [hands Mariana another block]. That's the <u>entrance</u> [puts a block into place].
Mariana: That's for the people. No, that's for the car! [Laughs]
Mother: They look nice.

When Todd and his mother were building with the blocks during the 4-year-old home visit, his mother used the rare word *railing:*

Todd: Mom, we have to have the other people that go . . .
Mother: Here, you want to go up through this?
Todd: What is that?
Mother: I'm making you a road with a <u>railing.</u> See, so you can go up like that. You know like when we're goin' over or somethin'— bridges.
Todd: Well, you gotta make the longest, the bridge that he can fit under?
Mother: Well, I don't know if I can make a bridge.

During the following tea party play, Rochelle's mother uses three rare words as she explains to Rochelle how to go about making coffee:

Mother: What are we making, tea or coffee?
Rochelle: Coffee and tea.
Mother: Okay you need to. . . . Let's make the coffee first.
Rochelle: Okay.
Mother: You need the little coffee <u>grinder,</u> remember?
Rochelle: Huh?
Mother: The stuff that I put in the white thing? You need those, and you pour the water in [makes a sound like water being poured]

and you put the top on, and you let it <u>brew</u>. Okay, now on the little <u>container</u>. . . . Here. Put it on here.

In all of these instances, the rare words are words that the mothers are introducing into the toy-play situation as part of the ongoing activity, so that the words are embedded in the context that is being played out by the mother and child. We can see how it would be possible for the children to begin to understand the meaning of the words when they are used in this way.

In the following examples, one can see how a word that Casey's mother uses during the 3-year-old home visit toy-play session becomes a word that Casey is able to use himself by the 5-year-old home visit. In the toy-play session at the 3-year-old home visit, Casey's mother uses the rare word *ramp* while playing with the toy cars:

Mother: I'll park mine here, you park yours there. Okay? Oh, look, we can make <u>ramps</u> and everything. We'll build a <u>ramp</u> and go jump. Right?
Casey: [Makes a noise as his car jumps over the ramp]
Mother: [Laughs]
Casey: [Checks the numbers on the race cars] This one's a 1 and this one is 7.
Mother: 1 and a 7?
Casey: Yeah. Mm-hm.
Mother: Oh yeah.
Casey: 4. 7.
Mother: What's that?
Casey: 10. No, that doesn't have a number.
Mother: Doesn't have a number?
Casey: [Makes engine noises]
Mother: Back down the same way, down the <u>ramp</u>.
Casey: You turn around.

By the 5-year-old home visit, Casey is the first one to use the word *ramp*, followed by his mother. Clearly, Casey knows the meaning of *ramp*.

Mother: Here's a couple of fast-looking cars.
Casey: And this is very fast.
Mother: This one's turbo. See, it's turbo.
Casey: This is a <u>ramp</u>.
Mother: Okay.

Casey: Maybe I'll try it, building a <u>ramp</u> [makes sound of car going].
Mother: You gonna make a big <u>ramp</u>?
Casey: I can't make a big <u>ramp</u>. How do I make one?
Mother: Do you want to do something else?
Casey: I can make a big <u>ramp</u>.
Mother: All right, let me see.
Casey: Gonna make one.
Mother: Oh, yeah.

Obviously, Casey has had lots of other opportunities to hear the word *ramp* in other conversations besides these with his mother, but his mother's use of the word and Casey's uptake of the term give an idea of how children can incorporate into their own vocabularies words that adults use.

Book Reading

As mentioned previously, book reading is a complex vocabulary situation because there are two sources of words: the words in the text of the book and the words spoken by the mother in discussing the book with her child. In order to look at the rare words in book reading, therefore, we needed to look at the rare words in the text of the books and how the mothers treated those words and then at the rare words that the mothers used when they were discussing the books with their children.

When we looked at the texts of the books that the mothers read to their children, we found that the different books had different numbers of rare words. *What Next, Baby Bear!* (Murphy, 1983) has only 4 rare words, including *chimney; The Very Hungry Caterpillar* also has 4 rare words, including *cocoon*; and *Elephant* (Hoffman, 1945/1984) has 21 rare words, including *ivory, tusks, squirt,* and *squirting.* When reading these books aloud to their children, the mothers in the study most often merely read the rare words along with the rest of the text, without pausing or commenting. When this happened, we had no way of knowing whether the mother assumed that the child already knew the word, whether she thought knowing the word was not necessary to understand the text, whether she thought the text already supported the meaning of the word, whether she thought the word was too hard for the child to learn, or whether she did not know the meaning of the word herself. Only when the mothers paused to discuss the word did we get an idea of how they might be helping their children acquire new vocabulary during book reading.

When the mothers did pause to talk about the rare words in the text, we found that they used a variety of techniques to explain these words, including referring to an illustration, giving a definition or a synonym, using an inference or comparison, or bringing up an example from the child's experience. Following are examples of each of these strategies.

Referring to an Illustration

Mother: "He built a small house called a <u>cocoon</u> around himself." And there he is now inside this cocoon [points to illustration].

Giving a Definition or a Synonym   Conrad and his twin brother, Joe, are reading *Elephant* with their mother at the 5-year-old home visit:

Mother: "Often they are killed for their <u>ivory tusks</u> even though this is against the law. Elephants deserve better treatment than this." That's really bad. They kill the elephant just to get their <u>tusks</u>. The <u>ivory</u>.
Conrad: Why do they need them?
Mother: Isn't that mean? 'Cause the <u>ivory,</u> um, they just make things out of the <u>ivory.</u>
Conrad: The horns?
Mother: The horns. The <u>tusks.</u>

Using Inference or Comparison   Mariana and her mother are reading *What Next, Baby Bear!* at the 5-year-old home visit.

Mother: "Home went Baby Bear—back down the <u>chimney</u> and onto the living room carpet with a BUMP." There he is! He came out of a <u>chimney</u> like Santa Claus, huh?
Mariana: [Laughs]
Mother: [Laughs] That's funny.

Using the Child's Experience   Riley and her mother are reading *Elephant* during the 5-year-old home visit:

Mother: "They suck up quarts of water into their trunks at a time, then <u>squirt</u> the water down their throats. They also bathe by <u>squirting</u> the water from their trunks all over their bodies." Remember at the zoo?
Riley: [Nods]
Mother: When they <u>squirt</u> themselves with the water? Huh? Do you remember?
Riley: I want to go there again.

The other source of rare-word use during book reading was the discussions that the mothers had with their children. Unlike the text of the book, the words the mothers used in discussion were words that they had in their own vocabularies. Many more rare words were used in the discussion during the book readings than were present in the text of the books. For example, the mothers used 23 rare words when discussing *What Next, Baby Bear!* during the 5-year-old home visit, including nine mothers who used the word *colander* when explaining what the bear was using as his space helmet, as in the following example:

Mother: Is that a space helmet, really?
  Greg: No.
Mother: What is it really?
  Greg: The thing that you wash.
Mother: That you wash, right. You put spaghetti in it when you're getting the water out, right?
  Greg: Mm-hm.
Mother: A <u>colander</u>.
  Greg: <u>Colander</u>.

Rare words were also introduced into the discussion of the other books. For example, when Sara and her mother were reading *Elephant,* her mother used the rare word *frolicking* as she referred to an illustration:

Mother: "This sea cow is called a manatee. Sea cows are shy creatures that never leave the water. Their skin and teeth are like an elephant's. Some sea cows even have small tusks." And there's a picture of them just <u>frolicking</u> in the grass.

When David and his mother were discussing *The Very Hungry Caterpillar* at the 5-year-old home visit, his mother introduced the word *metamorphosis:*

Mother: "He stayed inside for more than two weeks. Then he nibbled a hole in the cocoon, pushed his way out and [gasps] he was a beautiful butterfly!" Do you know what that's called? Have you ever heard of it before?
 David: What?
Mother: What that's called when a, uh, caterpillar turns into a butterfly?
 David: I never saw one.

Mother: You never heard of it before? <u>Metamorphosis?</u>
David: I never heard or saw a real caterpillar turn into a butterfly.

In two of these situations, the mothers can refer to the illustrations in the book when introducing the rare word during the discussion. In the conversation presented here, however, David's mother gives the definition first ("when a caterpillar turns into a butterfly") and then provides the actual word *metamorphosis.*

Mealtime

In the examples that have been presented so far in this chapter, we have shown how mothers and other family members introduce rare words into their conversations with the preschool-age children in the study. These examples also show that rare words can be introduced in ways that may be *informative* for the children so that the children can begin to understand what these words mean. There are also times, however, when rare words are read aloud or used in conversation and no effort is made to help a young listener begin to construct a meaning. We consider these uses of rare words to be *uninformative.* In order to get a better idea of how children could get meaning from rare words used in conversation, we decided to look specifically at how support for meaning might be provided by family members during mealtime.

All theories of word learning begin with the assumption that somewhere children hear someone else use the word and somehow make a connection between the word and at least some sense of the word. An important issue, then, is to clarify whether word-learning situations are relatively rich or impoverished in terms of the availability of information from which children can make inferences about the meaning of a word.

The work by Susan Carey and others (Carey, 1978, 1982; Carey & Bartlett, 1978; Dickinson, 1984; Dollaghan, 1985) on *fast mapping,* in which children quickly acquire at least some sense of a new word through a single exposure to it, has shown that children can learn words with only an incidental exposure. Mabel Rice (1990) expanded the model of fast mapping to what she calls *Quick Incidental Learning (QUIL)* of words. She examined how QUIL works in experimental settings with young children. Her main conclusion from these studies is that at about age 3, children no longer need to be looking at an object when a label is given for that object in order to infer the meaning of a new word. This leaves open the possibility of children's acquiring new words in a wide variety of everyday conversational settings, spontaneous interactions in which there is little or no planning for instructing children directly on word meanings. We decided to look more closely at mealtimes to see what sorts of contextual supports are actually available to children in everyday conversation and how frequently those supports are used.

To carry out this analysis, we first located all of the rare words used during the mealtimes. Then we looked more closely at the discussions around the use of the words—what we call an *exchange*—to see whether the context was informative to a young listener who may not have known the word. Then we coded the exchanges as either informative or uninformative. This coding was carried out by asking ourselves the question, "Could a 3-, 4-, or 5-year-old child gain some sense of the word's meaning from this use of the word if this was the first time the child heard the word?" The earlier example with Casey and his mother and father demonstrates an informative use of the rare word *oxygen*. We also found, however, that there were many times when rare words were used at mealtimes in uninformative ways. The two examples that follow present uninformative uses of rare words.

During the mealtime when Melanie was 3 years old, her aunt, uncle, grandmother, grandfather, and mother were all at the table with her. Apparently, at least one other person was expected: Darlene. The following conversation about what might have held up Darlene includes the word *cabinet* without any support being given Melanie about the meaning of the word:

Aunt:	I thought Darlene would be here.
Uncle:	Darlene? She's shopping. She's still shopping.
Grandmother:	She's shopping for what?
Uncle:	I don't know. Just to go shopping and spend money.
Grandmother:	Good. She's gonna get a new <u>cabinet.</u>
Uncle:	[Unintelligible] she's picking up a card and all that.

At Brad's 4-year-old mealtime, with his mother, grandmother, and grandfather, peas were on the menu. During the meal, the Jolly Green Giant commercial was mentioned, and Brad began singing the "ho ho ho" refrain from the commercial. His grandmother was thinking about something else, however, and used the word *advantage* without any support for meaning while Brad continued his singing.

Brad:	I want more peas.
Mother:	See? I knew you'd like them.
Grandmother:	Yeah. I was thinking that thing there is neat, 'cause, um, Blake could take <u>advantage</u> of that.
Brad:	[Singing] Ho ho ho ho ho ho.

It is easy to see from these examples that the use of rare words is not always supported by the context of the conversation. However, we also found many examples of informative uses of rare words in mealtime conversations.

To answer the question of what types of contextual support for learning new words is offered in spontaneous conversation, each instance of informative use of rare words was coded for one of the four different ways that we found that contextual support was being provided. These four categories were developed by using our experience with the strategies that the mothers had used for supporting children's understanding of new vocabulary during book reading as a starting point and then looking carefully at the informative exchanges from the mealtimes. The four categories were as follows:

1. *Physical context:* Indicating a demonstration or the presence of an object or action in the immediate environment

2. *Prior knowledge:* Calling on past experiences or general knowledge

3. *Social context:* Pointing to social norms or violations of norms

4. *Semantic support:* Giving some direct verbal information about the meaning of a word

Physical Context   As in some of the toy-play and book-reading examples, the most obvious way that a child might learn the meaning of a new word is from the physical context. In this example from a mealtime, 3-year-old Emily hears the word *twirl* as she sees the motion being demonstrated for her:

Emily: Me need butter on this!
Father: Yes, you do need butter on that corn.
Mother: Yeah, here's the butter. You twirl it over the top of the big cube of butter.
Emily: Oh.
Mother: Dad'll show you how.
Emily: Me?
Father: Um, I don't want your fingers all over it, though. There we go.

Prior Knowledge   As in the conversation during book reading that Riley and her mother had about the elephant at the zoo, we also found that at mealtimes family members used the child's prior knowledge to help in understanding a new word. For example, when 3-year-old Tommy and his mother were reviewing the events of an exciting trip to the park, Tommy already knew what kind of animal his mother was talking about—because he had been there, too—he just could not remember the name for that type of animal.

Mother: Tommy, you don't remember what you said you saw at the park?
Tommy: Oh, yeah.
Mother: What?
Tommy: Um, a . . . I don't know.
Mother: You don't remember the word?
Tommy: No.
Mother: An iguana.
Tommy: Oh, an iguana [unintelligible].
Mother: Yeah! Did its owner let you pat him?
Tommy: No, no.
Mother: Was he walking around all by himself?
Tommy: Mm-hm.

Social Context   A category that we had not come across before in the book-reading context came up at the mealtimes: social context. In this category, children's understanding of social rules and routines helps them understand new words. In the following example, 4-year-old Catherine's mother has time, in the midst of all of the other demands of the mealtime, to label her son's behavior as *rude:*

Mother: I'm talking about the soup, darling.
Sister: Ma!
Catherine: Good!
Mother: What?
Sister: Can you make me some more bread and butter, please?
Brother: [Hums and talks with food in his mouth] For me.
Mother: [In warning tone] Robert.
Sister: Ma, can you please?
Brother: [Hums and talks with food in his mouth]
Mother: Robert, don't do that, that's rude.
Sister: Ma! Can you please make me some bread and butter?
Mother: In 1 minute, dear.

In the following example, 5-year-old Tammy's family engages in a debate just before their mother labels it as a *debate:*

Brother: Can I have an ice cream sandwich please, Mom? Mama, please can I have an ice cream . . .

Sister: Just a minute! Someone scarfed the last ice cream sandwich, right?

Brother: Oh.

Sister: How about cookies?

Brother: Tammy, can I please have one of your twisters?

Tammy: That's the only one. Gary had two.

Mother: What's the matter? Is this the great ice cream <u>debate</u>?

Semantic Support   We also found that during mealtimes there were lots of examples of family members using semantic support strategies as well, using other words to help the child understand a new word. These strategies included using some of the types of help we noted in the book readings and toy play, including the use of definitions and synonyms.

In the next mealtime example, 4-year-old George says he wants to go swimming right after supper. When his mother uses the word *cramps* in her response, George asks for a definition, and his mother provides it:

Mother: You have to wait a little while so you don't get <u>cramps</u>.

George: What's <u>cramps</u>?

Mother: <u>Cramps</u> are when your stomach feels all tight and it hurts 'cause you have food in it. And you're in the water.

Interestingly enough, the rare word *colander* also came up at one of the mealtimes. In this example, Sara's grandmother uses a synonym (*drainer*), and then Sara's mother uses the rare word *colander*:

Grandmother: [In another room] Is this [referring to noodles] done?

Mother: Needs to be drained!

Grandmother: Oh, it needs to be drained in the [unintelligible] regular drainer?

Mother: <u>Colander</u> or just put the cover to the edge and drain the water out.

Results   In the 160 mealtime transcripts, rare words were used in 1,631 exchanges. Of the 1,631 exchanges, 65% were coded as informative uses of the rare words, 30% were uninformative, and 5% were considered uncodable due to unintelligible material immediately preceding or following the rare words in the transcript. The fact that almost two thirds of the exchanges around rare words were informative means that the children in the study were often hearing new words at mealtimes in contexts that would help them acquire meaning.

When we broke down the informative exchanges into the four categories, we found that the most frequent strategy used was that of semantic support (61%). Use of the physical context strategy accounted for 19% of the exchanges; use of the social context strategy accounted for 13% of the exchanges; and use of the prior knowledge strategy was surprisingly infrequent, having occurred in only 7% of the exchanges.

RELATIONSHIPS BETWEEN RARE
WORDS AND KINDERGARTEN VOCABULARY

The data presented so far have demonstrated that the children in the study were provided with a broad range of words and supports for learning those words. An important question remains: Does exposure to rare words affect a child's vocabulary? To investigate this issue, we decided to look at two sets of relationships: 1) the relationships between the *density of rare words* in the three conversational contexts and the children's scores on the Peabody Picture Vocabulary Test–Revised (PPVT–R; Dunn & Dunn, 1981) in kindergarten and 2) the relationships between the frequency of informative uses of rare words at all three mealtimes and the PPVT–R in kindergarten (see Table A5.7 in the appendix).

We found that there were relationships between the *density of rare words* used in many of the home conversational contexts and the children's PPVT–R scores. The densities of the mothers' use of rare words during the reading of *The Very Hungry Caterpillar* at the 3-year-old home visit, during the mealtime at the 5-year-old home visit, and during all three toy-play sessions are related to the children's vocabulary scores in kindergarten, as are the *densities of rare words* by all speakers but the child in both the mealtimes at the 3-year-old and 5-year-old home visits. This means that the richness of rare words that the children in the study were hearing in these conversational contexts probably was helping them to develop their own vocabulary knowledge.

The frequency of informative uses of rare words in all three mealtimes was also positively correlated with the children's PPVT–R scores. Furthermore, the use of the semantic support strategy at all three mealtimes was also correlated with the child's vocabulary scores in kindergarten. Children's exposure during the preschool years to informative uses of rare words, and especially semantic support strategies, appears to be a strong predictor of their later vocabulary.

CONCLUSIONS

Preschool-age children are provided with a great deal of information about rare words that are spoken in their presence. Specifically, they hear conversations that draw on their prior knowledge, point to the physical and social context, and provide verbal semantic support.

Although the Home–School Study has not attempted to show whether the target children actually learned some sense of these rare words, it seems reasonable to say that in light of the research on the rapid rate of word learning, much of the learning takes place within conversations of the sort presented here. Conversation that engages children in extended discussion around a topic offers many opportunities for children to hear unusual words being used by more knowledgeable speakers and to make the connections with what they already know.

SUGGESTIONS FOR PARENTS

Most of the rare words that we found parents in the Home–School Study using with their children were not highly technical or abstract words. On the whole, they were words that most parents could be expected to have in their vocabularies anyway. The difference may well be that some of the parents in the study chose to use those words in conversations with their preschool-age children and, furthermore, were careful about making sure that they used these words in ways that made it possible for their children to begin to understand the words' meanings. The following suggestions for parents are based on our findings about vocabulary acquisition:

- Do not hesitate to use words that your child has not heard before. Exposure to new words is important for young children's vocabulary development.

- Consider how you are using these words. What other information in the context or in what you are saying will help your child understand what the word means?

- When you are reading books with your child, use the vocabulary in the books as an opportunity to introduce new words. Talk about what these new words mean as you read the book together.

- Whenever you go someplace new or different, talk to your child about the new surroundings. Be sure to use vocabulary words that are connected to this new experience. We found that each conversational setting in the study (that is, book reading, toy play, and mealtimes) generated a whole new list of rare words, so any new situation that children are exposed to—even something as ordinary as a trip to the music store or the park—can be a source of new vocabulary.

Chapter 6

Home Language and Literacy Environment
Final Results

Patton O. Tabors, Kevin A. Roach, and Catherine E. Snow

When the research team of the Home–School Study of Language and Literacy Development designed the home visits, we specifically wanted to capture different types of talk used in the homes and to collect other information about activities in the home environment that might have an impact on the children's language and literacy development. As detailed in the previous chapters, we were able to identify four specific types of extended discourse related to three conversational settings: nonimmediate talk during book reading, pretend talk during toy play, and narrative and explanatory talk during mealtimes. Furthermore, we were able to identify the quality of the vocabulary, as measured by the density of rare words, in these different conversational settings. Finally, we were able to gather information about the types of literacy activities that the mothers reported doing with their children in order to gauge each family's home support for literacy. Each of the preceding chapters has taken one or more of these topics and has discussed how the amount of a particular type of talk, density of rare words, or support for literacy in the home environments was associated with the literacy-related abilities that the children displayed in kindergarten as measured by the School-Home Early Language and Literacy Battery–Kindergarten (SHELL–K; Snow, Tabors, Nicholson, & Kurland, 1995).

The results of these individual investigations demonstrate that each of these ways of sampling the home literacy environment can be said to be related at different times to various measures on the SHELL–K. What we do not know from these correlational analyses is how these three aspects of the home language and literacy environment—extended discourse, rare-word density, and home support for literacy—are related to each other within and across years. We also do not know from these analyses whether these aspects of the home language and literacy environment are better predictors of the literacy-related measures in kindergarten *singly* or *in combination*. Finally, we do not know what role other factors, such as income, race, or mothers' education, might have played in how well the children scored on the SHELL–K. This chapter reports on the further analyses that were used to answer these questions about the home language and literacy environments of the children in the Home–School Study.

MAGNET TASK AND SCIENCE PROCESS TALK

Before beginning the discussion about further analyses, however, we need to introduce one final type of extended discourse: *science process talk* (see Snow & Kurland, 1996). During the home visit when the children were 5 years old, we introduced a new task that we called the *magnet task*. This task was unusual because it was done only once, unlike the other tasks, which were done during each of the three visits. The reason for adding this task was to see how mothers and children would approach a task that involved more expository or analytic types of talk. For this task, we brought to the visit a 3″ × 3″ × 1″ sealed black plastic box that contained a magnet, and a variety of small objects, including ones made of material that would or would not be attracted to the magnet and a few that also contained small magnets that could be attracted or repelled by the magnet. These objects included ball bearings, small plastic balls with magnets inside, pennies and nickels, nuts, bolts, washers, paper clips, sponge sea animals, and a plastic crab and lobster. Our instructions to the mothers and children simply involved asking them to play with the magnet and the objects for about 10 minutes.

As with the other tasks, we audiotape-recorded and then transcribed and coded the conversations of the children and their mothers during the time they played with the magnets and other objects. We were particularly interested 1) in seeing whether the mothers and children would adopt an experimental science orientation to this activity and 2) in knowing whether their talk would include an investigation of magnetism and how it worked. The coding therefore included four main categories:

1. Talk related to the process of science, such as talk about magnetism
2. Talk related to the scientific properties of the objects, such as talk about whether objects would "stick"

3. Talk related to using the objects for artistic purposes, such as talk about constructing sculptures with the objects

4. Talk related to superficial properties of the objects, including labels or attributes such as number or color

The four portrait children and their mothers all played actively with the magnet and the objects. But, not surprisingly, each pair spent varying amounts of their time talking about the different properties of the objects and about magnetism. For example, Mariana, her mother, and her older brother spent a good deal of time labeling the objects before they investigated the magnet and what effect it had on the objects:

Mother: Oh, look at the money. You can stick that to the magnet. Oh, no.
Manny: [Laughs]
Mother: What's the matter?
Manny: No, that doesn't stick.
Mariana: Let me do it.
Manny: Like this.
Mother: Let me see, Mariana.

Although Mariana and her mother and brother spent time seeing which objects would "stick" to the magnet and building with the objects, there was very little talk speculating about what was happening. Finally, when Mariana's mother attempted to explain magnetism, she used an analogy to another difficult-to-explain scientific process:

Mother: It's like electricity, right? Electricity? It's like some power, right? It attracts metal things.
Mariana: Okay.

Casey and his mother also spent a lot of the time during the magnet play seeing whether individual objects would or would not stick to the magnet. It spite of this interest, there was little conversation about *why* certain objects do or do not "stick":

Mother: Do the marbles stick?
Casey: Mm, what marbles?
Mother: No.
Casey: I wanna put that, and that, and this, and . . .

Mother: Does the paper clip stick?
Casey: Yeah.
Mother: It does?
Casey: Yeah. See?
Mother: Oh, yeah. Does the hairpin stick?
Casey: Let's see. Um, no. And I don't know if that other one . . .
Mother: Does this one stick? It's a colored one. No, 'cause it has plastic on it.

When Astra and her mother played with the magnets, Astra brought up the term *magnet*, but she and her mother never engaged in any conversation about the magnetic process.

Astra: This is a magnet [puts objects on the large magnet].
Mother: It is?
Astra: Uh-huh.
Mother: And what is that? Try that.
Astra: They magnets. See? All of them are magnets [holds nuts together on the large magnet].

After a conversation about whether Astra had ever eaten a lobster (referring to the plastic lobster that came with the magnet), Astra began pretending the objects were talking to each other, using the opportunity to create a pretend situation.

Todd and his mother spent much of the time during the magnet task playing with the plastic marbles, but there was also some talk about metal and about which objects would "stick" and why. In this first sequence, Todd's mother had discovered that the marbles with magnets inside would "shake" when they were close to each other, and she showed Todd how to make this happen:

Mother: Watch, Todd, watch [picks up marbles with magnets inside].
Todd: I know. I know.
Mother: See that? It didn't even touch it. Look. I can feel it. I can feel it in here. Feel it? Watch. When you go like . . . Hold this in one hand [shows Todd how to hold the marbles].
Todd: I got it! [Laughs]
Mother: Got it? Now hold this in your other hand. Did you feel it?
Todd: Uh-huh.
Mother: Did you feel it shake? Want to do it again?
Todd: No! [Laughs]

Later in the session, Todd and his mother began to make some finer distinctions about the fact that some metal objects stick and others do not:

Mother: You know how you can tell if it's metal? See, pennies won't do it. I forget what these are made out of [tries to get pennies to stick].

Todd: That was metal?

Mother: *Certain* kinds of metal, put it that way. That won't do it. See? It won't stick. See? This will, though. Do you think this [indicates the paper clip] will? Why will it?

Todd: 'Cause it's metal.

Mother: Right.

Todd: What about this [indicates the crab]?

Mother: What do you think that is? It's not metal, it's plastic.

Todd: Is this metal [indicates the lobster]?

Mother: What do you think?

Todd: No! [Laughs]

Mother: No, I don't think so, either.

Todd: Gonna pinch you!

During their play with the magnets, then, Todd and his mother discovered that magnets can repel each other—although they did not label the process in that way—and they discovered that some metals are attracted to magnets and some are not.

Overall, the mothers in the study spent much more time talking about the superficial qualities of the magnets and objects (55%) than about the artistic possibilities (8%), the scientific properties (22%), or the scientific process that they observed (14%). As with other forms of talk, however, different mothers displayed different amounts of each of these types of talk during the magnet task (see Table A6.1 in the appendix for complete descriptive data on this task). To see how these different types of talk used during the magnet task were related to the kindergarten tasks, we again used correlations between the types of talk and the SHELL–K scores (see Table A6.2 in the appendix for complete results of the correlations).

Two types of talk—*artistic process talk* by the mothers and the children and *object science talk* by the children—were completely unrelated to any of the kindergarten measures. *Object science talk* by the mothers was related to three of the measures: Narrative Production, Superordinates, and Receptive Vocabulary. Mothers' use of *superficial talk* about the objects was *negatively* related to all of the measures except Picture Description, and children's use of this type of talk was *negatively* related to four of the measures as well. This means that the more of this type of talk that the mothers and children used, the lower the scores for the children on the kindergarten measures. This type of talk was clearly not very cognitively challenging for these 5-year-olds.

The type of talk that proved to be most strongly related to the kindergarten measures was *science process talk,* during which the mothers and children discussed the hows and whys of what was happening when they played with the magnets. In the following example, Mark and his mother use a lot of this type of talk (indicated by **boldface** type):

Mark:	Uh-oh! Sticks!
Mother:	**Yeah, what's that called?**
Mark:	Marble.
Mother:	**No, when it sticks. When metal sticks to metal.**
Mark:	**Don't know.**
Mother:	You don't remember, huh?
Mark:	No.
Mother:	How come I've seen your tag at school up on that table where all this stuff is? Huh?
Mark:	**Magnets.**
Mother:	Thank you.
Mark:	[Tries one of the objects] Nope, doesn't stick.
Mark:	**How come this d—** . . . Mom, look at this.
Mother:	**How come he doesn't stick?**
Mark:	**'Cause he's plastic.**
Mother:	Very good.

[Later in the conversation]

Mark:	**Mom, how come this sticks?**
Mother:	**How come what sticks?**
Mark:	**This. The lobster.**
Mother:	**Now, do you think he sticks?**
Mark:	**No [laughs], because he's lower.**
Mother:	**'Cause, look.**
Mark:	What?
Mother:	**You have two magnets, right?**
Mark:	**Mm-hm.**
Mother:	**And they're strong ones, so you can put one magnet on one side of him and the other magnet on the other side.**
Mark:	Let 'em go.
Mother:	See? **And it still works 'cause they're close enough together that the magnets [pauses] catching each other.**
Mark:	**Hmm.**

Of particular interest is the pause in Mark's mother's last sentence of the previous example. Perhaps she was trying to think of a way to talk about how magnets behaved without having to use words that she might feel her 5-year-old would have trouble understanding.

Science process talk by the mothers is moderately to strongly related to all of the children's scores on the kindergarten measures, except Picture Description. *Science process talk* by the children is moderately related to all of the kindergarten measures except Picture Description and Emergent Literacy. *Science process talk* during the magnet task, therefore, became an important type of talk to add to the other forms of extended discourse in the analyses we needed to do to develop an overall picture of the home language and literacy environments of the children in the Home–School Study. Therefore, we included the percentage of *science process talk* by the mothers as an additional measure of extended discourse in further analyses.

HOME LANGUAGE AND LITERACY ENVIRONMENT: PUTTING THE PIECES TOGETHER

Having established that we were concentrating on three specific aspects of the home language and literacy environments of the children in the Home–School Study—extended discourse, rare-word density, and home support for literacy—we then needed to think about how these experiences might work *together* to influence the children's later abilities. But before we could do analyses comparing the importance of these three aspects of the home language and literacy environment in relation to how the children scored on the kindergarten outcomes, we needed to look at each aspect individually to see how we could reduce the number of variables (across conversational settings and/or across years) and how we could account for missing variables so that we could keep as large a group of families in the analyses as possible.

Developing the Home Language and Literacy Environment Composites

Because the data we collected as part of the Home–School Study involved a variety of activities and contexts repeated over multiple years, we faced a potentially enormous number of variables to consider. None of these variables on their own captured precisely what we wanted to examine. For example, we were not particularly interested in the effect on children's development of, say, the mothers' pretend talk during toy play at age 3—in and of itself. We were interested in the bigger picture— what the relationship is between extended discourse and later literacy development. Pretend talk in toy play is only one type of extended discourse, and age 3 is only one of the ages we were interested in. To look at the big picture, then, we needed to choose which variables we wanted to use in further analyses, and we needed to combine those variables *together* into a single set of variables that would represent the three aspects of the children's language and literacy environment: extended discourse, rare-word density, and home support for literacy. The process of combining variables together into a new variable that represents a larger or more general concept is called *compositing*.

The first step in this process was to choose which variables we would use in the composites. Because we wanted the composites to represent the language and literacy *environment* of children in the Home–School Study and not the children's own contribution to the conversations, we chose to concentrate on the mothers' talk for the extended discourse and rare-word density variables. And because the home support for literacy variables were already derived from the interviews with the mothers, we believed that they would also work well in the next set of analyses.

The next step in the compositing process involved standardizing the variables so that they all would be on the same scale. The process of standardizing is no more than changing the scale of the variables so that they all can be compared. A similar situation would occur if you had one set of temperatures in degrees Fahrenheit and another in degrees Celsius. You could standardize them both (by converting the Fahrenheit temperatures into Celsius or vice versa) so that they could be compared directly. Standardizing is important because each of the variables in our study was on a different scale. Standardizing them makes them comparable to one another. In our case, we standardized the variables so that they had a mean value of 0. Any value greater than 0 would mean that the mother had a higher score on the variable relative to the other mothers in the study and that any value less than 0 would mean the mother had a lower score than the other mothers in the study. Standardizing the variables (because it makes them all comparable to one another) allows the variables to be considered together without one variable dominating the rest simply because it is measured on a different scale.

Finally, the three groups of variables for each of the composites were summed for each of the three aspects of the language and literacy environment. The Extended Discourse composite consisted of 16 individual variables summed together—the four types of *extended discourse* used by the mothers in the three conversational settings (toy play, book reading, mealtimes) across the three visits, plus the mothers' *science process talk* (which occurred only at the 5-year-old home visit). The Rare

Word Density composite consisted of six variables added together—the *density of rare words* used by the mothers in toy play and mealtimes across the three home visits. Finally, the Home Support for Literacy composite consisted of the answers to the questions from the age 3 and age 4 visits, combined (see Table A6.3 in the appendix for a detailed listing of the variables).

There are other, more statistically complex ways to composite variables apart from simply adding them together, such as in a principal components analysis. We should make two notes, then, about the way in which we composited the variables. First, we tried the more sophisticated methods and found that our results with those methods were, by and large, the same as the results we present here based on the composites derived from simple addition. Second, a decision to add the variables together is appealing because it represents something that we think is important about these kinds of talk: that is, that the specific context in which the talk occurs is *not* the most important factor. In other words, a mother who uses a number of rare words in toy play, a mother who uses that number of rare words at a mealtime, and a mother who splits the same number of rare words between the two contexts are all providing their children with the same opportunity to hear rare words. The three mothers would look the same if the individual variables were summed into the overall Rare Word Density composite; the context in which those rare words occurred is not very relevant.

Imputing Values for Missing Data

One of the issues that arose as we constructed the three composites was the question of missing data. In a longitudinal study with as many visits as the Home–School Study, it is not surprising that occasionally we missed some of the information that we would have liked to have collected during our visits to the mothers and children. Sometimes the home visitor had to end a visit early because family members had to be somewhere else and would be unable to reschedule the visit. Sometimes a tape recorder would break or a mother would forget to return the tape we had left for the mealtime recording. Also, sometimes we lost track of a family for a year because of a move or other circumstances and then we would reconnect with the family the following year. In the real world of research, these things happen. The fact that bits and pieces of data were missing meant that we were faced with many small holes of missing data as we composited the variables.

The correlational method that we used to analyze the data that appear in the earlier chapters works only on complete data. In the results presented in those chapters, this issue is dealt with in two ways: 1) in the book-reading and toy-play chapters, analyses were run on the families for whom we had complete data for all three home visits; and 2) in the mealtime chapter, the analyses were run on all of the families for whom we had a recorded mealtime at a particular home visit. Our use of each of these methods means that some families were not included in all of the analyses. In constructing the composites, however, we found that a little more than half of the families were missing at least one variable of interest. Unless we used a strategy for filling in some of the missing gaps, we would be reduced to using fewer than half of the families in the final analyses. Instead of accepting that unacceptable situation, we chose to develop more complete data through a strategy called *imputing*.

Imputation is a process of taking a best guess at what the data would have been if we had been able to collect it. It uses other information that we have about the families to construct an educated guess about missing data. For example, we found that there was a strong relationship between the density of rare words across the three visits. If we know what the mother's rare-word usage was at the 3- and 5-year-old home visits but not at the 4-year-old home visit, we can use the 3-year-old and 5-year-old data to construct a reasonable guess as to what the 4-year-old data would be.

Obviously, if this process is not done carefully, there is a risk of changing the nature of the data and the final results. In order to ensure that we were not changing the data, we went through a painstaking process known as *sensitivity analysis*. This procedure analyzes and re-analyzes the data with and without the imputed values, looking at the effects of imputation on all of the original variables one by one. Luckily, although we were missing at least one piece of information for more than half of the families, we were missing only a very small part of the total data for the vast majority of families. Thus, less than 15% of the data in the final analysis were based on imputed data. Furthermore, the act of compositing minimizes the effect of imputed data because the preponderance of real data in the composites overwhelms any effect that the imputed data might have had.

By using the two processes of compositing and imputing, we were able to construct the three home language and literacy environment composites for the 74 families in the kindergarten sample. This means that for each of those 74 families, we developed a separate value for Extended Discourse, Rare Word Density, and Home Support for Literacy that represented how each family compared with the other families in the sample across each of the three aspects of the home language and literacy environment across the years.

Relationships Among the Three Home Language and Literacy Environment Composites

One of the first questions that came to mind after developing the composites was how the different aspects of the home language and literacy environments were related to one another. Were mothers who provided a great deal of extended discourse in their conversations with their children the same mothers who provided a rich proportion of rare words? Alternatively, was it possible for a family to score high on one composite measure and not on others?

To examine this question we used correlational analysis (see Table 6.1) to compare the relationships among the three composite measures. The results of this analysis show that a relationship does exist— that is, a family with a high score on one of the composites is *somewhat likely,* on average, to have a high score on the others. But that relationship is only in the moderate range, indicating a lot of variation. To explore that variation, let's examine how each of the four portrait families looks on the three composite measures (see Figure 6.1; see also Table A6.4 in the appendix).

In Figure 6.1 we have charted the three aspects of the home language and literacy environment for each of the four portrait children. On these graphs, the bars indicate the range of scores, and the dotted line indicates the average score for each of the composite measures— Extended Discourse, Rare Word Density, and Home Support for Literacy for all of the families in the study. The darker lines on the bars indicate the values that the portrait children's families received on each of the composite measures. By looking at each of these graphs, we can see how the portrait children's families compared with the overall sample and with each other.

As shown in Figure 6.1, the four portrait families varied on the three different aspects of the home language and literacy environment. Mariana's mother provided an amount of Extended Discourse just above average during her interactions with Mariana across the 3 years,

Table 6.1. Correlations among the three aspects of the home language and literacy environment

Aspect of environment	Extended Discourse	Rare Word Density	Home Support for Literacy
Extended Discourse	—		
Rare Word Density	.31**		
Home Support for Literacy	.29*	.24*	—

*p < .05; **p < .01.

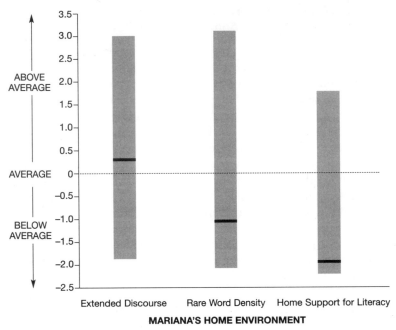

MARIANA'S HOME ENVIRONMENT

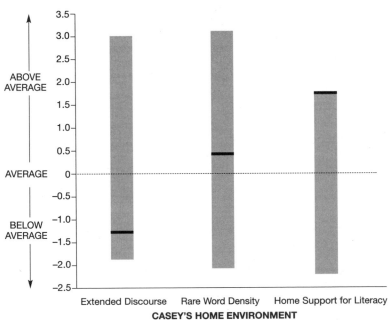

CASEY'S HOME ENVIRONMENT

Figure 6.1. Scores on the three home language and literacy environment composites of the four portrait children in the Home–School Study. (Bars indicate range of scores; dotted lines indicate average scores; darker lines on the bars inidcate values received by portrait families.)

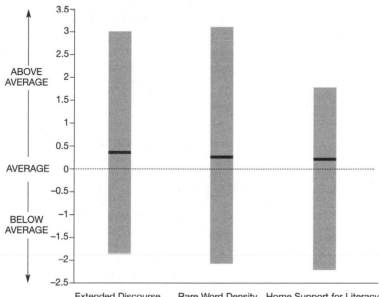

TODD'S HOME ENVIRONMENT

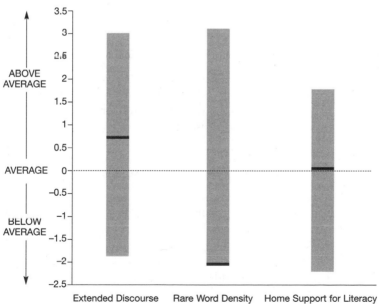

ASTRA'S HOME ENVIRONMENT

but she had a lower Rare Word Density and reported even lower Home Support for Literacy than other mothers in the sample (see Chapter 2). Todd's mother was more consistent than Mariana's mother, providing slightly above average amounts of all three aspects of the home language and literacy environment. Casey's mother used a well below average amount of Extended Discourse and slightly above average amount of Rare Word Density, but unlike the other portrait mothers, she reported a high level—in fact the *highest* level—of Home Support for Literacy in the sample. Astra's mother, though she provided a slightly above average amount of Extended Discourse and an average amount of Home Support for Literacy, scored the *lowest* in the entire sample in Rare Word Density.

When looking at these results, it is clear why the correlations in Table 6.1 are in the moderate range—some of the families, such as Todd's, provided similar levels for all three aspects of the home language and literacy environment. Other families, however, such as Mariana's, Casey's, and Astra's, provided different levels in different areas. So, our next question was, "What difference do these different patterns of home language and literacy environment make, if any, in how the children scored on the SHELL–K battery of tests that we gave them in the spring of their kindergarten year?"

HOME LANGUAGE AND LITERACY ENVIRONMENT AND KINDERGARTEN SKILLS

In order to simplify the analyses to be presented, we made the decision to limit the number of literacy-related tasks from the SHELL–K to be used in the final analyses linking the home environments and the children's kindergarten skills. We chose the following measures:

- The Narrative Production task, in which we asked the children to tell us a story after looking at three pictures of a bear family's adventures on a picnic

- The Emergent Literacy tasks from the Early Childhood Diagnostic Instrument: The Comprehensive Assessment Program (CAP; Mason & Stewart, 1989), which included Environmental Print In and Out of Context, Story and Print Concepts, Upper and Lower Case Letter Naming, Beginning and Ending Word Sound Awareness, and Writing

- The Receptive Vocabulary task (the Peabody Picture Vocabulary Test–Revised [PPVT–R]; Dunn & Dunn, 1981)

We believed that these three measures would capture three important aspects of the children's literacy-related skills: 1) oral language skill; 2) book concepts, phonological awareness, and print skill; and 3) word knowledge. Knowing how the children scored on these three different measures, we believed, would give us a relatively comprehensive view of their ability to take information from the kindergarten curriculum and a preview of their ability to embark on the beginning-to-read process.

To make sure that these three measures were, in fact, expressing different abilities, we examined the correlations among the scores on the measures. Table 6.2 shows that the correlations on the SHELL–K measures are higher than the ones between the three home language and literacy environment composites. This means that it is more likely that children who scored well on one measure also would score well on the other measures. These correlations are not high enough, however, to show us that we were sampling the same behavior twice in using any two of the measures. So, although the measures are moderately to strongly related, we believe that they still each express a distinct type of language or literacy skill.

Correlational Analyses Between Aspects of Home Language and Literacy Environment and Kindergarten Outcomes

To find out what the relationship was between the children's home language and literacy environment and their SHELL–K scores on the three chosen tasks, then, we examined a further set of correlations. The results are displayed in Table 6.3. These results support one of the assumptions that was a starting point for the Home–School Study: that factors in the language and literacy environment of preschool-age children would be related to how children perform on literacy-related tasks in kindergarten. Although this statement can be made for all three of the home environment composites and all three of the kindergarten measures, some of the relationships are stronger than others.

Home Support for Literacy is strongly related to all three of the

Table 6.2. Correlations between three of the SHELL–K variables

SHELL–K[a] variable	Narrative Production	Emergent Literacy	Receptive Vocabulary
Narrative Production	—		
Emergent Literacy	.26*	—	
Receptive Vocabulary	.44***	.59***	—

[a]School-Home Early Language and Literacy Battery–Kindergarten (Snow, Tabors, Nicholson, & Kurland, 1995).

*p < .05; ***p < .001.

Table 6.3.   Correlations between the three home language and literacy environment composites and three of the SHELL–K variables

	Narrative Production	Emergent Literacy	Receptive Vocabulary
Extended Discourse	.28*	.21~	.36**
Rare Word Density	.20~	.40***	.50***
Home Support for Literacy	.40***	.36**	.50***

SHELL–K, School-Home Early Language and Literacy Battery–Kindergarten (Snow, Tabors, Nicholson, & Kurland, 1995).

~p < .10; *p < .05; **p < .01; ***p < .001.

kindergarten measures, indicating that the time and effort that the mothers reported that they and other family members spent on literacy activities at home were apparently having an effect on a broad array of literacy-related skills for their children. Furthermore, all three home environment composites show clear relationships to the children's receptive vocabulary ability in kindergarten, demonstrating that for this group of children, more extensive word knowledge was developed in the context of higher levels of extended discourse, rare-word use, and home support for literacy. These findings indicate that it is clearly necessary to take into account the types of literacy-related activities and language that young children are exposed to at home if we want to have an idea of the abilities that children will bring to kindergarten.

Correlational Analyses Between Aspects of Home Language and Literacy Environment and Kindergarten Outcomes, Including Control Variables

The last statement of the previous section might have been our final conclusion of the investigation into the home language and literacy environments of the children in the Home–School Study. As social scientists, however, we also had to consider the possibility that *something else* might be responsible for the children's later development—that our three composites do not matter—or do not matter as much—when some other factor is taken into account. Thus, in addition to considering the home language and literacy environment composites when predicting the children's scores on the SHELL–K tasks, we knew that we would need to include other variables that might turn out to be related to the kindergarten scores. These other variables, called *controls,* are possible alternatives to the home language and literacy environment composites that we had investigated so far. The controls were included in the analysis because they might explain away our findings.

Perhaps, for example, mothers in this sample talked differently to boys and girls. If this were true, then we might be faced with the prob-lcm of saying that what was important was the children's home language and literacy environments, when in reality the important factor was the gender of the children. In order to prove that what is really crucial is the children's home language and literacy environment rather than other factors that we had not yet taken into account, we needed to include those factors in our analyses to see whether they made a difference.

For this analysis, we chose to include five different control variables. Gender and Race of the child are two of the five; these variables are included to test for the possibility that what is important in terms of the children's kindergarten scores is not their home language and literacy environment but their gender or race. The third control variable is Reported Family Income at the time when we first started visiting the families. As mentioned in Chapter 1, in spite of the fact that all of the families in the study had low incomes, some families had more resources than others. Perhaps families with more resources are better able to provide certain experiences for their children, which gives their children an advantage in kindergarten.

The fourth control variable is Mother's Education as reported at the first home visit. Other researchers (Coleman et al., 1966; Jencks et al., 1972) have found that this variable is often related to children's academic achievement, so it is an important variable to account for in our analyses. The fifth control variable is Child's Mean Length of Utterance (MLU) during toy play at the age 3 home visit. MLU is a measure of the complexity of a child's language and is included because children who are using longer utterances at this early age are using more advanced features of language. This control variable is included to test for the possibility that the children who were more advanced in terms of literacy-related abilities in kindergarten were already more advanced language users at age 3 and therefore that the home language and literacy environment during the preschool years did not make a difference.

Each of these control variables was included not because we necessarily believed that one or another of them is truly crucial but because they must be included for us to say with confidence that the important predictors come from the child's home language and literacy environment and not elsewhere.

To investigate the relationship between the control variables and the kindergarten measures, we first looked at the correlations that appear in Table 6.4. As can been seen in these correlations, in general, the controls are not strongly related to the kindergarten measures. In fact, for two variables—Gender and Mother's Education—there is no relationship to the scores that the children received on the selected SHELL–K measures.

Table 6.4. Correlations between the control variables and the SHELL–K outcomes

Control variables	Narrative Production	Emergent Literacy	Receptive Vocabulary
Gender (of child)	n.s.	n.s.	n.s.
Race (of child)	n.s.	n.s.	−.34**
Reported Family Income at 3-year-old home visit	.27*	.23*	.19⁻
Mother's Education at 3-year-old home visit	n.s.	n.s.	n.s.
Child's Mean Length of Utterance (MLU) at 3-year-old home visit	n.s.	.27*	n.s.

n.s., not significant.

⁻p < .10; *p < .05; **p < .01.

There are, however, some correlations of interest. Race, though not related to Narrative Production or Emergent Literacy, is negatively related to the Receptive Vocabulary scores of the children in the study. This negative finding is generated by the way in which the variable was defined: Children in this sample who were classified as minorities—including African American, biracial, and Hispanic children—were assigned a value of 1, and nonminorities—Caucasian children—were assigned a value of 0. This negative finding, therefore, means that membership in a minority group in this sample is associated with a lower PPVT–R score, on average. For the 47 Caucasian children in the kindergarten sample, the mean score on the PPVT–R was 97.8—close to the national norming average of 100. For the 27 children in the kindergarten sample who were members of minority groups, the mean score was 87—almost 1 standard deviation below the national norming sample. This difference is statistically significant.

This finding is consistent with other researchers' findings concerning the scores on vocabulary tests of young children who are members of minority groups. For example, in a sample of 294 preschool-age children of African American mothers who were on welfare, the average score on the PPVT–R was 67 (DeTemple & Tabors, 2000). For the sample of children of African American mothers on welfare in the National Longitudinal Youth Survey, the average score on the PPVT–R was 76. The average score for the African American children classified as "non-poor" in this survey, however, was 80 (U.S. Department of Health and Human Services and U.S. Department of Education, 1995, p. 62). This indicates that the primary factor involved in the PPVT–R scores is indeed race rather than socioeconomic status.

The children's MLU and family income also showed moderate relationships with one or more of the SHELL–K measures. The correlation that reaches significance for the child's MLU is, unexpectedly, with the Emergent Literacy measure rather than the Narrative Production measure. In a larger sample, however, we might have also found significant relationships with Narrative Production and Receptive Vocabulary. The correlations between family income and all three measures, though not strong, might well be strong enough to have an impact when included as a control variable in further analyses.

To find out what type of impact the control variables had, we examined the correlations between the three home language and literacy environment composites and the kindergarten outcomes with the control variables taken into account (see Table 6.5). These correlations, with the controls accounted for, answer a slightly different question than the original set of correlations. The first set of correlations between the three home language and literacy environment composites and the kindergarten outcomes answered questions such as, "Does a child whose mother has a high Rare Word Density have a higher Emergent Literacy score, on average, than a child whose mother has a low Rare Word Density?" Because there was, in fact, a correlation, the answer to that question turned out to be yes.

The question asked by the second group of correlations is slightly different: "Consider two children of the same race and gender, whose family incomes and maternal education are the same and who were equally sophisticated in language at age 3. For children matched in such a way, does a child whose home provides a high Rare Word Density have a higher Emergent Literacy score, on average, than a child whose home provides low Rare Word Density?" The second question thus takes into account those five control factors that we wished to consider: If the children are matched on those five factors and the three home language and literacy environment composites *still* show a relationship with the kindergarten outcomes, then we will be more confident that it is the composites that are important above and beyond the control variables.

Table 6.5. Correlations between the three home language and literacy environment composites and three of the SHELL–K variables, controlling for the five control variables

	Narrative Production	Emergent Literacy	Receptive Vocabulary
Extended Discourse	.20⁻	n.s.	n.s.
Rare Word Density	n.s.	.35**	.43***
Home Support for Literacy	.35**	.30*	.41***

SHELL–K, School-Home Early Language and Literacy Battery–Kindergarten (Snow, Tabors, Nicholson, & Kurland, 1995).

⁻p < .10; *p < .05; **p < .01; ***p < .001.

Table 6.5 shows that in fact the answer to that second question is yes. Even after taking those five control variables into account, children whose homes provide a higher Rare Word Density have higher Emergent Literacy scores, on average. The patterns in Table 6.5 do not match the patterns from the original correlations exactly, however. In particular, one can see that the relationship between Extended Discourse and the kindergarten outcomes is very weak or nonexistent. Extended Discourse only weakly predicts performance on the Narrative Production task and does not predict performance on the Emergent Literacy or Receptive Vocabulary tests at all when the control variables are taken into account. It is crucial to point out that such a finding does not mean that Extended Discourse is unimportant. It is, after all, related to the kindergarten outcomes. We cannot state with certainty, however, that Extended Discourse is a crucial feature of the child's language and literacy environment. We can only raise the possibility that it might be.

Although the effect of Extended Discourse on the kindergarten outcomes is curtailed after adding the five control variables, we found that the other two home language and literacy environment composites still do predict the kindergarten outcomes. Rare Word Density predicts Emergent Literacy and Receptive Vocabulary, and Home Support for Literacy predicts all three of the kindergarten outcomes. In these two cases, then, we are more confident that the use of rare words and support for literacy in the home are crucial elements of the home environment.

Regression Analyses Using Aspects of the Home Environment to Predict Kindergarten Outcomes

There is one final step to take to have the most complete picture of how the early language and literacy environment predicts how a child does in kindergarten. We established previously (see Table 6.1) that the three language and literacy environment composites are related to one another. The fact that they are related to one another could raise the question of whether they each are uniquely important in predicting a child's kindergarten outcomes. Perhaps, for example, only Home Support for Literacy predicts a child's kindergarten performance, but it *appears* that the other variables predict the kindergarten outcomes as well because they are related to Home Support for Literacy. We cannot easily account for this possibility using correlation, so we turn to a related method called *regression analysis.*

A regression analysis can answer the same questions as correlation ("Is a mother's rare-word use related to her child's later performance on the Emergent Literacy test in kindergarten?"). But the advantage of regression is that it can take several predictors together simultaneously and see whether they each uniquely predict an outcome. If one of the composites appeared to predict an outcome only because it was related to another predictor, it would not uniquely predict that outcome when combined with that other predictor.

Consequently, we constructed models for each of the three kindergarten outcomes using regression analysis. Our goal in constructing these models was to find which of the home language and literacy environment composites (if any) *uniquely* predicts the kindergarten outcome. Constructing a model is a step-by-step process. First, each of the three composites is put into a model on its own, and then they are combined to see whether they still uniquely predict the outcome when combined with the others.

Predicting Narrative Production   In Figure 6.2, the results of a set of regression analyses in which the three home language and literacy environment composites are used to predict the scores on the Narrative Production task are graphically displayed. The first bar at the left of the graph shows that the control variables discussed previously account for 14% of the variation in scores on the Narrative Production task before any of the home language and literacy environment composites are included in the analysis (see also Table A6.5 in the appendix). The next three bars on the graph show how each of the three individual home language and literacy environment composites relate to the Narrative Production task on its own, after the controls are taken into account. Both Extended Discourse and Home Support for Literacy are significant *independent* predictors of the children's scores on Narrative Production, each accounting for 23% of the variance.

The fifth bar on the graph shows the results of the analysis that combines the control variables and all three of the home composites to see whether any of them predict Narrative Production *uniquely*. In fact, Home Support for Literacy and Extended Discourse remain unique predictors of the children's scores on the Narrative Production task in the combined model that explains 28% of the variation in the scores (see Table A6.6 in the appendix).

Predicting Emergent Literacy   The same type of analysis was used to predict the variation in Emergent Literacy using the three home language and literacy environment composites. The results of this analysis are displayed in Figure 6.3.

Again, the first bar at the left of the graph indicates the amount of variation accounted for by the control variables. When predicting the children's scores on the Emergent Literacy task, the controls explain 17% of the variation (see Table A6.7 in the appendix). Among the three

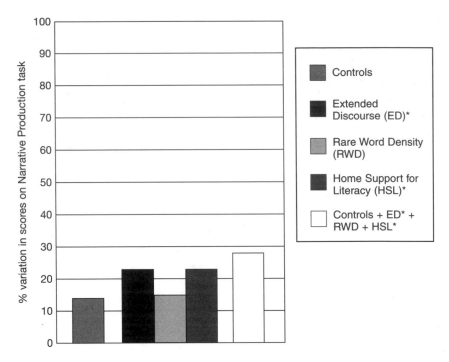

Figure 6.2. Predicting Narrative Production: Home language and literacy environment composites. (* indicates a significant composite.)

home language and literacy environment composites, Rare Word Density and Home Support for Literacy are independent contributors to the children's scores on the Emergent Literacy task, explaining 28% and 24% respectively. Furthermore, both Rare Word Density and Home Support for Literacy are also *unique* contributors to the children's scores because they, along with Family Income, remain significant in the combined analysis, explaining 32% of the variation in the scores on the Emergent Literacy task.

Predicting Receptive Vocabulary   Finally, the results of the regression analyses using the three composites of the home language and literacy environment to predict the Receptive Vocabulary scores are presented in Figure 6.4.

As can be seen in Figure 6.4, the control variables account for 18% of the variance in the children's scores on this test (see Table A6.9 in the appendix). In this model, all three home environment language and literacy composites are *independent* predictors of this kindergarten outcome. When the analysis includes the control variables and all three of the home language and literacy composites, Rare Word Density and

Home Support for Literacy remain unique predictors. Note that Rare Word Density and Home Support for Literacy are both stronger predictors of Receptive Vocabulary than they are of Emergent Literacy and that together they explain 44% of the variation in the children's scores (see Table A6.10 in the appendix).

DISCUSSION

What do we know now about the relationships between various aspects of the home language and literacy environment and the types of skills that the children in the kindergarten sample were able to demonstrate when they were 5 years old?

We know that all of the aspects of the home environment that we took into consideration—the ways that mothers talked to children (Extended Discourse), the level of vocabulary that the mothers used with the children (Rare Word Density), and the types of activities in which the mothers and other family members participated with regard to books (Home Support for Literacy)—were related to how children

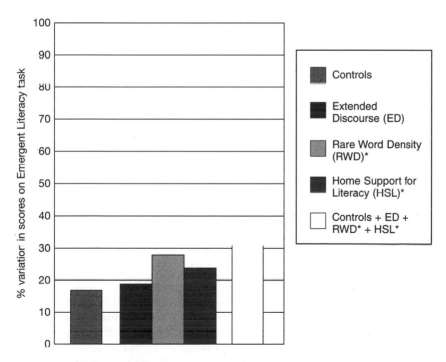

Figure 6.3. Predicting Emergent Literacy: Home language and literacy environment composites. (* indicates a significant composite.)

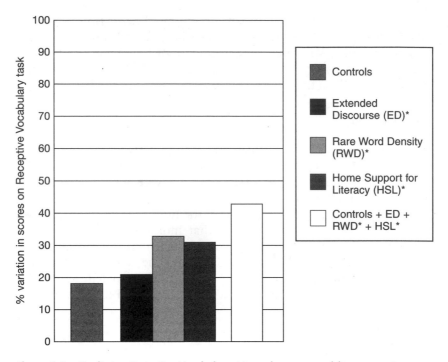

Figure 6.4. Predicting Receptive Vocabulary: Home language and literacy environment composites. (* indicates a significant composite.)

did on the kindergarten tests (see Table 6.3). Some of these relationships were stronger than others, but all were significant.

But it was also important to consider other factors that might influence the relationships between these aspects of the home environment and the SHELL–K results, including other features of the home environment such as race, income, or mothers' education or abilities that the children had already acquired by the time they were 3 years old, such as indicated by MLU. Furthermore, we wanted to see how these various aspects of the home environment would look if they were put into analyses *together* to see which ones proved to be unique predictors.

For these reasons we repeated the correlational analyses with the control variables taken into consideration and found that all of the relationships were affected by including the control variables. In fact, three of the relationships that had been significant before were now no longer significant (Extended Discourse with Emergent Literacy, Extended Discourse with Receptive Vocabulary, and Rare Word Density with Narrative Production) meaning that part of the relationship between those aspects of the home environment and the kindergarten measures was actually attributable to the control variables.

Finally, in the regression analyses, we found that Home Support for Literacy was a unique predictor of all three of the kindergarten measures, that Rare Word Density was a unique predictor of both Emergent Literacy and Receptive Vocabulary, and that Extended Discourse was a unique predictor of Narrative Production. This means that all three of the home environment language and literacy variables were important contributors to how the children in the study performed on these three tasks from the SHELL-K battery of tests. In other words, we found that the kinds of activities that the mothers and other family members engaged in around books with the children; the types of language that mothers used during book reading, toy and magnet play, and during mealtimes; and the level of vocabulary that the mothers used when they talked with their children during mealtimes and toy play were all crucial in helping the children develop certain language and literacy skills that are important in kindergarten.

Although we were able to develop significant predictive models for each of the three kindergarten outcomes, it is also important to note that we were only able to predict 28% of the scores on the Narrative Production task, 32% of the scores on the Emergent Literacy task, and 44% of the scores on the Receptive Vocabulary task. This means that there is still a good deal of the variance in each of these measures unaccounted for by the three aspects of the home language and literacy environment that we were able to sample. This raises the possibility that there are *other* factors in the children's environment that may influence how well they perform on the kindergarten measures. Not surprisingly, our guess was that the preschool classrooms that these children attended might be a good place to look for other influences on the children's language and literacy abilities. Chapters 7–11 examine the preschool classrooms that the children in the Home–School Study attended and look at the relationships between the classroom environments and the children's kindergarten skills. Chapter 12 looks at home and school relationships, and a final chapter reports on analyses that combine the information from home and school to gauge the combined influence of the two environments.

CONCLUSIONS

The results of the analyses on the home environment variables from the Home–School Study indicate that there are a variety of sources for the skills that children bring to kindergarten and that the children who demonstrated higher-level skills were, on the whole, those who had experienced interesting talk, with lots of new words, and literacy activities such as frequent and varied book reading with different people. All of these aspects of the home literacy environment, of course, take time—because adults and children need to be together, whether talking or reading—but none of them require extensive resources.

Children's book ownership has often been considered a stumbling block for low-income families. However, the mothers in the Home–School Study who scored high on Home Support for Literacy made use of libraries—more with 4-year-olds than with 3-year-olds (see Chapter 2), but they also actively searched out opportunities to buy books, often purchasing inexpensive books at grocery stores or at tag sales. Some mothers mentioned that they always asked for books from family members who inquired about what presents to give the child, and many of the families took advantage of school book clubs. Making time to read the books and talk about them, as well as making the time to discuss other compelling topics with interesting vocabulary at other times during the day, was what was required to help children prepare for kindergarten.

We end this section of the book with a mealtime transcript that demonstrates how one family made use of conversation to bring many of these aspects of the literacy environment into their home. In the following example, 4-year-old Ethan and his mother and father are planning to attend a parade in Boston that takes place near the Boston Common. Children dress up for this parade as characters from Robert McCloskey's 1941 classic children's book, *Make Way for Ducklings*. This is a book that Ethan and his parents clearly have read together in the past. During this conversation, Ethan and his parents use narrative talk (indicated by *italic* type), explanatory talk (indicated by **boldface** type), and rare words (indicated by <u>underlined</u> type). In addition to displaying these various features of extended discourse and rare vocabulary, the whole conversation could also be considered a literacy event because Ethan and his mother and father call on their knowledge of the story in the book as they plan Ethan's participation in the parade.

Mother: *I got the telephone number for the parade today.*
Father: *Yeah.*
Mother: *And, um, I walked by Boston Garden. I could see some ducks in there.*
Ethan: *Yeah?*
Mother: *Yep!*
Ethan: *Were they . . .*
Father: Did you wash your hands for dinner? Soap and water—those are dirty hands. Okay?

Ethan: 'Kay.

Mother: *Well, I told them* [the ducks], *"Ethan says 'hi'."*

Ethan: *What did they say?*

Mother: **I didn't walk right up to them, because I had to rush. I had a lot of things to do.** [Dishes rattle.] **But, um, yeah, and it was kinda raining out when I went by the first time.** *Okay, tomorrow, Ethan, I will call the place where you get tickets for the parade, okay?*

Ethan: *What place?*

Mother: *Uh, it's called the Boston* <u>Historic,</u> *uh,* <u>Foundation.</u> *I'll call 'em up and find out everything we need to know.*

Ethan: *Know what Susan* [Ethan's teacher] *thought where it was?*

Mother: *Where?*

Ethan: *Um, in Boston.*

Mother: *It is* [with emphasis] *in Boston. It's in Boston, right where the duckling in the story went. Remember, in the Boston Garden, in the story?* [Dishes are clanking loudly.] *Remember how they were on the Cambridge side of the river when she had made the nest? And then remember when she had to meet Mr.* <u>Mallard</u> *and, um, Michael the policeman had to cross them and everything? That was in Boston.*

Ethan: *And they thought, um, that bridge was a island?*

Mother: *Yeah, right. But then they did find an island right underneath the bridge. If I remember correctly.* Here we go. Now, this is hot. Let it cool off. You can pick it up and eat it right off the bone, but it needs to be a little cool.

[Later in the conversation]

Mother: Which duck [that is, which character from the book] are you gonna be, Ethan?

Ethan: Quack!

Mother: Quack still?

Ethan: Yeah.

Mother: *I stopped in the Dino store to see if they had any duck bills.*

Father: **In the Dino** [with emphasis] **store?**

Mother: **Well, they have other animal noses that aren't dinosaurs. So she went and got me a** <u>**duckbill**</u> **dinosaur.**

[Later in the conversation]

Father: **I was thinking maybe we could make a duck** <u>**costume**</u> **that looks sort of like Big Bird's birdketeer** <u>**costumes,**</u> **except duck colors.**

Ethan: **Nah. I wouldn't like it.**

Father: **Where they have wings?**

Mother: **Oh, yeah!**

Father: *And they have bird heads.*

Mother: *What is the <u>fabric</u> that you were thinking . . .*

Ethan: *Well, I was thinking of tissue paper.*

Mother: *I know.*

Father: *Well, I think that's a very good idea, but we have to have something somewhat firm to put the tissue paper on!*

Ethan: *Cardboard.*

Mother: *Make it, uh, <u>papier-mâché</u> or. . . . You know, Ethan was saying we could make a <u>piñata</u> that he could put on him.*

Father: *Yeah? Well, I think that's the right idea. I don't know if it's possible to get <u>selastic</u> any more.*

Ethan: *What's <u>selastic</u>?*

Father: *It's something that they use in theater to make things.*

Mother: *Well, where would we find out?*

Father: *I guess a theater <u>supply</u> store. It used to be very <u>expensive,</u> so let's just say it's gonna be <u>papier-mâché</u>* [laughs]. *For the crown of the head, we can use a balloon. So we can measure the distance around his head. Then we measure a balloon that's about a half-inch larger in diameter. And we <u>papier-mâché</u> the balloon. Then when it hardens, you pop the balloon. Then you just cut where you want it to finish. And then you can add another layer of <u>papier-mâché</u> to make the bill! Use the <u>crepe</u> paper to make the feathers.*

Ethan: *What's <u>crate</u> paper?*

Father: *That's the type of stuff that's on the <u>piñata</u> that we said we should use.*

Mother: *So, I imagine I should get whatever <u>supplies</u> I can at this store. Maybe on the weekend we can do it.*

Ethan: *Weekend! That will be too late.*

Mother: *No, no. It's the next weekend is the parade.*

Section II

Supporting Language and Literacy Development in the Preschool Classroom

David K. Dickinson and Miriam W. Smith

We now shift from looking at children's homes to considering their preschool experiences. All of the children in the Home–School Study of Language and Literacy Development attended center-based preschool before they went to kindergarten, with half of these children attending Head Start and the remainder going to private child care facilities or public preschool programs. Therefore, we have the opportunity to describe children's preschool experiences and gauge their impact on children's emerging language and literacy development. Of course, the possible ways in which one describes something as complex as preschool experience are endless. Not surprisingly, we have chosen to focus on classrooms in terms of their support for children's language and literacy development. We scrutinize the nature of children's and teachers' conversations in considerable detail. Chapters 7–11 relate our information about children's verbal experiences to insights about teachers' pedagogy that we gained from interviews and case studies and observations of the conversations, materials, displays, and organization of children's classrooms.

Although our examination of conversations and the curriculum of classrooms sheds a particularly bright light on aspects of classrooms linked to language and literacy development, we also gain valuable insight into how preschools foster children's social and emotional growth. After all, by the time children are 3 years old, it is primarily through conversations that they form relationships with teachers and other children. And children's emerging sense of competence is in part tied to their growing mastery of symbol systems such as print and their ability to express themselves with words and symbols. Furthermore, the emotional tenor of classrooms is largely influenced by how teachers talk to individuals and to the group. This emotional climate, in turn, has an impact on children's willingness to trust and relate to teachers and to engage in the activities provided in the classroom (Howes & Smith, 1995). Therefore, we believe that by taking a careful and multifaceted view of the nature of teacher–child and child–child conversations throughout the classroom day, we can learn much about the features of preschool classrooms that influence children's language and literacy development. We expect that many of the same factors that foster language and literacy are related to children's social development, but we leave it to other studies to explore these relationships.

PRIOR STUDIES OF PRESCHOOL SUPPORTS FOR LANGUAGE AND LITERACY

There have been numerous attempts to determine the effects of preschools on children. Studies examining the effects of program quality have used four general ways to measure quality:

1. *Structural measures:* These include issues such as the funding source of the program (such as private or Head Start), the teacher–child ratio, the size of the program, and the years of experience and education level of the teachers. We obtained such measures through our teacher interviews (see Chapter 7).

2. *Educational process assessed by rating tools:* Rating tools include some that focus on aspects of teacher–child interaction (for example, teacher sensitivity to children's needs). Other tools assess a broad range of classroom features such as the nature and organization of furnishing, materials made available to children, and the nature of teacher–child conversations. One such widely used broad-gauge rating tool is the Early Childhood Environment Rating Scale (ECERS; Harms & Clifford, 1980). We used items from the ECERS and created an observation tool that supplied additional information about the curriculum in the classrooms (see Chapter 7).

3. *Teachers' beliefs:* Researchers (for example, Bryant, Clifford, & Peisner, 1991) have developed tools to assess beliefs teachers hold about child development and appropriate classroom practices. These tools are structured so that the responses more consistent with develop-

mentally appropriate practice (Bredekamp, 1987) are more highly valued. We determined a teacher's beliefs from her responses[1] to a more open-ended series of questions about how she organizes her day, what activities she provides, and what she sees as being her most important goals. In addition, see Chapter 8 for case studies of teachers of two of the portrait children.

4. *Teacher–child and child–child interactions:* A few studies have coded ongoing child interactions in classrooms (Layzer, Goodson, & Moss, 1993; McCartney, 1984). We audiotaped and videotaped interactions and coded them using five different coding systems (see Chapters 7–11).

Structural Variables and Classroom Process Ratings

Some studies of the impact of preschool on children's development have found that stronger programs are more likely to have beneficial effects than programs rated less highly (Barnett, 1995). The clearest evidence of a relationship between classroom quality and children's development as measured by a rating tool (the ECERS) comes from a study done in North Carolina (Bryant, Lau, Burchinal, & Sparling, 1994). Researchers assessed 145 children from 32 Head Start classrooms and found considerably better intelligence test (Kaufman, 1983) scores among children from more highly rated centers. What is especially important is that this relationship remained even after the home situations of children were taken into account. In a similar study of 60 children drawn from 30 child care centers, Dunn (1993) found that ratings of classroom quality and structural variables, such as teachers' years of experience and college major,[2] helped account for children's growth even after characteristics of the children's homes were taken into account.

Although some studies (see reviews by Barnett, 1995, 2001) have found that preschool experience and program quality are associated with enhanced academic growth, it is not always easy to establish what aspects of a child's classroom are responsible for the beneficial effects of classroom participation. This challenge is best seen in results reported

---

[1]With only a few exceptions, the center-based preschool and kindergarten teachers of the children in this study were women; therefore, the teachers are referred to as female.

[2]Children's growth was greatest when they had a teacher with a moderate amount of experience (neither a new teacher nor a long-term veteran) and when their teacher had a bachelor's or master's degree in early childhood education.

by the impressive ongoing longitudinal study of Head Start classrooms across the United States called the *Family and Child Experiences Survey* (FACES). The FACES research team is conducting in-depth interviews with families, observing classrooms, and assessing children over several years (Zill, Resnick, & McKey, 1999). In an early report from this study, the research team reported that they gave 1,580 children the Peabody Picture Vocabulary Test–Third Edition (PPVT–III; Dunn & Dunn, 1997) once in the fall of 1997 and again in the spring of 1998. They found that in the intervening time the children had learned an average of 11 new words on the PPVT–III and that programs in which children had higher PPVT–III receptive vocabulary scores also were programs that received higher ECERS scores. When the researchers included data about the children's parents, however, it turned out that children in the better classrooms came from communities in which parents were somewhat less economically disadvantaged. In a smaller study involving 100 children from 10 child care centers, Susan Kontos (1991) also found that performance on a measure of classroom quality, the ECERS, related to stronger language growth but that children in more highly rated classrooms came from homes that were more able to support their development. Thus, although structural measures and ratings of classroom processes sometimes help predict children's development, they may not fully capture the essence of what distinguishes high-quality classrooms from others.

Teacher Beliefs and Teacher–Child Interaction

If we want to understand aspects of classrooms that affect children's development, it is likely that we need to understand how teachers think about teaching and how they relate to children. Of course, a major reason to determine a teacher's beliefs is that the manner in which a teacher relates to children is probably at least partly affected by his or her beliefs about development. There is some evidence that children make greater gains when they are in classrooms of teachers who subscribe to beliefs consistent with developmentally appropriate practices (Abbott-Shim & Lambert, 1997; Bryant et al., 1994).

Because it is the direct contact between teachers and children and among children that is most likely to affect an individual child's development, information about these interactions should be especially helpful in identifying the aspects of a child's classroom experiences that have enduring effects. On the basis of our theory of literacy development, we would expect that an important aspect of emergent literacy is skill using extended discourse. Children are most likely to acquire such skill by being part of conversations in classrooms that include varied words and that involve talk about topics apart from the ongoing activities of the classroom. Furthermore, beneficial conversations are most likely to be those that are with adults because it is adults who are most likely to be able to extend a child's thinking about topics and supply appropriate new vocabulary. That said, children likely also acquire skill using extended discourse as they talk with friends, especially as they engage in pretend play.

There is some support for our notions about features of classrooms most likely to foster language development. In the 1980s there was a major study of the effects of child care on the development of children in Bermuda (McCartney, 1984). This study was especially interesting because most children in Bermuda attended center-based child care programs. The research team gathered extensive information about children's families and classrooms using rating tools such as the ECERS. In addition, the team members recorded the amount and kind of verbal experiences children had with teachers and peers. Although they found some evidence of a relationship between the ECERS rating of quality and children's language development, they found strong links to children's language experiences. In particular, children benefited from having conversations with adults and showed reduced levels of development if they spent considerable time with peers. Interestingly, in a later effort to replicate the results of the Bermuda study in the mainland United States, Susan Kontos (1991) used a research design that was similar except that instead of examining details of children's language experiences, she coded teacher–child interactions at a somewhat more global level. For example, she coded interactions in terms of whether the teacher was attempting to accomplish particular goals such as promoting acquisition of skills, fostering self-esteem and positive identity, or providing choices. Her study did not find that this approach to coding teacher–child interactions enabled her to predict children's language or intellectual growth.

SUMMARY

Researchers have examined many aspects of classrooms that are likely to have an impact on children's language and literacy development. On the basis of these studies, we conclude that one is most likely to identify features of classrooms that relate to children's development if one adopts all four approaches to collecting information but that careful study of the details of teacher–child conversations is likely to provide the most useful information. This, of course, is precisely what we did in the Home–School Study.

CLASSROOM DATA COLLECTION

One Day of Data Collection and the Aftermath

Each year that the children participating in our study were in center-based child care or kindergarten (and were 3–5 years old), we attempted to visit them to collect the data that we outlined in Chapter 1. We arranged with the teacher for an observer to visit her classroom, and we informed the parents that we would be visiting their children's preschool classrooms. On the day the observer was to collect data, he or she arrived at the beginning of the classroom day and asked both the teacher and child to wear our backpacks with attached lapel microphones. After explaining what he or she would be doing during the visit, the observer tried to be as unobtrusive as possible. As the child moved around the room, the observer took notes about the child's activities. At the same time, the observer took notes about what the teacher was doing. When the class gathered for a full-group book reading, the observer videotaped the gathering to provide a visual record of the session. Because it was our intention to audiotape a child during mealtime, free play, and large-group times that included book reading, it was occasionally necessary for a researcher to visit a classroom over the course of 2 days to complete data collection.

When the observer had an opportunity, he or she moved around the room, coding for the presence of wall displays, books, and writing materials and evidence of ongoing thematic explorations. At a point when the teacher had time, the observer would sit with her and conduct the teacher interview. This interview elicited information about the composition of the classroom, the teacher's professional history and education, how she structured her classroom day, her approach to supporting children's language and literacy development, her views about the purpose of preschool education, and her approach to working with parents.

After the classroom visits, the teacher audiotapes and the videotapes of book reading were transcribed, with every transcription being checked by a second person who listened to the audiotape or viewed the videotape. These transcripts were then coded in ways that are described in the coming chapters. The audiotapes of children's conversations were coded directly from the tapes without being transcribed. The codes applied to all of our materials were checked to ensure that they were being assigned in a reliable manner.

Characteristics of the Classrooms and Children Visited

When the children in the Home–School Study were 3 years old, we visited 64 children in 55 classrooms. Half of the classrooms were in Head

Table II.1. Classroom data collected

Data source	Age 3	Age 4	Age 5
Child audiotapes (all settings)	$n = 63$ 5,684.52 min.	$n = 76$ 6,663.38 min.	$n = 66$ 5,686.09 min.
Teacher audiotapes			
Free play (15 min.)	$n = 42$	$n = 79$	N/A
Large group (15 min.)	$n = 45$	$n = 62$	
Mealtime (10 min.)	$n = 25$	$n = 49$	
Small group (10 min.)	$n = 7$	$n = 19$	
Book-reading videotapes			
Transcribed (15 min.)	$n = 42$	$n = 70$	N/A
Analyzed for reading quality	$n = 46$	$n = 62$	
Classroom curriculum observation	$n = 53$	$n = 79$	$n = 57$
Teacher interview	$n = 61$	$n = 77$	$n = 58$
Total amount of talk analyzed (in minutes)	7,939.52	13,303.38	5,686.09

Start programs, whereas the other half were in private child care centers or public preschools. (Some of the children in the study were in Head Start home-based preschool programs as 3-year-olds. In this model, the children received regular visits from a trained home visitor and periodically attended a morning program that focused on socialization in a group setting. We did not collect data on children who received home-based Head Start.)

For the children who were in classroom-based programs at age 3, the average number of children per class was 16, typically staffed by one head teacher and one teaching assistant. On average, across all of the classrooms, 44% of the children were Caucasian, 25% were African American, 18% were Hispanic, and 13% were Asian American. Teachers reported, on average, that 80% of their students were fluent in English. The average age range in each classroom was 1½ years, indicating that most of the classrooms truly were mixed-age groups, even though we characterize the children in our study as being age 3 during the first visit.[3]

When the children in the study were 4 years old, we visited 74 children in 61 classrooms. The average number of children per class was still 16, typically staffed by one head teacher and one teaching assistant.

---

[3]When the children in the study were 3 years old, the average age of children in their classrooms was generally lower than when the children were 4 years old; therefore, the overall trend was for children to be with older groups of children when they were 4 than when they were 3. This trend partly reflects the fact that some of the 3-year-old children were in a home-based program.

Across all classrooms, by teacher report, 53% of the children were Caucasian, 28% were African American, 10% were Asian American, and 9% were Hispanic. At this visit, teachers reported, on average, that 82% of their students were fluent in English. As in the previous year, the average age range of children was 1½ years, indicating that our children really were in mixed-age groups.

At our kindergarten classroom visits we visited 66 children in 58 classrooms. Most of these were public school kindergarten classrooms. Because we were now following children into schools and classrooms that had not previously committed themselves to participate in our research, we encountered some constraints related to data collection. In particular, although we could audiotape children, we were unable to audiotape teachers and teacher interviews were intentionally narrowed to provide information about the child's adjustment and performance in their classrooms. Thus, we were unable to report demographic data on these teachers and their backgrounds.

Characteristics of the Teachers Visited

The teachers we visited exemplified the range of educational backgrounds and experiences typical of early childhood educators today. At our 3-year-old classroom visits, we did not determine teachers' educational backgrounds. However, they reported working at their current position, on average, more than 4 years. Interestingly, teachers who reported more experience in their current setting were more likely to be teaching larger groups of children ($r = .31$, $p < .01$) and groups with a larger age range ($r = .36$, $p < .01$). At this visit, 59% of the teachers we visited identified themselves as Caucasian, 30% as African American, 9% as Hispanic, and 1% as Asian American. There was a very strong correlation between the race of the teacher in a classroom and the race of the children in the classroom. Teachers who identified themselves as African American were far more likely to have students identified as African American ($r = .77$, $p < .0001$).

At our 4-year-old classroom visits, teachers reported a mean education level equivalent to an associate's degree. In terms of experience, the average length of time in their current position was nearly 5 years. At the 4-year-old visits, teachers who identified themselves as Caucasian were much more likely to teach children identified as Caucasian ($r = .61$, $p < .0001$) and were more likely to teach with other teachers; that is, the total number of teachers in a classroom was slightly higher in classrooms with head teachers who were Caucasian ($r = .36$, $p < .01$). Teachers who had more experience in their current setting again were more likely to teach larger groups of children ($r = .28$, $p < .01$) and groups with a larger range of ages ($r = .34$, $p < .01$).

OVERVIEW OF THE CHAPTERS IN THIS SECTION

Now we will examine the classrooms the children our study attended and, through these classrooms, consider broader questions about the impact of preschool classrooms on the development of children from low-income homes. First, you will be introduced to these classrooms in a broad manner, as Miriam Smith describes the beliefs and classroom practices of three teachers. In subsequent chapters we examine specific classroom settings and present profiles of the classrooms of selected children from our study. The final chapter in this section returns to the big picture, drawing together the quantitative data about all of the classroom settings and presenting summary profiles of the classrooms that the children attended when they were 4.

Chapter 7

Children's Experiences in Preschool

Miriam W. Smith

Central to what happens in every early childhood classroom is the teacher. Providers of early care and education (whether we call them *preschool teachers, caregivers,* or *child care providers*) determine the nature, quality, and content of children's early learning experiences and therefore are in a position to greatly influence young children's learning and development. Given this important role of the early childhood educator, it is surprising that we have minimal information about how and why teachers teach in the ways that they do. From research (Drummond, 1995; Tizard & Hughes, 1985) conducted in similar teaching settings, we know that there are two key elements of practice to be considered: teachers' pedagogical beliefs and teachers' instructional practices. These elements cannot be considered independent of each other because they clearly exert reciprocal influence.

In the case of early childhood education since 1985, teachers' beliefs and practices have been strongly influenced by a single philosophical and practical perspective: developmentally appropriate practice (DAP; originally articulated in Bredekamp, 1987). Simply stated, the philosophy of DAP includes the Piagetian notion (Brainerd, 1978; Gruber & Voneche, 1977; Piaget, 1926) that young children learn best through direct manipulation of objects and ideas in the world and the related notion that the role of the teacher is to construct an environment in which children can independently explore and manipulate objects and ideas. Another key feature of the articulation of DAP is the separation of learning goals for children into different developmental areas (such as physical, socioemotional, language, cognitive, aesthetic), coupled with suggestions for practices that facilitate development in each area. Combined, this set of beliefs and goals for children gave rise to a particular set of practices that have become common in most preschool classrooms. For example, most classrooms are divided into distinct activity areas or learning centers, each supplied with materials that children can use independently or in small groups. Teachers circulate through the classroom, providing guidance and facilitating interactions among children and materials. Many teachers plan using the developmental areas as their focus, incorporating age-appropriate materials and activities into the learning centers.

When the position statement on DAP (Bredekamp, 1987) was released in 1987, it received immediate acceptance and was celebrated by early childhood educators because many believed that this important document articulated their long-held beliefs and associated practices. With this philosophy in mind, researchers associated with the Home–School Study of Language and Literacy Development were interested in learning how a more specific educational agenda (language and literacy development) might fit with or challenge the notion of developmentally appropriate teaching.

METHODOLOGICAL CONSIDERATIONS

Among the many goals of the Home–School Study was collection of data that would enable us to look broadly and deeply at the nature of children's language and literacy experiences in early care and education settings. It was always our belief that general aspects of children's preschool experiences would correlate with and perhaps predict their later language and literacy achievement (Dickinson & Snow, 1987). In addition, it was our contention that specific aspects of preschool experience—those directly relevant to language and literacy—would relate to children's subsequent outcomes. In the years since we originally collected our preschool data, other researchers (for example, Hart & Risley, 1995; Tizard & Hughes, 1985; Vernon-Feagans, 1996) have published results that lend additional support to these assertions. The goals of this chapter, in light of our assertion that general aspects of preschool experience exert some influence on children's later language and literacy, are to present a broad perspective on the experiences that children in the Home–School Study had during their preschool years, to articulate major dimensions of variation across the range of classrooms visited, and to correlate aspects of these dimensions with children's later language and literacy achievement.

To accurately describe life in preschool classrooms, we must consider the complex relationship between what teachers believe, how they organize the learning environment, and how they interact with students (Madison & Speaker, 1994; Neuman & Roskos, 1993a; Schickedanz, Pergantis, Kanosky, Blaney, & Ottinger, 1998). Traditionally, class-room-based research in early childhood settings has considered only one of these areas at a time, using a single methodology appropriate to the research focus (Pajares, 1992). For example, studies of teachers' be-liefs have typically used self-report methodologies, whereas studies of classroom organization have used classroom observation techniques. Furthermore, many studies of preschool life have employed qualitative and descriptive methods, yielding highly interesting results but not allowing the possibility of powerful statistical analysis or generalization of findings to a wider population. Though previous studies have been essential to our broadening understanding of the forces that shape life in preschool classrooms, they have not combined qualitative and quan-titative methodologies to integrate the many factors to develop a more comprehensive portrait of the preschool experience. The research and results to be reported in this chapter represent our attempt to collect data through multiple methodologies (qualitative and quantitative), with the goal of describing the preschool experiences of children in the Home–School Study broadly, deeply, descriptively, and predictively.

Pajares (1992) suggested that research concerned with teachers' beliefs and practices should be centered on "something"—some content or situational context. In the case of the Home–School Study, our focus was on children's language and literacy experiences. This focus was known to all participants in the study and framed the questions we asked, the observations we made, the ways in which our data were coded, and the analyses we conducted. In this chapter, I address three central issues relevant to the focus on children's language and literacy development: preschool teachers' expressed goals for their students (in-cluding but not limited to language and literacy); teachers' reports of how they organize children's learning in the classroom; and connec-tions between teachers' goals, organization, and children's subsequent language and literacy development. With regard to each issue, I report on the nature of the data we collected, how it was coded and analyzed, and my interpretations of group results. To illustrate particular portions of the group results, I present descriptive miniportraits of several teach-ers who were participants in both the Home–School Study and a later follow-up study I conducted several years after our initial visits to the teachers' classrooms.

FOCUS TEACHERS

Throughout this chapter, I present interview responses and observa-tional data from three teachers to help illustrate points. The data that I report for these teachers reflect responses that they gave to interview questions and classroom observations conducted when the children in the Home–School Study were age 4. I begin here with a brief overview of the focus teachers' programs and classrooms.

Brookdale Head Start

The Head Start program in Brookdale is a large, suburban program that serves almost 200 children in five different locations. About one quarter of the children served by the Brookdale program were of Hispanic descent, and many of these children spoke Spanish as their primary language. One director, one assistant director, and two education coordinators administered the program. Cami Johnson is one of the education coordinators in this program. She was formerly a classroom teacher whom we visited when Todd was in her classroom.

The administrative offices and six of the classrooms were located in an underused junior high school building in Brookdale. Very few modifications had been made to the building to meet the needs of its young residents—metal lockers lined the wide, echoing hallways; classroom doors were windowless, solid, and heavy; drinking fountains, sinks, and toilets were at heights suitable for adults; and the gym was located a quarter-mile hike from the classrooms. The six classrooms themselves had been somewhat modified for young children, with short, wooden bookcases used as dividers; small tables and short chairs scattered strategically; and early childhood materials available on open shelves in different activity centers. The classrooms were distributed along one side of a long hallway, with the classrooms for the youngest children at one end near the bathrooms, and the classrooms for the older children at the other end, near the entry. The administrative offices, parent lounge, resource center, and health coordinator's offices were on the opposite side of the hallway. The classrooms all had windows that looked into a small courtyard that served as the program's outdoor play area. The courtyard had two small crabapple trees, a 9' x 9' sandbox, two swings, a small wooden house, and several large rocks to climb on.

Midway down the hallway, between the 3- and 4-year-old classrooms, was Roz Mahoney's mixed-age group. When I entered this class in January 1993, the small group of 11 children had been in school for only 3 weeks, and they were still getting to know their teachers: Roz, the head teacher, and Kathy Brady, her assistant. During our previous visits to Brookdale, Roz was one of Todd's teachers.

Roz is a tall woman with short, gray hair and a deep, soft voice. At the time we visited her classroom, she had been a teacher at Brookdale

Head Start for 11 years and had served the program in several different locations. Roz first completed child development associate training through Head Start, then continued her education, completing both her associate's and bachelor's degrees in early childhood education over a 6-year period and working for Brookdale Head Start the entire time.

The children at Brookdale Head Start arrived at school on school buses. They lined up outside and walked in with the assistant teacher. The lockers outside the classroom were marked with each child's name and a picture of an animal. The children were assisted in finding their lockers, taking off their coats and boots, hanging them up, and entering the classroom. Each school day in Roz's classroom began with breakfast time; children sat at three small tables near the windows and had cereal, milk, and fruit. This was followed by a group trip to the bathroom for toileting, hand washing, and toothbrushing. Then the children returned to the classroom for a brief group time in which Roz described the activities that would be available during free-play time. A daily art project was planned and related to a theme of the week. Following free-play time, the group headed outside or to the gym. Then they returned to the classroom for circle time, which often included book reading. Finally, the teachers and children sat down together for lunch, which was followed by dismissal.

Park Hill Community Childcare

Park Hill Community Childcare is located on the corner of two busy city thoroughfares in the heart of downtown Boston. In 1990, the neighborhood surrounding the school was somewhat run down, according to observers. The Park Hill Community Building, which houses the child care program, is an older, multistory brick building with high ceilings and large windows. There is no playground at the school, although the children and their teachers could walk to a large nearby park. When one enters the school itself, there is an aura of purpose and activity. The bottom floors house a cafeteria and various offices (staffed by volunteers of the program), and the upper floors house a series of small classrooms. The school seems to be run rather strictly, as was evidenced by children walking in straight, quiet lines, wearing prescribed dress, and addressing adults by titles such as Mrs. Washington and Mr. Davis. The school is staffed by head teachers in each classroom, many classroom aides who are available for a small number of hours each week, a curriculum coordinator who spends a portion of each day in the classrooms, and a director who coordinates the administrative aspects of the program.

The school is composed of a number of individual classrooms, each of which is quite small. In fact, the rooms give a sense of being much taller than they are wide or long, with high windows and wooden paneling that extends from the floor to the base of the windows. The sizes of the classrooms help determine the number of children and teachers within them. During our visits to Mrs. Angela Washington's classroom, she had seven students (six African American and one Latino) ranging in age from 4 to 5 years old and one part-time aide.

Mrs. Washington is an African American woman who was about 50 years old at the time of our classroom visits. She had been teaching at Park Hill for 3 years. During our visits, she was one of Astra's teachers. Although her prior educational experience and teaching history were unknown to us, it was evident from observations and conversations that Mrs. Washington had been teaching for some time. Her classroom was a small square that she had divided into several areas by arranging desks and wall displays. There was an area with a table for using small manipulatives, another table adjacent to some puzzles and books, and a housekeeping area. There were also smaller sections of the classroom labeled as *Science, Math,* and *Arts,* with corresponding materials nearby.

In contrast to Brookdale Head Start, Park Hill was a full-day, full-year child care program. Most of the children walked to school, accompanied by their parents. Because different children attended the program according to different schedules, it was harder to describe a typical day at Park Hill than a typical day at Brookdale. The description that follows is a general portrait of how Mrs. Washington structured her time.

When the children came to school each day, they were offered breakfast. After breakfast, there was a long free-play period (1–1½ hours), which often was held in the multipurpose room of the school, with several classes merged together. Following free play, children went with their teacher to their own classrooms. The teacher–child ratio was very high. Mrs. Washington had only seven students. They began with more structured activities, usually designed to help the children learn and practice specific skills. Circle time followed and reinforced the skill-building portion of the morning. Typical circle time activities included book reading, calendar activities, and common preschool games and songs. Circle time also was a time when spontaneous discussion of plans and ideas occurred. The afternoon at Park Hill included lunch, resting time, snacktime, and then an extended free-play period. Mrs. Washington noted that sometimes children worked on finishing projects or activities that they had started during curriculum time. The afternoon also was the time when the classes walked to a park or went out into the neighborhood.

TEACHERS' PEDAGOGICAL BELIEFS

The beliefs that preschool teachers hold about young children, their development, and appropriate pedagogy are complex and intertwined. They are likely to result from teachers' own personal and educational histories, their past and current experiences with children, and the contexts within which they work. As noted at the beginning of this chapter, prevailing philosophies of practice strongly influence teachers' pedagogical beliefs.

During our visits to the preschool classrooms of children who participated in the Home–School Study, we interviewed teachers about their pedagogical beliefs, in general and specifically with regard to children's language and literacy learning. Among the questions asked were the following:

- What do you see as the two or three most important goals of preschool?

- What activities do you typically do during group times?

- How do you support the language development of non–English speakers?

- Are there ways you support children's development of reading and writing skills?

Teachers were free to answer these questions in their own words. That is, we did not provide forced-choice options. An initial review of the data began to reveal common themes across the sample. On the basis of these emerging themes, the data were coded and responses to the questions were separated into four dimensions: focus on the social aspects of preschool, focus on preacademic skills, focus on language and book use, and focus on integrated curriculum and content. Items within the dimensions themselves were mutually exclusive (that is, one response would not be coded as belonging in two dimensions). Each teacher, however, typically provided responses that fell into more than one dimension. For example, when asked about early literacy skills, a teacher might answer that rehearsing the letters of the alphabet was important *and* that writing down children's stories during a thematic unit was important. The first response would fall into the preacademic skills focus dimension, and the second would fall into the integrated curriculum and content dimension. We believe that the open-ended questions were a strength of our approach because they yielded a multidimensional profile for each teacher rather than categorizing the teacher as falling within a single dimension. In the following sections, each of these dimensions is described in greater detail, along with examples of typical responses.

Focus on the Social Aspects of Preschool

In response to our series of interview questions, almost every teacher gave highest priority to the social aspects of preschool, as reflected in the following statements:

> For me, I think getting them to socialize, to feel confident about themselves. To kind of build their self-esteem, to see that they can do what they want to do as long as they put their mind to it. (Roz)

> I think my conscious effort has gone to socialization . . . That [the children] would have a good school experience. That they felt good about themselves, as individuals. That they would feel part of the unit, as part of a group. (Cami)

> To teach them how to get along with each other, how to play together. For example, how to share, the Golden Rule . . . Good self-concept. To feel good about themselves and about *expressing* themselves. (Mrs. Washington)

Clearly, the social functions of preschool are paramount—learning to get along with others, learning to share, and feeling positive about school. This strong belief makes sense in light of the prevailing philosophy of DAP, which begins with a strong statement about the importance of safe and nurturing environments for young children. It is also strongly aligned with the primary goal of Head Start, which is to promote the social competence of young children. Table 7.1 lists the kinds of responses to our interview questions that were coded as falling within the social focus dimension. Teachers' responses within this dimension were weighted and summed, yielding a range from 0–9. Within the dimension, the mean scores were 4.83 at our first classroom visit and 4.35 at our second classroom visit. As Figure 7.1 shows, our focus teachers exhibited different profiles for this dimension. Notice that Roz had a rather low score on this dimension and that Cami had a very high score, further reinforcing the view she presented in my interview with her.

Focus on Preacademic Skills

Many of the teachers whom we interviewed contrasted a focus on the social aspects of preschool (which they believed were most appropriate) with a focus on academic preparation (which they believed was inappropriate). This strongly asserted belief is closely related to the DAP position statement, which argues that there has been a "trend toward increased emphasis on formal instruction in academic skills" (Bredekamp, 1987) in early childhood settings, with activities and expectations that are inappropriate to the ways young children learn best. Consider Cami's strong statement:

> When we're dealing with parents, especially kindergarten, you know, prekindergarten age, and they're looking at the screening. And then they come back and say, "My child's not ready for kindergarten." Well, that's not our job. And that's also not our responsibility in many respects. Because the child isn't ready. Our first and foremost is socialization, working with the family. We're giving them experiences, in both social ways and academic ways, that they may not be exposed to previously or in their own homes. If a child comes in and is not socially competent, and we try and sit down and teach them 1-2-3, A-B-C, they're not gonna hear it. They're busy doing other things with their head. (Cami)

The strength with which many teachers asserted their opinions against providing academic instruction for children is notable. Cami's assertion that "the child isn't ready" and that what Head Start is doing is "exposing" children to experiences they have not had at home clearly revealed some understanding of the goals of Head Start as well as limiting teachers' responsibility to helping children achieve social goals.

Table 7.1. Teachers' responses to interview questions within the social focus dimension

Interview question	Teacher response
Primary purpose of preschool	To help children get along with others
	To support emotional development
	To help develop children's independence
Group time activities (reported)	Verbal sharing (show and tell)
	Share feelings
Helping nonnative English speakers	Encourage verbal sharing
	Assign aide to "shadow" or translate
Helping children with literacy	Passive (children learn on their own)
	Traditional focus on letter names

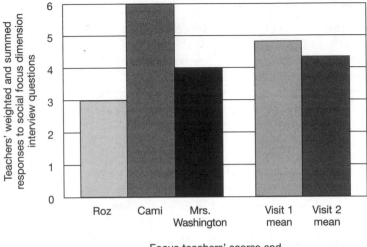

Figure 7.1. Teachers' pedagogical focus on socialization.

Some teachers, however, believed that helping children learn some preacademic skills was as much a part of their responsibility as helping children learn social skills. Mrs. Washington and other teachers in her program asserted this point of view. Though socialization was their most important goal, they also wanted to provide "the skills that will help children begin to learn to read and write." In Mrs. Washington's classroom (and in other classrooms at Park Hill), children were expected to spend a portion of each school day in skills-oriented activities such as tracing letters, counting, practicing writing their names, and playing games such as "Which one is different?" The time spent on these activities was short but planned and goal-directed. In our observations, children did not resist these activities and completed assignments as they were directed. Every child in Mrs. Washington's classroom knew the letters of the alphabet and could point to the letters in his or her first name.

Just as with the socialization focus, particular responses to interview questions were coded as having a skills focus, and each teacher received a score indicating her pedagogical orientation toward providing such experiences in the classroom. Responses coded in this orientation are displayed in Table 7.2. For this dimension, teachers' scores ranged from 0 to 9. Within the dimension, the mean scores were 2.97 at our first classroom visit and 3.47 at our second classroom visit. Interestingly, Figure 7.2 shows that all three of the focus teachers had fairly

Table 7.2. Teachers' responses to interview questions within the preacademic skills focus dimension

Question	Response
Primary purpose of preschool	To learn skills that will be needed in kindergarten
	To learn basic concepts, numbers, and letters
Group time activities (reported)	Reciting the alphabet, numbers, and names
	Attendance and daily calendar
Helping nonnative English speakers	Teach vocabulary
	Send to speech-language specialist
Helping children with literacy	Teach alphabet, numbers, and shapes
	Instruct children in writing skills

high scores on this dimension in relation to the group mean, with Cami again showing the highest score among the three teachers.

Focus on Language and Book Use

A third dimension that emerged from our teacher interview data reflected teachers' beliefs about the importance and use of books and oral language experiences for young children. Here are some typical comments that demonstrate this dimension:

> The first thing, especially with books, is looking at pictures. They picture a lot within their looking at books. Many times they'll come and ask you to read a story with them. They may not realize it, but I think indirectly they're coming to understand that letters mean words, and words mean stories or lines or sentences. And that relates to the picture . . . because that gives them an understanding as far as a reading and a language literacy. So they get an understanding . . . that words are written . . .[and] oral language [is] written down. (Roz)

Literacy for Roz was specifically related to book use and her perception that children would make natural connections between looking at books, seeing words in print, reading words, and writing words. A similar, more fully developed perspective, was articulated by the education coordinator in Roz's program, Cami:

> I think literacy is extremely important. I think it begins with being able to verbalize, being able to speak and understand what other people are saying. So, we're looking at really basics: Are they hearing okay? Are they understanding? Are they processing okay?

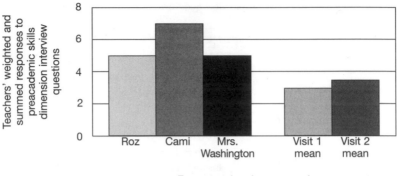

Figure 7.2.   Teachers' pedagogical focus on preacademic skills.

After you get past the verbalization part . . . I think any kind of experience that the children have can be reflected in literacy. We can get down to basics such as labeling everything in the classroom with letters, and this is *stove,* here's the symbolic representation of *stove* in letters. Here's the word. If we've gone on a field trip or somebody's had an experience of some sort, writing that down. Again, using the language, taking it that next step. Past being able to verbalize things, putting them into letters and words and sentences and paragraphs. Using tape recorders and speaking into tape recorders, singing activities, fingerplay activities, memory-type activities, labeling. (Cami)

For the teachers in this program, beliefs about language and literacy were connected to classroom practice through the use of books and through procedures such as labeling and writing things, subtly demonstrating to children the connections between spoken and written language. In the Park Hill program, reading books with children was a focus of some daily activities.

On the basis of responses to our interview questions, each teacher received a score for the degree to which she had a focus on language and book use experiences. Teachers' responses are displayed in Table 7.3. As with the previous dimensions, teachers' responses were weighted and summed, yielding a range for the group from 0 to 8. Within the dimension, mean scores were 3.44 at our first classroom visit and 3.27 at our second classroom visit. In Figure 7.3, our focus teachers' scores are compared with the group mean at each visit. Notice here that both Roz and Cami have relatively low scores on this dimension and that

Mrs. Washington's score is somewhat higher. Interestingly, all of these teachers' scores are below the group means.

Focus on Integrated Curriculum and Content

Most of the classrooms we visited followed a "seasons and holidays" approach to curriculum, a very common approach in early childhood classrooms (Katz & Chard, 1989). In this approach, each month is oriented thematically to the season and/or holiday of the month. Thus, September usually has a focus on the season of fall, including activities related to the changing colors of leaves, the harvesting of fruits such as apples, and changes in weather and temperature (drier, colder, frost appears). As critics have noted, this approach to curriculum tends to trivialize and compartmentalize children's learning, focusing on surface features and activities. Thus, in the fall theme, it is likely that children will engage in art projects such as printing with leaves and apples, learning that apples come in different colors, and that one should wear a sweater when it is chilly. Children's conceptual learning is not the focus of such a curriculum.

In contrast to this surface-level treatment of curriculum, several of the classrooms we visited, including Cami's at Brookdale and Mrs. Washington's at Park Hill, demonstrated a fuller, more meaningful approach to children's learning. In these programs, a curriculum theme based on a major concept was chosen and pursued over a long period. For example, in Cami's classroom, children spent nearly a month on an intensive study of dinosaurs. The theme was integrated throughout the classroom, including multiple readings of books about dinosaurs; use of small replicas in sand play; group construction of a "life-sized" dinosaur;

Table 7.3. Teachers' responses to interview questions within the language and book use focus dimension

Question	Response
Primary purpose of preschool	To learn to communicate effectively
	Early literacy development
Group time activities (reported)	Building oral language skills
	Reading, telling, and discussing stories
Helping nonnative English speakers	Intentional efforts to foster first language
	Small, mixed-language groups
	Engage in meaningful conversation
Helping children with literacy	Encourage purposeful uses of writing
	Read and discuss books
	Develop a love for books

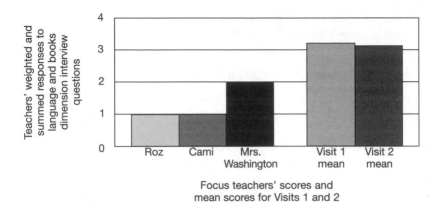

Figure 7.3. Teachers' pedagogical focus on language and books.

and small-group discussions of types of dinosaurs, their lifestyles and eating preferences, and why they became extinct. During this exploration, children learned and used extensive vocabulary about dinosaurs and engaged in considerable discussion of "big ideas" such as extinction, fossils, and the distinction between herbivores and carnivores. Integrated curriculum of this sort is fundamental to DAP.

During work time and curriculum time at Park Hill, Mrs. Washington spent considerable time interacting with individual children, made possible by the very small group size and favorable teacher–child ratio. Sometimes the interactions centered on the curriculum work they were doing, and at other times the interactions were about the children's personal experiences. As in Cami's classroom, we noted the focus on curriculum content at Park Hill. A large portion of each morning was devoted to pursuing particular themes or ideas such as Black history, not just through art activities but also through discussion, books, field trips, and other means.

In order to gauge teachers' pedagogical beliefs about curriculum, their responses to our interview questions were coded for curriculum and content orientation, and again teachers' responses were weighted and summed. Table 7.4 displays responses coded for curriculum and content orientation. The range of scores from the group was 0–12, the widest range across all four dimensions. Within the dimension, the mean scores were 2.47 at our first classroom visit and 2.74 at our second classroom visit. These means were the lowest of all four dimensions. Notice in Figure 7.4 that Mrs. Washington has a very high score on this dimension, which corresponds to the way that she described curriculum in her classroom. Interestingly, Cami's score is very low, which stands in contrast to the observed curriculum in her classroom.

Table 7.4. Teachers' responses to interview questions within the integrated curriculum and content dimension

Question	Response
Primary purpose of preschool	To instill intellectual curiosity
Group time activities (reported)	Discuss current unit
	Teacher and children write down ideas
Helping nonnative English speakers	Engage children in activities
	Concentrate on children's ideas and content of their talk
Helping children with literacy	Help children communicate their ideas in talk and in writing

This seeming contradiction may point to a weakness in the profile approach. If a teacher makes fewer statements about his or her beliefs, there are fewer statements to code; thus, the teacher may not be adequately represented by the profile. Also, the way that Cami in particular conceptualizes her curriculum may be through a different lens; thus, her higher score on the skills dimension may include her view of curriculum as being predicated on developing particular skills through an interesting curriculum. Thus, in the interest of fairly representing teachers' beliefs and practices, we believe it is necessary to broaden the scope of inquiry beyond teachers' *reported* pedagogical beliefs to include actual observations of classroom materials and practices.

TEACHERS' CLASSROOM PRACTICES

Organization and Materials

One of the strongest links between what a teacher believes pedagogically and what he or she does practically may lie in how he or she physically organizes the classroom and the ways in which the classroom day is structured (such as division of time into activity periods of different duration). All of the classrooms that we visited in the Home–School Study employed similar structures for classroom organization and time use.

Classrooms were arranged with a series of activity centers, which, at a minimum, incorporated fine motor activities (with puzzles, Legos, and pegboards), arts and crafts activities (with markers, scissors, glue, and paper), and dramatic play (usually a "housekeeping" arrangement with kitchen supplies). As in many early childhood classrooms, approximately half of each room was carpeted and half was durable linoleum flooring. Messy activities (with paint, glue, sand, and water) and meals took place at small tables arranged in the more durable area, and dra-

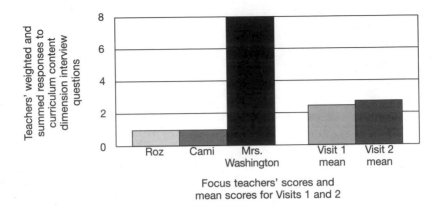

Figure 7.4.   Teachers' pedagogical focus on curriculum content.

matic play, block play, puzzles, games, and book readings took place in the carpeted sections of the classroom. This type of organization reflects some of the tenets described in the guidelines for DAP, as noted previously.

During our visits, we conducted specific observations to determine classroom materials and practices related to three areas in particular: books and book use, writing opportunities and materials, and curriculum content and materials. These foci were concurrent with our interest in experiences that might intentionally foster children's language and literacy development. For example, our observations of writing opportunities and materials included the following questions:

- Is there a writing area? $0 = no, 1 = yes$
- Are motivational materials accessible? $0 = no, 1 = yes$
- Can children see letters, words, other print? $0 = no, 1 = yes$
- Is children's written work displayed? $0 = no, 1 = yes$
- Is there a range of writing supplies? $0 = no, 1 = yes$
- Are materials available on request? $0 = no, 1 = yes$

On the basis of observers' descriptions of classroom areas and materials, teachers received a score for each of these observational categories. In addition, when the children in the study were age 4, we completed a portion of the Early Childhood Environment Rating Scale (ECERS; Harms & Clifford, 1980) in each classroom. The ECERS was created to provide a standardized way to determine the developmental appropriateness of preschool classrooms. The items were based on the tenets of

DAP (Bredekamp, 1987). For the three subscales we used (furnishings, social, and language), ECERS scores ranged from 33 to 86 with a mean score of 63.71, indicating that the classrooms as a whole were above average in developmental appropriateness. Table 7.5 shows the mean scores on our observation variables across all teachers when the children in our study were ages 3 and 4.

Here it is notable that, overall, classrooms were rated near the middle of the scale in all categories, with observations of the writing materials and opportunities consistently being the lowest of the three scores. In general, classroom scores on the content area observation were higher in the classrooms that children in the study attended at age 4 than they were in the classrooms that they attended at age 3. Teachers working with 4-year-olds may believe that introducing curriculum content is more appropriate with older children or that children of this age may require more content-oriented curriculum.

Time Use

Just as there were similarities across classrooms in terms of organization and materials, there were striking similarities in how teachers structured classroom time each day. Namely, the classroom day was divided into free-play times, large-group times (usually twice per morning), small-group activities, mealtimes, and outside or gross motor times. During free-play times, children were expected and encouraged to use the activity centers and materials independently, with a minimum of teacher supervision, involvement, or interaction. Typically, one large-group time was devoted to taking attendance, singing songs, and calendar activities, and the other large-group time was devoted to story reading or (infrequently) to discussions of ongoing curriculum and proj-

Table 7.5. Teachers' mean scores on classroom observation variables

Variable	n	Mean	Range
Age 3			
Book area observation	53	2.94	0–6
Writing area observation	53	2.06	0–5
Content area observation	53	2.77	1–4
Age 4			
Book area observation	73	3.38	0–7
Writing area observation	73	2.40	0–6
Content area observation	73	3.30	0–4
ECERS[a] observation score	73	63.71	33–86

[a]Early Childhood Environment Rating Scale (Harms & Clifford, 1980).

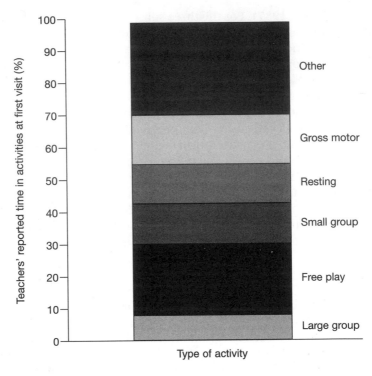

Figure 7.5.   Teachers' reported time in activities at first visit.

ects. Small-group times usually involved an art project or a skill game such as Bingo or Lotto.

During our interviews with teachers, we asked them to describe their daily schedules, how they divided class time, and what kinds of activities and materials were available during each time period. From their responses, we calculated the amount of time that teachers *reported* spending in different activities, which is shown in Figures 7.5 and 7.6. As these figures show, only about 50% of the day is represented by free-play, large-group, and small-group activities. The rest of the day is spent in resting, gross motor, or other activities ("other activities" included transitions such as entering, toileting, toothbrushing, lining up, and mealtimes).

Because we recognize that teachers' reports of how they spend time (ideally) and that the realities of daily classroom activity may differ, we also recorded the actual amount of time spent in various classroom activities during our visits. Figures 7.7 and 7.8 show the amount of *observed* time teachers and children spent in particular activity periods during our classroom visits. Please keep in mind that these results

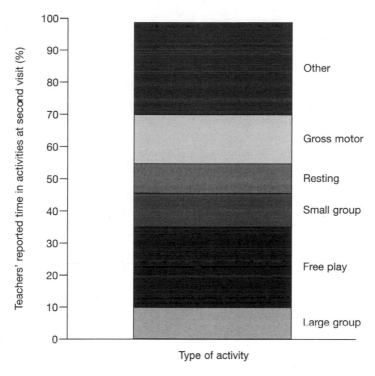

Figure 7.6. Teachers' reported time in activities at second visit.

do not necessarily represent the entire day because our visits were usu-ally limited to 3 hours. We believe, however, that they represent typi-cal patterns of time use on a typical preschool morning. Notice, in contrast to the graph of reported time use, that considerably more than 50% of the classroom day was actually spent engaged in free-play, small-group, and large-group activities. Overall, we found that teach-ers and children spent very little time in small-group activities. In fact, in many classrooms (25 of 74) we were unable to observe any small-group time at all.

Considering these graphs together indicates that the ways teachers *reported* spending their time was only minimally related to how we observed them actually *using* the time. For example, on average, when our target children were age 3, teachers reported spending about 10% of their time in large-group activities but were observed to spend closer to 25% of their time during our observation actually engaged in large-group activities. When we correlated reported time use with observed time use, there were no relationships. In other words, *how teachers* **reported** *using the time was not actually related to how they were* **observed** *to*

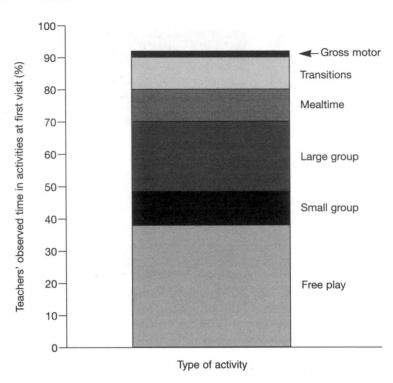

Figure 7.7. Teachers' observed time in activities at first visit.

use their time each day. Figures 7.9 and 7.10 depict the focus teachers' reported and observed patterns of time use. What is particularly interesting about these graphs is the inverse relationship that emerges—Roz reported that her class spent the least but was observed to spend the most amount of time in free play, and Mrs. Washington reported that her class spent the most and was observed to spend the least amount of time in free play.

Influence of Teacher Background on Classroom Practice

These data, when viewed in light of the pedagogical beliefs reported previously, beg the question of how beliefs relate to practices. To answer this question, it is important to know whether and how teachers' reported pedagogical beliefs relate to their observed curricular emphases (from our classroom observations) and to their reported and observed use of time. It is also interesting to consider whether expressed beliefs and observed practices are related to teachers' educational backgrounds, teaching experience, or aspects of their current teaching environments (such as number and age of children). Here we are asking two questions. First, do teachers' beliefs about the goals of preschool education relate to their reported or observed practices? Second, are there demographic or situational factors that relate to reported or observed practices?

To answer the first question—regarding whether teachers' reported pedagogical beliefs relate to their reported or observed practices—we conducted a series of correlation analyses. The results of these analyses are reported, by year. During our first observation year, when the children in the study were age 3, a teacher's strong pedagogical orientation toward socialization was negatively correlated with a skills focus ($r = -.44$, $p < .001$) and positively correlated with our observations of content area curriculum ($r = .37$, $p < .01$). Similarly, teachers with a strong pedagogical focus on curriculum scored higher on our observations of content area curriculum ($r = .35$, $p < .01$). In general, although teachers' pedagogical orientations were occasionally related to our observations of curriculum, they were not correlated with patterns of reported or observed time use. Patterns of observed and reported time use, however, were correlated with each other; teachers who reported spending more time in free play reported spending less time in small-group activities ($r = -.49$, $p < .001$) and large-group activities ($r = -.29$, $p < .05$). In addition, teachers who were observed to spend more time in free play were observed to spend less time in large-group activities ($r = -.45$, $p < .001$) and less time in small-group activities ($r = -.28$, $p < .05$). There

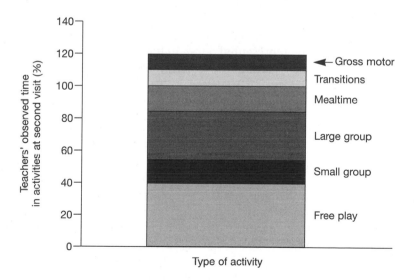

Figure 7.8.   Teachers' observed time in activities at second visit.

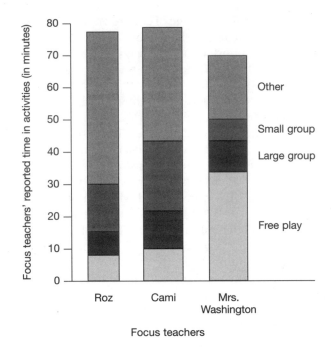

Figure 7.9.   Focus teachers' reported time in activities.

were no clear clusters of relationship among variables during this year, yielding a relatively unclear picture of teachers and curriculum.

During the second observation year, when the children in the study were age 4, a more consistent pattern of results emerged, with two clusters of variables being represented. First, in terms of pedagogical beliefs, teachers who asserted a strong socialization focus were likely to score higher on the ECERS ($r = .38$, $p < .01$), reported spending more time in free play ($r = .37$, $p < .01$), and were observed to spend more time in free play ($r = .35$, $p < .01$). In another cluster of findings, classrooms that were rated highly on our observations of the writing program also were rated highly on the content area curriculum ($r = .43$, $p < .001$) and the amount of time teachers reported spending in small-group activities ($r = .35$, $p < .01$). In a related finding, teachers who asserted a strong pedagogical focus on content area curriculum were observed to spend more time in small-group activities ($r = .31$, $p < .05$). Taken together, two patterns are clear: Teachers who valued the social functions of preschool tended to organize the day with an emphasis on free-play time (Roz was this sort of teacher); teachers who focused more strongly on content area curriculum tended to organize the classroom in ways that facilitated children's writing and content area explorations and spent more time in small-group activities (Mrs. Washington was this sort of teacher).

These two patterns are interesting to consider and raise a second set of questions: whether there are educational, experiential, or situational factors that affect teachers' beliefs and practices. For example, is it likely that teachers with more education emphasize content area curriculum? Or is it possible that classrooms with more children spend a greater proportion of time in large-group activities? In order to investigate these and other questions, we correlated some of our background variables (see page 146 in the introduction to Section II) with the same set of pedagogical beliefs and observed practices analyzed previously.

Results from correlation analyses conducted on data from our first year of classroom visits showed a strong difference between the expressed attitudes and patterns of time use reported by African American teachers and Caucasian teachers. African American teachers reported practices and attitudes most closely aligned with the preacademic skills dimension ($r = .52$, $p < .001$), and their attitudes were, in fact, negatively related to the socialization focus ($r = -.40$, $p < .001$). Furthermore, African American teachers were more likely to report spending a portion of their classroom day working on projects with the children ($r = .48$, $p < .001$) and were observed to spend somewhat more time actually working with small groups of children ($r = .28$, $p < .05$). Notice how closely this pattern of results mirrors the profile of Mrs. Washington, one of the African American teachers in our study. In con-

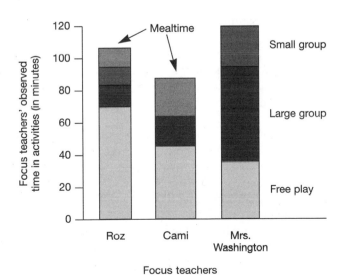

Figure 7.10. Focus teachers' observed time in activities.

trast, the pattern of results for Caucasian teachers was quite different. Caucasian teachers were less likely to report attitudes aligned with the preacademic skills focus ($r = -0.28$, $p < .03$) and more likely to report a focus on socialization ($r = .25$, $p < .05$). They reported very little or no time spent in project work ($r = -.52$, $p < .001$) but considerable time spent in free play ($r = .28$, $p < .03$). Notice here how the pattern of results mirrors the profile of Roz, one of the Caucasian teachers in our study.

A second pattern of results from the first year concerns the overall number of children in a given classroom. Classrooms with more children were observed to spend less time in free play ($r = -.34$, $p < .01$) and more time in meals ($r = .28$, $p < .03$) and transitions ($r = .23$, $p < .05$). Furthermore, teachers of larger groups reported spending more time in full-class activities ($r = .29$, $p < .02$).

Results from the second year of data were similar, although not as strong as those from the first year. For all teachers, their amount of reported education was strongly related to their attitudes and practices. Teachers with more education received higher scores on the ECERS classroom observation ($r = .42$, $p < .001$) and on the book area observation ($r = .31$, $p < .01$). African American teachers were again more likely to report spending more time in project work ($r = .51$, $p < .001$) and to report a focus on preacademic skills ($r = .37$, $p < .01$). They also received lower scores on the ECERS ($r = -.42$, $p < .001$). Caucasian teachers were observed to spend less time in full-group activities ($r = -.38$, $p < .01$) and reported less time working on projects with children ($r = -.36$, $p < .01$). They tended to receive higher scores on the ECERS ($r = .30$, $p < .02$).

In contrast to the first year of data, there were fewer correlations between group size and classroom activity. In classrooms with more children, overall, teachers reported spending more time in general purpose activities ($r = .34$, $p < .01$) and were observed to spend less time in large-group activities ($r = -.27$, $p < .03$). This may speak to the fact that when there are many children in a classroom, it is more difficult to get them all to do something together; hence, more time is spent in general-purpose activities and less time is spent in full-group activities.

Taken together, the patterns of results from the 2 years of preschool data are strikingly similar. There were strong differences between the reported and observed attitudes and practices of African American and Caucasian teachers, with African American teachers reporting a focus on preacademic skills and tending to spend more time engaging in project work with children and Caucasian teachers reporting a focus on socialization and spending more time in free play with children. These patterns beg the questions of whether and how such attitudes and practices relate to children's later achievements.

Given the strength of the beliefs expressed by the teachers in our study and the variability in practices reported and observed, it is natural to pursue the question of whether any of these variables relate to children's outcomes later in their school experiences. Do either beliefs or practices relate to children's language and literacy outcomes at the end of kindergarten? To determine this, we correlated pedagogical beliefs and reported and observed practices with children's scores on a series of outcome measures at the end of kindergarten. The measures reported here include the Narrative Production task (the Bear Story), the Emergent Literacy task (Early Childhood Diagnostic Instrument: The Comprehensive Assessment Program [CAP]; Mason & Stewart, 1989), a test of story comprehension (*The Snowy Day*; Keats, 1962), and the Receptive Vocabulary task (the Peabody Picture Vocabulary Test–Revised [PPVT–R]; Dunn & Dunn, 1981).

There were four variables from our first observation year that were correlated with children's outcomes nearly 2 years later. The amount of time that teachers reported spending in small-group activities was positively correlated with children's performance on the PPVT–R ($r = .39$, $p < .05$) and on the CAP ($r = .47$, $p < .001$). It is important to remember that reported time in small-group activities was unrelated to observed time in small-group activities. Thus, the correlations may reflect teachers' belief in the importance of small-group activities and their regular practices that we may not have observed during our limited visits to their classrooms. In contrast to these findings, teachers' reported time in large-group activities was negatively related to children's performance on the PPVT–R ($r = -.34$, $p < .02$) and CAP ($r = -.40$, $p < .01$). Furthermore, teachers' pedagogical focus on socialization and content area curriculum at our initial observations was negatively related to children's performance on the Bear Story task ($r = -.43$, $p < .001$ and $r = -.44$, $p < .001$, respectively). Taken together, a somewhat muddled picture of relationships between teachers' pedagogy and practice in relation to children's outcomes is evident. There may be a beginning hint of the importance of small-group learning experiences for children's subsequent development emerging, but, overall, the results are not compelling.

During our second round of classroom visits, when the children in the study were mostly age 4, a clearer picture of relationships between classroom variables and subsequent outcomes emerged. In fact, two classroom observation variables were repeatedly and strongly related to children's outcomes 1 year later—the amount of observed time in small-group activities and the quality of the observed writing program. Children's scores on the PPVT–R were correlated with the writing observation ($r = .37$, $p < .01$) and time observed in small-group activities ($r = .32$, $p < .01$). Scores on the CAP were also correlated with the writing observation ($r = .32$, $p < .01$) and time observed in small-group activities ($r = .27$, $p < .05$). Children's scores on *The Snowy Day* listening comprehension task were correlated weakly with observed time in small-group activities ($r = .25$, $p < .05$), though not with the writing observation variable. In addition, children's scores on the Bear Story task were correlated weakly with the writing observation variable ($r = .28$, $p < .05$), though not with the observed time in small-group activities.

It is interesting to note that despite the strong clustering of certain variables within the 4-year-old observation year (such as social focus, ECERS, and time in free play), *none* of these variables were related to children's outcomes at kindergarten. Thus, considering both sets of results (within-year and predictive), the variables that repeatedly emerge as important to consider are the content area curriculum (whether expressed as important by the teacher or observed independently), the presence of a writing program, and the amount of small-group time reported or observed.

CONCLUSIONS

Despite the different profiles reported here, from the socialization focus of Roz and Cami to the skills and curriculum focus of Mrs. Washington, there seem to be different potential pathways to positive outcomes for children. We are left with the conclusion that though some aspects of teachers' attitudes and practices seem potentially important to children's long-term growth, no single variable accounts for much. Perhaps what is most important is not what teachers believe or even how they spend their time but what happens during each day in the actual interactions between teachers and children. To determine whether this is true, we must look in more detail at those interactions.

Chapter 8

Book Reading
in Preschool Classrooms
Is Recommended Practice Common?

David K. Dickinson

When teachers explain how they help foster early language and literacy development, typically one of the first things they discuss is book reading. This response is not surprising, given the prominent place of books in teacher preparation programs and the fact that teachers often advise parents to read to their children. Research in preschool and primary grade classrooms has shown that special intervention programs that increase children's access to books and enhance the quality of how books are read can foster children's language development (Arnold & Whitehurst, 1994; Dickinson, 1989; Elley, 1989; Feitelson, Goldstein, Iraqi, & Share, 1993; Feitelson, Kita, & Goldstein, 1986; Karweit, 1994). Of course, book use is not confined only to group times; children read books on their own, with friends, or in small groups with the teacher. Some research also has shown the benefits of special efforts to provide more books to classrooms and to organize classrooms so that they make books more available (Neuman, 1999; Neuman & Roskos, 1997; Shimron, 1994). Despite the wide popularity of book reading in preschools, relatively little research has been done in typical classrooms examining the place of books in the course of the classroom day and how books are read and discussed. This chapter sheds light on typical book-reading practices in classrooms serving children from low-income families and makes suggestions regarding the effective use of books in preschool classrooms.

First, I discuss elements of book programs that are particularly helpful to children, drawing on data for 61 of the children in the

Home–School Study of Language and Literacy Development when they were 3 years old and for 70 children when they were 4 years old. I then illustrate how book reading unfolds within the overall flow of the day in two of the classrooms attended by the children in the study sample, sketching the place of books and book reading in Mariana's and Todd's classrooms, and relate what was found in their rooms to the results from the full sample. I then use this discussion of the details of book reading in Mariana's and Todd's classrooms as a starting point for examining the impact of different styles of book reading on children's development of language and literacy. In the final section, I give suggestions for enhancing the effectiveness of book use.

HOW EFFECTIVE BOOK-READING
PRACTICES SUPPORT LITERACY DEVELOPMENT

Most parents and teachers now believe that reading books to children helps prepare children to learn to read, but there is less general understanding of how this occurs. Some believe that book reading helps children learn to identify letters and read words, but research gives little support to this model, which assumes direct effects of hearing books read on children's reading (Whitehurst & Lonigan, 1998). What is more likely is that book reading supports the development of children's ability to comprehend stories and helps foster a love of books and reading. Growth in comprehension occurs as children learn vocabulary and concepts, become familiar with the language of books, and begin to learn strategies for taking meaning from books.

Book reading has special potential for fostering the type of language development that is linked to literacy. It is one of the few times during the preschool day when language comes to the forefront and words are central to the activity. Children must attend to the language of the book, integrating it with information from pictures as they construct an understanding of the world of the story. This reliance on language apart from ongoing activity is challenging and can be especially hard for children with limited experience with reading books at home. To best understand how book reading can support language growth, it is helpful to turn to what has been learned about features of mother–child conversations that support children's language growth.

Language development research has shown that mothers engage children in conversations that they can understand but that help them to stretch, supporting them as they learn new words and new grammatical structures. Adults do this by articulating words more clearly and tailoring their grammar and choice of words. These interactions often are part of routines such as book reading and games; this predictability helps children understand what is being said and provides a natural review of words, phrases, and grammatical structures. Also, because children are active participants in these interactions, they have a chance to try out new words and phrases, which gives the adult the opportunity to detect misunderstandings and provides clues about how to extend the topic in a way that will continue to hold the child's attention.

If research on mother–child interaction is applied to group book reading, one can see the problem teachers face: It is very hard to engage in conversations that are slightly challenging yet also comprehensible when talking with groups of children who have diverse levels of language skill and book-reading experience. As a result, skilled teachers need to be attuned to children's understanding, to find places in a book that are likely to be confusing, and to engage the group in conversations that are challenging but that they can understand. This is asking a lot! Because it is so hard to gauge children's understanding in full-group situations, individual and small-group reading sessions come much closer to creating the kind of environment for conversation that is found between mothers and children.

Child language research also shows that the number of conversations and the variety of words that children hear affect the speed of their language growth. Although research on book reading has not identified the precise links between the amount of book reading a child experiences and the rate of his or her language growth, it is likely that the amount of time children spend hearing and discussing books is important. Children can learn more from hearing books read once or twice per day than if they are read to only twice per week.

To fully understand the place of book reading in classrooms, one needs to look beyond the time when books are read aloud. Children may reenact the story in the dramatic play area, reread the book alone or with a friend, and discuss it at lunch with friends or their teacher. Because children learn language best when they actively take part in conversations, such opportunities to take the role of the characters, explore the plot, and use the language of a story support children's developing capacities to understand books (Rowe, 1998). Thus, if the impact of books is to be examined, the place of book reading in the entire preschool day must be studied.

As the varied ways in which teachers use books are examined, it is important to remember that book reading and the use of books are being discussed here in terms of what the research team saw when they observed in classrooms. This was not a carefully developed intervention designed to test the effectiveness of best practice on children's development. What the Home–School Study data most clearly show is how teachers typically use books. The data also give some sense of the impact of relatively effective practices on children's development, but they do not reveal the extent to which optimal approaches could support development because we found exemplary practice in relatively few settings. I next turn to descriptions of book reading and the place of books in two contrasting classrooms.

MARIANA'S CLASSROOM: A DIDACTIC INSTRUCTION APPROACH

When Mariana was 4, she attended preschool for the first time. She went to a prekindergarten classroom based in a public school. Her teacher, Roberta Williams, provided a range of experiences that focused on skills and knowledge commonly considered important for kindergarten (such as colors, counting). Books played an important part in her classroom day, and book-reading time was an important instructional time.

On the day she was observed in her classroom, Mariana's day began as she joined the other children in a circle on a rug around Ms. Williams for 45 minutes of group time. For the first 15 minutes of group time, Ms. Williams's class said the Pledge of Allegiance, discussed the calendar, selected classroom leaders, and sang songs. Ms. Williams then asked the children to recall what they had learned about robins the day before and elicited the information that robins are red, brown, and orange and have black eyes. Two children then told about giving their mothers the robins that they had made in school the day before. The final 15 minutes of group time were spent reading and discussing a book about robins.

After circle time, Mariana had 25 minutes for free play. During this time Mariana first used an alphabet puzzle, talking with her friend Sebastian about the shapes and identifying letters in her name. She then briefly played with some blocks, counting them as she put them away before joining Sebastian in a game that involved finding numbers. After a conversation with her teacher, Mariana moved to the dramatic play area, where she joined Sebastian and another girl in playing house until it was time for snack. Mariana had this type of free play 3 days per week; earlier in the year, she had more free-play time. On days when Mariana did not have this free activity time, Ms. Williams provided art-related activities and occasional worksheets designed to teach children the names and sounds of letters.

After free play, the children had a snack. The children gathered in a group, and Ms. Williams reviewed a discussion they had the day before about taking one's own medicine, not that of anyone else in the house. Ms. Williams asked children to indicate the correct responses to questions by pointing to *Yes* or *No*, words that she had written on the board. Ms. Williams then used demonstration and explanation to lead the children through the steps needed to draw a brown robin standing on green grass looking for a little brown worm.

Each child then selected a book and took it to a table. Mariana and a friend talked about whether they could read. They agreed that they could not. Nonetheless, Mariana spent much of the next 10 minutes sounding out words in the book. After book time, the children prepared to leave, taking a homework assignment with them.

The overall flow of Ms. Williams's day when she was observed was somewhat different from her usual day. In our interview with her, she told us that her initial daily group time typically lasts about 45 minutes but that usually she does not read during that time. Instead, her book readings usually occur after snacktime and take 15–20 minutes. As on the day researchers observed, children usually read on their own; Ms. Williams does not read with individual children or with small groups.

In Ms. Williams's room, one can see the strong influence of her concern for ensuring that children learn specific knowledge linked to academic skills. She had relatively little time for free play, and the choices she provided emphasized basic math and reading skills. She provided times when children were expected to read, and she assigned homework. Later, the similarity between her direct instructional approach to drawing and how she read and discussed books is evident.

TODD'S CLASSROOM: A CONSTRUCTIVIST APPROACH

In Chapter 7, Smith introduced the afternoon Head Start classroom that Todd attended when he was 4. Todd's teacher, Roz Mahoney, provides a contrast to Ms. Williams. Roz saw the most important goal of preschool as being to socialize children. She was not concerned about academic skills but did believe that her work on fine motor skills helped prepare children for kindergarten. Though she did not explicitly talk about fostering children's language and literacy development, her program provided varied opportunities for the rich use of language, with book reading being one important setting in which this occurred.

On the Thursday afternoon that Home–School Study classroom observers visited, Roz gathered the children to read to them while her assistant teacher set up lunch. In his half-day afternoon Head Start program, Todd typically heard Roz read books three times per week. As usual,[1] he was eager to hear the story and was especially excited about

---

[1]Teachers were asked to rate children's language use and interest in language-related activities from well below average to well above average. Todd's teacher rated him as being *well above average* in his attentiveness and responsiveness to books and *somewhat above average* in recalling and communicating the essence of the story.

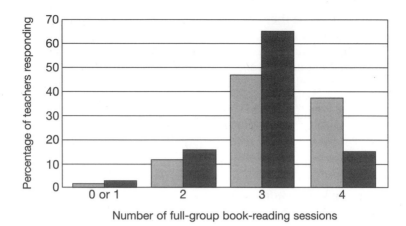

Figure 8.1. Percentages of teachers reporting the number of full-group book-reading sessions per week when children were ▨ 3 years old (*n* = 61) and ▦ 4 years old (*n* = 70).

this book because dinosaurs fascinated him. Indeed, he had been playing with toy dinosaur figures during the 15 minutes of settling-in time after he arrived and before circle time. The book was *Quiet on Account of Dinosaur* (Thayer, 1964), a book that Roz had chosen because it related to the classroom's dinosaur theme. Following the group time, children were given 5 minutes to look at books on their own on the rug. During this time, Todd looked at a book alone while Roz invited children to read a book with her. Pedro, whose first language is Spanish, and other children engaged Roz in a discussion about dinosaurs that was sparked by pictures in the book she was holding. After talking with Pedro, she moved to converse with other children about their books. After book time, children had lunch and about an hour of free play. During free play, there was a "dinosaur table" with dinosaur books and pictures, toy dinosaur figures in the blocks area, and an activity led by Roz that used a large dinosaur she had cut out. After free play, children went outdoors until departure time.

According to Roz, this day was fairly typical. Two or three times each week, she read one book to the full group during group time. She said that usually these books took about 5 minutes each, less time than on the day we observed. Each day she set aside time for children to read alone or with a friend as she circulated around the room. Roz enjoyed these chances to read with individuals or with small groups. She said that Todd especially liked to look at books alone or with a friend and did so two or three times per day.

In Roz's classroom, as in Ms. Williams's, the book that the teacher read as well as many classroom activities related to a core theme. In contrast to Ms. Williams's classroom, Roz's classroom showed no evidence of direct instruction on academic skills and relatively little evidence of children counting or identifying letters. In Roz's classroom there was, however, ample evidence of extended pretend play and rich teacher–child conversations during free play (see Chapter 11 for discussion of these conversations).

PLACE OF BOOK READING IN THE CLASSROOM DAY ACROSS ALL CLASSROOMS

When and How Long Teachers Read

Some aspects of book reading that were evident in Mariana's and Todd's classrooms were similar to most classrooms that the classroom observers visited. Typically, children heard books during group time two to three times per week. These group times lasted about 30 minutes and included time for book reading, singing, and discussion of the calendar (see Figures 8.1–8.3). During these sessions, teachers usually read one or two books. Despite these similarities, the amount of time devoted to book reading varied considerably across classrooms. When children in the study were 4 years old, about 25% of their teachers reported book-reading sessions of less than 8 minutes, and nearly another 25% had sessions of 16 minutes or longer. If the full week is considered, Todd heard books in full-group settings for about 20 minutes per week, Mariana for about 1 hour per week. This difference reflects the range observed. When children in our study were 3 and 4 years old, about one third

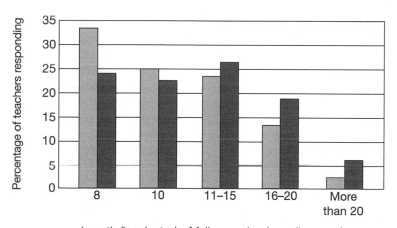

Figure 8.2. Percentage of teachers reporting full-group book-reading sessions of different lengths when children were ▨ 3 years old ($n = 61$) and ■ 4 years old ($n = 70$).

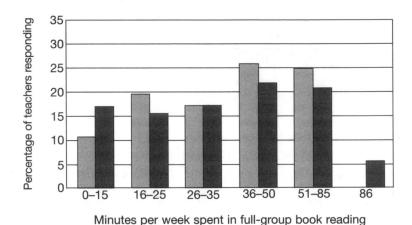

Figure 8.3. Percentages of teachers reporting how many minutes per week they spent in full-group book reading when children were ▨ 3 years old (*n* = 61) and ■ 4 years old (*n* = 70), estimated from teachers' reports.

spent 25 minutes or less per week listening to books in large groups, whereas another quarter were read to in groups for more than 50 minutes per week (see Figure 8.3). If it is assumed that these children were in half-day programs, they were in preschool for about 4 hours per day and 20 hours per week. Using teacher reports of time use across the entire day, Todd heard books for less than 1% of his time in preschool, as did 20% of the 3-year-olds and 11% of the 4-year-olds in the study. In contrast, Mariana heard books in large groups for 4% or more of her time in preschool, as did 6% of the 3-year-olds and 27% of the 4-year-olds in the study (see Figure 8.4).[2]

Of course, book reading was not restricted to group times. In both Todd's and Mariana's classrooms, as in nearly all classrooms visited, there were book areas that were available during free-play times. Also, as was observed in Todd and Mariana's classrooms, some teachers set aside times for children to look at books on their own or with a friend. During these times, some teachers circulated around the room and read to children. Most teachers reported reading with small groups of chil-

---

[2]It should be remembered that these data come from teacher reports and take into account all of the time across the full week. Data that we report from the audiotaping resulted in higher percentages of book reading time for two reasons. First, teachers were asked that book reading occur the day observers were present; thus, observers saw an activity that might occur only two or three times per week in many rooms. Second, only a portion of the day was taped, so calculations of the percentage of time reading books were much higher than would be the case if the entire day had been taped.

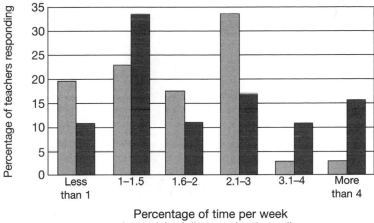

Figure 8.4. Percentages of teachers reporting differing percentages of the classroom day planned for full-group book reading when children were ▨ 3 years old (*n* = 61) and ■ 4 years old (*n* = 70).

dren and with individuals, but such individualized reading occurred much less often than teachers reported.[3] Although hearing books read in small groups or individually is the ideal way to experience books, the amount of individualized book-reading time often is not distributed evenly. Just as in Todd's room, typically the teacher responded to an individual child's request or invited those interested to join her. As a result, children who are interested in literacy—typically those who are read to at home—may receive powerful extra opportunities to hear and discuss books and those with limited interest in books may rarely receive such individualized attention. Teachers who are aware of this problem can devise ways to ensure that all children receive sufficient individualized book-reading time. For example, Roz set a time when children read books and she circulated among the groups, striving to read with as many groups as possible.

We also examined children's experiences with books using data from our audiotapes of the children's talk during the day. We taped children during mealtimes, choice times (similar to free play but with a

---

[3]During observations, the classroom observers rarely saw such individualized book reading experiences. In the time that David Dickinson has spent in Head Start classrooms in more recent years collecting data for other projects, he also has rarely seen such use of books. Thus, it seems likely that many teachers hope to read with individual children and small groups more often than they actually manage to. Because group times are more formal and planned than individual and small-group reading times, we believe that teachers are more likely to achieve the frequencies they reported to us during these times.

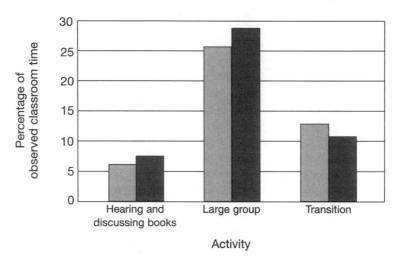

Figure 8.5.   Percentages of classrooms with differing amounts of classroom time use recorded on children's audiotapes when children were ▨ 3 years old (*n* = 53) and ■ 4 years old (*n* = 74).

limited number of activity choices), and large-group times (not indoor gross motor time, outdoor time, arrival, and departure) for an average of 1 hour and 36 minutes per child. During these prime times for interaction, children were listening to or talking about books an average of 6 minutes and 49 seconds (7% of coded time) when they were 3 years old and 7 minutes and 47 seconds (8% of coded time) when they were 4 years old. This time included any interactions dealing with books (such as reading books in large or small groups or talking at lunch about a book read earlier). Both years, children spent somewhat more than three times as long in full-group settings as they did in talk about books (see Figure 8.5). Because teachers tended to plan about one third of their group times for book reading, our audiotape data suggest that most of children's opportunities to hear and discuss books occurred during large-group times.

An indication of the relatively small amount of time spent reading and discussing books is that children spent more time in transition (such as cleaning up or moving from area to area) than they did hearing and discussing books. Transitions accounted for 13% of coded time when children were 3 (versus 7% in book reading) and 11% when they were 4 (versus 8% in book reading). This disparity is especially large when one remembers that classrooms were not audiotaped during major transition times such as when children left the room to go outdoors or when they came back inside. Thus, despite the high value that these teachers reported placing on books, reading and discussion of books often did not figure prominently in the classrooms visited for this study.

What Teachers Read

The books teachers choose to read aloud also have an important impact on children's language-learning opportunities. Teachers were asked what kinds of books they read, and each year many teachers reported reading picture books (see Figure 8.6). This category covers many different types of books but primarily refers to fiction. Teachers also often mentioned reading books about real-life experiences such as fears related to going to bed at night (33% when children were 3 and 49% when children were 4; see Figure 8.7). Such books provide good springboards for discussions because teachers can engage children in discussions that link their lives to the book. Books that communicate information also provide a way to deepen exploration of a current theme; but teachers of the 3-year-olds rarely (7%) reported using such books, though teachers of the 4-year-olds more often (43%) said they read books with specific informational content.

When teachers were asked which factors they took into consideration when selecting books, they most often mentioned the quality of the pictures (30% when children were 3 and 61% when children were 4). Also, many teachers reported choosing books that fit with their current theme (46% when children were 3 and 64% when children were 4). When teachers were asked which features of books they considered when selecting them, however, very few mentioned the informational

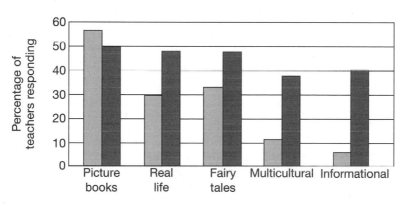

Figure 8.6. Percentages of teachers reporting use of different types of books when children were ▨ 3 years old (*n* = 61) and ▧ 4 years old (*n* = 70).

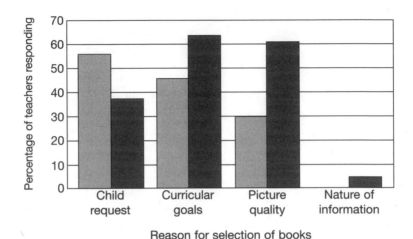

Figure 8.7. Percentages of teachers giving different reasons for their selection of books to read aloud when children were ▨ 3 years old (*n* = 61) and ▉ 4 years old (*n* = 70).

content of the book (0% when children were 3 and 5% when children were 4). What we noticed in teachers' book selection is that teachers often selected stories that were in some way related to their themes. For example, in Roz's room, when the class was studying dinosaurs, Roz read a story about a girl who found a dinosaur. Thus, in general, it appears that teachers select storybooks with high-quality illustrations that connect with their current themes. Although books provide a time for talking about theme-related material, they typically are not seen as a vehicle for introducing new information.

HOW TWO TEACHERS READ BOOKS

I now examine how teachers vary in terms of the conversations they have as they read to children. First, I examine in some detail reading sessions from Ms. Williams's and Roz's classrooms, then I discuss patterns of book reading that were observed in the full sample.

Ms. Williams's Reading: Using Book Reading for Direct Instruction

Ms. Williams read an informational book that was written in a narrative style. She used this book as a means to teach children information related to her robin theme. The book described one robin family and conveyed a considerable amount of information about how robins make nests and raise their young (see pages 187–188). Note that throughout

Book Reading in Mariana's Room:
A Didactic-Interactional Approach
The children in Mariana's preschool class are sitting in a circle around the teacher, Ms. Williams, who begins by asking children about a project that they did on the previous day (making a robin red breast). She asks them what colors it was and what each child did with it. Then she holds up a book with a bird on the cover.

1	Ms. Williams:	Okay, can anybody guess or raise a quiet hand—I think raise a quiet hand would be better—what this book is going to be about? [Almost every child silently raises a hand.] Hmm, let me see. We have such anxious children here. What do you think this book is going to be about, Christopher?
2	Christopher:	Robin red breast.
3	Ms. Williams:	Right, robin red breast, that's what this is going to be about. Let's give Christopher a hand. He guessed that; that was very nice. [They all clap.] Today we're gonna learn just a little bit about the robin [opens the book and creases its pages]. Okay, you all want to come just a little bit closer to me so you can see? [The children move in.] That's good enough, that's good enough, that's very good. Okay? Okay, great [rearranges her chair]. Could you please stop that, Jack? Sit down on your bottom, thank you. [Jack sits. Ms. Williams closes the book and shows the cover to the children.] Okay. How many robins do we have on this book? How many big robins?
4	Children:	Two.
5	Ms. Williams:	Two. Okay, now, if you think you know how many little robins are in the nest . . .
6	Child:	[Interrupting] Two, three.
7	Ms. Williams:	Raise a quiet hand.
8	Child:	Three.
9	Ms. Williams:	Raise a quiet hand. Karen?
10	Karen:	Three.

(continued)

(continued)

11	Ms. Williams:	Three, three baby robins. [Turns to first page] Okay, well, let's find out what the book is all about. [She begins to read the text, which tells about a father robin, called a male, who flew to a tree and started to sing. He is joined by his mate, the mother robin, called a female.] So, we have the male robin and the female robin [points out these birds on the page]. What was the male robin doing? Who can raise a quiet hand and tell me what was he doing? Brian?
12	Brian:	Sitting on a tree.
13	Ms. Williams:	No.
14	Ms. Williams:	What was he doing, Lauren?
15	Lauren:	Singing.
16	Ms. Williams:	He was singing. Because he wanted to tell everybody what? Because he wanted to tell everybody what, Desiree?
17	Desiree:	He lived there.
18	Ms. Williams:	Right. We've got good listeners. Okay. [She reads the next page, which describes how the robin made the nest and concludes by stating that it took her almost a whole week to construct it.] Is that a long time?
19	Children:	Yes.
20	Ms. Williams:	[Shows the book around as all children watch attentively] It took almost a whole week. [Looks at book, then points to the book] Okay, what color is her nest? Who can raise a quiet hand and tell me? [Almost all of the children raise their hands.] Michael?
21	Michael:	Yellow.
22	Ms. Williams:	It's yellow. [She continues reading another 4 pages, engaging in similar discussions after each page of text. She abruptly stops reading before the book is over and tells the children it is time to go outside.]

Book Reading in Todd's Room: A Co-constructive Approach
Todd's preschool teacher, Roz, has two children change where they
are sitting, quietly asks all children to look at her and settle, and
waits for their attention. She then begins the reading.

1	Roz:	I've got a book [holds up the cover to show the group] today because we're talking about what this week?
2	Children:	Dinosaurs this week!
3	Roz:	Dinosaurs this week. I have a story some of you might have already heard. It's called *Quiet on Account of Dinosaur.* Has anyone heard this story before?
4	Children:	Yes! No! [Mixed response]
5	Roz:	It was written by a woman named Jane Thayer, and the pictures were drawn by Seymore Fleishman. Look at this. What do you see?
6	Children:	Dinosaurs.
7	Roz:	Robert, look at this. What do you see?
8	Robert:	A brontosaurus.
9	Roz:	A brontosaurus. You remembered what his name was.
10	Robert:	[Makes comment that is hard to hear]
11	Roz:	What?
12	Children:	Duckbilled platypus. Brontosaurus rex.
13	Roz:	Looks like a duckbilled dinosaur, doesn't it?
14	Robert:	Yeah, and stegosaurus.
15	Roz:	Uh-huh. You know the names of all of them.
16	Todd:	Tyrannosaurus rex.
17	Roz:	Tyrannosaurus rex. Right. Well, let's hear the story. It's kind of a long one, so we need to listen. Are you ready?
18	Children:	Yes.
19	Roz:	[She reads several pages. The story is about a girl named Mary Ann, who loves dinosaurs and wants to find one. One day, she climbs a mountain and finds a dinosaur sleeping in a cave. She wakes it up and brings it back with her. As Roz reads, on three occasions, she briefly asks a child to be still or to

(continued)

(continued)

		attend. She then draws the children into the reading by varying the pace of her reading and the pitch of her voice.] Suddenly [loudly and abruptly] what went overhead [holds book up and points, with her eyes wide]?
20	Children:	An airplane!
21	Roz:	[Reads further, trailing off in the middle of a sentence so that children will explain what happens next]
22	Children:	A truck drove by!
23	Roz:	[She continues to read descriptions of their encounters with the truck and train that show the dinosaur's growing fear of large, noisy modern machines, using different reading patterns with each vehicle. Mary Ann then takes the dinosaur home.] What would your mom say if you brought a dinosaur home?
24	Jillian:	She'd scream!
25	Roz:	She would scream?
26	Jillian:	Yeah! And she'd run away.
27	Roz:	She would run away?
28	Juan:	Yeah. And you'd get no mother.
29	Roz:	Your mother wouldn't be there anymore? Jillian, can you believe that? Your mother wouldn't be there anymore? Let's see what Mary Ann's mom did.
30	Roz:	[She reads about feeding the dinosaur at home, pausing briefly to ask the children whether they would like to eat what the dinosaur ate. She then begins a longer discussion in which the book describes cars and planes that frightened Dandy, the dinosaur, and crowds that came to see him when he went to school.] How do you think Dandy feels, Susan?
31	Susan:	Bad.
32	Roz:	Why? Everybody take a look at the picture.
33	Roz:	I think he not only feels sad, he feels very . . .
34	Children:	Happy.

35	Roz:	I don't think so. What did Dandy do when the truck came?
36	Todd:	Shook.
37	Roz:	He was scared, he shook, and what did he do when the airplanes zoomed overhead? And when the train roared by? Did Dandy like loud noises?
38	Children:	No!
39	Roz:	How is Dandy going to feel with all this?
40	Children:	Bad. Sad.
41	Roz:	Not only sad. What else?
42	Children:	Mad!
43	James:	Scared!
44	Roz:	You got it, James! He's going to be very scared! [Returns to reading, describing Mary Ann's noticing that Dandy seems unhappy] What could be wrong with Dandy? Daryl, what do you think is the matter? Perhaps she should call up her famous scientist.
45	Daryl:	He's sticking his head in a hole.
46	Roz:	That's right.
47	Juan:	Boom boom. Boom.
48	Roz:	Boom boom boom. What a loud noise.
49	Children:	Yeah, they scare him!

[Roz continues reading, asking children for sound effects of machines. Then she stops for another discussion when they decide to help the dinosaur by taking him into the gymnasium. They talk about what a gymnasium is and the problems with having Dandy in the gymnasium. As soon as the last page is read, Roz moves the class on to lunch.]

Ms. Williams's discussion, the talk focused almost exclusively on low-level cognitive demands (such as counting, labeling, or reproducing story text that was just read) or on management issues (such as stating rules for participation).

Ms. Williams began by showing children the book's cover and encouraging them to state that the book would be about "robin red breast." After ensuring that the children were settled, she again showed the cover and had the children count the number of robins. She then read the first page and queried the children about what they had just heard, encouraging them to recall specific details from the text. Notice that in turn 11 she asked, "What was the male robin doing?" A boy answers,

"Sitting on a tree." Ms. Williams rejected this answer, even though it accurately described the information shown in the picture and was consistent with what she had read. Instead of accepting the boy's answer, Ms. Williams elicited a series of responses (turns 14–18) that provided a literal reconstruction of the text: The robin was singing because he wanted to tell everyone he lived there. After reading each page, Ms. Williams engaged the children in similar discussions that required recall of factual details. Ms. Williams did not finish the book; instead, she stopped abruptly after reading a page that discussed the difference between robins in the old and new worlds. When she stopped reading, children were still quiet but did not respond to Ms. Williams's questions with much enthusiasm.

The way in which Ms. Williams read this book reflected her general focus on skills, which she perceived as important for academic success. She consistently sought responses that repeated literal information from the text of the book. Children were not asked to make inferences of any kind or to reflect on the content by making connections to their personal experiences, for example. This type of book reading is called a *didactic-interactional style* (Dickinson & Smith, 1994). Such reading involves conversations with low cognitive demands and takes two forms. Some teachers used the interactional style seen in Ms. Williams's reading, an approach that is similar to what is seen in some teacher-directed first-grade basal reader lessons. Others encouraged children to chime in, producing familiar chunks of text. There was little reflective conversation about the story during these readings. Note that the style adopted was related to the type of book read; predictable textbooks lend themselves to the chiming style of reading. These books quickly become familiar, and their rhythmic, rhyming text does not lend itself to reflective discussions.

Roz's Reading: Supporting Children's Understanding

Roz read the book *Quiet on Account of Dinosaur* (Thayer, 1964), creating a very different overall type of book-reading experience. She also selected a book related to her theme, but her book was fiction, and she used it to help children understand the plot of the story and the characters, not to learn about dinosaurs (see pages 189–191). The book is about a little girl, Mary Ann, who finds a dinosaur that she adopts as a pet and names *Dandy*. The book describes the problems Dandy has in adjusting to the noisy modern world.

This reading began (turns 1 and 3) with Roz telling the children that the book was related to their current theme. In so doing, she reminded them of the theme and helped them realize that what they had learned about dinosaurs was relevant to the book. After she introduced the title, author, and illustrator, Roz gave the children a moment to tell what they knew about dinosaurs (turns 7–18), encouraging them to link their knowledge to the book. Note that this conversation lasted for several turns and included vocabulary that revealed their knowledge of dinosaur names. Once Roz started the story, she read several pages without stopping, drawing the children into the book. During each of the three discussion points that are included in the transcript (turns 19, 23, and 30), she tried to keep the children engaged by using questions that checked their understanding. On the first occasion, she asked for a low-level response—identification of the airplane. On the next two occasions, children made predictions that required them to link their understanding to their personal experiences. First, children were asked to link the character's mother's experience to predictions about their own mothers' actions. Second, Roz asked children how they thought Dandy felt, encouraging them to project their feelings onto the dinosaur. This sequence is especially interesting because one can see how Roz asked follow-up questions. In turn 44, she asked the children why they thought Dandy felt bad. Roz also gave the children a strategy by which to understand books by telling them to look at the picture (turn 32). In the ensuing talk, when asked how Dandy felt, one child replied, "Happy," revealing that at least this child completely misunderstood the dinosaur's emotional state. Picking up on this misunderstanding, Roz encouraged the children to refer to the text of the story by asking them to tell what Dandy did when the truck went by. She got the response she hoped for—"Shook"—and built on it by helping the children understand that, by his shaking, the dinosaur revealed that he was frightened. In the remaining interchanges, Roz reinforced this very important understanding about Dandy's growing fear. During the final exchange included in the excerpt, the children understood that Dandy was frightened (turn 43). As the story continued, Roz stopped for more discussions, with each being similar in content to those excerpted previously. Once she finished reading the last page, Roz put the book away and moved on to lunch.

Roz's reading of this book is typical of the co-constructive style of book reading (Dickinson & Keebler, 1989; Dickinson & Smith, 1994). She initiated a somewhat extended discussion before she started reading. As she read, she stopped several times and helped children understand the plot of the story and the characters by directing the children's attention to the text and the pictures. She helped them realize the importance of employing their own experiences and emotional reactions to understand the story. The way in which topics developed in Roz's discussion is also very important. Note that she picked up on cues indicating lack of understanding (the child's answering "Happy") and stayed with the topic for several turns. In the ensuing conversation, Roz led the children toward deeper understanding. There is a feeling of joint reflection, with the teacher and children engaged in an extended sequence of comments that stay on the same topic. Consistent with Roz's emphasis on the emotions of characters, her conversation supported an understanding of the links between Dandy's feelings and actions, not the teaching of concepts about dinosaurs. Thus, although the children learned relatively little about dinosaurs, they learned a lot about understanding stories.

OVERALL STYLE OF READING BOOKS

We have seen that Ms. Williams and Roz adopted distinct overall styles of reading books. Ms. Williams used a didactic-interactional style, with explicit instructional goals being dominant. When we did an in-depth analysis of the book-reading styles of teachers in the 25 classrooms attended by the first cohort of 4-year-olds,[4] we found that the didactic-interactional approach was used 40% of the time (Dickinson & Smith, 1994). We found that the co-construction approach used by Roz was less common, appearing in 20% of the classrooms observed. In these reading sessions, typically there was quite a bit of talk while the story was being read but relatively little talk at the end. Conversations tended to have a high level of cognitive demand, focusing on vocabulary, character motivations, and links between the book and children's experiences. A third style of reading, called *performance oriented,* was found in 40% of the classrooms. In these readings, the teacher read the story in a dramatic manner and stopped only occasionally for conversation. The content of conversations was similar to the co-constructive readings in that the conversations encouraged reflection. Thus, the goal of these teachers was to allow the words and pictures to create a story world with pauses inserted only to ensure that the children fully understood the story. Unlike the co-construction readings, there was considerable talk after the stories were finished, and these conversations tended to lead children to make links between the books and their experiences, to reflect on specific aspects of the story, or to guide them through a reconstruction of the story.

These three approaches to reading books provide children distinct experiences and introduce children to very different ways of relating to

---

[4]Because we were unable to obtain sufficient numbers of children and families in the first year of data collection, we went back to the same centers a second year to recruit a second group of participants. Because data from our first group were available first, these analyses included only the first cohort.

books. Naturally, we were curious about whether there was any relationship between the book-reading style of a teacher and children's later language and literacy development. Our sample size was quite small, but we did find that, at the end of kindergarten, children in the performance-oriented classrooms had better Receptive Vocabulary scores than children experiencing didactic-interactional readings ($p < .01$). Results for children from the few (only five) co-constructive classrooms were not significantly different from those for either of the other two groups.

BOOK-READING STYLES AND GROUP MANAGEMENT

Teachers use varied strategies to capture and hold children's attention. To understand the methods teachers used, we coded videotapes of the book readings for the management strategies that teachers used, for the dramatic quality of the readings, and for children's interest. In general, we found that these three dimensions went together.

We found several ways in which teachers attempted to draw children into the story worlds by injecting drama into their readings (Dickinson, Hao, & He, 1995). One technique was to vary the pitch and tone of their voice. For example, Ms. Williams changed the pace of her reading, varied the pitch of her voice, and drew out selected words and phrases when she wanted to convey important information. When reading about how long the mother bird took to make the nest, she slowed while reading that it would take nearly an entire week, and the pitch and volume of her voice rose and fell. All of these changes signaled the importance of that phrase. Other strategies used by Roz and others included using exaggerated facial expressions, giving characters distinctive voices, and highlighting the climax of the story by pausing or asking a brief question to ensure everyone was tuned in. About one quarter of the teachers observed used few such techniques, whereas about another quarter were far more dramatic, giving distinctive voices to characters and using extreme variations in pitch and volume to draw in the children. Interestingly, we found that use of these strategies was highly related: Teachers who employed one such strategy often tended to use others (see Table A8.1 in the appendix). This finding indicates that a dramatic approach to reading may come as a kind of package; use of dramatic techniques may largely reflect a general comfort level with reading aloud rather than mastery of specific discrete techniques. Dramatic readings did have the desired effect of engaging children. When teachers read in engaging ways, children were more interested and excited and gave more appropriate responses.

Children's engagement in group book readings was also affected by the way the teacher organized turn taking and the steps she took to redirect children or draw them in when their attention wandered. Ms.

Williams and Roz differed in how they dealt with rules governing participation. Ms. Williams often enforced rules by requiring children to "raise a quiet hand" and asking that only one child at a time respond. She talked about rules with the full group and made them the focus of the discussion for short periods of time. The flow of talk between Ms. Williams and the children in her classroom took a form typical of conversations between teachers and children in the primary grades (Cazden, 1988):

1.   Teacher asks a question that requests a specific answer.

2.   Child responds.

3.   Teacher evaluates the child's response as being right or wrong.

The carefully controlled turn taking seemed to flow from a concern about group management, revealed by her frequent reminders about the rules governing participation. When this teacher-determined conversational pattern is combined with Ms. Williams's concern for recall of literal details of the story, the result is a didactic-interactional style that has the feel of a traditional reading group.

In contrast, though Roz's discussions were orderly, she handled behavior management in a more fluid manner. For example, she accepted and responded to comments that were appropriate even if she had not called on the child. She also used a number of subtle, implicit behavior management strategies. For example, she did not call for attention prior to posing questions. Instead, she used questions to draw the children back into the conversation. She also altered the dramatic quality of her reading to draw children in and, on occasion, paused and looked at a child whose attention was straying. The only occasions when Roz dealt with behavior directly were the occasional quick comments she made to individual children as she was reading. Thus, we see that Ms. Williams used many explicit methods to structure participation, whereas Roz used more implicit methods. Looking across all of the teachers, we found that teachers who used an implicit approach to behavior management also tended to use many dramatic techniques. Children responded well when teachers used implicit strategies, showing high levels of interest and excitement (see Table A8.1 in the appendix). In classrooms in which explicit methods were used more frequently, children tended to be attentive but were less often actively engaged. Thus, it may be that use of explicit control strategies is more a reflection of the teacher's beliefs about the purpose of book reading and appropriate behavior than it is a response to children's behavior.

The way in which teachers bring books to life clearly influences children's involvement in the reading session. It is likely that the excitement that some teachers create increases the chances that children will become interested in books and reading. We could not measure this important but rather elusive aspect of children's literacy development. What was measured—language and literacy development—did not turn up any significant correlations between the dramatic quality of readings and children's later language growth.

CONTENT OF BOOK DISCUSSIONS ACROSS CLASSROOMS

In addition to examining the overall styles that teachers adopted, we were interested in the content of what teachers and children said. We anticipated that the book-reading conversations with the most long-term benefits for children's language and literacy growth would be those that engaged children's attention by responding to questions that they might have and by challenging their thinking. Especially valuable conversations would be those that helped children understand the more subtle and advanced features of books. For example, helpful conversations should be those that deal with characters' motivations, complex concepts introduced in books, and discussions about the meanings of words. In such conversations, children use language for intellectual purposes as they reflect on the meaning they are creating from the words and pictures of the book. Talk that we expected would be less valuable would be that dealing with group management and recall of known information (such as names of familiar objects, chiming in with familiar phrases, remembering factual details, or telling the name of the author). When we examined the content of the talk during book readings when the children being studied were 3 and 4 years old, it was found that about one third of the talk dealt with management issues and about one quarter of the talk was cognitively challenging.

The timing of such talk was different across the 2 years of this portion of the study. Teachers engaged in more complex talk about stories while the book was read when the children were 4, but such talk was more common before or after the book reading when the children being studied were younger (see Figure 8.8). As noted in Chapter 7, when the children involved in the study were 3, they tended to be in younger groups of children. Thus, it could be that these differences reflect changes in reading made by teachers in response to the ages of the children in the groups. With younger children, they may have been concerned about losing children's attention as they read; therefore, during the reading, they focused conversation on topics that they expected children to be able to understand easily.

Of course, the content of conversations varied among teachers, and this variation had implications for the children. In our analysis of the 25 first-cohort classrooms, we found a moderately strong relationship

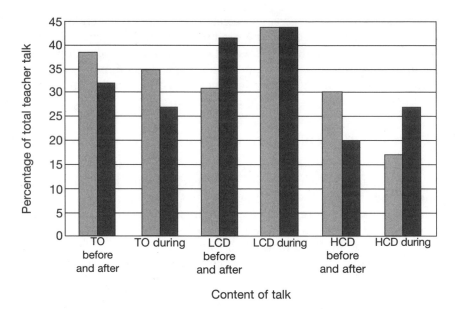

Figure 8.8. Percentages of comments by teachers during full-group book-reading sessions representing different content categories when children were ▨ 3 years old (*n* = 53) and ▦ 4 years old (*n* = 74) as percentages of total teacher talk. (TO, task organization; LCD, low-level cognitive demands; HCD, high-level cognitive demands.)

(*r* = .39, *p* < .001) between children's kindergarten Peabody Picture Vocabulary Test–Revised (PPVT–R; Dunn & Dunn, 1981) scores and their engagement in conversations that were both analytical and inter-active (Dickinson & Smith, 1994). Children benefited when there were links between what the teacher said and what the child said (that is, not simple statements unrelated to a prior question or comment) and in conversations in which the topic was the meaning of words, why things happened, or a prediction of coming events. This relationship remained even after we statistically took into account other aspects of classrooms that we knew were correlated with later performance (the writing cur-riculum in the classroom, time for reading with individuals and small groups). Children's story comprehension in kindergarten also was related to their opportunities to engage in interactive, reflective con-versations when they were 4 (R^2 = .25, *p* < .04, *n* = 25). When we took into account other classroom factors predicting story understanding, however, we found that the book-reading experience by itself no longer was significant. This suggests that children's ability to understand sto-ries was affected by a set of classroom experiences that includes in-teractive, reflective conversations during book reading. Analyses of the results for all classrooms that we conducted recently support these earlier-reported findings. We looked at the content of teacher and child talk from both cohorts when the children were 4 and at results of kindergarten assessments and found a positive correlation between the teacher's use of analytical comments and questions (such as "Why?" "How?" and "When?") during book reading and children's receptive vocabulary at the end of kindergarten ($r = .36$, $p < .003$, $n = 65$).

Thus, the types of conversations that we saw Roz leading tend to support children's developing language and story understanding. This finding provides a link to our earlier discussion of book-reading style and children's attention. Although we did not find a correlation between children's language and growth in kindergarten and stylistic features of the book-reading events, we did find relationships between these stylistic features and the content of conversations. Teachers of our 4-year-olds who engaged children in more analytical conversations and more talk about vocabulary, the type of talk that was correlated with children's later language growth, also used more dramatic techniques and more implicit management strategies. Furthermore, such analytic talk was related to sessions in which children were excited and attentive (see Table A8.2 in the appendix).

These relationships were not present in book-reading sessions with 3-year-olds. This lack of correlation between reading style and complexity of talk may indicate that teachers tend to avoid complex conversations while they read to younger children. Instead, they may engage in such talk after they have finished reading the book. In their conversations before and after the reading, teachers of 3-year-olds who engaged in significantly more high-level talk spent less time talking about management issues. Thus, in general, one can see that, during conversations in which children were attentive, teachers more often engaged children in interesting, cognitively challenging conversations. From our results, we cannot tell whether more complex conversations were made possible because children were attentive or whether children became more interested when they were challenged to think. Our detailed examination of Roz's and Ms. Williams's book-reading sessions suggests that conversations that challenge children to think rather than require them to recall familiar information actually draw children into the activity, thereby reducing the need to spend time on management issues.

CONCLUSIONS

Book reading is a special time because children create imaginary worlds in their minds as they listen to books. Using the book's words and pictures and the discussion with their teacher and friends, children

- Become involved in the lives of characters and begin to understand characters' motivations
- Think and talk about the meanings of words
- Expand their knowledge about the world
- Learn how to actively seek to make sense of books, predicting what will happen next and questioning why characters act as they do

In addition, in classrooms in which books are used regularly and effectively, children learn about the many kinds of books that exist and the ways that people can use books (such as for enjoyment, to learn about the physical world, or to learn about other cultures). Through these experiences, children develop a love of books and begin to see themselves as members of literate classroom communities. An added benefit of regular book-reading experiences is that children learn to attend to the details of what teachers and children say in group settings. Also, by participating in discussions, they learn how to connect their experiences to the book and contribute ideas to the discussion. Thus, book reading helps prepare children for school by building their vocabulary, introducing them to strategies for understanding books, and teaching them to participate in group activities that involve talking and listening.

Despite the many potential benefits of book reading, we have seen that the time spent reading books in these classrooms was limited, as was the range of types of books that teachers read. Children heard books read during full-group times as one activity among several and rarely were read to individually or in small groups. Furthermore, we found that even on days when book reading was scheduled, the reading might not occur if children were restless or if the group was late for other scheduled activities (such as outdoor time or lunchtime). Thus, on the basis of our data and the observations made in many classrooms as part of studies carried out after these data were collected, it may be rather common that children go through an entire day at preschool without hearing a single book read to them. The encouraging news is that even though this study did not reveal many teachers who were regularly incorporating books and book reading into their classrooms in optimal ways, some evidence was found that children benefited from being in classrooms with strong uses of books.

Taken together, our results suggest that, although most teachers in the study stated that book reading was an important way to support children's literacy growth and that books and book reading were a part of most programs that strive to be developmentally appropriate, rather few teachers seemed to approach book use in a carefully thought out, intentional manner. In some cases, teachers adopted effective reading styles but set aside relatively little time for books; in other cases, teachers allocated considerable time for books but failed to engage children fully in the book-reading experience. Despite shortcomings in the practices observed, in work with other Head Start teachers conducted after this segment of our research, we have found that once Head Start teachers begin to reflect on the place of books in their classrooms, book use moves from the background as a taken-for-granted part of the classroom day into the foreground as valued and important. When this happens, teachers find new and exciting ways of using books to capture children's interest and expand their language skills. The suggestions offered in the next section can serve as a starting point for teachers seeking to ensure that children receive the greatest benefits from the use of books in their classrooms.

SUGGESTIONS FOR TEACHERS

Schedule Sufficient Time for Book Reading

- In full-day programs, read aloud at least three times per day for a minimum of 45 minutes total. In partial-day programs, read once or twice per day for a minimum of 10 minutes per session.
- Divide the children into groups of 8–10 for one or two group book-reading times. Use these smaller groups to allow time for children to ask questions and for the group to engage in thoughtful discussions about books.
- Provide individual and small-group reading experiences every day. Keep track of which children are involved, and ensure that each child is read to in such a setting at least twice per week.
- Do not withhold book reading as a punishment, and do not drop book reading from the day's activities.
- Schedule time for children to look at books alone or with a friend.

Read and Reread Various Types of Books

- Share your enjoyment of books you love.
- Read books that are related to your theme. Be sure to seek out some that convey important information and contain varied vocabulary.
- Stretch children's attention to books by trying out longer books and books with more text than you typically read.

- Read favorite books several times. With rereading, be alert for opportunities to extend children's understanding by asking questions about features of the plot or characters that have not been discussed before.

Be Thoughtful About Book Discussions

- Think about the book you will read before you start. Identify important words and concepts that you want the children to grasp.
- Encourage children to think by talking about aspects of the story that might confuse them. Use the pictures and children's own experiences to help them understand the story. Tell children word meanings and clarify confusion when needed.
- Respond to children's questions, especially when they deal with matters directly relevant to understanding the story. Discourage extended conversations while the book is being read and conversations on topics with limited relevance to the book.

Enjoy Reading, and Minimize Time
Spent on Organizational Matters

- Establish clear routines for book reading—when it happens, who sits where, and how turn taking will be handled.
- Hold children's attention by reading with drama, asking questions when children are lost, and showing and discussing pictures.
- Be clear about expectations related to turn taking, but beware of stifling involvement and enthusiasm with overly strict rules governing participation.

Make Books and Book Reading Part of the Full Day

- Link books to your theme or current topic and strive to get children interested in rereading books on their own that you present in a group setting.
- Set up a listening center with tapes of books that you have read to allow children repeated opportunities to listen to favorite stories while looking at the books.
- Display books in multiple places around the room.
- Constantly introduce new books related to your theme.

Encourage Parents to Read to Children at Home

- Tell parents about the importance of regular reading. Encourage them to read with their child and to find others who can read to their child (such as big sisters, uncles, or grandparents).
- Strive to develop a classroom library with books that can be sent home.
- Encourage parents to use the library, buy books, and subscribe to children's magazines.

Chapter 9

Language Opportunities During Mealtimes in Preschool Classrooms

Linda R. Cote

Preschool teachers have long sought to make children's transition from home to school as easy as possible. One way they do this is by creating times during the day that are organized in ways that are familiar and responsive to children's rhythms and needs. For example, mealtime is an important setting in classrooms, and it has similarities to the home event. Much like at home, mealtime is a routine part of a young child's preschool day. Mealtime provides children with an opportunity to relax, eat a nutritious meal, and get to know each other better through conversation. Ever since its founding, Head Start has mandated that its programs provide family-style meals in which the teachers sit with the children. This requirement reflects the fact that meals provide opportunities for conversation that teachers should use. Although preschool practitioners recognize the importance of mealtimes as social occasions, researchers have not studied the potential role of mealtimes in classrooms in supporting children's language growth. It is reasonable to expect that classroom mealtimes have beneficial effects on children's language. After all, during meals, teachers have relatively few distractions because everyone is seated and involved in what is hopefully a pleasurable activity. Teachers typically sit at tables with only a few chil-

The research discussed in this chapter was supported by a U.S. Department of Health and Human Services Administration for Children and Families (Head Start Bureau) Graduate Research Fellowship, Grant No. 90-CD-0961, awarded to the author while at Clark University. Material in this chapter was presented at research conferences and appears in the following publications: Cote (1993, 1995, 1997) and Dickinson, Cote, and Smith (1993).

dren. In such a setting, teachers can hear each child, ask questions and pursue topics of interest, and ensure that everyone interested in the topic has a chance to contribute. During mealtime, talk can be a source of entertainment.

The fact that teachers generally *do not* have competing educational goals during mealtimes means that they can be more flexible and use mealtimes as opportunities to sit with and engage children in extended discussions and narratives about events that occurred in the past (for example, "What did you do after school yesterday?") or that will occur in the future (for example, "What are you going to do over vacation?"). Although different researchers have used different words to describe this narrative skill, the features of this skill are the same; namely, such discussions require that the child speak explicitly about nonimmediate events in order to communicate information. Because the events of the narrative are not readily observable, the individual must rely on language alone to convey his or her story.

In this chapter, I examine the preschool mealtime experiences of children involved in the Home–School Study of Language and Literacy Development, comparing the quality of conversations between different classroom mealtime settings. First, I take a careful look at how mealtimes were organized and discuss the remarkable impact that the structure of mealtimes had on children's language-learning opportunities. Next, I examine patterns of language use during mealtimes in comparison with other times of the day, then discuss results showing the link between mealtime conversations and measures of literacy development. In closing, I discuss interactional strategies that encourage children's talk.

ROLE OF MEALTIMES IN THE HEAD START DAY

Mealtimes play an important role in the life of a child attending a Head Start program. In half-day programs, the day begins with breakfast and ends with lunch. Among the 59 children I observed during center-based mealtimes for the Home–School Study, children typically spent 15% of their day at mealtime. Interestingly, the amount of time varied greatly from one room to the next (3%–31% of the classroom day). In a separate study of 119 preschool classrooms for 4-year-old children, Layzer, Goodson, and Moss (1993) reported that about 9% of the classroom day was spent in mealtime (eating lunch or snacks). Regardless of the exact amount of time children spend in mealtimes, it is clear that this activity plays an important role in the life of the classroom.

The way in which mealtimes are used most likely is related to how teachers view the purpose of meals. Thus, it is noteworthy that when teachers in the Home–School Study were asked in an open-ended interview to name the two or three most important functions of preschool, the Head Start teachers emphasized the importance of good nutrition and ensuring that children consume well-balanced meals. This goal is illustrated in the following mealtime excerpt from the classroom of Roz Mahoney, Todd's teacher:

Child 1:   Tuna fish. Tuna fish, I like.
Child 2:   Ah, Mina needs one of those.
    Roz: Why, thank you. That was very thoughtful. Will you give it to her for me? Thank you, Jerry. And you can start eating your sandwiches. Do you want a pickle or a carrot?
Child 1:   [Unintelligible]
    Roz: I can't hear you.
Child 1:   No.
    Roz: Okay.
Child 1:   I took a piece, and I didn't like it.
    Roz: Okay, thank you for tasting. One pickle. Did everybody get a carrot?
Child 2:   Yeah.

This excerpt shows how the teacher, Roz, makes sure that each child gets to sample all of the food (that is, everyone gets a tuna fish sandwich, a pickle, and a carrot). Roz also encourages each child to take a bite of the food and try it, even though a child may not like the looks of a particular food. Because these preschool classrooms serve children from low-income homes, the teachers are particularly concerned that the children eat their fill of a well-balanced meal. Some teachers, however, tend to restrict themselves to these nutrition-related concerns, whereas others address these concerns in the context of relaxed and intellectually enriching conversations.

   In addition to providing children with a well-balanced meal, classroom mealtimes contain great potential for enhancing children's development in other areas, such as social and language development. As the previous example shows, one way that teachers assist children's social development is by modeling polite forms of speech to children ("Okay, thank you for tasting"). When asked to name the most important functions of preschool, the teachers universally spoke of enhancing children's social skills, such as learning to get along with each other, to express themselves, and to develop friendships and enhancing self-esteem (see Chapter 7). Though some teachers emphasized literacy readiness skills such as learning to read and write, some unequivocally said that academic preparation was neither their goal nor their responsibility. Furthermore, when teachers were explicitly asked about academic goals, they spoke of developing children's oral language skills, such as communication and self-expression skills, through engagement in small-group times.

My interest in mealtimes in preschool classrooms was inspired by the work of Blum-Kulka (1993), Blum-Kulka and Snow (1992), Teale and Sulzby (1986), and Tizard and Hughes (1985) and the unfolding results of the Home–School Study analyses of mealtimes in the home (see Chapter 4). In order to better understand mealtimes in Head Start classrooms, I visited classrooms at Great Brook Valley in Worcester, Massachusetts. The classrooms that I observed are not included in the Home–School Study corpus, but they did help to inform my research questions and conclusions. For example, I noticed that some teachers sat down at tables with their children and ate with them, others served the children their food while the children sat down and ate, and still others took their own lunch break while the children ate. I became curious as to whether these differences in mealtime settings or setups would have an effect on mealtime conversations. In addition, I wondered whether the mealtime settings that were most like mealtime settings in the home (that is, when teachers sat down and ate with the children) would include the same types of beneficial conversation as mealtimes at home. On the basis of these observations, I analyzed mealtime data collected as part of the Home–School Study.

COMPARISONS OF THE
QUALITY OF MEALTIME CONVERSATIONS

Given my observation that teachers use their time very differently during mealtimes, I examined data from children's mealtimes when they were 4 to learn whether their use of nonpresent talk (that is, talk about past or future events or experiences) differed according to the way in which their teachers organized the mealtime. My research team coded all classroom transcripts that contained a mealtime, 59 of the 76 four-year-old children (34 girls and 25 boys), or 77.6% of our total sample. The racial background of the 59 target children was 7% African American, 74% Caucasian, 14% Hispanic, and 5% unknown; the racial background of the teachers was 4% Asian American, 4% African American, and 92% Caucasian. Transcripts were coded for the amount of nonpresent talk and the type of mealtime setting. *Nonpresent talk* was defined as discussions about past or future events and experiences, including narratives (Dickinson & Smith, 1991). In the following example of nonpresent talk from a child transcript, one of the portrait children, Casey, is telling his teacher, Ms. Ann Greenbaum, about a trip he will take the following weekend:[1]

Ann: Does anyone have any special plans to go away on the weekend?
Casey: I'm going to New York.
Ann: Do you mean next weekend?
Casey: Yeah. My dad is coming, too.

Discussions about past and future experiences such as this one, which I call *nonpresent talk,* seem to be a natural part of mealtime discussions when the teacher is stationary and sitting with the children while they eat.

Next, the mealtime transcripts were classified into one of two categories: *teacher stationary* or *teacher circulating. Teacher stationary* mealtimes were ones in which the teacher was present and seated at the children's table during mealtime. These mealtimes were characterized by a small teacher–child ratio. *Teacher circulating* mealtimes were ones in which the teacher was in the classroom with the children but was walking around, attending to the children's needs. Occasionally these mealtimes took place in a school cafeteria. The following mealtime groups were observed: 33 children were in *teacher stationary* mealtimes and 26 children were in *teacher circulating* mealtimes (see the appendix for statistical information about coding). Of the portrait children discussed throughout this book, Astra did not have mealtime in her classroom and therefore is not mentioned in this chapter. Mariana and Todd were in *teacher circulating* mealtimes, and Casey was in a *teacher stationary* mealtime.

The type of mealtime observed in a given classroom may be the result of several factors. One major factor is the location where the meals are served. When children eat lunch in a cafeteria, the teachers there are responsible for a large number of students. This type of mealtime seems to be a function of the structure of the school building (for example, whether there is a cafeteria) as well as the teachers' schedules (for example, whether the teachers take their break while the children eat). The division between mealtimes in which teachers are stationary or circulating when the class eats in the classroom seems to be less clear-cut. Observations of Head Start mealtimes suggest that factors such as the number of children and staff present on a given day influence whether it is possible for teachers to remain stationary during mealtime, even

---

[1]In the excerpts from the transcripts, silences of only 10 seconds or more are noted.

if that is their intention or the norm for them. Also, the physical surroundings in which mealtimes take place may have an effect on children's language. For example, mealtimes that take place in a cafeteria tend to involve large groups of children and yield little teacher–child interaction. Thus, to some degree, teachers' decisions with regard to which type of mealtime to have in their classroom may be constrained by forces beyond their control.

Topic of Conversation

Children whose teachers were stationary during mealtimes engaged in significantly more nonpresent talk than children whose teachers were circulating during mealtimes (see the appendix for details about the statistical analyses; see also Figure 9.1). These differences were obtained even though there were no significant differences among the children in each of the two mealtime groups in their talkativeness throughout the classroom day or in the amount of time that each group spent in mealtimes (see the appendix). Furthermore, there were significant dif-

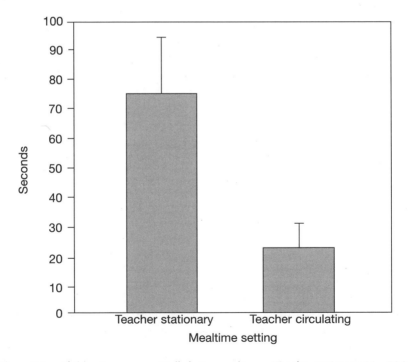

Figure 9.1.   Children's *nonpresent talk* during mealtimes. (*Teacher stationary,* $M = 76.30$, $SE = 18.18$; *teacher circulating,* $M = 23.77$, $SE = 7.74$.)

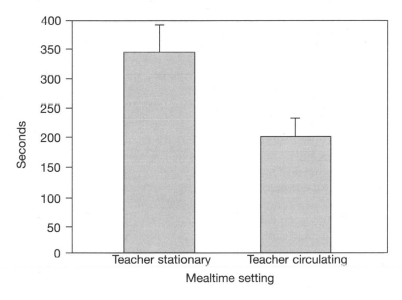

Figure 9.2.   Amount of time children talked during mealtimes. (*Teacher stationary, M =* 348.76, *ST – 45.37; teacher circulating, M – 201.81, ST – 29.85.*)

ferences between the mealtime groups in the amount of time the 59 children spent talking overall. Specifically, children whose teachers were stationary during mealtimes spent more time talking than children whose teachers were circulating during mealtimes (see the appendix; see also Figure 9.2).

Why was it, though, that children whose teachers were stationary during mealtimes spent more time engaging in nonpresent talk than children in the other mealtime group? A final analysis was performed in order to determine with whom children were engaging in nonpresent talk. Children engaged in significantly more nonpresent talk with teachers as their conversational partners than when children were their conversational partners, suggesting that children tend to use nonpresent talk during discussions with adults but not with other children (see the appendix). The following example is from a mealtime in which the teacher was present and stationary. In this example, one of the portrait children, Casey, and his teacher, Ann, discuss what Casey will do during the coming weekend. Ann has gone around the table and asked each child whether he or she has anything to share. This example shows how teachers have the luxury of engaging children in conversations during *teacher stationary* mealtimes and also how these conversations tend to go beyond the here and now. Also notice how this conversation

(1 minute and 23 seconds of interaction) is shared by Casey and Ann, rather than being monopolized by the teacher:

Ann:	Does anyone have any special plans to go away on the weekend?
Casey:	I'm going to New York.
Ann:	Do you mean next weekend?
Casey:	Yeah. My dad is coming, too.
Ann:	That's great, Casey. That's in 1 more week. You know, I'm going to New York, too. Remember that we will not have school for 10 days. That will be your vacation.
Casey:	I am not going to New York City.
Ann:	No? Where are you going, Casey?
Casey:	Villaroma, we call it that.
Ann:	Oh. That's in upstate New York. Do you know someone who lives there? Will you visit someone when you go to New York?
Casey:	No.
Ann:	How are you going to get there?
Casey:	In my mom's car.
Ann:	Oh. I'm going to go in an airplane.

The following example comes from a mealtime during which the teacher is circulating. In this example, the teacher is Roz. The target child is Todd, one of the portrait children profiled throughout this book. Notice that the quality of the adult–child interaction changes when the teacher circulates during mealtime. During this mealtime, Roz walks around the classroom, putting food on children's tables, passing out milk, and attending to individual children's material needs. Thus, the teacher's attention is split between several tables and a classroom full of children, rather than dedicated to five or six children, as in a *teacher stationary* mealtime. This example of a teacher circulating during a mealtime (5 minutes and 55 seconds of interaction) illustrates how teacher–child interaction during mealtimes of this sort tends to revolve around eating, the mealtime routine of teaching children how to pass the food, and behavior at the table:

1	Todd:	I want to move. I want to move.
2	Roz:	Okay, you gonna sit with me.
3	Child:	Todd needs a chair over here.

[Todd is silent for 74 seconds.]

4	Roz:	I don't have my [unintelligible]. Okay, Todd, you need to use words to ask for

5   Todd: [Interrupts] Pass it to me, please. And you need bread.
[Todd is silent for 96 seconds.]
6   Roz: Todd, pull your chair up to the table. Did you like the story
             today?
7   Todd: Yeah.
8   Roz: What would you do if you found a dinosaur in the cave?
9   Todd: I would leave it alone.
10   Roz: Why would you leave it alone?
11 Todd: 'Cause I don't want to bring it home.
12   Roz: No?
13 Child: He won't fit through the door.
14 Todd: They would have to make a big door.
15   Roz: A gigantic door.
16 Todd: And a bigger house.
[Roz continues to talk to the children about what they would do if they
found a dinosaur, but Todd does not participate and is silent for 90 seconds.]
17 Todd: I want another carrot. Last one.
18   Roz: What do you say?
19 Todd: Thank you.
20   Roz: You're welcome.

Todd is quiet for long periods of time (after turns 3, 5, and 16). Todd
spent 24% of his classroom day in mealtime, and during mealtime he
was silent 71.5% of the time and engaged in only some nonpresent
(9%) and cognitively extending talk (that is, conversation about world
knowledge and current events and reflection on language; 8%).[2] In
contrast, though Casey spent only 13% of his classroom day in mealtime, he was silent only 31% of the time and spent a much greater percentage of his time engaged in nonpresent (34.5%) and general talk
(that is, talk about likes and dislikes and miscellaneous "small talk";
31.5%) than Todd did.[3] Todd's mealtime transcript also shows that when
the teacher did talk with Todd, they discussed a book the teacher just
read to the class, and thus their conversation did go beyond the here-

---

[2]The rest of Todd's talk during mealtime was as follows: general talk (5%),
controlling (that is, commands or talk intended to manage children's behavior;
4%), didactic (that is, instruction or explanatory talk; 0.5%), language routine
(that is, routinized activities such as counting, reciting the alphabet, and singing; 2%). Mariana, whose teacher also circulated during mealtime, spent 16%
of her day in mealtime. She was silent 97% of the time and engaged in didactic talk 3% of the time.
    [3]Casey spent the remaining 3% of his mealtime in controlling talk.

and-now (turns 6–16). Because of Roz's need to feed and oversee all of the children in the classroom, however, her interactions of this sort with individual children are limited. Although teachers may engage children in conversations during mealtimes in which the teacher is present but circulating, these conversations often seem to be cut short or interrupted because the teacher must attend to a child's physical needs. For example, the following excerpt transpires during Roz's *teacher circulating* mealtime:

1	Roz:	So what kind of things would you play with a dinosaur in a cave?
2	Child:	I would talk to him.
3	Roz:	What kinds of things could you talk to a dinosaur about?
4	Child:	Dinosaurs.
5	Roz:	I think . . . about dinosaurs.
6	Child:	Yes.
7	Roz:	I'd bring a book and read him a story.
8	Child:	Like what real dinosaurs do.
9	Roz:	Tell him what real dinosaurs do.
10	Child:	Yup.
11	Roz:	Uh-huh. What do you see, Kenny? Kenny? I'd really rather that you did not do that, do you understand? I don't like it when you put wet paper on the milk carton. Please stop.
12	Child:	Can I have more milk?
13	Roz:	A little bit later I'll be passing out seconds on milk.
14	Child:	[Unintelligible]
15	Roz:	Okay.
16	Child:	I don't know when's mine.
17	Roz:	What do you think is in this?
18	Child:	Carrots.
19	Roz:	Uh-huh.

You can see that in turns 1–10, Roz and the children were talking about a book they had just read at circle time. Notice how the talk goes beyond the here-and-now by reflecting on the book they had just read and adding some imaginative ways that they would cope if they, like the main character in the story, found a dinosaur. Furthermore, notice how this talk is interrupted when the teacher must speak to a child who is playing with his milk (turn 11) and from there on is focused on the here-and-now aspects of mealtime.

Summary

In summary, children whose teachers were stationary during mealtimes engaged in significantly more nonpresent talk than did children whose teachers were circulating during mealtimes. This finding supports the idea that mealtimes in school, like mealtimes at home, can encourage children's telling of narratives. The finding of relationships between *nonpresent talk* and having a teacher as a conversational partner also supports this viewpoint. These findings are especially interesting because there were no significant differences between the children in the two mealtime groups in the amount of overall talk each engaged in throughout the day. That is, the differences between these three mealtime groups do not seem to be attributable to individual differences in children's talkativeness. Rather, the way in which mealtimes are organized is responsible for differences in the conversations that occur during mealtimes at school. Furthermore, as illustrated in the mealtime transcripts, the constant presence of a teacher who can encourage children to narrate nonpresent events during mealtimes and is not preoccupied with other organizational goals can facilitate children's engagement in narratives and other forms of nonpresent talk and thereby strengthen children's oral language skills and facilitate their literacy development.

Patterns of Language Use During Mealtimes

To better understand the details of language use during mealtimes, I examined results of our analyses of children's use of rare words. I used the same general approach that was used to study patterns of word use in the home (see Chapter 5). After transcribing our audiotapes, I used a computer-assisted analysis system to check our words against a list of relatively common words. This common-word list contains 7,881 words and was generated by adding plural noun forms and expanding the verb forms found in Chall and Dale's (1995) list of 3,000 words known by fourth graders. In addition, any words that the children or teachers used that were listed as slang or informal words in *The American Heritage Dictionary* (1982) and all proper names, forms of address, exclamations, incorrect forms, and child culture words were added to this common-word list. As mentioned in previous chapters, *rare* vocabulary words were defined as words not appearing on this list of words thought to be common to the vocabularies of preschoolers (see the appendix for further details). Our analyses allowed us to determine a number of details about children's language use. Specifically, I was able to learn how many words the children and teachers used during meals as well as how many

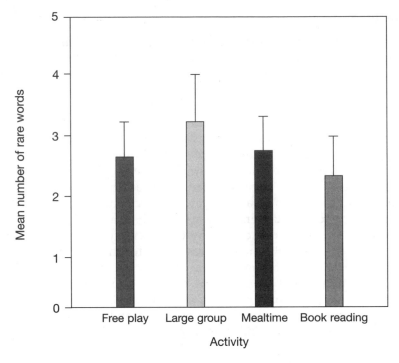

Figure 9.3. Children's use of rare words by activity. (Free play, *M* = 2.70, *SE* = 0.55; large group, *M* = 3.22, *SE* = 0.81; mealtime, *M* = 2.74, *SE* = 0.54; book reading, *M* = 2.32, *SE* = 0.73.)

of those words were relatively unusual or rare (such as *dinosaur* or *broccoli*).

These analyses of patterns of word use allowed me to explore the idea that mealtimes in preschool classrooms can enhance children's language and literacy development by exposing children to novel or rare vocabulary words (by hearing teachers say rare vocabulary words) and through children's own use of rare vocabulary words. Furthermore, I compared patterns of word use during mealtimes with patterns in the other settings for which there were data (that is, book reading, free play, circle time) to determine the extent to which mealtimes provide special opportunities for language use. Transcripts of 23 teachers' conversations during each of four classroom settings (that is, mealtime, book reading, free play, and circle time) were examined.

Vocabulary Use and Exposure

When mealtimes were compared with the other settings, free play was found to be the setting in which children talked the most. Circle time was the setting in which children used the most rare words. There were no significant differences in the amount of rare words children said during mealtimes and the three other classroom settings (see the appendix for details about the statistical analyses; see also Figure 9.3).

Thus, mealtime seems to provide children with an equally good opportunity as several other classroom settings to use a large variety of common words and to use novel or rare vocabulary words. This finding suggests that children's vocabularies can be enhanced during mealtime at least as well if not better than in classroom settings that have traditionally been geared toward children's vocabulary and language development (that is, book reading).

The vocabulary that teachers use in the classroom constitutes the most sophisticated vocabulary to which children are exposed while in school. Teachers' vocabulary use seems to follow a slightly different pattern than children's vocabulary use. Similarly to the children, teachers said significantly more words overall during free play than during

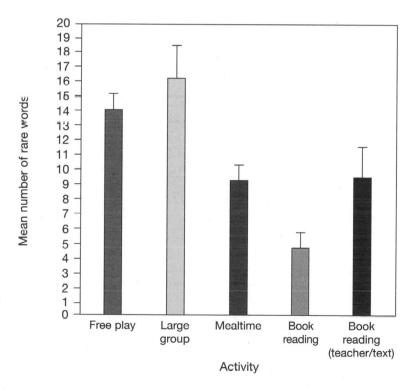

Figure 9.4. Teachers' use of rare words by activity. (Free play, $M = 14.09$, $SE = 1.51$; large group, $M = 16.22$, $SE = 2.33$; mealtime, $M = 9.39$, $SE = 1.07$; book reading, $M = 4.82$, $SE = 1.15$; book reading [teacher and text], $M = 9.55$, $SE = 2.00$.)

mealtime. They also used more words during circle times than during mealtimes (see the appendix for details about the statistical analyses; see also Figure 9.4).

Teachers also used significantly more rare words during free play than during mealtime. In a surprising result, I found that teachers also used significantly fewer rare words during book reading than during mealtime. This difference disappeared, however, when the text of the book was included as part of the teachers' talk. Thus, it seems that mealtime provides at least as good an opportunity for children to be exposed to novel vocabulary words as settings traditionally oriented toward children's language development (for example, book reading).

The finding that teachers' vocabulary use during circle time was greater than during mealtime suggests that teachers talk more and introduce more new vocabulary terms when giving lessons than when engaged in more casual conversation. During free play, teachers were usually anchored to the activity table and directed classroom behavior from this spot. Thus, teachers seemed to talk more and to use new vocabulary when instructing children in an activity. The high proportion of teachers' overall talk during circle time and free-play time also suggests that teachers engage in more interactive (rather than one-way) discussions during mealtime, leaving more room for children to speak, than they do during other activity times (for example, circle time or free play). The interactive nature of mealtimes thus allows children to engage in the conversation and use rare words themselves, as illustrated by the following mealtime transcript:

Teacher: So, Mummy said that you guys went out last night? Where did you go?

Child: Um, we went to a [unintelligible] with my cousin, Jay.

Teacher: How old is Jay?

Child: Um, 16.

Teacher: He's 16. He's a big cousin.

Child: No, he's a fat.

Teacher: He's the one that's fat? Oh, I remember, you told me about him. He likes to eat, huh?

Child: I know, like he was gonna . . . he was on a diet that morning, and now he's eating [unintelligible] ice cream. We went to the ice cream shop. But he was on a diet. They lived in a big building last morning, but they moved in a other house now.

Teacher: Oh.

Child: So he . . . he was eating popcorn, and he spilled the popcorn on my dad's car. And then, and my mom said, um, oh my . . . my [unintelligible]. Wait.

Teacher: What did your mom say?
Child: Um, I don't remember [unintelligible]. It's my, ah . . .
Teacher: It's my husband, is that what she was gonna say?
Child: My husband will get so mad.
Teacher: So did Jay . . .
Child: [Interrupting] [unintelligible] yup.
Teacher: He cleaned it up?
Child: Yeah, it was still on the floor on the floor of it. But he didn't clean the floor.
Teacher: Oh, boy. So who did—who went shopping with you?
Child: Um, my mom and my sister named Diana.

In summary, this comparison of classroom settings in terms of children's vocabulary use and exposure suggests that classroom settings in which the teacher is not engaged in a lesson but rather is engaged with the children in a more personal and interactive way may facilitate children's vocabulary development.

LONG-TERM IMPLICATIONS OF LANGUAGE USE DURING MEALTIMES

It seems clear that teachers play an important role in shaping children's language experiences during mealtime and that mealtime is a setting that is at least as well suited as other classroom settings to helping children acquire language. The question that naturally arises is whether the data provide evidence that children's language experiences during mealtimes are related to their language and literacy growth at the end of kindergarten. The answer is yes.

Our analyses of mealtime conversations when children were 4 revealed several results pointing to the impact of mealtime conversations. Specifically, children's exposure to *nonpresent talk* during mealtimes when they were in preschool predicted their performance on literacy tasks when they were in kindergarten (that is, *The Snowy Day* [Keats, 1962] Story Comprehension task, $r = .32$, $p < .05$, and the Receptive Vocabulary task, $r = .34$, $p < .05$).

SUGGESTIONS FOR TEACHERS

Teachers can do the following during mealtime to enhance children's language development:

- Sit with children during mealtime and have family-style meals (1:5 adult–child ratio)

- Encourage children's discussions about nonimmediate events by asking children to share personal experiences and by asking open-ended questions
- Encourage children to use novel vocabulary during mealtime by using new words learned during class lessons in mealtime conversations

In the following example (a portion of a transcript discussed previously), notice that a closed-ended question such as, "Did you like the story today?" (turn 6), is likely to produce a monosyllabic response from the child, as it does here in turn 7:

6	Roz:	Todd, pull your chair up to the table. Did you like the story today?
7	Todd:	Yeah.
8	Roz:	What would you do if you found a dinosaur in the cave?
9	Todd:	I would leave it alone.
10	Roz:	Why would you leave it alone?
11	Todd:	'Cause I don't want to bring it home.
12	Roz:	No?
13	Child:	He won't fit through the door.

However, Roz follows up Todd's monosyllabic response with an open-ended question (one that does not have a right or wrong answer and one to which the teacher does not know the answer) in turn 8. If Roz had followed her initial question to Todd (turn 6) with another closed-ended question, such as, "If you found a dinosaur, would you take it home with you?" Todd would have given another monosyllabic response. Through the use of an open-ended question, Roz elicited a thoughtful and elaborate answer from Todd.

In addition to the style of the question, the topic of the question is also an important aspect of the way teachers initiate conversations. For example, the first question that Ann asked in an exchange that appeared previously was, "Does anyone have any special plans to go away on the weekend?" Ann's question focused the topic of the conversation on future events, whereas the question, "What do you say?" focuses the conversation on the readily observable present. Discussing past events is more challenging for the child because the teacher probably does not know what the child did over the weekend, when he or she was away from school. Thus, through the use of language only, the child must communicate to the teacher what he or she did. A discussion of something that the teacher can readily observe, however, allows the child to rely on the physical environment to communicate to the teacher what he or she is doing and is thus less likely to challenge or extend the child's language skills.

In addition, by controlling the topic of the conversation in the previous example, Roz encouraged Todd to use a specific new vocabulary word (that is, *dinosaur*). Thus, by asking Todd about something beyond the bounds of the physical environment, Roz asked him about a broader range of topics and settings and thereby encouraged him to use varied and novel vocabulary.

CONCLUSIONS

The Home–School Study draws attention to the informal learning opportunities of a classroom setting during which academic and social learning opportunities have largely gone unnoticed: mealtime. The results of this study suggest that a lot more than eating may be happening during mealtimes. Specifically, mealtimes provide an opportunity for children to enhance their vocabulary and narrative skills through discussions with teachers while also enhancing children's social skills by improving their communication skills. This seems to occur when teachers are not engaged in a lesson and are therefore free to engage children in extended discussions about decontextualized (that is, nonpresent) events or activities. Mealtimes provide good opportunities for teacher–child discussions because teachers are not working on overt educational goals at these times. However, not all mealtimes are created equal. Although mealtimes in which teachers are stationary and sit with the children in small groups while they eat seem to foster these types of extended discussions between teachers and children best, remember that it is not the activity or the presence of an adult in itself that results in children's discussions of nonpresent events. Rather, what is necessary is the presence of an adult who values and encourages children's discussions.

Chapter 10

Large-Group and Free-Play Times
*Conversational Settings Supporting
Language and Literacy Development*

David K. Dickinson

Chapters 8 and 9 examine two settings in preschool classrooms that we expected would be particularly important for children's language development: book reading and mealtime. In Chapter 8, Miriam Smith takes a broad view of classrooms, considering their overall structure and organization. This chapter also takes a broad view, this time looking in detail at children's conversations during group times and free play. Surprisingly few studies have examined the nature of children's interactions with teachers and peers throughout the day. In one noteworthy study that took on this task, the researchers spent 1 week in each of 119 classrooms serving 3- and 4-year-olds across the United States. While in the classrooms, the researchers observed the overall classroom, examined individual children's patterns of activity, and tested children (Layzer, Goodson, & Moss, 1993). They found that children spent about 29% of their day in large-group settings and 20% in free play. Thus, in general, the two settings on which this chapter focuses typically account for nearly half of a preschool child's classroom day.

This chapter begins by describing prior research about these two times of the day and then visits Astra's and Casey's classrooms. After giving an overall sense of their classrooms on the days when researchers from the Home–School Study of Language and Literacy Development visited, this chapter looks at the large-group and free-play times. After these two portrait children's particular experiences are examined, results from the broader sample are reported to give readers a sense of how representative the children's experiences were. Also, particular features of their experiences are selected for more detailed discussion to provide concrete images of the kinds of interactions that were found to be related to our kindergarten assessments. This chapter then turns to a discussion of the data collected and discusses which features of teacher–child conversations were linked to the children's kindergarten test scores. A concluding section summarizes the Home–School Study's findings, and suggestions for classroom teachers are given.

BACKGROUND RESEARCH

Large-Group Times

Group times can be used to accomplish different goals, with the organization and content of meeting times carrying different meanings for children and supporting children's development in different ways (Dickinson, 1984). Although children spend considerable time in large-group settings, the portions of these events that do not include book reading have received little attention from researchers. Chapter 9 discusses the book-reading portion of large-group times and notes that book reading accounts for only a small part of the time spent in groups. As in Casey's and Astra's classrooms, singing and group discussions often occupy much of the remaining time. Because of the sparse attention to group times apart from book reading, there is almost no research examining the potential benefits or drawbacks of varied ways of using group time. There is some indication, however, that these settings might have more impact on children's language development than many would suppose.

A study conducted with many of the 3- and 4-year-old children attending preschool in Bermuda examined patterns of language use and their relationship to children's language development (McCartney, 1984). The researchers found that children's language growth was strongly associated with the amount of time that they spent talking with and listening to adults. The most beneficial type of talk was that which the researchers called *representational talk*—talk that communicated information and was not used to control children's behavior. This is much the same as the type of talk that we refer to in this book as *decontextualized language*. The proportion of time that speech was addressed to children in large-group settings was strongly related to the amount of such talk children experienced. This study did not code language experience by setting; thus, the nature of children's language experiences during group times is not clear. Nonetheless, these findings suggest that the amount and type of language that children experience as members of a group—during book reading and all other large-group settings—may have beneficial effects on their language growth.

Free-Play Times

At the heart of traditional early childhood programs in the United States are periods when children are allowed to move about the classroom, selecting activities that they want to do. We refer to these times as *free play* because most teachers in our study employed this term themselves. Some children also had *choice time,* during which they could choose from among a limited range of activities. Some classrooms offered both choice time and free play, with the latter being a time when children had access to all of the materials and areas in the classroom. For analytic purposes, these times are combined in this chapter because children were able to select activities of their choosing and engage in child-initiated play at both times.

Free play has been considered from varied angles by different re-searchers, with dramatic play being a favorite setting because of inter-est in the symbolic abilities that children display through their words (for example, role play), actions (for example, building with blocks), and art. Such play is of interest in the Home–School Study because chil-dren's talk while they are pretending is a type of decontextualized talk that has been linked to literacy development (Galda, Pellegrini, & Cox, 1989; Pellegrini & Galda, 1993; Pellegrini, Galda, Dresden, & Cox, 1991). Because symbolic play has long been a hallmark of cognitive growth in the preschool years, researchers have studied the conditions under which children are likely to engage in this type of high-level play. Stud-ies of symbolic play have found that it is most likely to occur when chil-dren are playing with blocks, are involved in fantasy play, or are doing open-ended art projects (Kontos & Wilcox-Herzog, 1997; Layzer et al., 1993). Not surprisingly, children more often engage in this type of play when they are with friends and less often when they are with teachers (Kontos & Wilcox-Herzog, 1997; Layzer et al., 1993; Wilcox-Herzog, 1999). Although the presence of teachers tends to diminish such play, the nature of a child's relationship with his or her teacher makes a dif-ference because the child engages in more such play when in a class-room in which he or she has a warm relationship with the teacher (Howes & Smith, 1995). This chapter does not examine the emotional tenor of teacher–child interactions, but early analyses of our data also indicate that the emotional tone of teachers' conversations with chil-dren contributes to children's long-term growth (Densmore, Dickinson, & Smith, 1995).

Researchers have begun to look closely at children's patterns of conversations during free play. This has resulted in some surprises. Layzer and her colleagues (1993) found that children interacted with other children only about 50% of the time. They also found that teachers spent only 10% of their time with individual children, considerably less than the 30% of their time spent interacting with the class as a whole or with groups. Thus, for considerable periods of time, children are alone and are not interacting with other children or with adults. Another study that was carried out in university-affiliated preschool classrooms found surprisingly low levels of conversation between children and teachers (Wilcox-Herzog & Kontos, 1998). Researchers coded teacher–child interactions when teachers were within 3 feet of a child being studied and found that 81% of the time, teachers did not talk to the child whom they were near. When teachers did engage children in extended, complex discussions, the children were less likely to engage in high-level play. That is, their energy went into talking with the teacher and not into sustaining complex, imaginative play (Wilcox-Herzog, 1999). Teachers may be aware that their presence can disrupt high-level play. Another study (Kontos & Wilcox-Herzog, 1997) found that teachers were less likely to talk with children who were engaged in high-level play. Thus, teachers who value children's play may be concerned about the possible negative impact of their presence on children's play. This pattern of avoiding children may result in unintended negative consequences for children. The previously mentioned study (McCartney, 1984) done in Bermuda found that children's initiations of interactions with adults were positively related to language outcomes, whereas a tendency to initiate conversations with other children was negatively related to children's assessment scores. Because the Home–School Study data provide information that is drawn specifically from free play and describe the experiences of the child and the teacher, our findings can provide some guidance to teachers as they struggle with the tension between a desire to foster children's play and a desire to provide support to children's language and literacy growth.

Though prior research provides some sense of the patterns of interaction between teachers and children, it says relatively little about the quality of teacher–child interactions during free play. Studies that I directed as part of research by the New England Quality Research Center shed some light on this area. In 28 Head Start classrooms, the research team for that project coded[1] 354 minutes of teacher–child conversations during mealtimes and free play (Dickinson, Rafal, & Merianos, 1998) and found that teachers spent 18.5% of their time engaged in decontextualized talk (2.4% about literacy or math, 5.2% in talk

---

[1]The researchers observed interactions for 30 seconds and then just coded what they saw for 60 seconds and then observed for another 30 seconds. This approach eliminated the need to transcribe data while still providing a detailed description of teacher–child interactions.

about general knowledge topics,[2] and 10.9% in talk about the past or the future). During these conversations, teachers shifted topics often, as indicated by the fact that they developed a topic over several turns in only 11% of the 30-second intervals that were coded.

If we put together what is known about children's preschool classroom language experiences, several general trends are evident:

- Individual children have relatively few extended conversations with other children or with adults during the course of the day.

- During free play, children tend to engage in complex play with other children and are less likely to engage in such play when they are talking with adults.

- Conversations that occur between children and adults only occasionally deal with topics that draw on decontextualized language skills, and conversational topics change frequently.

- Children's language growth is supported by interactions with adults, including the time spent in large-group teacher-led activities. Some evidence suggests that children's language growth may be undermined by extensive time spent talking with peers.

PROFILE CLASSROOMS:
ASTRA'S AND CASEY'S CLASSROOM DAYS

This chapter draws from portions of Astra's and Casey's preschool experiences to illustrate important features of free-play and large-group activities in the classrooms we studied. These children represent interestingly different experiences. Astra attended a full-day private program all of whose attendees were African American, whereas Casey attended a half-day program with 12 Caucasian children and 1 Caribbean American child. Casey's classroom was designed specifically to provide children with enriched language opportunities. For Astra, the schedule from when she was 3 and 4 is included because, owing to equipment problems, we do not have a recording of free play from when she was 4. When she was 3, Astra was in Mrs. Angela Washington's classroom, the teacher described in Chapter 7, and when Astra was 4, she was in Ms. Dorothy Howard's classroom. Casey's experience when he was 4 and in Ann Greenbaum's room also is described. Though both Astra's and Casey's classrooms have roughly similar structures in terms of pacing and general types of activities, they represent distinctly different ap-

---

[2]Talk about general knowledge topics comprised expanding on concepts and the meaning of words and discussing why things are the way they are.

proaches to supporting children's development. In the following pages, Astra's and Casey's experiences in large-group times are discussed first, then free-play times are examined. Small pieces of conversation are selected to be discussed in some detail.

Astra's Morning Routine

Astra was in full-day child care; therefore, the schedule for her day stretched from early in the morning until the late afternoon. This chapter focuses on only the morning portion of the day because that is when we collected our data. The daily schedules for Astra's classrooms when she was 3 and 4 years old (see Figure 10.1) indicate that her teachers planned for the children to spend about 22% of their morning time in large-group meetings. Her teachers distinguished between free-play/choice time and unit project time. When she was 3, Astra's teachers allocated 37% of the morning to free play and 19% to projects. When Astra was 4, her teacher planned to spend 27% of the day in free play and set aside 24% for projects.

On the day the Home–School Study researcher visited Astra's classroom when she was 4, she had free play until 9:00 A.M. The education director of Astra's preschool then gathered children into a group for an instructional activity. After some songs, he engaged the children in a brief discussion of a piece of shiny plastic and encouraged them to dance along with the shimmering reflections of the sun. He then gave

Astra's reported classroom schedule		Casey's reported classroom schedule
(when she was 3)	(when she was 4)	(when he was 4)
7:30 Group time	7:00 Breakfast	8:00 Free play
8:00 Breakfast and free play	8:00 Free play	8:45 Circle
	9:30 Teacher-led activity (group for 30 minutes)	9:00 Choice time
9:00 Circle		10:30 Story time
9:30 Teacher-assigned projects		10:45 Snacktime
	10:30 Circle	11:00 Small group
10:00 Choice time	11:00 Unit projects	11:00 Small group music and movement
10:20 Free play	12:00 Lunch	
11:15 Lunch	12:30 Nap	12:00 Dismissal
12:00 Nap	2:30 Snack	
2:30 Gross motor, outdoors	2:45 Teacher-led activity	
5:00 Dismissal	3:15 Free play, outdoors	
	4:00 Departure	

Figure 10.1. Daily schedules for Astra's and Casey's classrooms.

each child a piece of reflective plastic to play with. At about 10:30 A.M., there was a second group time during the slot identified as "unit project" time. This group time was used for about 40 minutes and included book reading. After book reading, children were allowed to select activities of their own choosing.

Casey's Morning Routine

Casey's teacher planned to spend 13% of the day in large-group activities, less time than Astra's teacher had planned for large groups. On the day the researchers observed Casey, however, he spent about 25% of his day in group settings because most of the final gross motor and movement period was used for a teacher-directed activity done in a group setting. Ann planned for only about 19% of the day to be used for free play, but she also set aside 38% of the morning for choice time. Thus, Casey was scheduled to spend about 56% of his time in child-initiated activity periods.

On the day that researchers observed, the day flowed in a way that was generally consistent with the schedule Ann had told them. For the choice time following circle, Casey's teachers had created activities that might be of special interest: colored water and bubbles in the water table and cookie cutters and a rolling pin in the playdough area. Casey and his friend Bryan spent nearly an hour in the block area, where they engaged in vigorous pretend play that involved a battle between them and some "menacing sharks." At one point, Ann joined and redirected their fantasies. Later, during choice time, she invited the boys to observe another child's performance. She then sat down and read with them. In quick succession, the children read *The Very Hungry Caterpillar* (Carle, 1979) and *Brown Bear, Brown Bear, What Do You See?* (Martin, 1967/1983). During the group book reading that followed choice time, Ann and her assistant teacher divided the class into two groups. Ann read *Nicolas, Where Have You Been?* (Lionni, 1987), a story about a mouse, in an engaging, interactive manner. After snacktime, Ann gave the children board games, which they played until she led the group in a brief closing gross motor activity.

EXAMINING LARGE-GROUP ACTIVITIES IN OUR CLASSROOMS

Overall Time Spent in Groups

Many of the classrooms we visited had two or three group times per day. For example, if a book was not read during the first circle time, the reading often would occur in one of these later group times. Similarly, later group times tended to include music or movement activities if they were not part of the first circle time. These later meetings also were sometimes used to review what children had done during the day, discuss problems that had arisen, and talk about what the group would be doing the next day.

Large-group times occupied significant amounts of time in children's classroom days. When the children in the study were 3 and 4 years old, their teachers reported spending roughly the same percentage of classroom time in large-group meetings (9% when 3, 11% when 4), but when the children were in kindergarten, this figure jumped to 32% of the day (see Figure 10.2). We calculated the time the children spent in different settings on the days when their conversations were recorded and found a steady increase in group times across the years. When the children were 3, we observed them in group settings an average of 20 minutes and 45 seconds ($n = 55$). This figure rose to nearly 25 minutes at age 4 ($n = 76$) and to 36 minutes and 30 seconds at age 5 ($n = 66$).

Group Times in Astra's and Casey's Rooms

This chapter focuses on only one meeting time from each of two rooms; nonetheless, these two meetings illustrate most of the content included in group times. They also depict some of the differences in orientation

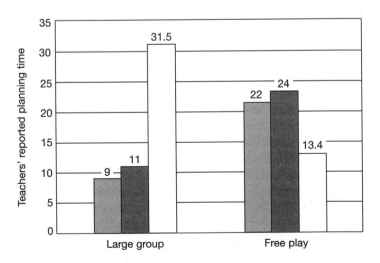

Figure 10.2. Percentages of time teachers reported planning for large groups and free play when target children were ■ 3, ■ 4, and ☐ 5 years old.

to the governing purposes of group times. Figure 10.3 summarizes the content of the first meeting in Astra's and Casey's rooms when they were 4 years of age.

These two meeting times share some general features. In each case, the full class gathered on a rug area, and the teacher led the discussion. In both cases, the teachers discussed the days of the week and the coming weekend (both visits were conducted on Fridays) and meetings included group singing. Beneath these similarities, however, there were marked differences. Astra's teacher, Mrs. Washington, held a long meeting (40 minutes), using it as a time for instruction and review of academic material, whereas Casey's teacher, Ann, held a rather brief meeting (12 minutes) and used this time to draw the group together, converse about the day, and set the stage for choice time.

The academic thrust of Mrs. Washington's meeting can be seen as she led the children through reviews of the days of the week, numbers, and shape names. Her instructional intention is clearly shown in her willingness to correct children when their responses were incorrect:

Mrs. Washington:	All right, we're going to just review the days of the week. Who'd like to stand up and name the days of the week for us? Douglas? Okay, you need the ruler? Here you are, Douglas. All right, Douglas. Nice and loud, so we can hear you.
Douglas:	Monday, Tuesday, Wednesday, Thursday [unintelligible].
Mrs. Washington:	Why don't we start all over again, Douglas. You forgot the very first one. Sunday, go on.
Douglas:	Sunday, Monday, Tuesday.
Mrs. Washington:	I don't think you're loud enough. We can't hear you.
Douglas:	Monday.
Mrs. Washington:	No, Sunday.
Douglas:	Sunday, Monday, Tuesday, Wednesday, Thursday, Friday, Saturday.

Mrs. Washington also used her book-reading time as an opportunity for a lesson on personal safety. She engaged children in an extended conversation about the issue of talking to strangers after she read the book *Never Talk to Strangers*. Thus, during Mrs. Washington's group time, she mixed singing and book reading with group review of academic material. There were several relatively long stretches when children listened silently as other children rehearsed information.

Astra's group time	Casey's group time
(40 minutes)	(12 minutes)
Children gather, and individual children say the days of the week with the teacher's help, occasional group involvement, and occasional comments about what they do on selected days (especially weekends).	Teacher discusses visitors and their equipment (uses words *microphone, video camera, tape*).
	Group sings *Here We Are Together.*
Teacher asks children whether they have things to share. Teacher assists as children discuss plans for the next day (Saturday).	Group discusses who is present and who is absent.
	Group briefly discusses that it is Friday and the weekend will follow.
Teacher asks children to suggest a song for them to sing. Together they sing *Teapot, Old MacDonald Had a Farm, The Alphabet Song.*	In response to child comment, group talks about coming school vacation and about an accident a child had at home.
Children are given a ruler and point to selected letters that are on display. One child is helped to point to the letters in his name one at a time. Next child asks to point to and say the alphabet. Astra says the alphabet and points to the letters in her first and last names. Same routine continues with other children.	Children sing *Open Them Shut Them* and *Where is Thumbkin* while doing associated finger plays. Group briefly discusses each finger as they sing second song.
	Children sing *One Little Bird* followed by counting birds.
	Children say rhyming poem together: *Ten Little Fingers.*
Children (one at a time) review shapes, pointing and naming them.	Teacher reads a rhyming riddle and children guess answer.
Children (one at a time) review numbers, pointing and naming them.	Group discusses mystery box for children to examine during the day.
Teacher reads and discusses the books *Never Talk to Strangers* and *Corduroy.*	Children sing *Twinkle Twinkle Little Star.*
Group discusses people who wear uniforms.	Teacher describes activities available for choice time: water table with green water and soap bubbles, art table with playdough and tools, blocks, books, detective game, and dramatic play area.

Figure 10.3.   Group times in Astra's and Casey's classrooms.

In contrast, during her meeting times Ann did no explicit review of academic content, but she did challenge children's thinking. When talking about who was present, she engaged children in problem solving as she asked them to determine who was absent. She also encouraged children to think about the days of the week in the context of a discussion of the fact that it was Friday and the weekend was coming. The activity demonstrating the most explicit academic intent was Ann's giving the children a riddle to solve. In this playful activity, she encouraged the children to focus on language as they guessed what was being described, exposed them to rhyming text, and used a novel word, *riddle*. (Rare words are underlined in the transcripts that follow.)

> Ann: Yes, we don't want to forget about the <u>riddle</u> today, and it's right behind Bella. We could take a look at that and see if you can guess what this <u>riddle</u> is.
> Child 1: Bella.
> Ann: It says, "I can grow very tall. I can grow very high. My branches and leaves . . . "
> Child 2: [Interrupts teacher] I know what it is!
> Ann: " . . . can touch the sky."
> Children: Tree.
> Ann: What am I?
> Children: Tree.
> Ann: Boy, you guys really did a great job guessing all these <u>riddles</u>. You did all of them.

Another type of talk that occurred during large-group times was explanation. Usually, explanations appeared as teachers explained to children the reasons for something the teacher was going to do. An example of such an explanation comes from when Ann was negotiating with children about which song they would sing next:

> Ann: Well, how about if we do that one another day?
> Child: Do what one?
> Ann: You want to do "Twinkle, Twinkle"? Sure. That's a short one. We'll do that one today. And we'll do "Five Little Monkeys" another day because that's kind of a long one. Okay?

In her group time conversations, also notice how Ann used group times to expose children to new words. Earlier her intentional use of the word *riddle* was noted, but such novel vocabulary could be used at any time. For example, when Ann introduced the activities that would be available during choice time, she used several such words:

> Ann: The book area has the tape story of *The Three Bears* and the <u>flannel</u> board with the *Three Billy Goats Gruff*. In the game area, we're going to have the "What's Missing?" tray, so we need <u>detectives</u> to

figure out what's missing. And the writing table's open, and the <u>dis-</u> <u>covery</u> table. So, think about where you'd like to choose.

Even though Ann generally did not engage in explicit instruction of academic content, she, like Mrs. Washington, corrected children when needed. For example, when the group was talking about coming events, the following interaction occurred:

Child: We have 10 days off.
 Ann: No, not yet. That school vacation's coming up soon but not yet, okay?

Later, she corrected children as they were discussing a song they had just sung:

Child: I can do Ring Man.
 Ann: You can do Ring Man? Good. Okay. Where? . . . No, the next finger.

One final type of talk that was relatively common during large-group times was explanation. Typically, teachers offered explanations as they stated why they were going to do something in a particular way.

Thus, instruction in Ann's large-group time is indirect and occurs in the context of other activities. There are relatively few occasions when children quietly listen to the teacher or to other children for long periods of time.

EXAMINING FREE-PLAY ACTIVITIES IN OUR CLASSROOMS

Overall Time in Free Play

In the classrooms visited as part of the Home–School Study, teachers sometimes allocated time for both free play and choice time. These distinctions reflected the extent to which teachers provided special options and limited children's choices. From the children's perspective, however, in both such settings, they were free to move about the room, talk with friends, and choose an activity that appealed to them. As mentioned before, because the conversational opportunities were comparable across all such child-initiated settings, we did not distinguish these times. Among the range of activities children typically could select was one that would support pretend play (such as blocks, sand and water, or dramatic play area), some type of art activity (such as painting or gluing) or art area (such as using the easel), construction materials (such as Legos or blocks), toys (such as vehicles of varied types), and puzzles or games.

Teachers' reports indicated that, when the children in the study were 3 years old, 22% of their classroom time was set aside for free play and/or choice time. When they were 4 years of age, 24% of their day was scheduled for such time, but only 13% of the time during kindergarten was planned for child-initiated activities. On days the researchers observed, when children were age 3, the children spent 1 hour and 35 minutes in free play; when they were 4 years old, they spent 1 hour and 31 minutes in free play; and in kindergarten, the children spent 25 minutes in free play. Just as for group times, the percentage of the day that children were observed in free play was inflated by the lack of outdoor time in our recordings.

Conversations in Astra's Classroom

When Astra was 4 years old, we were unable to record a free-play time in her classroom because of equipment problems. Therefore, Astra's free play that was observed in Ms. Howard's room when Astra was 3 is discussed. On the day observations were made, free play in Astra's room lasted from about 9:45 A.M. to 11:15 A.M. During this time, Ms. Howard spent time observing the children, talking to the researcher and other teachers, and interacting with the children. No special activities were provided.

During free play, Astra kept herself well occupied. For much of the morning, she held a doll. Her play shifted between bursts of conversation with children and extended periods of silence when she was engaged with her doll. For example, at the beginning of the observation, Astra initiated a "going to church" event, then another child noticed that Astra was wearing earrings:

Child 1:   Why you wearing those [referring to Astra's earrings]?
  Astra: I'm going to church!
Child 1:   I'm going to church with my baby.
Child 2:   Hurry up, Courtney, I'm going to church now. Hurry up, I can't wait for you.
Child 3:   I'm not going to church. I'm staying home.
  Astra: You have to go to church.

The children talked about going to church for about 1½ minutes, after which Astra lapsed into silence as she carefully put playdough on her baby's eyes so that the baby could sleep. This period of activity during which she was silent most of the time lasted about 2½ minutes. She then began quietly singing to her baby saying, "Baby has to go to church." Once again, the other children picked up their cues from her and began singing along for 35 seconds. Children then asked her why her baby's eyes were covered. After explaining, Astra invited more children to "come to the church" with her. She then led a small group to the rug. The burst of talk about her baby and going to church lasted another 2 minutes, after which she and the others sat silently for half a minute before Astra initiated a new theme by announcing, "I'm on the bus sitting down."

In this glimpse of Astra's free play when she was 3, there are several important features to point out. Astra was an organizer who used language to draw other children into new activities. The novel scenes she established helped to provide a context for conversations with the other children. Despite Astra's generally verbal nature, she exhibits bursts of talk interspersed with silence. These silences occurred even during dramatic play episodes and occupied nearly half of the time that was coded. Such periods of silence were characteristic of all children. As shown in Table 10.1, during free play when children were 3, they were engaged in no sustained talk for 63% of the time. Such periods of silence accounted for 59% of their time when they were 4.

Also note that the teacher was not involved in any of Astra's conversations. Indeed, Ms. Howard had only brief, passing conversations with Astra during this free play. This type of limited contact with teachers was common. As shown in Table 10.1, the children's conversations with teachers accounted for 21% of their free-play time when they were 3, 17% of their free-play time when they were 4, and 17% of their free-play time when they were in kindergarten. When children were in preschool, there was a decrease in the amount of time they spent talking with teachers and a slight increase in the percentage of time that they spent talking to other children (13% at 3 years old, 18% at 4 years old). This shift from talk with teachers to talk with children

Table 10.1. Percentage of time children talked with teachers, other children, or no one during free play, based on observational data from child audiotapes

Free play	3 years old (n = 52)	4 years old (n = 75)	5 years old (n = 72)
Talk with teacher	21	17	17
Talk with child	13	18	10
No sustained talk	63	59	71

In some cases, we could not determine the conversational partner and had to code the partner as *unknown.* The result is that the percentages do not total 100.

likely reflects children's growing conversational skills. When children were younger, they were more likely to sustain conversations over longer stretches of time when talking with teachers. The role of the teacher in extending conversations is illustrated in a conversation between Ms. Howard and Frankie, a child in Astra's room, while he was building with blocks:

Ms. Howard:	What is that you're buildin', Frankie? What is it, Frankie?
Frankie:	A bank.
Ms. Howard:	A bank? Oh, that's a tall bank. That's a tall bank for a small bottom. That bank don't have anything to stand on, look. You got two feet to stand on one body. This one don't have one foot.
Frankie:	Oh.
Ms. Howard:	It needs some more. It needs some more body.
Frankie:	Here's one.
Ms. Howard:	Okay, put another small one over here, Frank. You need another one somewheres around here. Let's see. That won't work. Give me another. Do you have another small one?
Frankie:	[Unintelligible]
Ms. Howard:	Now, that looks better, doesn't it?
Frankie:	Those—these are doors.
Ms. Howard:	These are doors? Oh, all right. Now what color is this one?
Frankie:	Green.
Ms. Howard:	This is what?
Frankie:	Yellow.
Ms. Howard:	This is what?
Frankie:	Red.
Ms. Howard:	This is what?
Frankie:	White.
Ms. Howard:	This is what?
Frankie:	Blue.
Ms. Howard:	Okay.
Frankie:	Green.
Ms. Howard:	Right there. If these are doors, right, this is the street floor, right?

There are several important things to note about this conversation. First, consider the balance in the amount of talk between the teacher and the child. Ms. Howard speaks far more than Frankie, who mostly responds to questions. Despite the child's limited conversational role, Ms. Howard is striving to challenge his thinking. First, she directs Frankie's attention to the structure of his "bank," noting, "That's a tall bank for a small bottom. That bank don't have anything to stand on, look." Then she makes a comparison between his block structure and his body: "You got two feet to stand on one body. This one don't have one foot." Through this exchange, she challenges Frankie to think about his structure and uses complex metaphorical language to push him to reconsider his structure. Later, at the end of this exchange, Ms. Howard uses a logical construction to lead Frankie toward articulating further information about his structure: "If these are doors, right, this is the street floor, right?"

Although Ms. Howard urged Frankie to engage in high-level thought about his structure, she used no low-frequency vocabulary herself. Thus, though she was clearly concerned that Frankie know basic color terms, she did not expose him to more challenging vocabulary as she discussed his block structure. For example, she might have used a whole range of words such as *balance, tower, top-heavy, unsteady, stable*, and *structure*, words that one can safely assume were in her own vocabulary. She used a limited range of vocabulary, even though it is clear that she was concerned about Frankie's vocabulary growth because she led him through a review of the colors. It seemed that conception of vocabulary was focused on a narrow range of words typically considered to be part of the "school readiness" knowledge package that children are expected to have as they enter kindergarten. She is not alone in this respect, as we noted many occasions when teachers rehearsed color names with children and few instances when teachers explicitly discussed the meanings of other words. Ms. Howard's overall use of a relatively limited range of words was common in other classrooms. When children were 3 and 4 years of age, we found that only 1% of the total words they used during free play were among those counted as rare words (see Table A10.3 in the appendix for details regarding total teacher word use across settings).

Conversations in Casey's Room

Free play in Casey's room immediately followed circle time. He spent nearly the entire time with his close friend Bryan, a common pattern, according to his teacher. Casey and Bryan together constructed an extended fantasy that alternated between fighting with and then saving sharks. The fantasy also was liberally sprinkled with "bad guys" who alternated between being threatening and being vanquished. Through much of their narrative, Casey and Bryan were in a "lifeboat" equipped with various "weapons." The following excerpt gives a flavor of their conversation:

Bryan: I'm going out on the lifeboat. I'm jumping out on my lifeboat, Casey.

Casey: Me, too.

Bryan: Someone's dead in the water. Get in the lifeboat! The life . . .

Casey: Jump in. I'll jump in. Bad guy.

[More talk about "bad guys" follows, then they begin talking about fish and sharks.]

Casey: I got the fish.

Bryan: I killed the shark.

Casey: We're fish savers. Jump in the lifeboat. There's an emergency.

Bryan: Emergency.

Casey: I'm underwater, don't throw it to me.

Bryan: Throw it back.

Casey: A fish is attacking. Bad guy.

[Their play continues with action-packed conflicts involving sharks and bad guys.]

In this glimpse of Casey's free-play fantasy, note that Casey and Bryan have the ability to construct an almost seamless narrative. They are so completely attuned to each other that they sustain talk within the narrative frame nonstop for nearly 30 minutes. They do this while shifting the plot of their fantasy abruptly, using dialogue that stayed in the fantasy: "Someone's dead in the water. Jump in the lifeboat. There's an emergency." This type of highly evolved play in part reflects the fact that the two boys played together often and had sufficient time to develop elaborated fantasies. In their use of words such as *lifeboat* and *emergency*, one can see how children can introduce interesting and varied vocabulary into their play.

Casey's teacher, Ann, spent relatively little time talking to the boys during their play. She entered their play when the two boys were "killing sharks," characters that they called "bad guys." Notice in the next excerpt how deftly she helps make explicit the elements of their fantasy and suggests a possible alternative direction for them to pursue:

Ann: Oh. So you're going to get the sharks. Do you need to kill them, or do you move them to a different place so they can't hurt anybody?

Casey: Kill them.

Ann: Kill them. You have to kill them?

Bryan: Yeah.

Casey: There's water already in the cage.

Ann: Oh, so they're in cages that are filled with water?

Bryan: Yeah, it's a water cage.

Ann: And they don't get to eat <u>spinach</u>. Do you think sharks miss eating <u>spinach</u>?

Casey: Sharks think they could get out with <u>spinach</u>.

Ann: You <u>must</u> be very <u>brave</u> and <u>daring</u> men to go down there and take all these sharks back to this special place.

Casey: We're protecting them.

Ann: Do you have to wear special suits? What kind do you wear in the water?

Bryan: I wear climbing.

Ann: A climbing suit?

Casey: Yeah.

Ann: What do you wear?

Casey: A shark suit.

Ann: Those things on your back. Are those the <u>oxygen tanks</u>? To help you breathe underwater?

Bryan: They can breathe underwater.

Ann: Wow, that's a special trick to learn how to do.

Note that Ann observes that they are "killing sharks," and after finding out why, she restates what she understands: "Oh. So you're going to get the sharks." Building on this, she further clarifies where the sharks are being held and which type of food they eat, then she discusses the equipment the children need. In the course of her comments, Ann uses two words that are relatively uncommon: *spinach* and *oxygen*. Her use of *oxygen* is especially noteworthy because she models the correct use in a context that children may have had prior exposure to ("oxygen tanks") and then she makes explicit their purpose ("To help you breathe underwater"). She then departs their play, leaving them with an interesting word that they might pick up and incorporate in their play, much the way that skilled teachers seed dramatic play areas with new props to encourage elaborated play.

Later, Ann speaks with other children who were engaged in dramatic play related to cooking. Again we see how she joins into their play and introduces new vocabulary. In the following interaction, she also gently introduces an explanation of how ovens work and discusses scientific concepts:

Child: I'll check the oven.

Ann: What <u>temperature</u> does it have to be put at? When you put on the <u>oven,</u> you have to put it at a <u>certain temperature</u> to see how hot it is. So, you might turn it to 100 <u>degrees,</u> or 200, or 300, or 400, or 500.

Child: 500.

Ann: 500? That's usually—that's the hottest, and that's usually <u>broiling.</u>

In a few words, Ann has provided an explanation of what ovens do, how the temperature is set, how hot 500 degrees is, and what *broiling* means. These sentences were coded as dealing with "science and world" concepts. Unfortunately, the type of explanation that Ann used here— to explain a physical phenomenon—was quite rare during free play. Most of the time, explanations were used either when teachers were resolving problems or when they were explaining procedures. Following is an example of how explanations (in boldface in the next excerpt) were used in connection with reinforcing rules in Ms. Howard's room:

Ms. Howard: I don't want these blocks thrown all over the floor, please.

Child: Okay.

Ms. Howard: **Because you might hit someone.**

Next we see Ann responding to a child's complaint that she did not get a turn by providing an explanation of why she is going to give the child another turn:

Child: I didn't have a turn.

Ann: Well, we'll do it again, **so that everybody gets a turn.**

SHIFT BETWEEN PRESCHOOL AND KINDERGARTEN

Space does not permit an extended discussion of similarities and differences between preschool and kindergarten, but it is important to point out that the data clearly suggest that, on average, life in preschool is quite different from what children experience in kindergarten. One way in which this change can be seen is in the scheduling of the day. Figure 10.2 reveals the dramatic drop between preschool and kindergarten in the amount of time that teachers plan for free play (23.8% in preschool versus 13.4% in kindergarten) and the dramatic increase in time set aside for large groups (11% in preschool versus 31.5% in kindergarten). Also, we found an increase in the amount of time scheduled for children to do seatwork, with teachers of 4-year-olds reporting about 2.5% of their time was scheduled for such activities compared with 5.8% of the kindergarten day. There also was a decrease in the amount of time set aside for gross motor or outside time (14% in pre-school versus 8.5% in kindergarten). Thus, when children move into kindergarten, they typically encounter environments that more often require them to attend to the teacher and less often to move around freely and talk to peers.

We also noted shifts in the nature of children's interactions during free play. As shown in Table 10.1, observation of children's talk during free play revealed that kindergarten children spent considerably less time talking with other children (10%) than they did in preschool as 4-year-olds (18%) and were more likely to be silent (59% as 4-year-olds, 71% as 5-year-olds). Thus, when children enter kindergarten, they typically have considerably less time scheduled for free play, and, during the time provided, they spend less time conversing with peers. This sudden drop in time spent talking to other children, paired with an increase in silence, comes at a time when children are gaining conversational competence. The likely interpretation of these findings is that there are important changes in their classrooms. It may be that teachers are more likely to discourage audible talking and/or that they are less skilled in organizing their classrooms in ways that foster interactions among children.

HOW WE EXAMINED CHILDREN'S CONVERSATIONS

Next, this chapter turns to the statistical analyses of the links between children's large-group and free-play experiences and their performance on tests that were administered at the end of kindergarten. First, the array of information we drew upon is reviewed, then patterns of results are discussed. Where possible, the findings are discussed in the context of Astra's and Casey's classrooms.

Data and Variables Used

Extensive information about children's conversational experiences is available (see Table A10.3 in the appendix). Audiotapes of the children included 299 hours and 33 minutes of audiotapes of children's conversations that were coded[3] and timed directly from the audiotapes (age 3 = 5,634 minutes, age 4 = 6,640 minutes, and age 5 = 5,686 minutes). In addition, when the children were 3 and 4 years old, their teachers'

---

[3]The reliability of our coding was checked to ensure good interrater reliability.

conversations were audiotaped during the day (see Table 10.2). We transcribed[4] portions of these tapes, selecting the same amount of time from each setting across rooms: 15 minutes of free play per room and 15 minutes of large group per room. Our data were coded in the following ways:

- Children's audiotapes were coded by setting (large group, free play) for the following:
  - The number of seconds of conversations with different kinds of *content*. Examples of important content categories included pretending and talk about the past or future.
  - The number of seconds a child spent talking to different *conversational partners*. We coded for three kinds of partners: other children, the teacher, or no one (that is, the child was not engaged in any conversation for a period of 5 seconds).
  - The number of seconds that a child spent in different *activity settings* (for example, free play, mealtime, or large-group time)

The following data were obtained from teachers' audiotapes (see Table A10.2 in the appendix), focusing on large-group times and free play:

- Patterns of *vocabulary use* by teachers and children as they conversed with teachers. These patterns of use are considered to be *rare-word* usage as determined in the manner described in Chapter 9. We learned about the *amount of talk* that teachers and children used by counting the number of utterances[5] of teachers and children.
- The *content* of teachers' conversations with children. By *content*, we mean what was talked about. Examples included talk about past or future events, talk about science-related topics, or efforts to reprimand children or control their behavior.
- The *function* of a teacher's or child's comments. By *function*, we mean what the speaker was attempting to accomplish. For example, some

---

[4]All audiotapes were transcribed by one person and then listened to and corrected by a second person (that is, no one person both transcribed and corrected the same transcript).

[5]An utterance may have been a single word, a phrase, or a full sentence. We based coding decisions on units of speech in which the rise and fall of intonation was that of a distinct utterance.

comments are intended to explain something, others ask for or provide clarification, and others simply extend a topic. A single comment was coded for its content and its function.

What We Learned from These Different Kinds of Data

The audiotapes that were made of children's conversations focused on the patterns of time use and conversations of the children being studied. The tapes indicate how much time children spent in different activity settings, to whom they talked, and the content of their conversations. The tapes demonstrate how much the teacher talked during group times and what she was talking about. The child tapes provide information about each child's pattern of conversation during free play. Because these tapes reflect the target child's particular language-using habits, they allowed us to examine how the child's own language skill and conversational preferences shaped his or her classroom experience and subsequent development. Thus, by seeing how much children talked to other children and how much time they spent in verbalized fantasy play, one gets a sense of a child's patterns of language use.

The tapes of teachers' conversations provide a portrait of the classroom's language environment. The Home–School Study's analysis of patterns of use of individual words provides a fine-grained picture of language in the classroom as a whole. Unlike the data for the children's language use at home, the data about patterns of vocabulary use do not reflect any particular child's conversations because the teacher spoke only occasionally with the child whom researchers were simultaneously recording with the tape recorder in his or her backpack. Language experiences were examined at the level of the individual word (rare-word analyses), in terms of the meaning of the conversations (content codings of teacher and child tapes), and in terms of the purposes or functions of each utterance (for example, explaining). We wanted this multifaceted view of children's language experiences because individual words can be used in many ways. For example, an interesting word such as *oxygen* can be used to explain what oxygen is (for example, "It's the gas in tanks that helps you breathe underwater"), in a command (for example, "Give me oxygen!"), or in an accusatory question (for example, "Why did you throw the oxygen tank?"). In each case, the word used is the same; but for the listening child, the utterances are quite different. They require the child to assume a different stance in relationship to the teacher. The child may simply listen to the explanation, may have to carry out an action in response to the command, or may have to offer an apology or explanation in response to the question. Furthermore, these utterances convey different amounts of information about the word's meaning and appropriate usage.

RELATIONSHIPS BETWEEN LANGUAGE
EXPERIENCES AND DEVELOPMENT IN KINDERGARTEN

We examined many variables describing children's language experiences as we sought to identify links between children's early experiences and their kindergarten level of development. Here I report what we found as we looked at correlations between children's language experiences and the kindergarten assessments. When one examines the correlations among many variables, it becomes increasingly possible that one will find a statistically significant relationship between two variables by pure chance. There are two ways that we guarded against the possibility of mistaking chance findings for real relationships. First, analyses were guided by theory. That is, we only expected certain variables to relate to children's later development, so we only examined certain relationships. Second, in discussing the results, I highlight and discuss only the findings that exhibit a consistent pattern across multiple kindergarten outcomes and classroom variables.

In an effort to provide as complete a picture of overall patterns of results as possible, we provide results that are likely to have occurred by chance fewer than 5 times in 100 ($p < .05$), the usual point at which findings are considered to be statistically significant. We also display results with a probability of occurring by chance fewer than 10 times in 100 ($p < .10$) (see the appendix). In this discussion, much greater weight is placed on results at or below the $p < .05$ level and less significant results are considered only when they are part of a broader pattern of similar results. The full set of correlations is overwhelming; therefore, the overall pattern of findings that is shown in Table 10.2 is the focus. Each finding reported in Table 10.2 reflects evidence that the behavior listed was related to two or more child outcomes in kindergarten.

CONTRIBUTIONS OF GROUP TIMES TO
LANGUAGE AND LITERACY IN KINDERGARTEN

The results reveal relationships between children's group time experiences and their kindergarten performances on the assessments. In Table 10.2 we display the overall pattern of results that show significant and consistent patterns across different data sources for all 3 years of data collection (see Tables A10.1–A10.4 in the appendix for detailed statistical results). Large-group experiences that benefited children can be summarized as follows:

- Group times were well organized.
- Teachers avoided extended interactions with a single child.

Table 10.2. Patterns of large-group and free-play conversational experiences during preschool and kindergarten that relate to kindergarten language and literacy development

3-year-old visit			
Free play		**Large group**	
Positive correlation	Negative correlation	Positive correlation	Negative correlation
% child talk to child	*% no talk by child*	% group focus	% extending: teacher
			% extending: children
% pretend by child		*% talk by teacher*	
% literacy talk			
# child rare types		*% cognitive extending*	
# rare words			
% teacher rare types		% explaining: teacher	
% rare words		% explaining: children	
		% cognitively challenging: teacher	

4-year-old visit			
Free play		**Large group**	
Positive correlation	Negative correlation	Positive correlation	Negative correlation
# child types	% explaining: teacher	% group focus	% extending: teacher
# child words			% extending: children
# child rare types			
# child rare words			
% child rare types			
% teacher rare words		# children's words	
		# children's types	
Teacher–child ratio (more children is better)		# teacher types	
		# teacher rare types	
		% teacher rare types	
% extending: teacher		*% cognitive expanding*	
% extending: children		*% nonpresent*	
% cognitively challenging: teacher		% explaining: teacher	
		% explaining: children	

Kindergarten visit[a]			
Free play		**Large group**	
Positive correlation	Negative correlation	Positive correlation	Negative correlation
% child talk to child			
% pretend by child			
% literacy talk			

Note: Italic type is used for results from the audiotaping of the children's conversations. Plain type is used for results that come from the audiotaping of the teachers' conversations.

[a]In kindergarten, we did not have tapes of the teachers' conversations; therefore, we could not code for rare-word usage or patterns of the content of teachers' conversations.

- Teachers and children engaged in intellectually stimulating conversations.

- Teachers used a variety of vocabulary words.

Content of Teacher's Talk During Group Times   Central to effective group times seems to be the effort of the teacher to use the time for instructional purposes. Evidence of this effort can be seen in the pattern of significant relationships between strategies indicating attempts to keep the group focused and children's scores on our kindergarten assessments. Strategies for holding the group's attention that were grouped included asking children to attend, taking steps to control their behavior, evaluating children's responses, and, when necessary, correcting their incorrect responses. Each year, such group-focusing strategies were strongly related to several of the kindergarten assessments. In the two classrooms illustrated in the transcripts in this chapter, both Mrs. Washington and Ann kept their groups on task and were willing to stop children and correct them when necessary.

Of course, it is not enough simply to keep a group orderly; the teacher also needs to provide children with opportunities to learn. Data from the teacher tapes provide evidence of the value of teachers' efforts to engage children in stimulating conversations. We analyzed teachers' patterns of engaging children in cognitively challenging conversations and used statistical procedures to identify those types of talk that tended to go together. When the children were 3, we created two such clusters. One cluster, called *cognitive abstractions,* combined talk about generalizations about the physical world (for example, "Why does it snow?") and about human motivations (for example, "Why do you think he is sad?"). A second cluster, called *nonpresent talk,* combined talk about nonpresent topics (for example, "What are you going to do this weekend?") and talk about books. When the children were 3, both of these clusters of cognitively challenging types of conversation were related to kindergarten assessments of early literacy and storytelling.

Further evidence pointing to the aspects of group times that were beneficial comes from the audiotaped data collected from the microphones the children were wearing. These data were coded using different systems, but the results point in directions similar to the teacher data. We found evidence of beneficial effects on Definitions, Story Comprehension, and Emergent Literacy if teachers talked more and some evidence of benefits when children heard more conversations that we coded as *cognitive extending* (that is, about the past and future or about ideas and language) and more *didactic talk* (that is, talk used to impart specific factual content knowledge).

When children were 4 years old, we saw similar kinds of talk by teachers correlating with later achievement of study children. Group times with more cognitive extending talk and talk about literacy were associated with somewhat stronger literacy scores a year later, and conversations that included nonpresent topics were associated with stronger vocabulary scores. Also, group meetings with extended periods of no "codable" talk (that is, periods of silence or side conversations between the teacher and other adults or individual children) were linked to lower performance on Narrative Production. A year later in kindergarten, even though children spent more time in group settings, we found fewer relationships between their experiences and our assessment of their literacy skills. The two significant findings that did emerge are noteworthy. Just as when children were 4, more talk about literacy was linked to better early literacy development. In contrast to findings when children were 3 and 4, more talk by teachers was related to lower child performance on our Narrative Production task, possibly reflecting a surfeit of group experiences and a shortage of time for children to use language themselves.

Across all 3 years, our coding of the content of talk during group settings indicates that these occasions can benefit children. The details vary somewhat year to year, but general patterns emerge: Orderly group times that have a cognitive orientation are beneficial. We now look at these times through the lens of vocabulary use and again will see indications of the impact of these settings on children's literacy development.

Vocabulary Use During Group Times The nature of teachers' and children's use of vocabulary revealed the importance of providing children with linguistically as well as intellectually rich experiences during group times in both years. When children were 3 and 4 years of age, their teachers' use of a variety of words was related to kindergarten development because the percentage of rare words that their teachers used out of all of the words they spoke during group times was related to the children's later development. Also, when the children were 4 years old, their teachers' use of varied words (teacher types) and varied kinds of rare words (rare types) was predictive of the children's later development. Ann's incidental use of words such as _flannel_ and _detectives_ is a prime example of how teachers could introduce many such words in a relatively short period of time. In addition to enriching the language-learning opportunities of group times with their own words, skilled teachers also could support children's language by providing room for children's voices in group times. This conclusion is based on the finding that the amount of children's talk and the variety of words that they used were correlated with their kindergarten test scores.

Further evidence of the potential of group times for supporting children's development comes from our finding that the percentage of talk coded as performing the function of explaining was related to all five child measures administered in kindergarten, with this result being strongest for Receptive Vocabulary. Earlier it was noted that during group times, explanations were used most often when teachers were telling children their reasons for particular decisions. This result suggests that children benefited when teachers included them in discussions about the reasons for teachers' actions. Thus, it may be that a willingness by a teacher to provide explanations during large-group times, a time when some teachers may be inclined simply to assert their authority, is associated with a tendency to listen to and be responsive to children. Such behavior appears to have long-term benefits for children's language and literacy growth.

Though we found considerable evidence of ways in which large-group meetings benefit children, there also can be a darker side to these events. Across both years, we found that group conversations with more turns coded as *extending* the same topic rather than *explaining* were associated with lower scores on all five of our kindergarten measures. These negative associations were strongest for Narrative Production and Receptive Vocabulary. Such extending can occur in conjunction with any topic, but repetitious reviews of information such as those seen in Mrs. Washington's room as she led children in a review of the days of the week was a common way that teachers fashioned long stretches of talk that we coded as "extending" a topic.

CONTRIBUTIONS OF FREE PLAY TO LANGUAGE AND LITERACY IN KINDERGARTEN

The results from the analysis of free play are interesting to compare with what was found for large-group times. One point of contrast between the two settings is that it was only when the children were age 3 that data from the child audiotapes provided evidence of long-term effects of the child's language-using skills and proclivities. When the children were 3 years old, those who were found talking with other children and not remaining silent for long periods later were most likely to do well on our literacy and language assessments (for example, Narrative Production or Receptive Vocabulary).

Similarly, children who engaged in more pretend talk were more likely to perform well on the assessments. These results reflect a complex interplay of the language-using skills that the children brought with them to preschool and the opportunities that teachers provided them. The data were collected in the spring; thus, children had several months to establish patterns of interacting and play that reflected the opportunities that their teachers provided them. To make this concept concrete, think of Astra's play when she was 3. Her teacher allowed an extended period of time for pretend play, which Astra made good use of. Furthermore, her peers apparently recognized Astra's power as a story creator because they quickly joined her in discussing new topics, thereby helping her to extend them. When Casey was 4, he showed evidence of having well-established patterns of play with his best friend. An association between time spent pretending and kindergarten outcomes when children were 4 also was found, as was a trend toward a positive association in kindergarten.

Evidence suggesting the impact of the children's preschool classroom experiences during free play on long-term language growth comes from results from both years indicating the beneficial effects of being in classrooms rich with varied vocabulary. We found consistent links between our kindergarten measures and the total number of words and the variety of words that children used during free play. We also found that the pattern of vocabulary use by teachers that was most beneficial included higher percentages of rare words. Unlike during group times, when the sheer number of interesting and varied words that teachers used also was beneficial, during free play, the most effective teachers were those who were selective in their choice of words as indicated by the fact that it was the relative amount of rare words used that was more predictive than the total number used. Further evidence of the importance of thoughtful teacher engagement with children during free play came from examination of the balance of talk between teachers and children. We found better kindergarten performance when the children as 4-year-olds had teachers who limited their own talking and gave children more time to talk. The way Ann talked to children during free play provides an example of effective free-play conversations. She listened to children, then spoke to them about the topic of their play, using interesting and varied words that were relevant to the theme of their play.

The free-play results from when children were 4 years of age present another interesting contrast to the large-group findings. When we examined the function of teachers' comments during free play we found a pattern that was the opposite of what we found for large-group times. That is, children who had experienced free-play times in which teachers did more explaining tended to have lower kindergarten outcomes, and when teachers did more extending of topics, the children tended to have stronger kindergarten outcomes. This is the exact reverse of what we found for group times, when explanatory talk was beneficial and extending talk was not. To make sense of these findings, one needs to think about the differences between the two settings. During free play, if a teacher is extending a topic, the conversation is occurring with a single child who presumably is actively engaged in the conversation. When a teacher develops an extended topic with an individual child in a large group, however, many children are likely to tune out the conversation. Thus, the data indicate that children benefit when teachers engage them in extended conversations one-to-one during free play. Such conversations are especially likely to be beneficial when teachers allow children many opportunities to talk. The negative relationship between explanations during free play and later language development likely reflects the pattern discussed previously: Teachers tended to engage in long explanations during free play when they were resolving problems and explaining why a particular rule was being enforced. Though explanations during free play tended to have negative effects on later vocabulary and literacy skills, children tended to do better on kindergarten Emergent Literacy tasks if their teachers had engaged them in conversations that included personal narratives, talk about past and present events, and discussion of ideas. In the same vein, in kindergarten, the amount of time that children were observed talking about literacy-related topics was related to our assessment of their early literacy skills.

CONCLUSIONS

The Home–School Study's examination of relationships between the details of teachers' and children's conversations during the classroom day and their performance on measures of language and literacy development near the end of kindergarten has yielded a host of results that point to the importance of conversations during the classroom day for children's later language and literacy development. In looking across the full array of our data, three major points stand out:

1. The conversations that children have during the classroom day when they are 3 and 4 years old are related to a broad range of skills using oral language and print at the end of kindergarten. Thus, efforts to support early literacy development must not have an overly singular focus on print and print-based activities to the detriment of providing rich opportunities for oral language development.

2. There are important differences among activity settings. We found more evidence of effects of teachers' behaviors during group times and more evidence of children's impact on each other during free play. Also, we found that the same behavior may have opposite

effects, depending on whether it occurs in a large-group setting or during free play (for example, extending a topic). Thus, teachers need to tailor strategies to particular settings, and researchers need to be cautious about combining data across settings.

3. The full conversational environment that children experience needs to be kept in mind, considering both the input of the teacher and that of other children. We found that the talk of both teachers and other children is related to children's long-term development. The finding of the effects of children on each other has far-reaching policy implications because it speaks to the multitude of decisions that determine which children are placed in the same classroom.

These major points are discussed in more detail in Chapters 11 and 12. Next, I turn to consideration of what the study's findings suggest about the effective use of large-group and free-play times.

SUGGESTIONS FOR TEACHERS

Large-Group Times

Effective large-group times include focused and purposeful conversations. Teachers who are effective do the following:

*   They hold the attention of the group by asking for attention, calling on individuals, evaluating children's contributions, and, when necessary, correcting misinformation that children produce.
*   They avoid long stretches of talk during which they simply extend the same topic or encourage a single child to review information.
*   They incorporate varied vocabulary into what they say and encourage children to use novel words.
*   They ensure that their talk is informative, challenges children to think, and provides explanations of what they and the group are doing.

It is worth noting that we did not find a relationship between the length of meetings and children's outcomes. This lack of finding suggests that what matters most is the activities that teachers employ and how they interact with children.

It would be helpful if our data could link specific common large-group practices such as discussing the calendar, taking attendance, and reviewing academic material to children's outcomes. Though we cannot do this directly, the study's results provide some basis for speculation. For example, the pattern of negative effects of talk that extends a single topic during large-group times suggests that teachers should avoid interactions that engage a single child in a long conversation. Asking individual children to engage in extended reviews of information (for example, days of the week) results in the type of extended sequences that the data indicate are counterproductive.

The evidence of the beneficial effects of using varied vocabulary leads to the recommendation that activities that provide occasions for talk about varied topics and introduction of new words are valuable. This could occur during sharing and calendar times if the teacher were to take steps to vary the content of what is discussed.

Singing also is a way that teachers may introduce varied vocabulary into group times. Songs often include interesting and varied vocabulary. Although we did not find evidence of a relationship between time spent singing and children's language and literacy growth, this could be because the songs that teachers selected had only a limited range of words or because teachers did not draw children's attention to novel words. For children, unfamiliar words sung in songs may be so tightly linked to the rhythm, tune, and phrasing of the songs that they are unable to identify distinct words. Thus, to take advantage of the word-learning opportunities that songs provide, teachers should use unfamiliar lyric words in sentences and briefly discuss them to help children understand their meanings. Even fleeting exposure to the meanings of words can lay the foundation for children's eventual acquisition of the complete meaning of a word (Dickinson, 1984).

Free-Play Time

Free play is the time when children flex their linguistic and conceptual muscles and contribute to each other's development. Major findings that point to effective practices during free play are as follows:

- Children's pretending provides them with important opportunities to develop literacy-related language skills. Across all 3 years, we found associations between the amount of time that children engaged in pretending and their performance on our outcome measures.

- Children need to be allowed to talk to other children during free play. Across all 3 years, we found indications of positive outcomes that were associated with time spent talking to other children.

- Teachers need to encourage children to use varied vocabulary as they talk with adults in the classroom and as they play with each other. Children benefited from playing with other children who used varied vocabulary.

- Teachers should engage individual children in conversations that are sustained over several turns and should ensure that there is "space" in the conversation for children to talk.

- Teachers should use a variety of words, striving to include a high percentage of relatively novel words.

- Teachers should engage children in conversations that are intellectually challenging.

So, what are some strategies that are consistent with these general guidelines and that teachers can adopt during free play? Clearly, teachers should provide time for children to engage in pretend play, spur children's pretending, and encourage children's use of varied vocabulary by supplying attractive props and interesting play areas. To increase the chances that children will introduce varied vocabulary into their play, classroom areas and props should be changed periodically because new objects and play topics will naturally result in changes in children's conversations. When areas and props are linked to an ongoing theme, teachers can introduce new words and play themes during story times and in large-group discussions. Also, providing materials that spark literacy activities (see Linder, 1999, and Neuman & Roskos, 1993b, for guidance) will help increase the amount of literacy-related talk, a topic of conversation during free play that was found to be linked to outcomes for the children when they were 3 and 5 years old. A small caveat about free-play time should be noted: Results from teachers' reports of how they used time during the day when the children were 3 suggest that that too much free play can have negative consequences. Teachers need to retain a balance between free play and more structured times.

The other clear message regarding free play is that teachers should strive to engage children in extended conversations. Data that I have collected for another study[6] show that teachers often move quickly from one topic to the next, limiting the extent to which a single topic is developed. Teachers need to be aware of this tendency and strive to sustain their interactions with individual children. I also have found that some teachers often move about the room, organizing activities and managing behaviors. Not surprisingly, when teachers are moving around, they are unlikely to engage children in meaningful conversations. Teachers need to attempt to remain in one place for a time so that more extended conversations with individual children can develop.

---

[6]These data were collected for work being done by the New England Quality Research Center, one of four Quality Research Centers supported by the Head Start Bureau.

The results reported in this chapter make apparent how challenging it is to be a successful preschool teacher. What teachers do with children throughout the day can make a difference—group times as well as free play provide important opportunities to foster children's language and literacy development. Furthermore, the effective teacher needs to shift his or her interactional style between large-group times and one-to-one conversations, changing from being a strong organizer and provider of information to being a good listener. He or she also needs to push him- or herself intellectually, providing children with interesting activities. When talking to children, the preschool teacher needs to draw on his or her knowledge of the world and use varied words to express thoughts and feelings rather than rely on a comfortable familiar repertoire. Finally, the effective preschool teacher needs to create a classroom community in which children have many interesting subjects to talk about because they are provided with a curriculum and classroom environment that enable them to support their friends' language and understanding of the world as they converse and play.

Chapter 11

Putting the Pieces Together
Impact of Preschool on Children's Language and Literacy Development in Kindergarten

David K. Dickinson

The previous chapters reporting data from preschool classrooms visited during the Home–School Study of Language and Literacy Development examine the classroom experiences of our children through selected lenses. Chapter 7 describes three teachers in some detail and considers the connections between their practice and reported pedagogical beliefs. Chapters 8–10 examine conversations during different classroom settings—book reading, mealtimes, and free-play and large-group times—and identify key features of these settings and describe the kinds of conversations that relate to our children's later language and literacy development. By this point, the reader may be wondering how these pieces fit together. Do teachers who engage in supportive conversations during mealtimes also have effective book-reading times? Do teachers who plan for small-group times and support children's writing also engage in good conversations during free play? As one strives to answer these questions, one will gain a better understanding of the factors that influence teachers' instructional practices. Our search for factors that have an impact on teachers includes aspects of their personal histories (for example, education and racial and ethnic identity) as well as en-

Kathleen Holmes provided invaluable assistance with the data analyses conducted for this chapter. Kevin Roach and Patton Tabors also assisted with analyses. Linda Cote and Miriam Smith played invaluable roles with many aspects of the preschool classroom effort from data collection, to coding, to the initial data analyses. Margo Sweet spent many hours helping construct tables and working on figures. I thank them all for their assistance.

vironmental factors associated with their classroom (for example, teacher–child ratio or number of children learning English), and the families they serve (for example, income or education).

Of course, ultimately we are interested in children's preschool experiences; therefore, this chapter investigates factors that shape preschool classrooms by looking at children's conversations with teachers and other children and identifying the impact of dimensions of classrooms and of home background on their classroom experiences. The chapter concludes by discussing the impact of preschool on children's subsequent development. To do this I combine many of our different ways of capturing children's experiences in preschool and determine how much they affect children's development in kindergarten. I conclude by summarizing the portraits of teachers that we have been developing in earlier chapters and link them to what we have learned from our quantitative analyses about how children's classroom experiences contribute to different aspects of their emerging literacy skills.

All of the analyses reported in this chapter discuss data from when the children in our study were 4 years old. We chose to focus on this age to simplify our reporting and because it is the age for which we have the most complete data. From a policy point of view, this is an important age because it is when many children are beginning to attend center-based programs.

DIMENSIONS OF CHILDREN'S CLASSROOM EXPERIENCES

Aspects of Teachers' Conversations

During free play and mealtimes, we considered teachers' *rare-word use*.[1] The frequency with which teachers used relatively uncommon or "rare" words was especially interesting because, as discussed in Chapter 5, rare-word use by parents is an important predictor of children's later development. Interestingly, similar to what we found in the home, exposure to conversations that include low-frequency vocabulary words has a beneficial effect on children's language development. We found that the percentage of rare words that teachers used in free play and mealtimes was related to three of our kindergarten assessments: Formal Definitions, Emergent Literacy, and Receptive Vocabulary (see Figures 11.1 and 11.2 and Table A11.1 in the appendix).

An important aspect of teacher–child conversations is children's contributions. Our analysis of rare-word use revealed that the use of

---

[1]*Rare words* are words that were not included on a list of words that children this age would commonly be expected to know. See Chapter 9, which discusses the procedures used to identify these words.

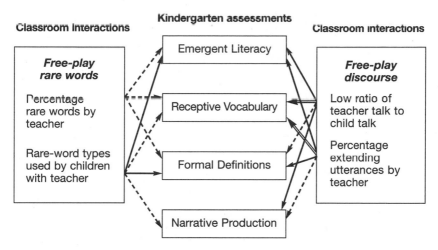

Figure 11.1. Correlations between selected aspects of teacher–child interaction when children were 4 and kindergarten language and literacy assessments. (‑‑▶ $p < .05$; ▶ $p < .01$; ⟹ $p < .001$.)

rare words by the children in the classroom while talking to their teachers also related to all four kindergarten assessments (see Figure 11.1).

We also considered two aspects of teachers' conversational styles during free play. One interesting feature of teachers' talk was the *ratio of teacher talk to child talk*. Research on mother–child conversations has shown that children acquire language best when their mothers listen to them and tailor their comments to the interests and needs of their child. Therefore, we expected that teachers who spent relatively less time speaking and more time listening to children would be better able to support children's development. We found support for this hypothesis: In classrooms where teachers had a lower rate of teacher talk to child talk during free play, children had stronger scores on all four of our kindergarten assessments of Narrative Production, Formal Definitions, Emergent Literacy, and Receptive Vocabulary. A second feature of teachers' free-play conversations was their inclination to speak to children in ways that extended children's comments. Teachers did this by indicating interest, asking questions designed to encourage children to clarify themselves, and by commenting on children's efforts. The number of such "extending" utterances was related to all of our end-of-kindergarten assessments.

We also examined teachers' conversational styles in group settings. In group book-reading sessions, as discussed in Chapter 8, teachers' comments that involved *analysis of books* were associated with children's subsequent Receptive Vocabulary scores (see Figure 11.2). These con-

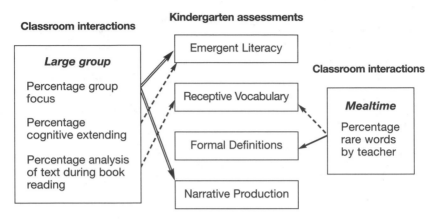

Figure 11.2. Correlations between selected aspects of teacher–child interaction when children were 4 and kindergarten language and literacy assessments. ($--\blacktriangleright$ $p < .05$; $\longrightarrow$ $p < .01$; $\Longrightarrow$ $p < .001$.)

versations often dealt with such issues as the setting and the attributes and motivations of characters. Another aspect of teachers' approach to conversing with children in large groups was their tendency to *focus the attention of the group*. Talk designed to focus the attention of the group included use of children's names and brief comments calling for attention. Such comments reflect teacher efforts to keep all of the children focused on what was being discussed and indicate that the teacher values child attentiveness during group times. We found that group focusing was strongly related to growth in Emergent Literacy and Narrative Production. It was marginally related ($p < .10$) to growth in Receptive Vocabulary and Formal Definitions. A third important feature of teachers' conversations during large-group activities was the extent to which they engaged children in intellectually challenging conversations. Discussions that involved talk about ideas or the meanings of words are examples of this kind of talk and were related to stronger Emergent Literacy scores.

Aspects of Classroom Environments and Pedagogical Beliefs

Several of our measures of the curriculum in children's classrooms were correlated with later performance on our assessments (for extended discussion, see Chapter 7). Noteworthy aspects of classrooms included a well-equipped writing area (for example, a distinct area or needed tools), a curriculum with strong content (for example, a theme that changed or displays indicating recent work by children), and teachers' support of language as ascertained from the language subscale of the Early

Childhood Environment Rating Scale (ECERS; Harms & Clifford, 1980; see Table 11.1).

Other information about teachers' pedagogy came from the interview, during which they told us how they scheduled their classroom day and indicated what they saw as being the most important benefits of preschool for children. One feature of teachers' use of time proved to be positively related to children's later growth—the amount of time they planned for small-group and individual activities. On the other hand, we found that children whose teachers placed heavy emphasis on the socioemotional benefits of preschool tended to do somewhat less well on our kindergarten assessment of Narrative Production.

Consistency in Pedagogy   With richly varied descriptions of the classroom practices of teachers, I am able to examine the extent to which teachers display consistent instructional approaches across the multiple dimensions of classroom instruction that we have examined. To identify aspects of teachers' approaches to children that provide evidence of consistency, I first examine how teachers talk with children across different settings. Next I examine the curriculum teachers provided, and then I consider the pedagogical beliefs teachers expressed to us. As a result of examining these many dimensions of teachers' instructional practices and beliefs, I identify two general orientations. One orientation I call a *Traditional Child Development Orientation,* and the other I call an *Academic Orientation.*

Table 11.1. Relationship between kindergarten assessments and observations of teacher pedagogy as revealed through observation of classrooms and interviews about teacher pedagogy

	Narrative Production	Formal Definitions	Emergent Literacy	Receptive Vocabulary
Writing area	.315** $n = 75$		.231* $n = 74$	.431*** $n = 75$
Curriculum Content		.194⁻ $n = 75$	.214⁻ $n = 74$	.234* $n = 75$
ECERS[a] language		.293** $n = 75$		.214⁻ $n = 75$
Small-group time			.234⁻ $n = 59$	.23⁻ $n = 60$
Socioemotional pedagogical focus	−.252* $n = 67$			

For these analyses we are employing data that include imputed values when selected observations were missing. As a result, values reported here may differ slightly from those reported in previous chapters. In no case does this affect the general findings being reported. This is the data set that is used in partial correlational and regression analyses reported later in this chapter and in Chapter 13.

[a]Early Childhood Environment Rating Scale (Harms & Clifford, 1980).

⁻$p < .10$; *$p < .05$; **$p < .01$; ***$p < .001$.

Consistency in Conversational Strategies   Are teachers consistent in how they talk with children throughout the day? To answer this question, we examined teachers' conversations across settings to see whether we could find evidence of consistency in how teachers talk to children in different settings (for example, free play, mealtimes, book reading, and large-group times) and found relatively little evidence of consistency across dimensions or settings. When we compared teachers' rare-word use in free play and mealtimes, two situations that allow for informal one-to-one and small-group conversations, we found no statistically significant indications that teachers who use rare words in one setting are more likely to do so in the other setting. Similarly, we found no relationship between teachers' use of rare words during large-group times and free play and mealtime.

With regard to measures of teacher conversations in large-group settings, book reading, and group meeting times, we found some evidence of consistency within these settings across these two behaviors. During book reading, teachers who engaged in more analytical talk about books also tended to use more rare words as they discussed books ($r = .29$, $p = .03$, $n = 55$) and in large-group conversations ($r = .26$, $p = .03$, $n = 68$). With regard to a different aspect of large-group conversations, group focusing strategies, we found no relationship between group focusing during mealtimes and text analysis during book reading. We found some evidence, however, that teachers who did more focusing during group times were less likely to use rare words when talking with children during large-group times ($r = -.27$, $p = .02$, $n = 69$).

Thus, when we examined both small- and large-group times, we found only limited evidence that teachers who used one type of effective verbal strategy more often in one setting also used other strategies in that same setting. We also found little evidence that teachers were consistent in their use of the same effective strategy across settings.

Consistency in Literacy Support   We now turn to our classroom observation data about the support teachers provided for children's language and literacy, use of print and books, and provision of a rich curriculum. In these data, we found evidence of relationships between our rating of classrooms' support for writing and other variables (see Table 11.2). Teachers who received high marks for their environmental support for writing also were rated highly for the content of their curriculum and the quality of their book-reading area. Strong writing support also was linked to provision of time for small groups. This set of results suggests that teachers' support for children's writing may reflect a more generalized orientation toward actively fostering literacy and language development.

Table 11.2. Interrelationships among variables reflecting teacher pedagogy and instruction related to supporting language and literacy development

	ECERS[a] language	Curriculum content	Small-group time	Socioemotional focus	Book area
Writing area	.40***	.29*			.260*
	n = 73	n = 63			n = 72
ECERS language			.21⁻	.28*	.340**
			n = 73	n = 73	n = 64

[a]Early Childhood Environment Rating Scale (Harms & Clifford, 1980).
⁻$p < .10$; *$p < .05$; **$p < .01$; ***$p < .001$.

The other evidence of interrelationships among classroom curriculum data was the links among the language subscale of the ECERS (Harms & Clifford, 1980), the quality of the book areas, and a socioemotional pedagogical focus. When a teacher received a high ECERS language score, this indicated that the observer judged her to be actively engaged in conversations with children and providing activities that support language development. This tool values responsiveness and intentional efforts to engage children in informal conversations as well as instructionally focused talk. It seems that teachers who are perceived as adopting such strategies tend to hold a pedagogical orientation that is marked by concern for social and emotional aspects of development. With the exception of the ratings of the book area, no variables in the ECERS clustering of scores were also in the cluster related to writing. These two sets of variables seem to reflect different orientations in how teachers work with children: a more academic and instructionally focused approach versus an approach more attuned to children's social and emotional development.

Relating Pedagogy and Curriculum to Conversations

I now bring together two dimensions of classroom instruction, conversational strategies and our measures of classrooms and teachers' pedagogical beliefs. Looking across these dimensions, one can find a cluster of language variables that are associated with the ECERS language scores (see Table 11.3). Teachers with higher ECERS scores were much more likely to engage children in analytical conversations about books, to use rare words during mealtimes and free play. As discussed previously (see Table 11.2), ECERS scores also related to our pedagogy variable that indicated emphasis on the importance of socioemotional development and of the presence of an attractive book-reading area. Thus, there is further evidence of a pedagogical style that we refer to as a *Traditional Child Development Orientation*. It includes the following:

Table 11.3.   Relationships among teacher–child conversations and measures of classroom curriculum

	ECERS[a] language	Writing area	Curriculum content	Percentage of small-group time	Socioemotional focus
Group times					
Book reading: text analysis	.40*** $n = 71$				
Large-group focus	-.30** $n = 73$		.39*** $n = 73$		−.32** $n = 73$
Large-group teacher cognitive extend- ing		.24* $n = 73$			
Free play					
Percentage of rare words by teacher	.378** $n = 62$	.30** $n = 69$			.20⁻ $n = 69$
Percentage of turns teacher extends child		.30** $n = 73$	.32** $n = 73$		
Ratio of teacher talk to child talk in free play					
Mealtime					
Rare words used by teacher	.37** $n = 69$				

[a]Early Childhood Environment Rating Scale (Harms & Clifford, 1980).
⁻$p < .10$; *$p < .05$; **$p < .01$; ***$p < .001$.

- Use of rare words by teachers during mealtimes, free play, and large-group times

- Analytical conversations about books during group book reading

- An inviting book area

- High scores on the language section of the ECERS rating scale

- A tendency to place a high value on children's social and emotional development

Figure 11.3 depicts aspects of practices included in the Traditional Child Development Orientation and the Academic Orientation.

We noted that three classroom curriculum variables tended to go together: teachers' provision of a strong writing area, having a curriculum with varied content, and planning for small groups. When we relate these variables to our measures of classroom interaction we find another cluster of variables that seem to be rather distinct from those linked to the Traditional Child Development Orientation. We called this second dimension the *Academic Orientation*. The language variables that tend to go with the classroom curriculum variables are as follows:

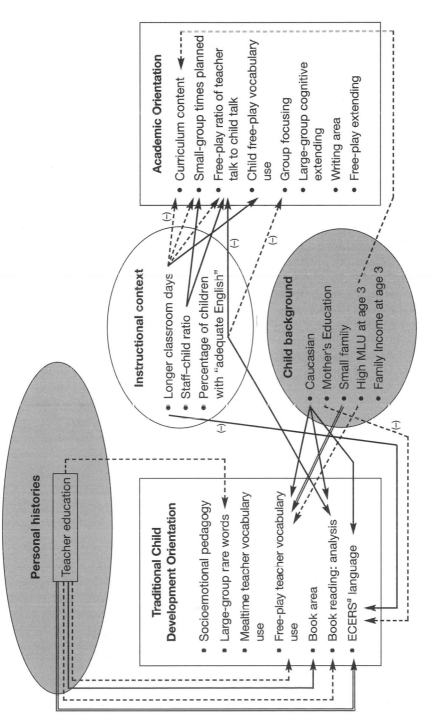

Figure 11.3. Ecological model of the impact of personal history, instructional context, and family and child background factors on classroom instructional practices. (- - -▶ $p < .05$; ───▶ $p < .01$; ═══▶ $p < .001$; (-) indicates a negative relationship.)

- Percentage of teacher utterances during free play that extend a child's talk (correlates with the ratio of teacher talk to child talk during free play [$r = .37, p = .001, n = 73$], curriculum content [$r = .32, p = .006, n = 73$], and quality of writing area [$r = .30, p = .01, n = 73$])

- Ratio of teacher talk to child talk during free play (correlates with teacher efforts to help children extend their talk during free play [$r = .37, p = .001, n = 73$] and group focusing [$r = .28, p = .02, n = 73$])

- Teacher engagement of children in cognitively rich conversations during large-group time (correlates with quality of the writing area [$r = .24, p < .04, n = 73$])

Thus, it appears that some teachers adopt what we are calling an Academic Orientation, a pedagogical approach characterized by a concern for children's language and intellectual development (see Figure 11.3).

FACTORS AFFECTING TEACHERS' CLASSROOM PRACTICES

Having identified significant teaching behaviors and two general instructional orientations, each of which includes practices that support children's language and literacy development, I now seek to identify factors that might help account for these patterns. First, I examine the relationship between classroom practices and aspects of teachers' personal histories and contextual factors, including information about a teacher's program and the families and children she teaches.

Aspects of Teachers' Personal Histories

One possibility is that the teacher carries sets of beliefs or interactional patterns with her that reflect the impact of important dimensions of her personal history. I consider two such possible sources of influence: teacher education and the racial composition of the staff in the center.

The years of education teachers received were related to our measures of teacher–child conversations and classroom curriculum. We found that more highly educated teachers used more rare words during free play and engaged in more analytical conversations during book reading (see Table A11.2 in the appendix). Figure 11.3 displays relationships between teachers' personal histories and classroom practices in a graphic form. Teachers with more education also had more inviting book areas and received higher ECERS language scores. Thus, aspects of teachers' personal histories that are reflected in their having more college education play an important role in how they talk with children in different settings throughout the day.

Another personal history factor that might account for aspects of teacher practice is the racial and ethnic identity of an individual. One's racial and cultural identity can have important and subtle effects on how an adult uses language as he or she relates to other adults and children (Heath, 1983; Smitherman, 1977), and the racial background of a teacher has been found to be related to his or her pedagogical beliefs in some cases (Heaviside & Farris, 1993). Therefore, when we visited classrooms we asked teachers how many teachers and assistant teachers were from different racial groups. When we visited classrooms, we neglected to record the race or ethnicity of the teacher we were interviewing and recording. As a result, we do not attempt to relate specific aspects of teachers' practices to these background variables.

We did seek to understand how the type of classroom (i.e., Head Start, private preschool) might be related to the racial backgrounds of the staff. Therefore, for our analyses we created a variable that described the staff of classrooms in one of three ways: 1) all Caucasian, 2) Caucasian and minority backgrounds, and 3) all from minority groups. Usually the minority group represented was African American; our sample was too small to allow us to analyze any single non-Caucasian group. We found that the staff in preschool centers where we were collecting data were most likely to include teachers from minority groups when the center was not a Head Start center ($r = .412$, $p = .0004$, $n = 71$) and offered extended day services ($r = .493$, $p < .0001$, $n = 71$). It is important to remember that this finding reflects only the pattern seen in our sample, which unfortunately did not include the Head Start programs[2] based in nearby areas with the largest numbers of African American families. We anticipate that both the racial and ethnic composition of the staff in preschools have important and complicated effects on how teachers realte to children as well as to parents, but careful consideration of these issues is beyond the scope of this study.

Classroom, Center, and Family Factors and Teachers' Instructional Approaches

We found some evidence of consistency across dimensions of teachers' practice and evidence that aspects of teachers' personal histories help account for some of their classroom practices. But we also found considerable variability from one setting to the next and one aspect of prac-

---

[2]Despite our best efforts we were not able to gain permission to conduct our research in certain key locations that would have provided us a more representative mix.

tice to the next, suggesting that important environmental influences may shape teachers' pedagogical practices. First, I consider whether teachers' instructional practices are affected by the centers and programs in which they work. The nature of teacher–child conversations could be affected by center-related factors such as group size and teacher–child ratio. Also, accepted ways of doing things within a classroom[3] could play a role in shaping teachers' decisions about such issues as time use, the organization of the room, and the importance placed on supporting writing. A pedagogical culture in classrooms and centers also may affect how teachers relate to children. For example, when beginning to work in a classroom, new teachers may observe the extent to which other teachers engage children in discussions as they read books or use varied vocabulary during free play and then may adopt practices consistent with other staff. I also consider the possibility that children's families and the language skills of children may have an impact on classroom conversations and curriculum. For example, families with higher incomes and educational backgrounds may send children to preschool more inclined to tell stories and use varied vocabulary. Teachers then may be more inclined to engage in high-level conversations with children having such language skills. Parents also may influence teachers' pedagogy by expressing a desire that their children learn certain knowledge and skills while in preschool. Such expressions of parental concern might have special impact on private programs because they depend on parent fees to support the program.[4] Thus, even though our families represent a rather narrow range of income levels and educational backgrounds, we might find some evidence of home effects on how teachers relate to children and structure their classrooms.

Center Effects on Instructional Strategies   Child care centers might affect the nature of teacher–child conversations during free play. Three such factors that we consider are teacher–child ratio, the average level of English fluency of the children in the class, and the length of the program day. One might expect that teachers working in classrooms with more favorable staff–child ratios and higher proportions of children who speak English proficiently would face fewer management

---

[3]The terms *classroom, center,* and *program* can be confusing. In our use of these terms, the highest organizational unit is the program. Some programs are large enough to have several centers, with each center having one or more classrooms.

[4]Half of our children were in private programs, but most were supported by state preschool vouchers. Thus, the parents of our children may not have been paying for their child to attend preschool, but the parents of other children in these programs certainly were paying fees.

challenges and might use a broader range of vocabulary because they could become more deeply involved in high-level conversations. We found no evidence of such effects. We also found no connection between word use and the type of the program, suggesting that teachers' patterns of using rare words are determined by factors specific to the teacher and not by the instructional setting.

The second variable that described teacher–child talk during free play that we examined was the ratio of teacher talk to child talk. This aspect of classroom conversations was related to the number of teachers per child (see Figure 11.3 and Table A11.2 in the appendix). The better the teacher–child ratio (more teachers per child), the more likely it was that the teacher would allow the child "space" to participate in the conversation. We also found that the number of children whom teachers deemed as able to speak English reasonably well was related to the ratio of teacher talk to child talk. If teachers rated more children as being able to converse in English, they were less likely to stop and listen; rather, the teachers tended to talk more. When teachers had more children they deemed to have limited English skills, they tended to speak less and listen more. This tendency to listen to children learning a language is a valuable strategy given that it can take especially keen listening skills to understand children who are struggling to communicate in a new language. We also found that the type of program that children were in related to the ratio of teacher talk to child talk. Teachers in programs with a longer day and in private child care centers were somewhat more likely to allow children more time to speak.

We also found evidence that conversations during large-group settings are affected by classroom factors (see Figure 11.3 and Table A11.2 in the appendix). During book reading we found that teachers engaged in more analytical talk when they rated more children as having "adequate" English language skills, suggesting that when teachers are reading to children in classrooms with significant numbers of children with limited English skills, they may reduce the cognitive demand level of their conversations. They may tend to ask questions designed to ensure basic understanding rather than challenging children to reflect on the story.

When we considered possible effects of classroom factors on our measures of classroom learning environment curriculum, we found evidence of some relationships between the curriculum and the length of the classroom day. We found that in full-day programs, teachers were more likely to plan time for small groups and less likely to receive high ratings for the content of their curriculum as reflected in ECERS scores and ratings of the content of their curriculum. Thus, the effort to plan times for small groups suggests that teachers in longer programs strive to provide children instructional opportunities, but that they are somewhat less successful in providing varied curriculum opportunities.

Family Effects on Teacher–Child Conversation   When we considered possible effects of family and child backgrounds on classroom interactions, we found a cluster of results that indicate the impact of such factors on important aspects of teachers' practices. But before these results are discussed, it is important to emphasize that our sample is small and far from ideal. In particular, due to difficulties we had in involving Head Start programs with sizable numbers of African American families, in our sample children from different backgrounds are not evenly spread across different kinds of programs. When we compared children in our sample who were in Head Start with those in private or school-based programs, we found that the Head Start children had the following characteristics: More were Caucasian ($r = .32$, $p = .002$, $n = 71$) and more economically disadvantaged ($r = .44$, $p < .001$, $n = 69$), and their mothers had less education ($r = .37$, $p = .002$, $n = 71$). Head Start programs tended to have shorter days ($r = .58$, $p < .001$, $n = 71$) and more children per teacher ($r = .37$, $p = .003$, $n = 63$). Teachers in Head Start centers received higher ECERS language scores ($r = .24$, $p = .04$, $n = 71$) and were more likely to be Caucasian ($r = .41$, $p < .001$, $n = 71$). These features of our sample are mentioned because they affect all of our efforts to relate classroom and family contexts to children's classroom experiences.

When we looked at the indirect effects of family and child background factors on the quality of classroom conversations, we found strong evidence of effects of these factors on patterns of classroom interaction. We were particularly interested in determining whether the backgrounds of children's families were related to the level of intellectual and linguistic challenges of teacher–child conversations as measured by the frequency with which teachers used varied vocabulary when speaking with children. What we found was somewhat disturbing. During free play, the time when teachers can most readily adjust their conversations to match children's needs and interests, teachers were more likely to use rare words when they were talking with children who came from smaller families, were Caucasian, and had a higher Mean Length of Utterance (MLU)[5] at age 3 (see Figure 11.3 and Table A11.2 in the appendix). Finally, classrooms that were given higher ECERS language scores tended to be those attended by children involved in the study who were Caucasian and whose mothers had more education.

---

[5]In this study, Mean Length of Utterance (MLU) is a measure of the child's verbal production at age 3. It is based on the child's conversations during toy play at home at the end of his or her first year of preschool.

These findings pointing to relationships between children's home experiences and their classroom experiences suggest that children who enter preschool with some slight social and linguistic advantages may be more likely to benefit from the teacher–child interactions that we found to be beneficial to their long-term development. Thus, it could be that teachers are more inclined to engage somewhat more linguistically advantaged children in the kinds of interactions that foster long-term development.

Summary   In the Home–School Study, we examined patterns in teachers' use of strategies that are correlated with children's end-of-kindergarten progress. One of our goals was to understand patterns in how different contextual factors influence classroom experiences. We found rather limited evidence of consistency in the conversational strategies of teachers at different times of the classroom day but somewhat more coherence in measures of their approach to curriculum and classroom organization. Taking all aspects of teachers' practice into account, we identified two loosely related clusters of instructional behaviors and beliefs and created a model that depicts the ecological factors that affect the instructional variables in these two pedagogical orientations.

We found multiple sources of relationship between the Traditional Child Development Orientation and variables relating to teachers' personal histories and children's personal and home backgrounds. The frequency with which teachers used varied vocabulary was associated with aspects of teachers' personal histories and with children's home backgrounds. Teachers' approaches to book reading also were associated with teachers' education and with the English-speaking skills of children in their classrooms. The ECERS language scores assigned to these classrooms showed similar patterns of association with contextual factors. These multiple sets of association indicate that the nature of teacher–child conversations in classrooms partly reflects patterns of conversing related to features of the teachers' personal histories, including their educational experiences. However, when one also recalls that teachers showed relatively little consistency from one setting to the next in their approach to language use, it is apparent that in many cases, how teachers converse with children is strongly determined by contextual features. This context sensitivity suggests that teachers often are not aware of the need to use varied vocabulary as they converse with children, and teachers do not generalize their skills in engaging children in good discussions about books to other settings and other conversational strategies.

We found that measures of teacher–child interaction associated with the Academic Orientation were linked to features of the instructional context of the classrooms. Teacher–child ratio of talk and children's use of rare words when talking to teachers during free play were associated with the staff–child ratio, the length of the classroom day, and the English language skills of children. These results suggest that structural features of classrooms can affect how teachers converse with children and point to some potential benefits that may accrue from having children in classrooms with more teachers per child and for more hours than are typical in half-day programs.

It is interesting that key features of the Academic Orientation, such as the writing area and several teacher conversational strategies (group focusing, large-group cognitive extending, free-play extending talk), were linked neither to contextual variables nor to any personal history variables. Use of these strategies may reflect adoption of a relatively self-conscious pedagogical orientation by teachers. Teachers who employ these approaches may not be drawing on strong, externally provided instructional methods; rather, they may be employing methods that reflect their own pedagogy that they developed in an effort to support children's learning.

EXAMINING THE OVERALL IMPACT OF PRESCHOOL

I now turn to one of the key questions guiding our study: What is the overall impact of teacher–child interactions and the quality of the classroom curriculum on children's subsequent language and literacy development? To address this question, we used data from when the children in our study were 4 years old. In the following pages, I describe how we analyzed our data and then report correlations between outcome variables and classroom experiences while taking into account the effects of the child's home background and earlier language skill. Finally, I report results that describe the overall impact of preschool on children's kindergarten assessments.

Creating Variables that Describe Classrooms' Language Environments and Curriculum

How We Created Composite Variables   We were interested in the impact of classroom experiences on children; therefore, we used variables that describe features of the children's classrooms, teacher–child conversations, and teachers' pedagogical beliefs. We faced several methodological challenges as we moved into this phase of our data analyses. To conduct regression analysis, the procedure required to answer our question, we could only use children for whom we had complete data. This meant that we had to focus our efforts on the second year of preschool, the year for which we had the most complete classroom data. Also, when we were missing data about children, we used the information we had about a child's classroom experience to estimate the values we were missing.[6] This process of imputing data enabled us to increase the number of children for whom we had full data while causing no noteworthy impact on the overall results reported in this and previous chapters.

Once we had complete data for as many children as possible, we combined our multitude of potential variables into three clusters to create composite variables describing children's experiences in their preschool classrooms. This compositing step was necessary because it is not statistically acceptable to use too many different variables when carrying out regression analyses. When we created these composite variables, we worked under several constraints. First, we wanted our composite variables to be conceptually sound. To this end we put variables together that reflected similar aspects of classrooms (for example, variables describing exposure to varied vocabulary). Second, we wanted composite variables that provided good estimates of the full impact of preschool. To accomplish this we tried to include variables that described as many dimensions of children's classroom experiences as possible. Third, we wanted psychometrically sound composite variables. Therefore, we created composites in which all of the individual variables worked together in ways required by this type of analysis. When composites are created, the variables that are put together all contribute to the new variable, but some are more central to the newly created variable than others. Those that are most central are given additional weight and play a more critical role in the final composite. As I discuss the three composite variables that we created, I explain which variables were combined and indicate how central they are to the composite variable in which they are included.

Control Variables   We know that children's home experiences had an impact on their development. Because our goal was to identify the effects of classroom experiences on children's development, we first took into account contributions made by important dimensions of their home backgrounds. Therefore, in the analyses reported below, we controlled for several home background variables. Variables that are specific to the child included the child's Gender, Race, and MLU during toy play with the mother when the child was 3. Other control variables describe the circumstances of the family as they were reported to us during our first home visit: Mother's Education and Family Income.

---

[6]This data imputing process often strikes nonresearchers as very odd, but statisticians have determined that by imputing data, one arrives at more valid conclusions because more of the available information is used fully.

Extended Teacher Discourse   The first composite variable that we created describes the teachers' use of Extended Teacher Discourse in different settings. The following variables were included:

- *Group focusing:* teachers' use of management and control strategies during meeting time (from teacher audiotapes)

- *Large-group cognitive extending:* the amount of time during large groups when the conversational topics conveyed information or required children to talk about past, future, or hypothetical topics (from child audiotapes)

- *Book analysis:* the percentage of talk during book reading that involved analysis of the text (from book-reading videotapes)

- *Free-play extending utterances:* the percentage of teacher utterances during free play that involved the teacher's building on and extending what the child had said (from teacher audiotapes)

In the final composite variable, free-play extending utterances carried considerable weight, large-group focusing and book analysis were moderately important, and large-group cognitive extending was modestly weighted.

We examined the correlations between our measure of teachers' extended discourse and kindergarten outcomes after taking into account home background variables: Race of the child, Family Income, Mother's Education, Gender of the child, family size, and child's MLU during toy play at the 3-year-old home visit. We found strong evidence of relationships between all of our measures of childrens' language and literacy development at the end of kindergarten and teachers' conversations with children across the day when children were 4 years old (see Table 11.4). The magnitude of these relationships is especially striking for Emergent Literacy ($r = .55$, $p < .0001$) and Receptive Vocabulary ($r = .52$, $p < .0001$). The power of these associations clearly suggests that the quality of teachers' extended conversations with children throughout the day has a significant bearing on the child's long-term language and literacy development.

Exposure to Rare Words   Our second composite variable provided a description of children's Exposure to Rare Words in three different settings: mealtime, large-group time, and free play. Three of the variables reflected the percentage of all teacher words that were rare words in these settings. The fourth variable was the number of different kinds of rare words that children used during free play as they talked with the teacher. Information about children's use of rare words came

Table 11.4. Partial correlations between composite variables describing children's classroom experiences at age 4 and kindergarten assessments ($n = 64$)

	Narrative Production	Formal Definitions	Emergent Literacy	Receptive Vocabulary
Extended Teacher Discourse	.25*	.34**	.55****	.52****
Exposure to Rare Words	n.s.	.40**	.31*	.28*
Classroom Curriculum	.31*	.24⁻	.35**	.42***

Partial correlations control for Gender, Race, Family Income at age 3, Mother's Education, and child's Mean Length of Utterance (MLU) during toy play at home with mother when 3 years old.

n.s., not significant.

⁻$p < .10$; *$p < .05$; **$p < .01$; ***$p < .001$; ****$p < .0001$.

from our transcriptions of the teachers' tapes and reflects our coding of children's patterns of word use. This variable provides information about the kind of conversations children had with teachers during free play and sheds some light on the contributions of children to each other's language learning. When we combined these four variables, the two free-play variables—teachers' and children's use of rare words—carried considerable weight. The other two variables, teachers' rare-word use during mealtime and in large groups, were given similar weights to each other and were of secondary overall importance. Using the resulting composite variable, we found significant correlations between rare-word exposure and our assessments of children's kindergarten literacy skills, receptive vocabulary, and use of formal definitions (see Table 11.4). These data suggest that vocabulary use by preschool teachers and patterns of vocabulary use by children as they converse with teachers can make a difference to children's long-term vocabulary development.

Classroom Curriculum   Our third composite, Classroom Curriculum, included two variables describing the teachers' curriculum, quality of writing program and curriculum content, and the pedagogical belief variable describing the teachers' focus on children's social and emotional development. The two curriculum observation variables were equally weighted and the social and emotional variable was of somewhat less importance. Children received higher values for this composite if their classroom was given high marks for the two curriculum variables and if their teacher was given a low score for emphasis on social and emotional development. Using this composite variable, we found that the classroom experiences of children when they were 4 are related to their subsequent literacy skill, receptive vocabulary, and storytelling skill and perhaps to their performance on the Formal Definitions task (see Table 11.4). Thus, in classrooms with a curriculum that is designed to support children's learning, children acquire a broad range of language and literacy-related skills.

Summary   The results using the composite variables show that three broad dimensions of preschool classroom experiences, exposure to rare words, the nature of extended discourse of teachers, and the classroom's curriculum, made significant contributions to the end-of-kindergarten language and literacy development of the children in our study after controlling for several important home variables. It is noteworthy that the nature of associations we found is quite broad ranging. That is, each dimension of classroom practice is related to multiple aspects of children's later development, and each aspect of children's development is supported by multiple kinds of classroom experiences. These findings point to the interconnected nature of early literacy development. Our data have allowed us to slice the life of classrooms into fine pieces, and these detailed analyses have enabled us to see how classrooms foster multiple aspects of children's growth. Although specific types of interactions may directly support a selected aspect of a child's developing language abilities, the overall nature of language and literacy development may be so interconnected that when a teacher supports one aspect of this web of knowledge, skills, and inclinations to use language and print, there are echoes throughout the web such that other aspects of children's emerging literacy skills are affected. Chapter 13 considers the overall nature of early literacy development in more depth.

Preschool Experiences and Kindergarten Assessments

Having examined the relationship between classroom variables and kindergarten language and literacy skills for the Home–School Study children separately, we combined our different variables to assess how predictive the children's preschool experiences were of their language and literacy skills when they were 5 years old. I discuss results for children's Emergent Literacy, Receptive Vocabulary, and Narrative Production. Formal Definitions is not included because too many children received scores of zero on this task. The distribution of scores on this task was acceptable for correlations, but did not allow us to carry out regression analyses.

Narrative Production   When we combined our measures of children's classroom experiences with the control variables, the overall set of variables accounted for 29% of the variation in children's end-of-kindergarten narrative skills (see Figure 11.4 and Table A11.3 in the appendix). Both Extended Teacher Discourse and Classroom Curriculum were independent predictors of Narrative Production, but neither were significant predictors in the combined model. The only control

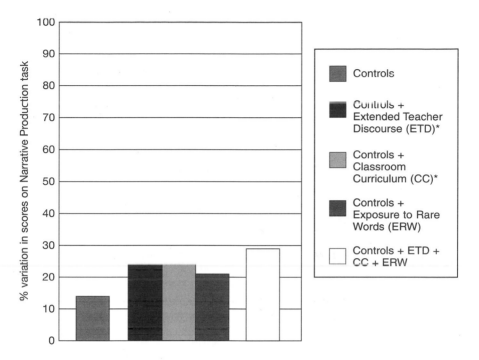

Figure 11.4. Predicting kindergarten Narrative Production using information about children's classroom experiences. (*indicates a significant composite.)

variable that proved to be a statistically significant predictor of narrative skill was Family Income.

Emergent Literacy We were able to predict almost half of the variability in children's Emergent Literacy scores at the end of kindergarten (49%) (see Figure 11.5 and Table A11.4 in the appendix). In the case of Emergent Literacy, all of the classroom dimensions made independent contributions, and in the final model, significant predictors of Emergent Literacy were Extended Teacher Discourse and Exposure to Rare Words. Control variables that were important in accounting for children's Emergent Literacy were Family Income and the child's Gender (boys had better Emergent Literacy scores). Thus, our children's classroom experiences when they were 4 made important contributions to children's emerging literacy skills.

Receptive Vocabulary We were able to predict almost half (49%) of the variability in children's end-of-kindergarten Receptive Vocabulary scores from our regression model that combined all three classroom variables along with the control variables (see Figure 11.6 and Table A11.5 in the appendix). Each of the composite variables describing dif-

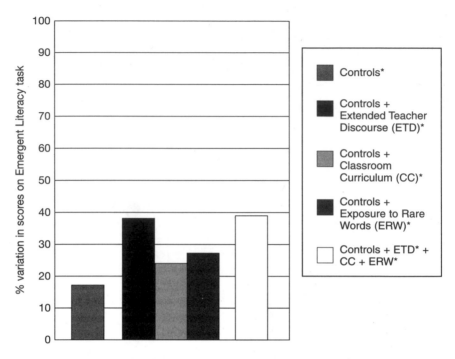

Figure 11.5. Predicting kindergarten Emergent Literacy using information about children's classroom experiences. (*indicates a significant composite.)

ferent dimensions of children's classroom experiences played important and independent roles in predicting children's vocabulary scores. In the final model, the quality of teacher discourse (TT) and the quality of the curriculum were significant predictors. The control variable that made a significant contribution to predicting children's vocabulary scores was Family Income ($t = 2.09$, $p = .041$). Thus, we have strong evidence that multiple aspects of children's classroom experiences when they were 4 play an important role in shaping their end-of-kindergarten receptive vocabularies.

Summary We created three composite measures of children's preschool experiences, one describing their exposure to varied vocabulary, one describing the quality of extended teacher discourse they experienced, and one describing the quality of the curriculum in their classroom. When we correlated these variables with our four outcome measures and controlled for the impact of home experiences, we found that all three aspects of the preschool environment contribute to children's emerging literacy-related abilities. When we combined all of our information about classrooms and homes in regression analyses, we found that we were able to account for almost half of the variability in children's kindergarten scores on our assessments of Receptive Vocabulary and Emergent Literacy. One strong predictor was our composite measure of teachers' discourse. This variable reflected teachers' use of strategies that were effective in one-to-one conversations with children: listening to children and extending their comments and strategies in large-group settings that reflected efforts to engage children in focused discussions that required children to think about books and experiences. Our measure of children's exposure to rare words was also a potent predictor, with teachers' rare-word use across settings and children's rare-word use during free play as being important. Our measure of the classrooms' curriculum also played a role in predicting kindergarten vocabulary levels.

UNDERSTANDING HOW CLASSROOMS SUPPORT CHILDREN'S DEVELOPMENT

To this point a number of the factors that shape children's classroom experiences have been discussed, and we determined that the nature

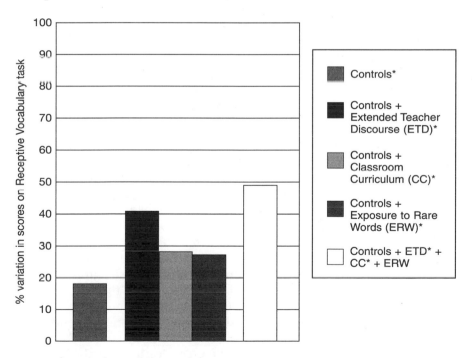

Figure 11.6.   Predicting kindergarten Receptive Vocabulary using information about children's classroom experiences. (*indicates a significant composite.)

of their preschool environments may have a profound impact on children's emerging language and literacy skills. Here now are nettlesome questions: Why do classrooms have such an impact? What are the mechanisms by which children's language and literacy skills are bolstered by their classroom experiences? Naturally I cannot provide full responses to these questions, but I lay out some thoughts that could guide future explorations. I do this by first turning back to the classrooms attended by the four portrait children in our study and by summarizing the nature of their experiences. Using these portraits as a grounding in classroom dynamics, I speculate about some of the possible pathways by which classroom experiences may translate into kindergarten successes.

Summary Profiles of the Portrait Children's Teachers

I now review the four portrait children's teachers, who were introduced in transcripts in previous chapters that highlighted aspects of the children's experiences that our analyses identified as being of special importance. We provide an overall feel for each portrait child's experiences by briefly describing their classrooms and summarizing our judgment of the overall pattern of experience of each child given our somewhat limited information.

Angela Washington and Dorothy Howard, Astra's Teachers

Angela Washington, Astra's teacher when she was 4, is first introduced in Chapter 7. When she was 3, Astra had Dorothy Howard, who was introduced in Chapter 8, the chapter on free play and large-group times. Mrs. Washington and Ms. Howard worked in a private, full-day, full-year child care center in downtown Boston that had very small classes. Mrs. Washington's classroom day included group time, structured times for skill development in the areas of literacy and numeracy, and a long free-play period. In Astra's center, the children ate meals in a large central cafeteria and teachers did not eat with the children. Given Linda Cote's analyses in Chapter 9 of the effects of classroom dynamics during mealtimes on language use, we can conclude that Astra had little exposure to varied vocabulary during her mealtimes.

In Chapter 7, Miriam Smith notes that Mrs. Washington valued children's social and emotional development but found that the teacher was quite concerned about the content of her curriculum and the need to build children's academic skills. Although Mrs. Washington encouraged literacy-related activities, she did not have a writing area for children to use during free-play times. One can learn more about Mrs. Washington's instructional style in Chapter 10, which discusses large-group times. Mrs. Washington had children in large-group meetings for extended periods of time, with considerable time being spent reviewing academic material. Her book reading included relatively little analytical talk as the book was being read. During the follow-up conversation, Mrs. Washington led an extended conversation about personal safety issues. When considering Astra's free play, we observed Ms. Howard. During the long free-play period provided, Astra engaged in extended imaginative play. During this free-play period, Ms. Howard spent time talking with individual children. We examined one extended interaction between Ms. Howard and a child who was building a block tower. This conversation was noteworthy for the manner in which Ms. Howard engaged the child in analytical thought about his structure while using a very narrow range of vocabulary.

Roberta Williams, Mariana's Teacher   Roberta Williams is introduced in Chapter 8, which describes children's book-reading experiences. Ms. Williams teaches in a prekindergarten classroom based in a public school. Prior to the year when we visited her, she had been a first-grade teacher. Her classroom had very little print displayed and no writing table. In the spring when we visited, Mariana had free play only 3 days per week, a reduction from the 5 days Ms. Williams had planned for earlier in the year. This reduction in free-play time reflected Ms. Williams's general concern for the children's preacademic development. During the morning Mariana participated in group activities such as calendar time, which her teacher used as an occasion to practice basic numeracy skills. Mariana moved from one activity to the next during the 20-minute free play, primarily spending her time with activities that Ms. Williams made available that emphasized practice with letters and numbers. During free play, the one conversation between Ms. Williams and Mariana was brief and limited in depth. The only meal Mariana had in school was a light snack. During snacktime, Ms. Williams did not sit with the children and there was very little talk among the children. We examined Ms. Williams's book reading in some detail. She read a book about robins and used it as an occasion to teach children facts about robins. She employed a didactic-interactional style, asking many questions that focused on the recall of details but required very little analytical thinking by the children.

Roz Mahoney, Todd's Teacher   We first met Roz Mahoney in Chapter 7. She teaches in a half-day Head Start in a suburban program that has a sizable Latino population. Her classroom day had two meeting times and free play that usually included art activities related to a theme. Roz's supervisor, Cami Johnson, strongly valued the social and emotional benefits of preschool, and Roz's statements about her practice and beliefs reflected a similar emphasis. She stated that she did not make special efforts to support literacy development. On the day we visited, the class was in the midst of a unit on dinosaurs, a topic that intrigued Todd, who spent free-play time playing with plastic dinosaurs provided by Roz. During free play Roz showed Todd how to put together a plastic dinosaur, using words appropriate for discussing dinosaurs, and then spent an extended time overseeing children as they brushed their teeth and went to the bathroom.

We learned more about Roz's classroom in Chapter 8. Roz said that she reads books two to three times per week, reading one book at a time and spending about 5 minutes on book reading. In the book reading that we observed, she and the children jointly constructed the meaning of the book as she required the children to think analytically about the story. In Chapter 9 Roz is shown moving between groups of children during mealtimes. While she was present she expressed concerns about children's nutrition and learning of manners but also engaged Todd and his friends in an interesting conversation about the book they had read. During the times she was absent, Todd said very little.

Ann Greenbaum, Casey's Teacher   We first met Casey's teacher, Ann Greenbaum, in Chapter 9. During her mealtime Ann made a special effort to draw children into a conversation about a recent trip. She was careful to provide Casey time to speak, encouraging him to elaborate on his experiences. Ann stayed at Casey's table through the mealtime, an arrangement that enabled the group to have several interesting conversations. Chapter 10 recounts more about Ann and how she handled free play and large-group times. Free play occupied a major portion of the classroom day in her room. During this period Casey spent considerable time engaging in elaborate and highly creative dramatic play with his good friend Bryan. When Ann joined them, she extended their play and stimulated use of varied and novel vocabulary by the children. Ann's group meeting time was brief and primarily focused on organizing the group for the day. Although she did not drill children on facts, she did encourage the group to engage in problem solving and analytical thinking.

Summarizing the Portrait Children's Classroom Experiences

When the classroom environments that portrait children experienced are compared, one gets some sense of the range of environments that children in preschools experience (see Table 11.5). At one extreme is Casey's classroom, a room that was specially designed to support children's language development. His teacher, Ann, provided time for small-

Table 11.5. Patterns of support for language and literacy in portrait children's classrooms when they were 4 years old

	Astra	Mariana	Todd	Casey
Varied vocabulary				
Free play	−	−	~	+
Mealtime	−	−	~	+
Time for free play	+	−	+	+
Analysis of books	−	−	+	+
Instructional pedagogical focus[a]	+	+	−	+
Writing area	−	−	−	+
Private program and extended day	+	−	−	+
Caucasian teachers	−	+	+	+

− limited opportunities.

~ intermittent (strong when occurred, but evidence of inconsistency).

+ clear evidence.

[a]*Instructional pedagogical focus* means the teacher did not express a primary focus on the importance of children's social and emotional growth. Absence of this social and emotional orientation was beneficial.

group teacher-directed activities, sat with children at mealtimes, and allowed ample time for free play. Throughout the day her conversations with children were responsive to children's interests and intellectually challenging. She created a language environment in which children used varied vocabulary freely. She provided only minimal time, however, for reading and discussing books with the full group, reflecting her general avoidance of large-group settings.

Mariana's teacher, Ms. Williams, fell at the other extreme from Ann. She was very concerned about children's mastery of skills and filled her day with opportunities for children to practice early numeracy and literacy skills. Her large-group times and book reading were used as occasions to teach children skills and knowledge that she deemed important (for example, specific facts about robins). Ironically, in her effort to support children's development, throughout the day, she failed to engage children in the kinds of conversations that foster language development, did not encourage children to use such language when talking with her, and failed to provide the time and materials the children needed to engage in productive dramatic play. Furthermore, although she was very interested in supporting literacy growth, she did not have a writing table or other means by which to encourage children to experiment with print. On the basis of the activities she provided, she appears to believe that children acquire literacy by practicing isolated letters and therefore saw no value in encouraging playful uses of print.

The classrooms of our other two portrait children reflect the mixed bag of features that our quantitative analyses indicated were beneficial as well as gaps in support for children's language and literacy development. Astra's teacher, Mrs. Washington, shared Ms. Williams's concern for children's academic development but allowed children considerable time for independent play. During her free-play time, she engaged the children in interesting and intellectually stimulating conversations but neither used nor encouraged the children to use varied vocabulary. Similar to the experiences of children in Ms. Williams's classroom, children's experiences with print in Mrs. Washington's classroom primarily involved recognizing and producing letters; Mrs. Washington did not have a writing table. Todd's teacher, Roz, was similar to Ann except that she seemed to lack an intentional focus on supporting children's language growth. She provided children an interesting curriculum and displayed an ability to engage children in good conversations, but these were brief and sporadic. Of all four teachers, Roz was least likely to directly attempt to support children's literacy development. This reluctance to teach literacy skills may have been linked to the high value she placed on children's social and emotional growth and a fear that attention to academic matters might undermine children's broader personal growth.

Implications for Supporting Literacy Development in Preschool Classrooms

Our results indicate clear and consistent patterns of relationship between children's language and literacy development and opportunities for children to engage in extended conversations with their teachers and friends throughout the day, to write and learn about varied topics, and to engage in dramatic play with friends. From the maze of correlational data that we have discussed in this chapter, we can distill some lessons about classrooms as learning environments and important dimensions of how teachers work with children.

Classroom Learning Environments We gained several important insights into how classrooms support children's learning. One lesson is that teachers such as Ann support children's learning throughout the day by using varied vocabulary, challenging them to think, and stimulating their curiosity and imaginations. This means that teachers have an important role to play during informal times such as mealtime and free play as well as during more formal, structured times like book reading and group time. But teachers cannot use the same conversational style throughout the day; they need to make adjustments in how they converse with children. Adjustments are necessary to allow teachers to take advantage of the constraints of different conversational settings.

During group times, children benefit when teachers work to keep the group focused, provide children new information, and engage them as a group in thoughtful reflection on books. In group times, teachers need to follow the lead of those such as Ms. Williams, who takes a directive role in determining the content and direction of the conversation while at the same time being responsive to children's questions and comments. In contrast, in less structured settings such as free play and mealtimes, teachers need to emulate the skill of Ann, who is able to listen to children and encourage them to extend their ideas.

A second lesson is that teachers need to be conscious of the important role children can play in supporting each other's language development. We found that the variety of words that children used when speaking with the teacher was a powerful predictor of the later growth of the children in our study. This finding suggests that teachers can create classrooms in which children freely and frequently use a relatively broad range of words as they converse with teachers and each other. We suspect that teachers could do much to raise children's general awareness of the value of using new words and could find creative ways to reinforce children's use of novel words when talking with teachers and with friends. In addition, by allocating sufficient time and providing the space, props, and support that children need to engage in complex dramatic play, teachers can enable children to practice their language skills through play.

We also found that factors that are beyond the control of teachers can have an impact on how they relate to children. Characteristics of classrooms that seemed to pose challenges to teachers include the presence of large numbers of children learning English as a second language and less favorable teacher–child ratios. On the plus side, we found that in full-day programs and programs with better teacher–child ratios, teachers were more able to listen to and extend children's conversations, pointing to the possible benefits that can accompany deeper teacher–child relationships. Although such environmental issues do play a role in shaping the classroom language environments, they do not appear to be of overriding importance. What is of paramount importance is the teacher—how the teacher views his or her role, how he or she converses with children, and the supports he or she provides children for using language and literacy in varied ways.

Teachers and Teaching in Preschool Classrooms   We found strong evidence that teacher–child conversations play an important role in shaping children's language and early literacy development. One key aspect of how teachers work with children is the extent to which they make themselves available to children. Children benefit from having conversations with teachers; therefore, teachers need to organize their classroom day to ensure that they have time to engage children as individuals, as well as in small and large groups, in extended conversations that encourage children to explore new ideas as they clarify and express their own thoughts.

Running through our data is evidence of the need for teachers to make intentional efforts to push children's thinking and support their literacy development as they converse with children throughout the day, plan their classroom day and the content of the curriculum, and organize their classroom environment. For a teacher to provide children optimal supports in all these areas, he or she must have a deep understanding of what children need, skillful ability to provide appropriate experiences throughout the day, and the willingness to expend the energy needed to support children's development all day long. These are the qualities of intentional teaching.

Chapters 7–10 reported findings showing that relatively few teachers currently provide children optimal support for learning across all settings. Overall use of rare vocabulary was quite low as was the frequency of intellectually challenging conversations. Not only do teachers run the risk of failing to stimulate children's thinking and language, but teachers who are not guided by a clear understanding of their role in fostering children's development also are likely to fall back on ways of relating to children that are shaped more by environmental factors and their perceptions of children than by their pedagogical beliefs. For example, we found that teachers' use of varied vocabulary and their inclination to listen to children were affected by a variety of contextual factors. Also, we found some indication that teachers' use of varied vocabulary may be related to the backgrounds of the children in their classrooms. Everyone's conversations are very sensitive to contextual factors: The words people use, the amount they speak, and the complexity of their syntax all reflect unconscious decisions that are shaped by the context. Our findings suggest that teachers need to elevate their awareness of how such factors shape their language use, become conscious of how they converse with children, and strive to engage children consistently in rich conversations.

In closing, in the chapters examining the preschool classroom experiences of the children in our study, we have explored multiple settings and varied dimensions of how teachers relate to children. Our findings make clear that preschool teachers play a vital role in supporting young children's early literacy development and that the strategies needed for fostering optimal growth require considerable sophistication and energy. Unfortunately, our society has yet to recognize and appropriately reward preschool teachers. It is no accident that many of the teachers we studied were not able to demonstrate the type of skillful, intentional instruction we found to be most beneficial. Few were highly educated, and no doubt many had second jobs and carried heavy responsibilities for caring for children and parents at home. Finally, like so many other preschool teachers, they tended to have little understanding of the developmental nature of early literacy development, of the place of oral language in supporting literacy, or of the critical role they as teachers play in fostering children's long-term language and literacy growth. Our data make clear the pressing need for pre- and in-service training for preschool teachers—training that provides teachers guidance as they strive to foster children's language and literacy development using methods that engage children's natural interests and skills and provide them needed materials, instruction, and encouragement.

Section III

Bringing Homes and Schools Together

David K. Dickinson and Patton O. Tabors

In the first section of this book, we have discussed the contributions of the home environments of the children in the Home–School Study of Language and Literacy Development to their later language and literacy development, and in the second section we have examined ways in which preschool classrooms supported these children's development. Now we turn from considering children's homes and classrooms separately to look at the connections between these two settings and the contributions each makes to fostering children's development. As all parents know, when their child first leaves home to attend preschool or school, both the child and parent may find the separation difficult. The difficulty of this transition has long been recognized by preschool educators, who have traditionally made special efforts to form relationships with the parents of the children in their classrooms. Head Start, for example, believes strongly in the importance of working with parents, maintaining staff with special responsibilities for families, and mandating that teachers make visits to the homes of the children in their classrooms.

Early childhood educators hope that the relationships they form with families will enable teachers to better understand children and provide a means to give parents information and support that will help them raise their children. Also, teachers hope that they can help parents acquire confidence and strategies that will help them in dealing more effectively with schools and teachers as their children enter the public school arena. Thus, Head Start and other preschool programs hope that information will flow in two directions, from parents to teachers and from teachers to parents, and that parents will acquire an orientation toward relating to schools that will have long-term benefits.

In Chapters 12 and 13, we take very different approaches as we bring together the home and school strands of this book. First, Michelle Porche blends qualitative and quantitative information as she examines how parents and teachers view and value parent involvement from their separate perspectives. Then, in the concluding chapter we take one last look at our quantitative data as we consider the mutual contributions of homes and classrooms to children's long-term development. In this chapter we also address the policy implications of the findings of the Home–School Study for interventions at home and in preschools, for staff development, and for national policy related to the early childhood period.

Chapter 12

Parent Involvement as a Link Between Home and School

Michelle V. Porche

The number of children enrolled in preschool programs across the country has grown tremendously since the late 1970s (McGill-Franzen, 1993). This early schooling for 3- and 4-year-olds has become an important component of preparation for later school achievement, whether through private child care centers, public preschools, or federally funded programs such as Head Start. It can also be a critical introduction for parents as they form relationships with their children's teachers for the first time and begin what is hoped will be a productive and enduring practice of involvement in the schools. Much has been made of attempts to form partnerships between parents and school personnel. Whether these attempts for true collaboration have been successful has been a topic of debate. But just as the quality of early schooling (for example, teaching, curriculum, and resources) may affect children's ability to learn, the quality of early parent–teacher interactions and programmatic attention to parents of children in early childhood programs may influence the quality of later parent involvement.

Many educational researchers have provided evidence of a relationship between parents' involvement in elementary school programs and their children's school achievement (Epstein, 1983, 1986; Lightfoot, 1978; Snow, Barnes, Chandler, Goodman, & Hemphill, 1991). Anne Henderson described the following outcomes in her annotated bibliography:

> Programs designed with strong parent involvement produce students who perform better than otherwise identical programs that

do not involve parents as thoroughly, or that do not involve them at all. Schools that relate well to their communities have student bodies that outperform other schools. Children whose parents help them at home and stay in touch with the school score higher than children of similar aptitude and family background whose parents are not involved. (1987, p. 1)

James Comer (1984) characterized the home as a social network that interacts with other social networks such as the school. When parents are actively involved in positive relationships with the school, children experience reduced behavioral problems and increased attention to classroom learning. Stevenson and Baker (1987) reported that children with more involved parents had higher teacher ratings of school performance. As the influence of parent involvement on children's school achievement has become more accepted, there are a growing number of programs and research interventions that seek to encourage this involvement.

This raises the question of what types of parent involvement were available to the participants in the Home–School Study of Language and Literacy Development and whether they were able to take advantage of those opportunities. As mentioned previously, almost half of the families in the study sent their children to Head Start for preschool. Head Start has incorporated parent involvement in its mission since the inception of the program in 1965, and it was clear that the Head Start participants in the Home–School Study knew that Head Start encouraged their involvement. Not all of the Head Start parents in the Home–School Study, however, were equally involved in their children's preschool education, nor were all of the families equally involved in the other preschool and kindergarten programs attended by the children in the study. What difference did these differences make for the relationship between the families and the schools? And were these differences related to the academic achievement of the children in kindergarten?

The purpose of this chapter, then, is to describe early patterns of parental participation in the preschool and kindergarten activities of the children in the Home–School Study. First, from the point of view of the mothers, I examine the types and frequency of involvement in activities that they reported in their interviews. Second, from the point of view of the teachers, I examine how involved they felt the parents were in the schooling programs and with their children's learning. Finally, I look for relationships between the mothers' and teachers' descriptions of parent involvement and the children's language and literacy skills at the end of kindergarten.

MEASURING PARENT INVOLVEMENT IN THE HOME–SCHOOL STUDY

Measures of parent involvement used in this study are context specific and age appropriate for preschool and early elementary school settings. By obtaining information from parents *and* teachers, we were able to assess the meaning and importance that each stakeholder attributes to involvement, triangulate reports of involvement, and test for associations between involvement and child outcomes.

Reports from Mothers

All of the mothers who were participating in the Home–School Study were interviewed during the home visits when the children were 4 and 5 years old (the age 3 visit did not include extensive questions about parent involvement at school and thus is not included in these analyses). Among the questions asked were some that were specifically crafted to gauge parent involvement with the children's preschool or kindergarten program. At home visits when the children were 7 years old, the mothers were asked retrospective questions about their experiences with the preschool and kindergarten programs that their children had attended. The retrospective interviews were semistructured and meant to elicit observations and ideas of particular interest to the mothers while gathering basic information regarding the children's language development, school progress, and parent involvement with the school.

Parental involvement, as reported by the mothers, varied from minimal involvement, consisting of attending annual or semiannual teacher–parent conferences, to a much greater degree of involvement, such as being a teacher assistant, a classroom parent, or a policy council member. There was also variation between paid positions and volunteer positions. For example, some mothers opted to work as bus drivers or aides so that they could be close to their children. The interviews contain information regarding time commitment of these activities, as it relates to ease of participation, as well as the mothers' understanding of the importance of different activities, both for themselves and for their children's well-being.

Frequency of Contact with Teacher   First, a *frequency of contact with teacher* variable was coded for degree of parent–teacher contact by estimating an average number of visits per month based on the mothers' interviews (see Table A12.1 in the appendix). Visits included formal meetings requested by the teacher or parent, scheduled classroom participation activities, or informal exchanges that were part of a day-to-day routine of dropping off or picking up a child. This *frequency of contact with teacher* variable ranged from 0.25 (conference visits only) to 20 (daily) visits per month. The overall pattern of contact with teachers was determined for all the mothers.

When children were 4 years old, mothers reported an average *frequency of contact with teacher* of 8 times per month. When reviewing average mother–teacher contact by program affiliation during preschool, surprisingly, mothers whose children were enrolled in Head Start tended to have lower levels of contact on average. As described later, however, *frequency of contact with teacher* was influenced by mode of transportation to school. When the children were age 5 and in kindergarten, the number of times that mothers were in contact with teachers dropped to 6.6 per month, on average.

From the interviews with the mothers, we know that contact between mothers and teachers was an important way of building rapport and respect. When mothers in the study were able to be in contact with their children's teachers by visiting the preschool or kindergarten classrooms, they often gained a perspective not available to the other mothers. In fact, there were many instances throughout the interviews when mothers expressed respect and admiration for teachers after observing their work in the classroom. They gained an appreciation of the difficulties that teachers faced, especially with overcrowded classes, and when conflicts arose between the teacher and their children, they tried to see the situation from the teacher's perspective. Although protective of their own children, they spoke as though they were able to make more informed assessments of situations, compared with mothers who had not spent as much time in the classroom. Zenia's mother even expressed the opinion that her daughter's preschool teachers had taught her how to be a more involved parent:

> [The] teachers are the ones that helped me learn how to do the parent–teacher interaction. Because remember, I never knew the first thing about being a parent. I didn't have a clue, you know. [Laughs] I didn't know what you were supposed to talk to those folks about. I never planned on having any kids. At least not early. . . . So, I'd have to say they helped me out, learn how to see my responsibilities as a parent. I mean, as far as interacting with them. You know, the rules and the regulations that go on. How can I put it? Like . . . when you was in school they was just somebody else's mother or whatever. They were just your teacher. [Laughs] You'd say whatever you had to and you left. And now you had to sit here and go into depth with these people about your child. You had to make them tell you about your kid. . . .

> And that was the hardest part, trying to interview these folks about what my daughter was doing. I mean. . . . So I think . . . I think they . . . sort of helped me communicate better.

As mentioned previously, there was a definite drop in how often mothers were in contact with teachers between preschool and kindergarten. One of the reasons for this drop may be that opportunities for contact between mothers and teachers became more formalized in the public schools attended by the children. In the interviews, mothers talked about disappointments in having only brief contact with teachers during conferences and open house meetings when their children were in elementary school, during which they had to compete with other parents for the attention of teachers. In this example, Kera's mother talked about these difficulties:

> I haven't had a chance to talk to her teacher. We had a meeting— Open House—when you get report cards and she had this long line of parents. It wasn't a point where you just walked in. And you had to wait. So, I couldn't—I didn't have a chance to speak to her. She had like seven people ahead of me and it wasn't a timed meeting. It was just talk. . . . I had been down to see my other daughter's teacher first and she just had so many students' parents in the waiting room. I mean, when you have all these people waiting you just can't sit there and keep going on and going on with this [one] parent.

Some mothers told of teachers who had other strategies for dealing with crowds of parents, such as giving a short talk about the class in general, asking for questions, and finally addressing concerns from parents on a more individual basis as time allowed. But when parents had much more informal access to teachers, they were not as reliant on conferences or open houses to discuss their children's progress. The more productive conversations happened on a regular basis, and formal meetings were just a reinforcement of what had already been discussed.

Level of Responsibility   Second, we asked mothers about their responsibilities at their children's schools (see Table A12.1 in the appendix). This variable measures the level of activities that the mothers (or, in a few cases, fathers) engaged in. The categories for responsibility in ascending level of involvement were

1. Contributes supplies, visits classrooms, and/or attends parent–teacher organization meetings

2. Volunteers for special events such as field trips

3. Acts as a classroom parent who volunteers on a regularly scheduled basis in the classroom or volunteers in the school library

4. Serves as a classroom aide who holds a part-time paid position either in the child's classroom or in another classroom in the school

5. Is a school staff member who may hold a full-time paid position and be peer to the child's teacher

6. Is a policy council member or parent–teacher organization officer who helps make policy regarding the school operation

This range represents the amount of influence the mothers might have had in interactions with school personnel, both on a personal level with teachers and in terms of decision-making for the school's operation. These categories were deliberately ranked to reflect the power dynamic between the mother and the teacher or other school personnel. The rankings of the sorts of involvement that the mothers engaged in measured the position of power or status that a mother might have had in conflicts between her and her child's teacher or administrator. As Delgado-Gaitan suggested, "'power' undergirds the knowledge required on the part of parents to deal with schools. How one utilizes power determines the extent to which individuals or organizations access valued resources" (1991, p. 22). One of her main assumptions about parent involvement highlights the potential benefit of increased responsibility: "Learning new roles provides people with access to resources, and the learning of those roles occurs through participation in those new settings" (p. 22).

Each mother received points for her reported activities and then the category ratings were added together to form a total *level of responsibility* score for each mother. For the *level of responsibility* variable at preschool, I found that many of the mothers scored in the low range, although the scores did extend to an unusually high value of 14. The mother who scored 14 was involved in Head Start, and her score reflected her participation through visiting the classroom, going on field trips, holding a paid position as a bus driver for Head Start, and being a member of the Head Start Policy Council. The average score for the group of mothers in the study was 3.06, reflecting a level of participation that combines classroom visits, contributions of supplies, and volunteering for special events such as field trips or the taking on of the position of a classroom parent.

When the children were 5 years old and in kindergarten, the mothers' responsibility scores ranged from 0 to 6, indicating that most mothers had only minimal responsibility, with only a few reporting that they volunteered for special events or field trips. Unfortunately we do not have extensive data on why this drop in the mothers' level of responsibility occurred between preschool and kindergarten. A number of mothers, however, expressed frustration with elementary school teachers or other personnel, in that they felt they were treated with disrespect or were excluded from the educational process of their children. This type of experience was a source of frustration as noted, for example, by Mark's mother:

> I think Head Start is a really good program but I think that if your child is going into the public school system that it's more detrimental than helpful. I'm on the Head Start Policy Council, and I told them that they really need to do something [to prepare parents]. [In public school] they really sever the ties as far as being involved in the education—all you find out about the education is like the quarterly parent meeting with the teacher and what your child tells you. Other than looking through their paperwork, you have no idea where they're at or where they're headed. I've found you really have to force yourself on the school. Being involved with the PTA helped, but for parents who only have access to the teacher once every quarter, it's a big shock. For 2 3 years in Head Start, they get you to call yourself the primary educator of your child—and then you go into the public schools, and they [tell you to] back off.

In fact, this mother made sure that she got a part-time job at her son's school so that she could monitor his progress and maintain contact with his teachers. Although this might seem an extreme case, she had cause to feel protective of him after an earlier instance in which his kindergarten teacher had mistakenly assessed him as needing remedial reading instruction. Standardized tests administered during school visits by Home–School Study researchers confirmed the mother's assessment of his high abilities. The process between the mother and teacher was not one of partnership, but rather was a battle for ultimate authority. In fairness, both parties might have been acting in what they perceived as the best interests of the child, but had there been more coordinated efforts, they would have reached the same results without as much disruption of the child's schooling. Moreover, this mother had been strongly influenced by Head Start's philosophy of involvement and advocacy. Another mother more inclined to a strategy of deferring to the teacher's authority and expertise might not have fought so hard on behalf of her child.

Mode of Transportation   When asked to describe the frequency of contact with teachers and the types of activities at preschool and kindergarten that the parents were able to engage in, mothers often reported the importance of transportation as a factor, which prompted a closer investigation of the effects of proximity. If the child's school was in close proximity, seeing the teacher on a regular and informal basis would have been relatively easy. If the child was bused to a school outside of his or her neighborhood, then the ease with which mothers were able to communicate with their children's teachers was diminished. The following interview excerpt gives a description of Shondra's mother's experience regarding the influence of transportation:

Interviewer: So, how did you feel about the interactions that you had with Shondra's preschool teacher versus the interactions you have with her current teacher?

Mother: Well, because we, with the preschool, we dropped her off and picked her up, we had more interactions because I knew her more. You know, so we were able to establish a rapport, whereas with her current teacher, because she takes the school bus . . . we've only met maybe four times— once at a parent conference and a couple of times, well, three times when we—I had brought Shondra to school.

In addition, when a parent's visits to the school consist of rare formal meetings or exceptions to the child's usual routine of taking the bus, there are fewer opportunities for the parent to see the child in his or her classroom environment or to get a sense of the child's peers. Responding to immediate problems or issues also is more difficult. As one mother related, she had difficulty attending meetings across town on short notice to discuss a budget crisis in her child's school district.

Head Start has, in fact, noted the problem of access as a barrier to involvement and suggested that centers "provide transportation and child care to increase accessibility to the program for parents" (Kracke, 1993, p. 4). Although the rare exception, one Head Start mother did take advantage of opportunities for parent involvement while relying on the program's transportation. She described fitting in school visits around her own college class schedule, in order to accompany her son, George, to Head Start:

Well, I didn't have a car. But I would take him. They had a bus that would go there on a very regular basis, and I would take that in the morning. I had half a day on Friday, then I would get there and come back without losing classes and stuff. And I would go in the morning, and then I'd come home with the lunch bus. That's where they made the lunches and they'd bring them back for the Girls' Club and stuff. So I'd ride with them back to [the Girls' Club] and then take the bus from there back to school. So I'd spend half a day. I liked that because I got to see what was going on, and otherwise I never would've even seen it because I couldn't get out there. And I got to see how they were, you know, doing things, and what they were doing, and talk to the teachers, get to know the teachers and all the rest.

Although Head Start's goal may be to have more mothers taking advantage of these sorts of opportunities, it did not seem to occur often for the mothers in the study.

Given the importance of this factor for parent involvement, mode of transportation to school was coded for each child, as either bused or transported by parent. Taking into account the influence of the *mode of transportation* on *frequency of contact with teacher,* busing had a significant effect. On average, there was a much lower frequency of parent–teacher contact for those children who were bused to school. The pattern of decreasing frequency of parent–teacher contact as children grew older was similar for both bused and transported-by-parent groups, but mothers who took their children to school had consistently higher frequency of contact with teachers. This is in keeping with research done by Powell (1978) that showed that most communication between parents and teachers happens when children are picked up or dropped off. Overall, a higher percentage of Head Start children in the study were bused compared with children who were in private child care and public preschools when they were 4 years old (see Table 12.1). In contrast to the results for *frequency of contact with teachers, mode of transportation* had no significant effect on mothers' level of responsibility at either preschool or kindergarten.

It could be argued that mode of transportation is really a proxy for distance, which might be a more meaningful predictor of parent–teacher contact. The relationship of distance[1] between home and preschool when the children were 4 years old and the frequency of parent–teacher contact did in fact approach significance ($r = -.24$, $p < .07$). To test this alternative explanation further, I compared a simple correlation between *mode of transportation* and *frequency of contact*

---

[1]Using a mapping program, distance was calculated to one tenth of a mile door-to-door using the home and school addresses for each child and the shortest route on public streets.

Table 12.1. Percentages of children bused to preschool and kindergarten, by preschool program affiliation

Preschool program affiliation	Bused to preshool	Bused to kindergarten
Head Start	59	31
Private child care and public preschool	15	22

with teacher ($r = .50$, $p < .0001$) with one which partialled out the effect of distance ($r = .41$, $p < .01$). Even controlling for the effect of distance, *mode of transportation* had a significant moderate relationship to *frequency of contact with teacher.* Mothers in the Home–School Study who took their children to school, no matter what the proximity of the home was to the school site, tended to have more contact with teachers, whereas mothers whose children were bused tended to have less contact. This was the case regardless of Mother's Education, Family Income, Race, and Gender of the child.

Four Portrait Families and Parent Involvement   Data from the four portrait families highlight the range of very involved to minimally involved parents represented in the participants in the study and provide some insight into reasons for this range of experiences. As can be seen in Table 12.2, both Todd's mother and Astra's mother held a steady pattern of involvement between preschool and kindergarten, although Todd's mother had few interactions with teachers, whereas Astra's mother reported daily contact. Mariana's and Casey's mothers had similar reports of more contact with preschool teachers than with kindergarten teachers, but their description of relationships with teachers was very different.

Todd's mother, Mary, talked about her experiences with Head Start as very positive:

> I think it is a very good program. I think the whole point to Head Start was to build up their self-esteem. This is the case for children as well as parents. Some mothers who had no self-esteem—they go in and start doing things and helping out at the program and you could see it in their self-esteem.

Although she reported that she herself did not need that sort of psychological boost, she described being able to benefit from Head Start in other ways:

> I think it helped me in a financial way sometimes because this woman, she used to help out a lot you know. I don't know whether she was like a social worker. She helped whoever needed it, like

if they needed a ride to the dentist, you know. I mean and she did help me at times with I think Christmas. . . . And you know, she just helped out in many ways, just if you wanted to talk to her.

Mary only volunteered a couple of times when Todd was in Head Start because she was providing child care in her home and was unable to fit volunteering into her schedule. As Todd progressed into elementary school, Mary went back to school, which also took up much of her time, and she expressed regret that she wasn't helping him with reading as much as she would have liked; she felt she "should do more." Similar to other women in the study, Mary was a single mother struggling to make ends meet while also trying to improve her situation by going back to school, leaving less time for involvement with her child's schooling than she would have liked.

Mary's interactions with Todd's kindergarten teacher were limited to regular conferences, and although her first impression of the teacher was not good—she described the teacher as "abrupt with parents" and "impatient"—she saw that Todd liked her and that "she did seem to be all right with the kids." Perhaps more discouraging to Mary in her efforts to be more involved at the school were her interactions with other parents. When asked whether the school made it easy for her to get involved, she replied,

I don't think so. I mean it does to a certain extent, but . . . then in another extent it's all the same, the same group of women, same group of people involved with the school. . . . [That] makes it hard. The parents that are involved are just like a clique of parents and doesn't make it easy for—I don't think—for an outsider to come in. Not that I'm an outsider, really, but I'm not the type of person who wants to go to every single thing. I want to do certain things and that's it, and as far as the classrooms, I know you're allowed in them, but I would feel like I was intruding, you know, so I would never do that, you know. . . . I go to field trips. The kids like that.

Table 12.2.   Portrait mothers' reports of parent involvement

Child	Average preschool contact with teachers per month	Average kindergarten contact with teachers per month	Preschool level of responsibility	Kindergarten level of responsibility
Todd	2	3	1	1
Mariana	8	1	3	1
Casey	20	1	3	3
Astra	20	20	6	6

Mary described herself as an "easygoing person" who avoided getting into arguments, although she was willing to advocate for her children when she felt it was necessary. She was unwilling, however, to force her way into a situation in which she felt unwelcome and so, after several attempts to join with other parents, had decided to limit her involvement at school.

Mariana's mother, Elena, also reported limited involvement with her children's schooling, although she expressed the importance of parent involvement as one of the reasons she transferred them to a new school:

> At this school they really work on parents. . . . You know that helps the kids a lot. They feel supported. . . . I'm not there that much, but you know, when [parents] come they can say it's something [the children] remember.

She mentioned that Mariana's kindergarten teacher had asked her to come read to the class but that she had had to decline because she was busy with final exams at her own school. Even so, she appreciated the opportunities to get involved that were offered by the school.

Much of Elena's story, however, was about being misunderstood and discriminated against by various teachers and administrators. She attributed this to her being Mexican and having a heavy accent. Originally from the Southwest, she was particularly sensitive to experiences of racism in the Northeast. Her biggest concern was about potential prejudice her children would face in school from other children and from teachers; she felt strongly that racism was entrenched in the local school systems.

Although she reported some positive interactions with teachers and believed that her daughter had some good experiences in preschool and kindergarten, much of Elena's focus was on conflicts with school personnel:

> When Mariana was in preschool, I went down and spoke to the teacher. She ignored me. Then I spoke to the principal, and then she tried to ignore me too. So, I had to get really angry at her and I—they had to call the teacher out of the classroom and I don't know if it did much. You know, the truth is they found out that I really care about what's going on and how they treat my kids and how that affects, you know, their learning.

Many of these conflicts centered around arranging bus transportation for her children, and Elena did not hesitate to contact the superintendent and transportation director to get her problems resolved. Unfortunately, her negative experiences and subsequent mistrust of school personnel diminished the possibilities for meaningful interactions that might have enhanced her children's education.

When Astra was enrolled in child care, her mother, Solange, was employed as a teacher at the same center while also attending college. Being an employee of the center facilitated Solange's involvement with Astra's teachers. Because of physical proximity it was easy for Solange to stay in daily contact to monitor Astra's progress and to respond to any concerns. More importantly, Solange was a peer of the other teachers and was able to address academic issues in a way that other mothers in the study felt unqualified to do. She was one of the few mothers in the study who saw herself in an informal teaching role, working *with* teachers and not sharply delineating roles of parent and teacher in her child's education.

As with Elena, racism was also a theme in Solange's interview, although the outcome was different. In kindergarten Astra was assigned to a school in which she was one of the few black children. Solange was keenly aware of the isolation and potential for discrimination that Astra faced going to school "out in the suburbs" while living in an urban neighborhood where "in our immediate environment there was only blacks." However, when Astra came home saying, "[My teacher] don't like me, she don't want me to talk," Solange told the interviewer, "I had to tell her no, not because she didn't like her, but because she wants her to do her work." Having a good relationship with Astra's teacher was extremely important in this case, as was having plenty of opportunities to observe Astra in the classroom. Solange knew the teacher well and knew from classroom visits that Astra liked to talk. In addition, in this and another incident she described, Solange took the opportunity to discuss racism with her daughter ("I didn't want it to fester and then she would feel bad") and at the same time instill pride in her Jamaican heritage. In this way, Solange's high level of parent involvement had a direct and positive effect on a potentially troubling problem.

Casey's mother, Stacy, reported a much less complicated relationship with Casey's school situation than either Elena or Solange. Casey went to preschool and kindergarten at the same neighborhood elementary school ("It's right down the street") that his parents expected him to attend through eighth grade. This school was located in the community where his mother had also gone to school; in fact, Stacy reported, "Casey's art teacher is the same art teacher I had all through grammar school." This school was located in a close-knit neighborhood where many parents knew each other and had formed close relationships with teachers. Teachers from this school were even known to attend children's outside-of-school activities, such as watching the children play sports or attending their First Communions.

Stacy reported much more contact with her son's preschool teacher than his kindergarten teacher, but given her son's successful adjustment to school and her positive relationship with teachers at the school, she felt that she had adequate contact with them. When asked whether she felt the school made it easy for her to be involved, she replied,

> Very easy, very easy. They're always asking if anybody wants to come in and help out with the class, or do an activity with the class. Anything that you want to do, you know, share and bring in or come in and read stories. . . . Some people go in on a weekly basis or a monthly basis. Whenever you can, you can go in and . . . help out, and, oh yeah, I mean you can call these teachers, call them or meet with them any time at all . . . it's good.

Stacy enjoyed helping out at school when opportunities arose, such as helping with field trips and other special events, although she had to limit her involvement when her third child was born.

In this rich community setting, attending regular conferences and open houses, along with helping in class and school events, went a long way to provide ample opportunity for meaningful parent involvement. When asked if there had been any time "where you felt like you were able to get the school to listen to you, to intervene or make changes that you thought were important for (Casey's) education," Stacy replied,

> I haven't come across anything yet, 'cause we haven't had any problems, really. . . . I haven't noticed anything that I thought should be changed, but I'm sure if I did, they would, you know, if I felt like something needed to be addressed, I know they would.

Reports from Teachers

During the same period each year when mothers were being interviewed, the teachers of the children in the study were interviewed regarding their teaching practices, their assessments of the children in the study, and their evaluations of the study families' school involvement. Data from the teacher interviews were coded to reflect teacher assessments of parent involvement, which were compared with maternal reports of contact with teachers. The coded data contained some consistent overlap with maternal reports of contact with teachers, and some critical divergence, which have implications for future parent involvement efforts.

Preschool Teachers   When the children in the study were 4 years old, 69 preschool teachers were interviewed about their interactions with parents. *Frequency of contact with parents* was measured categorically as *never, occasionally, often,* and *daily* (see Table A12.1 in the appendix). All but three of the teachers surveyed reported having some contact with parents, although, on average, preschool teachers in private child care centers and public preschools reported higher frequency of contact with parents than Head Start teachers reported (*often* compared with *occasionally*) (see Table 12.3).

Reviewing results by preschool program affiliation revealed clear differences in practices between the two groups of teachers (see Table 12.3). Both the Head Start and the private child care and public preschool centers relied on parent volunteers (75% and 67%, respectively). Head Start teachers, however, reported greater contact with parents as a result of parent involvement in the classroom or centers than did the other preschool teachers. In contrast, teachers in the private child care and public preschool programs were much more likely to see parents on drop-off and pick-up.

Teachers were also asked about their strategies for encouraging involvement (see Table 12.3). Again, there were differences in preferred strategies to contact parents, as Head Start teachers were more likely to initiate face-to-face or informal direct communication with parents, in the form of home visits or telephone calls. Teachers who conducted home visits usually did so about three times per year and used these visits to inform parents about the children's progress. To a lesser degree, Head Start teachers stressed the importance of getting to know the families, and some explained the need to involve social service representatives in the home visits. In contrast, the teachers in the other programs were more likely to rely on newsletters, notes, and formal conferences. Goals of conferences and more casual interactions with parents centered mostly around progress reports, in addition to follow-ups about children's illnesses and behavioral concerns.

Kindergarten Teachers   All of the kindergarten teachers of the children in the kindergarten sample received surveys that included a section on parent involvement. In all, 52 teachers returned them. Even with the limitations of missing data in the kindergarten year, we were able to gain important information about teacher assessments of parent involvement and how those assessments are related to mothers' assessments of their own involvement. Teachers reported that they were most likely to speak with parents at drop-off or pick-up times (62%) or dur-

Table 12.3. Teachers' reports of parent involvement

	Preschool program	
	Head Start (n = 42)	Private child care and public preschool (n = 27)
Average frequency of contact per month	1.5 (.92) > occasionally	2.0 (.88) often
Use of parent volunteers at center	75%	67%
Type of contact with parent		
Parent involvement in classroom or center	24	4
Contact at drop-off or pick-up	26	74
Home visit	41	4
Strategy for parent contact		
Class newsletter	67	15
Notes home	55	74
Telephone calls home	69	56
Formal conference	48	59
Home visit	74	4
Informal chats	5	26
Purpose of parent contact		
Exchange information about program and child	63	59
Address child's problems and concerns	54	52
Provide progress report through formal conference	54	67
Remind/discuss/plan school events	68	59
Act as liaison for social services	15	7

ing routine conferences (64%). About one quarter (23%) reported scheduling special conferences in response to a particular child's circumstances, whereas fewer reported speaking with parents as they performed volunteer activities while helping in the classroom (17%) or on field trips (17%). Some teachers reported telephoning parents at home (17%) and a few established contact during special school performances or programs (12%). Teachers' reports of *frequency of contact with parents* varied: one quarter (25%) reported seeing parents only a few times per semester, though more than half (58%) reported frequent or daily contact with parents. Overall, the practices of kindergarten teachers to promote involvement more closely resembled the practices of teachers in private child care and public preschool programs.

In contrast to preschool teachers, few kindergarten teachers reported strategies of using home visits to make contact with parents (7%), which had been a common practice of Head Start. Kindergarten teachers had a much heavier reliance on formal avenues of communication such as conference meetings (85%) and notes or letters sent home (70%). Half of the teachers (50%) reported calling the parents at home to establish contact, which is consistent with reports from the preschool teachers. When asked to name various purposes of parent involvement, most kindergarten teachers (85%) cited the importance of sharing progress reports about the child, and almost as many (78%) reported that it was an opportunity to discuss problems the child was experiencing. More than half (54%) stated that it was a chance to provide general information to parents, and a similar number (49%) reported that contact was an opportunity to remind parents about special events, such as field trips. A small percentage (12%) held a dual role in their contact with parents, acting as teacher and also as a liaison for social services.

Most telling from the kindergarten teacher interviews were teacher assessments of what types of activities parents used to support their children's learning. When teachers were asked whether they felt that parents read to the child at home, one teacher stated that the child was never read to, whereas almost half (48%) reported that parents did "some" reading with the child, and the rest (50%) stated that they were "absolutely" sure that parents read with the child "often." The answers to this question resulted in a variable for teacher assessment of the *child being read to at home*. Previous research with the mothers and children in the Home–School Study has shown that providing a rich literacy environment in the home, termed *home support for literacy*, is related to positive reading outcomes for children (see Chapter 2; see also Dickinson & DeTemple, 1998). Home support for literacy also is further investigated in this analysis of parent involvement.

Teachers were additionally asked to assess three areas of family support for the child: academic growth, child development, and support for the school program. Responses on a 4-point scale provided ratings of *well above average* to *far below average* support. In each case, more than three fourths of teachers rated family support as above average, though a number of families were rated as *far below average*. Because these three support variables were highly correlated with each other (Cronbach's index of internal consistency = .89), a composite variable of teacher assessment of *parent support for children's learning* was created for use in further correlational analyses.

Correlations Between Teachers' and Mothers' Reports of Parent Involvement

When I looked for relationships between the teachers' and the mothers' reports of involvement, correlational analyses (see Table A12.2 in the appendix) revealed that teachers' reports of *frequency of contact with parents* during preschool was strongly correlated with concurrent reports by mothers about how frequently they were in contact with the teachers ($r = .52$, $p < .0001$). When children were in kindergarten, however, the mothers' reports of *frequency of contact with teachers* was *weakly* correlated to teacher reports of *frequency of contact with parents* ($r = .26$, $p < .10$). Also in kindergarten, the mothers' reports of *frequency of contact with teachers* was weakly correlated with teacher assessment of *parent support for children's learning* ($r = .29$, $p < .10$) but strongly associated with teacher assessment of the *child being read to at home* ($r = .48$, $p < .01$). Mothers' reports of their *level of responsibility* at preschool were not related to any of the preschool teachers' assessments of parent involvement. Mothers' reports of *level of responsibility* the following year, however, were significantly correlated with kindergarten teachers' reports of *frequency of contact with parents* ($r = .38$, $p < .05$) and with teachers' assessments of *parent support for children's learning* ($r = .32$, $p < .05$). And finally, the *home support for literacy* variable was positively related to preschool teachers' reports of *frequency of contact with parents* ($r = .24$, $p < .10$), and with kindergarten teachers' assessments of the *child being read to at home* ($r = .38$, $p < .05$) and *parent support for children's learning* ($r = .45$, $p < .01$).

Kindergarten teachers' assessment of *child being read to at home* had a strong positive relationship with teachers' assessment of *parent support for child's learning* ($r = .57$, $p < .0001$). In contrast, teacher reports of *frequency of contact with parents* had a weaker relationship with their assessment of *parent support for child's learning* ($r = .33$, $p < .05$). This suggests that teachers attached more importance to their perception of parent involvement practices in the home centered around literacy activities than to volunteer efforts in the schools.

Correlations Between Parent Involvement and Children's Language and Literacy Outcomes

As described in previous chapters, children were given a battery of language and literacy tests at the kindergarten year of data collection, which included measures of Narrative Production, Emergent Literacy, and Receptive Vocabulary, tasks from the School-Home Early Language and Literacy Battery–Kindergarten (SHELL–K; Snow, Tabors, Nicholson, & Kurland, 1995). To investigate the relationship between parent involvement and children's language and literacy skills, correlational analyses were conducted between mother and teacher reports of parent involvement from preschool and kindergarten and children's language outcomes at kindergarten (see Table A12.3 in the appendix).

Results from data collected when the children were 4 years old showed that neither teacher reports of *frequency of contact with parents* nor mothers' reports of *frequency of contact with teacher* or of *level of responsibility* were related to any of the kindergarten language and literacy outcomes. Results from the following year, however, did show significant correlations between parent involvement and language outcomes. Mothers' reports of involvement were positively related to children's language and literacy outcomes in several areas. Mothers whose children tended to do better on Receptive Vocabulary also tended to report more frequent interactions with kindergarten teachers. Higher levels of responsibility at kindergarten were also related to better Receptive Vocabulary scores and better scores on Narrative Production.

Kindergarten teachers' assessment of *parent support for child learning* was positively related to all three measures of children's language outcomes: Narrative Production, Emergent Literacy, and Receptive Vocabulary. Teachers' assessment of the *child being read to at home* was also associated with all three measures, most strongly with Receptive Vocabulary scores.

A review of demographic variables indicated that Family Income was positively related to teacher assessment of *parent support for child learning* ($r = .32$, $p < .05$) and assessments of the *child being read to at home* ($r = .35$, $p < .05$), whereas Mother's Education was negatively associated with teacher reports of *frequency of contact with parents* ($r = -.31$, $p < .05$). This latter finding may reflect a constellation of circumstances in which mothers with less education tended to receive welfare and were less likely to work, having fewer of the scheduling concerns that hindered contact with teachers and opportunities for involvement in activities at school for the working mothers in the Home–School Study.

These results suggest again that kindergarten teachers value parent efforts that are more focused on academic development. Teachers are likely to view mothers who consistently read to their children as more involved and supportive than mothers who spend a lot of time volunteering at the school site. One might question whether teachers assume that children who are doing better in school are getting more support at home. Our data show, however, that even when preschool teachers and mothers give consistent reports of parent involvement, the influence of these preschool-based activities does not carry over to elementary school outcomes. Given significant relationships between kindergarten teachers' assessments of support and kindergarten language and literacy outcomes, this suggests that teachers do have a good idea of which parents are implementing academically based involvement activities. Previous research that examined correspondence between parent and teacher reports of involvement also showed that teacher reports were stronger predictors of achievement in elementary school (Reynolds, 1992).

CONCLUSIONS

Across the preschools and kindergartens attended by the children in the Home–School Study, there were structural differences in philosophical approaches to and expectations about parent involvement. Within each program there were also individual differences in the ways in which teachers implemented program expectations. From their interview data, we can see that mothers perceived a broad range of responses from the teachers—some teachers were more consistent in promoting parent involvement, whereas others articulated less-developed goals and seemed to be at a loss to move beyond their own negative stereotypes of particular mothers. Given this variety of opportunities for involvement by parents and attitudes on the part of teachers about parents, it is still interesting to note that there are relationships between some of the parent involvement variables and the language and literacy skills that the children in the Home–School Study displayed in kindergarten.

For parent participation as defined by this study, peak involvement occurred at the preschool level, with involvement declining as children moved into kindergarten. Transition into kindergarten also appears to mark an increased distance between mothers and their children's teachers. Teacher–parent contact moved from an informal exchange to a more formalized process centered around progress reports, and mothers took on fewer classroom-related responsibilities. In addition, qualitative data suggest that involvement should not be defined in static terms. Parents' activities within the school and with their children reflected different school structures and their children's changing developmental needs.

It is also apparent that for the most part the mothers in the Home–School Study wanted to be involved in their children's education and were willing to engage with teachers and school personnel in a variety of different ways. The rapport that mothers were able to establish with teachers as a result of informal contact was helpful in responding to any difficulties their children experienced and allowed more mutual decision-making on the children's behalf. Mothers who spent a good deal of time visiting their children's classrooms and volunteering in the schools also expressed an understanding and empathy for the difficult job that many teachers have. They related a strategy that entailed listening to both sides when conflicts came up, whereas mothers who spent little time in the classroom seemed to approach conflicts from a more adversarial position.

Teacher assessments of parental support were more strongly related to children's language and literacy outcomes than were maternal reports of involvement, which suggests that teachers have a specific understanding of the importance of the particular parent involvement activities necessary to enhance children's learning. Interestingly, by kindergarten, these activities are more home based (for example, reading to the child) or generally supportive (for example, support for child's academic growth or child development) than classroom based (for example, acting as an aide in the classroom or parent coordinator).

Given the heavy load that elementary school teachers must already manage, it is unlikely that adding more structured interactions with parents would necessarily be productive or welcomed. In addition, it is unrealistic to expect that parents will indulge in spending the same amount of time at their child's school in later grades as they did during the initial preschool period that marked the child's first days away from home. Indeed, the developmental expectation is that of greater independence for the child, which might mirror an increase in parental participation in homework-type activities.

Teachers and school administrators, however, might be well served by increasing the kinds of opportunities for *informal* interaction that could be available to parents, incorporating those opportunities into the school day, and promoting options to parents. Special consideration should be paid to parents of children who are bused to school, who may have to travel long distances to meet with teachers, or who may lack cars for transportation. Occasional visits might be facilitated by inviting parents to accompany children to school and providing return bus transportation after brief exchanges with teachers. Despite the best efforts of teachers and school administrators, there will certainly be parents too constrained by other commitments to participate to a great degree or others who prefer to put their energies elsewhere in terms of their children's development. But judging by responses in the interviews of the mothers in the Home–School Study, parents would like more opportunities for informal involvement. (See Edwards, Pleasants, and Franklin, 1999, for detailed suggestions regarding ways to encourage these opportunities and how teachers' relationships with parents can enhance literacy development.)

Given the relationship between parent involvement and children's language and literacy outcomes in this study, the most important aspect of any effort to facilitate parent involvement would seem to be to establish mechanisms for teachers to communicate clearly to parents about the sorts of activities that are most beneficial to children's learning. Parents may not necessarily see themselves as able to contribute to children's formal learning and may be more comfortable in fundraising or chaperone-type roles. Yet, many of the mothers in this study were enthusiastically supportive of their children's schooling and deeply committed to their own volunteer efforts. Intervention studies have shown that parents want to work with schools in promoting their children's education and given a well-designed program to encourage literacy-based activities between parents and children, the results are quite positive (Gallimore, Goldenberg, & Weisner, 1993; Jordan, Snow, & Porche, 2000).

Programs designed to enhance parent involvement must not focus solely on increasing participation, but rather in directing it toward children's academic outcomes. Teachers can take the initiative by providing guidance to parents in emphasizing reading activities with children. As children's language skills increase, parents with limited educational and financial resources may begin to feel that they are less capable in being able to help their children with school. Both formal and informal interactions with parents can provide opportunities to reinforce the value of involvement and curtail parents' declining participation in their children's education.

Chapter 13

Homes and Schools Together
Supporting Language and Literacy Development

Patton O. Tabors, Catherine E. Snow,
and David K. Dickinson

In this book we have looked at many different environmental factors at home and in preschool that we have shown are related to performance on language and literacy tests administered to the children in the Home–School Study of Language and Literacy Development when they were in kindergarten. In Chapter 12 we began looking at the perceptions of parents and teachers about the relationship between homes and schools, about their efforts to bridge the distance between homes and schools, and about how these efforts were related to how the children in the study performed on language and literacy tasks in kindergarten. In this chapter we combine the information we have about the home and the preschool environments of the children in the Home–School Study to begin to understand how homes and schools *together* may shape the skills that children bring to the literacy challenges of the early grades in school. Furthermore, we discuss implications of our findings for parent education, staff development of teachers, and overall public policy support for children's early language and literacy development.

Before investigating these important topics, however, we would like to take advantage of the fact that we have longitudinal data on the children in the study well beyond kindergarten. First, therefore, we look at the relationships between the kindergarten scores and later language and literacy scores of the children in fourth and in seventh grade, to see how critical the skills that children have in kindergarten may be for lasting school success.

LONG-TERM IMPORTANCE OF
KINDERGARTEN LANGUAGE AND LITERACY SKILLS

In Chapter 1 we talked about the battery of tests called the SHELL–K (the School-Home Early Language and Literacy Battery–Kindergarten; Snow, Tabors, Nicholson, & Kurland, 1995) that we administered to the children in the study at home when they were 5 years old. In later chapters we chose to restrict our analyses to three (see Chapter 6) or four (see Chapter 11) of the SHELL–K tests that involve skills most closely related to later literacy acquisition. In this chapter we again restrict our analyses to Narrative Production, Formal Definitions, Emergent Literacy, and Receptive Vocabulary and see what the relationship is between scores on these early tests and the language and literacy tests that we administered to the students in the study when they were fourth and seventh graders. This analysis will allow us to see how predictive the kindergarten scores may be of later language and literacy abilities for this group of children.

Fourth- and Seventh-Grade Language and Literacy Tests

Every year after kindergarten we visited the children from the Home–School Study in their classrooms, interviewed their teachers, and had the children complete a battery of tests for us. Each year, the SHELL battery contained a different configuration of tasks, although we did repeat many of the tasks from one year to the next. In both fourth and seventh grade, among other tests, we administered the Peabody Picture Vocabulary Test–Revised (PPVT–R; Dunn & Dunn, 1981) to measure Receptive Vocabulary as we had done in kindergarten, and we administered the Reading Comprehension section of the California Achievement Tests (CAT; CTB Macmillan/McGraw-Hill, 1992). These two nationally normed tests gave us an idea of how the children who were participating in the Home–School Study were doing in relation to other students around the country on Receptive Vocabulary and Reading Comprehension.

As we had anticipated at the outset of the project, we experienced a drop-off in the number of families participating in the study as we followed the children into elementary and then junior high school. In fourth grade, 54 students completed the Reading Comprehension section of the CAT and 56 students completed the PPVT–R, including all four of the portrait children. In seventh grade, 51 students completed both tests, including Astra, Todd, and Casey but not Mariana, as she had returned to Texas with her mother and brother by that time. In spite of having fewer students in the sample, we still found that the scores on these tasks were normally distributed with considerable variation on each task (see Table A13.1 in the appendix for full descriptive statistics). On the PPVT–R in fourth and seventh grade, the mean for the Home–School Study sample was extremely close to the national average of 100; on the Reading Comprehension section of the CAT, the mean was just below the national average in fourth grade and was at the national average in seventh grade. These results mean that we still had a well-distributed sample, even though it contained fewer individuals than in kindergarten.

When we examined correlations between the kindergarten language and literacy measures and the fourth- and seventh-grade outcomes, we found considerable stability across time for these measures (see Table 13.1). The strongest correlation was between kindergarten Receptive Vocabulary and the fourth-grade scores on the same test, although the correlation between the kindergarten and the seventh-grade Receptive Vocabulary scores was also strong. Furthermore, kindergarten Receptive Vocabulary was also strongly correlated with fourth-grade Reading Comprehension and even more strongly with seventh-grade Reading Comprehension. This means that how well children did on the PPVT–R in kindergarten was a strong predictor of how they would score on Receptive Vocabulary and Reading Comprehension 5 and 8 years later.

Scores in Emergent Literacy, which consisted of Writing Concepts, Letter Recognition, Story and Print Concepts, Sounds in Words, and Environmental Print, were also strongly correlated with Reading Comprehension and Receptive Vocabulary scores 5 and 8 years later. How children scored on Formal Definitions in kindergarten was also correlated with the fourth- and seventh-grade outcomes. And finally, scores on the Bear Story (the Narrative Production task) were significantly but less strongly related to scores in Reading Comprehension and Receptive Vocabulary in fourth and seventh grade.

Table 13.1. Correlations between scores on kindergarten language and literacy tasks and fourth- and seventh-grade language and literacy tasks

	Fourth-grade Reading Comprehension	Seventh-grade Reading Comprehension	Fourth-grade Receptive Vocabulary	Seventh-grade Receptive Vocabulary
Kindergarten Narrative Production	.47***	.45***	.28*	.31*
Kindergarten Formal Definitions	.55***	.51***	.64***	.61***
Kindergarten Emergent Literacy	.62***	.63***	.58***	.61***
Kindergarten Receptive Vocabulary	.60***	.71***	.76***	.63***

*p < .05; ***p < .001.

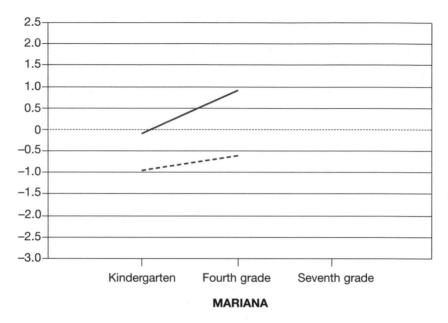

MARIANA

Figure 13.1. Standardized scores for Mariana's Receptive Vocabulary and Emergent Literacy/Reading Comprehension for kindergarten and fourth grade. (——— Emergent Literacy/Reading Comprehension; - - - - Receptive Vocabulary; horizontal dotted line indicates sample mean.)

Even though these correlations demonstrate that the scores that the children in the Home–School Study received on the kindergarten measures are strongly predictive of the scores they received on the language and literacy tasks in fourth and seventh grade, this does not mean that the skills that an individual child displayed in kindergarten determined how that child scored on the later measures. For example, when we look at the four portrait children (Figures 13.1–13.4), we see that there are a number of different patterns to their test results, and in no case was there a one-to-one relationship between how they had performed previously and their later results.

Mariana's Receptive Vocabulary and Emergent Literacy/Reading Comprehension results are displayed in Figure 13.1. Between kindergarten and fourth grade, Mariana continued to attend Boston public schools as she had for her 2 years of kindergarten. As mentioned before, however, Mariana left the Boston area and returned to Texas with her family after fourth grade, so we do not have seventh-grade results for her. In Figure 13.1, we can see that Mariana was below the mean for the Home–School Study sample in Receptive Vocabulary in kindergarten and fourth grade. She was only slightly below the mean on Emergent Literacy in kindergarten but was well above the mean for the

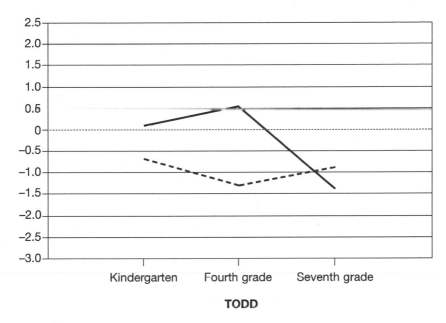

Figure 13.2. Standardized scores for Todd's Receptive Vocabulary and Emergent Literacy/Reading Comprehension for kindergarten, fourth, and seventh grade. (——— Emergent Literacy/Reading Comprehension; - - - - Receptive Vocabulary; horizontal dotted line indicates sample mean.)

sample on the fourth-grade Reading Comprehension test, scoring in the 70th percentile. Unfortunately, we have no way of knowing whether this upward trend continued as she reached the upper elementary grades.

Todd's Receptive Vocabulary and Emergent Literacy/Reading Comprehension results are displayed in Figure 13.2. Throughout the period from kindergarten to seventh grade, Todd continued to attend public school in the town where he lived outside of Boston. Todd scored somewhat below the mean for the sample on the PPVT–R in all 3 testing years. However, his results for Emergent Literacy/Reading Comprehension were not as consistent. In kindergarten his score on the CAP fell right at the average for the sample. But his fourth-grade Reading Comprehension was above the mean at the 61st percentile, whereas his score on the seventh grade Reading Comprehension test plummeted to the 16th percentile, perhaps due to lack of effort.[1]

---

[1]Field notes taken by the assessor during the seventh-grade testing session indicate that Todd "didn't seem to be reading the passages. He seemed to be just circling the answers. . . . On p. 14 he looked ahead to see how many pages he had [left] and how much longer the test would be. . . . Overall, it took him about 18 minutes . . . to finish the [test]." The time limit on this test is 50 minutes.

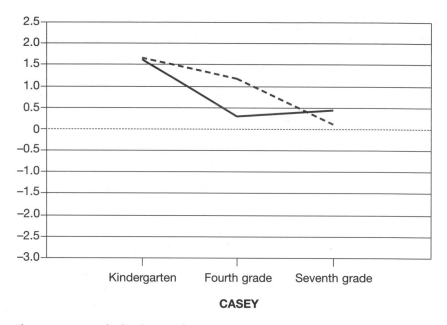

CASEY

Figure 13.3. Standardized scores for Casey's Receptive Vocabulary and Emergent Literacy/Reading Comprehension for kindergarten, fourth, and seventh grade. (——— Emergent Literacy/Reading Comprehension; ---- Receptive Vocabulary; horizontal dotted line indicates sample mean.)

After attending the public preschool program in his community, Casey continued in the same public school system throughout elementary school. The pattern of results for Casey (see Figure 13.3) shows a surprising decline in vocabulary, as well as a decline and then a plateauing between kindergarten Emergent Literacy and Reading Comprehension in fourth and seventh grade, which were in the 58th and 64th percentile, respectively. Having started out in kindergarten as one of the higher-scoring children in the study on Receptive Vocabulary and Emergent Literacy, Casey was only scoring at the mean for the sample in these two areas by seventh grade.

Although Astra, like Mariana, attended public schools in Boston from kindergarten to seventh grade, she moved around among several different schools, including attending an exam school[2] that specialized in math and science for seventh grade. In Figure 13.4 we can see that Astra, like Todd, had very stable PPVT–R results across the years, although Astra's scores were clustered around the average for the sample, whereas Todd's were slightly below average. Astra's Emergent Lit-

---

[2]To be admitted to an exam school in Boston, a student must pass an entrance exam.

cracy score was above the mean in kindergarten, her fourth-grade Reading Comprehension score was right at the mean, but her seventh grade Reading Comprehension score rebounded and was the highest among the portrait children, at the 76th percentile.

What these results tell us is that although how the children in the sample scored on the kindergarten measures can give us a good idea of how they *might* score on language and literacy tests later on in their elementary and junior high careers, their later scores were also subject to a variety of other influences. These other influences, no doubt, include the types of reading programs that the children were exposed to in school, the amount of reading children did outside of school; the types of experiences the children might have had with their families or other adults; and, increasingly, the impact of their peer groups on their attitudes about school. Even their ability and motivation as test takers could have influenced how they scored on all of these tests. Consequently, we think of these correlations between the kindergarten language and literacy skills and the fourth and seventh grade outcomes as being *indicative* but clearly not *determinative* of later literacy development.

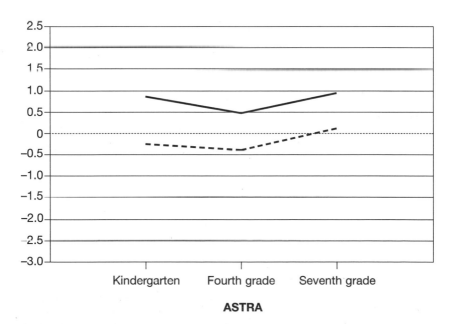

Figure 13.4. Standardized scores for Astra's Receptive Vocabulary and Emergent Literacy/Reading Comprehension for kindergarten, fourth, and seventh grade. (———— Emergent Literacy/Reading Comprehension; ---- Receptive Vocabulary; horizontal dotted line indicates sample mean.)

LINKING HOME AND SCHOOL DATA

When thinking about how to combine the home and school data, we decided that we would want to answer three main questions:

1. To what extent do children who come from homes with greater support for literacy attend classrooms with higher quality language and literacy environments? In other words, do families who are providing a home rich in language and literacy seek out or, perhaps, have easier access to preschool programs that emphasize language and literacy preparation as well?

2. What is the contribution of the home environment to children's language and literacy skills above and beyond the control variables, and what is the contribution of the preschool environment above and beyond the combination of control variables and home environment? In other words, did collecting data from a variety of sources, in fact, increase the information we had about the factors that were related to the children's language and literacy skills in kindergarten?

3. How do home and school environment factors work together? Can strength in one of these environments help offset shortcomings in the other? In other words, what happens when a child from a home high in language and literacy support attends a preschool without a strong program? What happens when a child from a home that does not provide an enriched environment attends a high-quality preschool program?

Each of these questions are considered in the following sections.

Relationship Between Home and Preschool Environment Variables

In order to answer the first of these questions, we ran correlational analyses between the home and preschool environment composite variables. The results of these analyses are presented in Table 13.2.

Interestingly, what we found was that although there are relationships among many of the home and preschool environment composites, those relationships are in the moderate range. This means that the answer to the question we posed about whether children's home language and literacy environments are similar to the language and lit-

Table 13.2. Correlations between home and preschool environment composites (n = 65-69)

Home environment composite	Preschool environment composite		
	Extended Teacher Discourse	Classroom Curriculum	Exposure to Rare Words
Rare Word Density	.30**	.34**	.30**
Extended Discourse	n.s.	.22⁻	n.s.
Home Support for Literacy	.43***	.24*	.25*

⁻$p < .10$; *$p < .05$; **$p < .01$; ***$p < .001$.

eracy environments in their preschool classrooms is neither a strong "yes" or "no," but a more guarded "sometimes." This is perhaps not too surprising when we realize that individual homes and individual preschool environments were already not consistent in terms of how well they were rated on the language and literacy aspects that we sampled, demonstrating different strengths and weaknesses even within the array of opportunities each could offer (see, for example, the individual graphs for the portrait children in Figure 6.1). What these results tell us is that in this sample of families, the types of experiences that the children have at home and at preschool may be similar, but they could also be quite different.

Combining Home and Preschool Environment Factors to Predict Kindergarten Language and Literacy

In order to answer the second question, we needed to do regression analyses that would combine the home and school environment composites to see which factors remain as unique predictors of the children's kindergarten scores and to see how homes and preschools *in combination* predict children's outcomes (see Table A13.2 in the appendix).

In Figure 13.5, the results of the regression analysis to predict Narrative Production are displayed. This graph incorporates the information from previous analyses discussed in Chapters 6 and 11, including the amount of variation explained by the control variables alone (the first bar on the left), the home environment variables taking into account the control variables (the second bar from the left), and the school environment variables taking into account the control variables (the third bar from the left). The final bar on the right indicates the amount of variance in Narrative Production that is explained when we combine the home and preschool composites in the same analysis. The

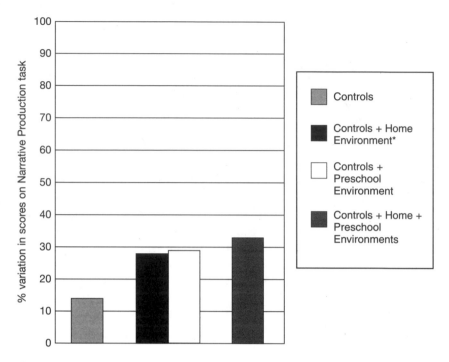

Figure 13.5.   Predicting Narrative Production: Home and preschool environment variables. (*indicates significant increment to R^2.)

final model for Narrative Production explains 33% of the variation in the children's scores on the Bear Story task.

In further analyses we found that the home environment composites together added significant explanatory power to the model above and beyond the control variables, whereas the preschool environment composites did *not* add significant explanatory power to the model when they were combined with the control and home environment variables. The only unique predictor in this model when all of the variables are included in the analysis is Family Income at the first home visit. In the case of Narrative Production, then, it is the control variables, particularly Family Income, and the home environment variables, that carry the predictive power.

The regression analysis to predict Emergent Literacy is displayed in Figure 13.6. In the final, combined model, Gender, Family Income, Extended Teacher Discourse, and Exposure to Rare Words at preschool all remain unique predictors. This combination of variables explains 52% of the variation in the children's scores on the CAP in kindergarten.

We tested again to see whether the home environment composites added explanatory power beyond the control variables and whether the preschool composites added explanatory power beyond the combination of the control variables and the home environment composites. In the case of Emergent Literacy, we found that significant additional explanatory power was added to the model each time. This means that we gained information about which factors contributed to the children's emergent literacy skills above and beyond the control variables by collecting home environment data and that we gained *further* information about which factors contributed to their emergent literacy skills by collecting data in their preschool classrooms.

And, finally, in Figure 13.7 we have displayed the models that predict the scores on the PPVT–R in kindergarten. In the final, combined model, we found that Rare Word Density at home and Home Support for Literacy, as well as Extended Teacher Discourse at preschool, all remain unique predictors of Receptive Vocabulary. The combination of all of the control, home, and preschool variables explains 56% of the variation in Receptive Vocabulary.

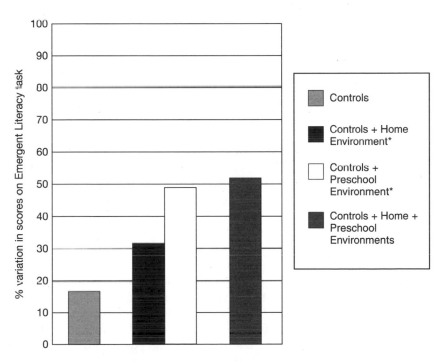

Figure 13.6. Predicting Emergent Literacy: Home and preschool environment variables. (*indicates significant increment to R^2.)

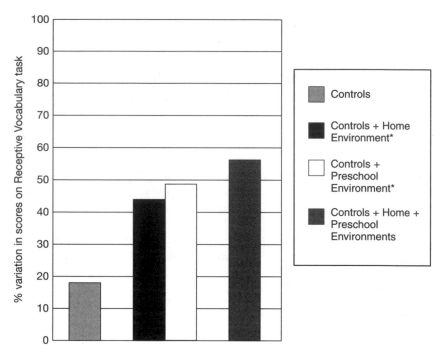

Figure 13.7. Predicting Receptive Vocabulary: Home and preschool environment variables. (*indicates significant increment to R^2.)

For this model, as with Emergent Literacy, we found that the home environment composites added explanatory power beyond the control variables, and that the preschool composites added explanatory power beyond the combination of the control variables and the home environment composites. Again this means that it was important for us to have collected data from multiple sources (maternal interviews, home environment, preschool environment), as each of these sources provided significant new information about the factors that influenced how the children scored on the PPVT–R.

The answer to the second question, then, is that by collecting home environment data we had more information about all three of these kindergarten outcomes for the children in the Home–School Study than we would have had if we had only had the information in the mothers' interviews and the children's Mean Length of Utterance. Furthermore, by collecting preschool environment data, we had more information about Emergent Literacy and Receptive Vocabulary than we would have had if we had not visited the preschool classrooms of the children in the study.

Home and Preschool Environments:
Can One Compensate for the Other?

In order to answer the third question, we used the regression analyses that we had completed to answer the second question and looked at the scores that would have been predicted for children from certain combinations of home and preschool environments. In fact, in this analysis, we are not talking about *actual* children in the Home–School Study, but how children similar to these children might have scored on the outcome measures *under certain conditions*.

In order to set up this analysis, we decided to define a high value on the home and preschool environment composites as being the 90th percentile value and a low value as being the 10th percentile value. In this way we could say that a child would have a *high home–high preschool language and literacy environment* if all six composites (Extended Discourse, Rare Word Density, and Home Support for Literacy in the home environment, as well as Extended Teacher Discourse, Classroom Curriculum, and Exposure to Rare Words in the preschool environment) were in the 90th percentile. Obviously, although some homes and preschools scored at this level on one or more of the composites, none of them scored that high on *all* of the composites. By the same token, a *low home–low preschool language and literacy environment* was defined as having all six composites in the 10th percentile. Again, although some homes and preschools scored at this level on one or more of the composites, none of them scored that low on *all* of the composites. In each of these cases, however, we can imagine that there might be children who would experience this type of situation, and we can predict what their scores would be on the kindergarten outcome measures based on the Home–School Study sample's results. Furthermore, and perhaps more interestingly for the question we are answering, we can also predict kindergarten language and literacy scores based on the two other combinations of environments: *high home–low preschool language and literacy environment* and *low home–high preschool language and literacy environment*.

Figures 13.8, 13.9, and 13.10 display the results of these analyses for the three kindergarten language and literacy measures. In each of these analyses, we can see that the high home–high preschool combination predicts that children will do well above average on the measure and the low home–low preschool combination predicts that children will do well below average. Neither of these findings is surprising. But how would children do if they were exposed to one of the high–low combinations? In other words, do we have evidence that one of these environments might be able to compensate for the other?

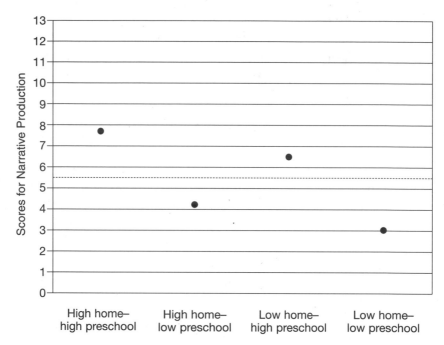

Figure 13.8. Predicting Narrative Production under varying combinations of home and preschool environments (dotted line indicates sample mean).

Again the results are consistent for all three of the kindergarten measures. Coming from a high home–low preschool combination predicts that a child will score slightly below average on all three measures, but coming from a low home–high preschool combination predicts that a child will score *above* average on all three of the measures.

The implication of these findings is that excellent preschools can compensate for homes that offer well below average access to language and literacy support, at least as those environments are reflected in children's kindergarten skills. This is a striking finding, as earlier studies of elementary school–age children (Snow, Barnes, Chandler, Goodman, & Hemphill, 1991) found that home factors had greater predictive strength during the early years of school. It is also a finding that offers considerable hope for improving child outcomes, as interventions to improve the quality of preschools may be easier to implement than interventions to change language and literacy practices in low-income homes.

IMPLICATIONS FOR PRACTITIONERS AND POLICYMAKERS

What are the implications of the findings of the Home–School Study for practitioners and policymakers who are interested in the influence of the early childhood period on language and literacy development? How can the findings presented in this book be applied to planning preschool and primary classrooms, as well as prevention and intervention services for children from low-income families? We discuss the implications of the results of the study under the headings that have organized our thinking throughout the book: homes, classrooms, and their interaction.

Thinking About the Home

Our results indicate that activities in the home make a considerable contribution to children's ultimate literacy success, both by providing opportunities for children to engage in specific literacy-related activities such as book reading and by developing language skills, including vocabulary, that show immediate and long-term relations to literacy. As mentioned throughout the book, the language and literacy environments in the homes of the children in the study were extremely varied,

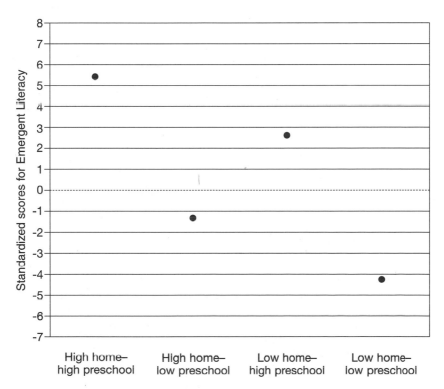

Figure 13.9. Predicting Emergent Literacy under varying combinations of home and preschool environments (dotted line indicates sample mean).

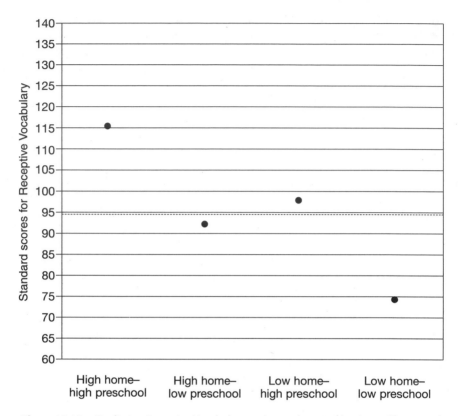

Figure 13.10. Predicting Receptive Vocabulary under varying combinations of home and preschool environments (dotted line indicates sample mean).

with some homes providing more or less of the environment factors that we have found were important for helping to develop kindergarten skills. These findings, of course, are specific to the perspective that we took when visiting the homes of the children in the study: We were measuring aspects of the home environment that were related to language and literacy. When we say a home environment was not as high on support for literacy, for example, as the other homes in the study, we are not, of course, saying that a child raised in that home was not being provided with a great deal of other kinds of support. We are merely focusing on one aspect of the home environment that we believe can affect how a child performs later in school.

The importance of the home environment factors naturally leads to the question how we might help parents engage more often in the activities shown in this study to be important. Fortunately, many efforts along these lines have already been undertaken by a variety of organizations and agencies. Programs such as Reading is Fundamental (RiF) and Reach Out and Read (ROAR) have focused considerable effort on getting books into low-income homes and on emphasizing the importance of regular parent–child book reading. The public emphasis on book reading has evidently worked, at least for some groups, as recent findings about home literacy activities from the National Household Education Survey (Nord, Lennon, Liu, & Chandler, 1999) demonstrate. As mentioned in Chapter 2, the survey included a variety of questions related to home literacy activities. One of the striking findings in the report is that when comparing the answers to this survey in 1999 with answers to the survey in 1993, a higher percentage of families with preschoolers reported routine book reading (81% versus 78%); storytelling (50% versus 43%); and teaching letters, words, and numbers (64% versus 58%). Unfortunately, however, the report indicates that there were no statistically significant increases in families' engagement in literacy activities for children with two or more risk factors. For these children, routine book reading, for example, occurred in 64% of the families in 1993 and 66% of the families in 1999.

As admirable and evidently effective as book-reading intervention programs can be, they have tended to ignore findings that *how* parents read is as important as whether and how often they read. Greater attention by groups such as RiF and ROAR to guidelines for enriched conversations during book reading would be of great value. Indeed, intervention programs such as Dialogic Reading (Whitehurst et al., 1994) have been developed to teach parents about how most effectively to read with their children and have been shown to work. Similarly, Neuman (1996) found that parents are able to make significant contributions to their children's development when helped to become more skillful in how they read and discuss books.

Our findings, however, show that it is not the frequency of book reading or even the quality of the talk that accompanies book reading *alone* that is related to children's language and literacy abilities in kindergarten. What we have found is a much broader pattern of parent–child activities and interactions that support children's language and literacy development. How aware are parents of the importance of this broader pattern of parent–child activities and interactions? In 2000, ZERO TO THREE: National Center for Infants, Toddlers and Families, an advocacy and training organization based in Washington, D.C., sponsored a national survey that asked parents of young children, and others, broad questions about child development. One of the findings of this survey, as reported in *What Grown-Ups Understand About Child Development: A National Benchmark Survey* (2000), was that 69% of parents of young children agree that children's capacity for learning is not determined at birth and can be increased by how parents interact with them. Although this would seem to be good news, it also means that the remainder of the parents surveyed did *not* believe this was true. Furthermore, there is no way of knowing from the survey how parents interpreted the phrase "how parents interact with their children." Clearly, there is still the challenge of getting the message across to *all* parents, and particularly to low-income and low-education parents, that everyday activities of all sorts, accompanied by interesting talk with lots of new vocabulary words, can play an important part in their children's language and literacy development.

Thinking About Classrooms

The findings of the Home–School Study reveal with great clarity the power of preschool classrooms to contribute to children's language and literacy development. Several recent policy initiatives, from the expansion of Head Start under the Head Start Amendments of 1998 (PL 105-285) to the recommendations of the National Research Council's *Eager to Learn* (Bowman, Donovan, & Burns, 2000), are consistent with our findings that preschool can contribute enormously to later academic achievement, in particular for children from low-income families.

Our findings make the additional point, though, that access to *particular* language and literacy learning experiences in preschool makes a big difference to child outcomes. Teacher language use and curricular focus are crucial to optimal effects. We also found evidence suggesting that children benefit from hearing conversations that other children have with their teachers. This finding of the impact of children on each other has implications for teachers, pointing to the need to support children's learning from each other. It also has implications for policy, pointing to the potential value of mixing children from different backgrounds. Some Head Start programs are blending funding in ways that enable children from different backgrounds to be in classrooms together, and the Head Start initiative, Quality Improvement Through Linking Together (QUILT), is seeking to draw together the child care and Head Start communities.

Although we found that classrooms can play a major role in supporting children's language and literacy development, just as is the case for homes, many preschool classrooms that are pleasant, safe, friendly, and attractive are still not attending sufficiently to building children's language and literacy capacities. The need for improvement in the quality of programs has been noted by policymakers in recent years. The 1998 Head Start reauthorization introduced higher levels of education for Head Start staff as a performance standard and established child performance standards in domains such as letter knowledge and oral language. *Eager to Learn* (Bowman et al., 2000) noted the importance of a planful curricular model with some clear and important content within any good preschool program, without endorsing any particular curriculum. *Eager to Learn* and *From Neurons to Neighborhoods* (Shonkoff & Phillips, 2000), another National Research Council report focused on early childhood, both strongly recommend that all the adults dealing with the care and education of young children meet new, higher standards of general education and of knowledge about early development and optimal practices for young children.

Until such recommendations have their full impact on the population of early childhood educators, we must think of ways to improve the practice of the current cadre of Head Start and preschool teachers, especially those serving children from low-income families. One approach is to strive to ensure that classrooms are organized and supplied with needed materials. During the 1990s, we learned a great deal about principles of how to organize classroom environments so that children have optimal opportunities to use books and print and engage in conversations (reviewed by Roskos & Neuman, 2001). Related work has shown the value of supplying classrooms with the needed books. For example, Susan Neuman (1999), noting the paucity of books and of child access to books in many preschool settings, launched an intervention called Books Aloud. It involved giving lots of books to preschool classrooms but also providing training to the classroom staff on ways to make the books accessible to children (low bookshelves, displays of book covers, regular shifting of available books). Classroom staff also received training in ways to read with children (reading in small groups as well as with the whole class, leaving time for child questions, posing open-ended questions). The impact of this intervention on classroom practice was impressive in introducing precisely the kinds of interactions that the findings of the Home–School Study suggest are helpful to children.

Of course, such changes cannot be made unless teachers understand the nature of early literacy and the strategies required to bolster young children's development. Although preservice training programs ultimately must help supply preschools with skilled teachers, there is an urgent need for effective in-service training now. Recognizing this need, Head Start and various state agencies are undertaking new models for staff professional development, such as *Heads Up! Reading*, a teacher-training course designed to enhance teaching practices and improve literacy outcomes for young children that is being delivered to Head Start centers, child care programs, and prekindergarten classrooms via satellite and Internet connections. Such professional development efforts, if sufficiently intense, individualized, integrative, and long term, have been shown to have an impact on teacher knowledge and teacher practice, even when the teachers involved do not have advanced training or education.

Another approach to providing in-service training to Head Start and child care teachers is the Literacy Environment Enrichment Program (LEEP; Dickinson & Sprague, 2001). Building on early results from the Home–School Study, David Dickinson and his colleagues at the Education Development Center created an intervention that carries college credits and is delivered by Head Start training and technical assistance providers throughout New England. Teachers take this course with their supervisors, who refine their supervisory skills while also deepening their knowledge of language and literacy development. Teachers learn about language and literacy development by reading articles and college textbooks and applying their learning in their own classrooms. Research that compared classrooms of teachers taking the course with comparable teachers who were not enrolled found that between the fall and spring, those teachers taking the course showed far more improvement in classroom quality related to language and literacy. Equally important, children in classrooms of teachers involved in LEEP were found to show more growth in language skills. Because of its success, this course is now being put into a format that will enable it to be taught using two-way interactive television in concert with a web site.

The success of researchers in identifying strategies that foster children's growth and constructing professional development experiences that translate into improved classroom instruction challenges early childhood programs in general to systematize and improve professional development activities for their staff. And it also challenges policymakers to provide the funding and support systems required to enable programs to engage in the level of sustained effort that is required to transform early childhood classrooms into settings where all children receive optimal support for language and literacy before they enter kindergarten.

Thinking About Home–School Links

We have seen that home factors make crucial contributions to child outcomes and that preschool factors contribute to outcomes above and beyond the home environment. For the average preschool-age child, though, home and school do not operate as separate predictors but interact both literally and statistically in producing outcomes. Given the limitations of our data, we could not separately consider cases in which the *specific* predictors at home and at preschool were compensatory versus reinforcing. For example, is a child better off if both home and preschool provide high densities of rare words even with low scores on the other predictors, or is it better if one environment has high rare-word density while the other provides more access to extended talk? Further research is needed to answer questions like this.

In contrast, we already have considerable evidence that homes and preschools can operate in ways that are synergistic, in particular when there is direct contact between them. An important effort along these lines was undertaken by Gail Jordan, a curriculum director in White Bear Lake, Minnesota. Inspired by early findings from the Home–School Study concerning the importance of rich parent–child talk, Gail developed an intervention program with parents of kindergartners called *Project EASE* (Early Access to Success in Education). The intervention involved both direct instruction to parents concerning different modes of interacting verbally with their children and regular assignments from the kindergarten teacher that built on the parent instruction.[3]

The intervention was highly successful. Parents in the intervention group participated actively and evaluated the experience very positively, and children in the intervention group showed significantly greater gains from beginning to end of kindergarten than the control group on precisely the same measures of language and literacy skill as those in the SHELL–K (Jordan, Snow, & Porche, 2000). Since the Project EASE intervention uses widely available books, builds on parents' eagerness to help their children as they start school, and can be implemented relatively cheaply, with Title I funds, for instance, it could be widely replicated in other school districts.

CONCLUSIONS

We have presented in this book evidence leading to the conclusion that individual children are already well launched on a particular pathway of literacy acquisition by kindergarten. We do not mean to suggest, though, that they cannot deviate from that early pathway. Indeed, we fully expect that exposure to excellent schools and to dramatically enriched language and literacy environments in the elementary years, whether at home or school, could redirect an individual child's developmental pathway upwards. In fact, when analyzing the results for a subsample of children in the Home–School Study who increased their Word Recognition[4] and Receptive Vocabulary scores by one standard deviation or more between kindergarten and sixth grade, we found that

---

[3]Details of the intervention itself and the materials used in it can be accessed at http://gseweb.harvard.edu/~pild/projectease.htm

[4]As measured by the Wide Range Achievement Test–Revised (WRAT–R): Reading Subtest (Jastak & Wilkinson, 1984).

a high percentage of them had received special services in their schools (DeTemple, 1999). Thus we have to interpret our overall findings as suggesting that, in general, the elementary and middle schools that the children from the Home–School Study attended were adequate rather than excellent language and literacy environments, and, thus, that most of the school programs simply helped the children continue along in the pathways on which they had started.

It seems clear, then, that until and unless elementary reading instruction is improved, in particular for children from lower-income, lower-education households, attention to quality of preschool environments is an excellent investment. We know right now what needs to be better in those environments, and we have a number of strategies for upgrading them that have proven successful.

Given the powerful effects of preschools above and beyond home contributions, our results also suggest the wisdom of expanding the availability of preschool, particularly for children from low-income families. Some states are already offering 4-year-old kindergarten classes to children growing up in poverty. This is a wise policy if those 4-year-old classes are not seen simply as opportunities to introduce formal reading instruction 2 years early, but precisely as contexts for focusing on language and on preliteracy skills. In fact, we would argue that kindergarten classes for 5-year-olds should also be protected as places to focus on the prerequisites to literacy development, as recommended in *Preventing Reading Difficulties in Young Children* (Snow, Burns, & Griffin, 1998), rather than as a chance to start a year earlier on phoneme–grapheme correspondences. Our results demonstrate that children do begin literacy learning with language and that enhancing their language development by providing them with rich and engaging language environments during the first 5 years of life is the best way to ensure their success as readers.

Appendix
Home–School Study Data

CHAPTER 1—LANGUAGE DEVELOPMENT IN THE PRESCHOOL YEARS

Following is information about the scoring procedures applied to the School-Home Early Language and Literacy Battery–Kindergarten (SHELL–K; Snow, Tabors, Nicholson, & Kurland, 1995) as well as descriptive statistics on the results of the SHELL–K (see Table A1.1).

Narrative Production Task

The Bear Story was coded for structure, for story elements, and for syntactic complexity. First, each story was divided into clauses, and clauses that described a complicating action, such as "The kite got stuck in the tree," were coded (see Peterson & McCabe, 1983; see also Chapter 4). Next, the stories were scored for the presence of certain story elements:

1. Was there a classic opening or closing (e.g., "Once upon a time," "The end")?
2. Was the kite mentioned in the orientation?
3. Were there evaluative elements?
4. Was a problem stated?
5. Was there a resolution proposed?
6. Was there a climax mentioned?
7. Was there any coda material?

Finally, the number of words in the story was divided by the number of clauses to yield a words-per-clause measure of syntactic complexity.

The words per clause and the number of complicating action clauses were distributed on 5-point scales (0–4), and these scores were added to the total points for the story elements (*yes* = 1) to yield the total score for the Narrative Production task.

Picture Description

The picture descriptions were scored for the total number of words; for the number of adjectives, verbs, and locatives; and for the presence of

Table A1.1. Summary statistics for School-Home Early Language and Literacy Battery–Kindergarten (SHELL–K)

Task	Mean	Standard deviation	Median	Range	Interquartile range
Narrative Production	5.43	(3.07)	5	0–14	3–8
Picture Description	6.99	(2.82)	7	1–13	5–9
Informal Definitions	1.39	(0.58)	1.28	0–3	.92–1.55
Formal Definitions	1.96	(3.02)	0	0–9.43	0–4.21
Superordinates	5.92	(2.79)	6	0–11	4–8
Story Comprehension	6.46	(2.14)	7	2–10	5–8
Emergent Literacy (standardized) total	0	(4.01)	–.43	–7.11 to 7.73	–3.28 to 2.90
Writing Concepts	8.54	(4.39)	8	1–17	4–13
Letter Recognition	32.93	(11.34)	38	0–41	31–40
Story and Print Concepts	12.72	(6.49)	11	0–24	8–17
Sounds in Words	7.14	(3.64)	7	0–12	5–10
Environmental Print	7.15	(4.76)	6	0–20	4–8
Receptive Vocabulary	93.86	(15.49)	91	69–133	83–103

$n = 74.$

five key theme words (*circus, balloons, clown, tent,* and *tickets*). The number of adjectives, verbs, and locatives was placed on 5-point scales, and the total number of words was distributed on a 12-point scale. The scores on these scales were added together and then added to the number of theme words to provide a total score for the Picture Description task.

Definitions

The answers given for the Definitions task were scored using Snow's (Snow, Cancino, Gonzalez, & Shriberg, 1989) scoring method. Each definition was coded as either formal—marked by the presence of a superordinate (often followed by a relative clause)—or informal. Formal Definitions were further coded for the quality of the superordinate and the relative clause, and Informal Definitions were coded for the quality of the descriptive, functional, or definitional features mentioned in the definition. The score for Formal Definitions was derived by dividing the total score for formal definitional quality by the number of definitions attempted. The score for Informal Definitions was derived by dividing the total score for informal definitional quality by the number of informal definitions.

Superordinates

The child received 1 point for each correct answer in the Superordinates task.

Story Comprehension

The total score for the Story Comprehension task was the number of questions answered correctly by the child.

Emergent Literacy

The scoring of the tasks from the Emergent Literacy strand was done as prescribed by the Early Childhood Diagnostic Instrument: The Comprehensive Assessment Program (CAP; Mason & Stewart, 1989). Each child received individual scores on each task as well as a total score. The total Emergent Literacy score was derived by standardizing each subtest score, then adding all of the subtest scores together.

Receptive Vocabulary

The Peabody Picture Vocabulary Test–Revised (PPVT–R; Dunn & Dunn, 1981) was administered and scored according to the manual. The standard score equivalent was computed for each child.

Descriptive Statistics for the School-Home
Early Language and Literacy Battery–Kindergarten

The scores that the kindergartners received on the SHELL–K measures are displayed in Table A1.1. The maximum score possible on the Narrative Production task was 15. The range of scores for kindergartners on this task was 0–14, with a mean of 5.43. The maximum score possible on the Picture Description task was 28, but the top scorers received a score of only 13.

The range of scores for the Informal Definitions was 0–3, with a mean of 1.39.

The range of scores for the Formal Definitions at kindergarten was 0–9.43; however, 40 of the 75 children who took the SHELL–K did not produce any formal definitions, so the mean was only 1.96.

The range of the scores on the Superordinates task was 0–11 (with a maximum of 12), with a mean of 5.92. The scores on this task were correlated with Formal Definitions ($r = .52$, $p < .001$), indicating that children who were able to provide a superordinate when asked directly were more likely to provide a superordinate (the basic requirement for a formal definition) when giving a definition.

The Story Comprehension measure from SHELL–K elicited nearly a full range of possible scores (maximum possible score was 10), and half of the sample scored 7 or higher.

The scores on the Emergent Literacy task also showed a great deal of variability, indicating a wide range of preliteracy skills among the children. The scores on the Story and Print Concepts and the Sounds in Words subtests were normally distributed across the entire range of possible scores. Scores on the Letter Recognition and the Environmental Print subtests also were distributed across the entire range of possible scores, but there was a strong ceiling effect on the Letter Recognition subtest (half of the children scored between 38 and the maximum of 41 points on this subtest) and a preponderance of low scores on the Environmental Print subtest (half of the children scored 6 or lower out of a maximum possible score of 20). The range of scores on the Writing Concepts subtest was slightly restricted (1–17 rather than 0–19), but the scores were normally distributed within that range.

The PPVT–R, a standardized test of receptive vocabulary, generated a mean score (93.86) that was somewhat below the population mean of 100. It is important to note, however, that the PPVT–R scores extended into the highly talented range.

SECTION I—HOME LANGUAGE AND LITERACY ENVIRONMENT

HOME VISIT #3 INSTRUCTIONS

SETTING UP THE INTERVIEW

1. Ask for a time when the mother and child will be ALONE for about 2 hours.

2. Get instructions for getting to their house. We have a map book here to help in this process. You should have a map in front of you when you call if possible. **Check the folder for the second home visit and see if there is a map and possibly some instructions available. MAKE A XEROX OF THE MAP PAGE TO TAKE WITH YOU. DO NOT TAKE THE MAP BOOK.**

3. Call back to confirm your appointment the evening before you are to go and make sure everything is OK. **THIS IS VERY IMPORTANT.** If the appointment has to be changed, be flexible and cheerful and try again.

4. **BEFORE YOU GO, READ THE INFORMATION ON THE CHILD FROM LAST YEAR'S VISIT SO YOU WILL BE "UP TO DATE" ON THE FAMILY SITUATION.**

WHAT YOU WILL NEED TO TAKE WITH YOU

1. Dictating tape recorder and FOUR tapes
TEST TAPE RECORDER BY IDENTIFYING YOURSELF AND YOUR PARTNER AND THE DATE AND WHERE YOU ARE GOING AT THE BEGINNING OF THE TAPE. Red light should be on while you are recording and playing back. If light does not go on when you push play, replace batteries and try again.

2. Lender tape recorder: SIGN OUT THE LENDER BY #, DATE, AND NAME OF FAMILY; SIGN IT BACK IN AFTER YOU RETRIEVE IT. Check battery level by pushing play and checking the red light.

3. Extra batteries, just in case

4. Toys

(continued)

Figure AI.1. Instructions for the 5-year-old home visit tasks.

Figure AI.1. *(continued)*

5. Our books (*The Very Hungry Caterpillar; What Next, Baby Bear!* and *Elephant*)

6. Magnet and assorted objects that go with it. **DO NOT PLACE THE MAGNET ANYWHERE NEAR THE TAPE RECORDER OR TAPES AS IT WILL SCRAMBLE THE TAPES.**

7. Clipboard, pen, and forms for context notes

8. Interview schedule—SPECIFIC TO THIRD HOME VISIT

9. Payment voucher (yellow)—make out in advance except for Social Security number and signature

10. Stamped, addressed envelope for return of tape—if needed with 75¢ postage

11. Present—beautifully wrapped

12. Mealtime instructions to leave at subject's house

WHEN YOU GET THERE

1. **GETTING STARTED**—Take it slow so that everyone has a chance to get acquainted before "formal proceedings" begin. Establish a **relaxed, friendly atmosphere.** Talk about yourself a bit if that seems appropriate so the whole event isn't entirely one-sided. Tell the mother what is going to happen (i.e., "We would like you and your child to look at some books together, to tell us about something that has happened to you, and to play with some toys we have brought with us"). First, we need to ask you some questions.

2. **INTERVIEW**—Administer the interview schedule. **Tape the interview.** If the interview starts to get overly long (i.e., if the child is upset at long distraction of mother's attention), suspend interview, saying, "We can come back to this later." Try again later or make arrangements to telephone and do the rest of the interview then.

3. **BOOK READING**—

   a. Take out *The Very Hungry Caterpillar* and ask if the mother would **look at this book with (name of child)** while you tape-record them together.

   TAPE AND TAKE NOTES

b.   Follow the same procedure with *What Next, Baby Bear!*

TAPE AND TAKE NOTES

4. **ELICITED REPORT—Begin by recounting a "scary" thing that happened to you on the way over** (an "almost" car accident, perhaps). Then ask (BOTH) of them if anything like that had ever happened to them ("Can you and your mom tell me about anything like that that's happened to you?"). The purpose here is to have mother and child talking, NOT THE EXPERIMENTER. Nod or smile if you want to show you're following the conversation but do **NOT** jump in verbally.

5. **BOOK READING #2—**Hand the *Elephant* book to the mother and child and ask if they would "look at it together."

TAPE AND TAKE NOTES

6. **TOY PLAY (10–15 MINUTES)**

Ask the mother: **Where would you like me to dump out the toys?**

Tell child: **I have brought some of MY toys for you to play with, with your mom. Would you like to do that? When you get finished, you can help me pack them all up, because I have to take them home with me.**

Tell mother: **Just play with (name of child) like you would if I weren't here.**

TAPE AND TAKE NOTES

After the toy play, you should ask the child to help you pick up the toys and put them away. Then invite the child to come and read *The Very Hungry Caterpillar* to you.

7. **BOOK READING #3—**Ask the child if she or he will read *The Very Hungry Caterpillar* to you. If the child says, "I can't read," just ask her or him to tell you what's going on in the book. Let the child take the lead in holding the book, turning the pages, and deciding when she or he is done.

TAPE AND TAKE NOTES

(continued)

Figure AI.1.   *(continued)*

8. **MAGNET TASK (10 minutes)**—Take out the magnet task—hold the magnetized base in one hand and all of the small objects in the other hand. Hand them to the mother, and ask her to play with them with her child.

TAPE AND TAKE NOTES

Let the child continue to play with magnet task objects while you explain mealtime to mother.

9. **MEALTIME TAPE**—Ask if you could leave a blank tape (and tape recorder, if needed) with them so that they can make a recording during a meal when the family is together. **WRITE NAME OF FAMILY ON TAPE BEFORE LEAVING IT. DEMONSTRATE USE OF TAPE RECORDER—REMEMBER RECORD REQUIRES PUSHING DOWN BOTH *PLAY* AND *RECORD* BUTTONS.**

Instructions for the mother: **Set the tape recorder up near (name of child) when everyone is eating a meal together in the next few days and let it run during the meal.**

Make arrangements to retrieve the tape recorder (if needed) **THE FOL-LOWING WEEK.** Otherwise, leave an envelope with instructions to mail the tape back to you. **FOLLOW UP ON TAPE IF IT DOESN'T SHOW UP IN THE MAIL IN A WEEK.**

10. **PAYMENT**—Get Social Security number and signature.

11. **PRESENT**—Give present to child as the packing-up process begins.

12. **ON THE WAY HOME:** Tape an oral description of the home visit while it is fresh in your memory. Include description of neighborhood and house (exterior and interior), location of activities during the visit (kitchen, living room, etc.), general atmosphere of visit, and thumbnail sketch of personalities.

INTERVIEW SCHEDULE FOR PRIMARY CAREGIVER
THIRD HOME VISIT

NOTE: Be sure to fill in question #14 (primary caregiver's occupation as of HV2) before administering this interview.

Name of child (TC): _____ SUBJID: _____
Name of primary caregiver (PC): _____
Relationship to child: _____
Date and time of interview: _____
Racial code: (PC) _____ (TC) _____
Name of interviewer: _____

A. TC'S SCHOOLING AND CARE

  1. Schedule

     Let's talk a little about TC's school schedule. Does she or he go to school 5 days a week? [If not] Which days?

     Does she or he go all day [or mornings or afternoons]?

     How does she or he get there? get home?

     How long does that take?

  2. Teacher and school

     Name of TC's school:

     City/town:

     Name of TC's teacher:

  3. Choices and decisions about TC's schooling

     Did you have any choices about which school TC would go to?

     What were they?

     How did you decide?

     How about choices for which classroom (teacher)?

     What were they?

     How did you decide?

(continued)

Figure AI.2.   Interview schedule for the 5-year-old home visit. (PC, primary caregiver; TC, target child; HV2, second home visit)

Figure AI.2. *(continued)*

---

4. Teacher contact

   Have you spoken with TC's teacher?

   When/how/who called who? [Get PC to describe conversation.]

   Any other contact with the teacher? Written letters or notes to or from teacher? Notices about school events, activities?

5. Classroom visit

   Have you visited TC's classroom?

   When?

   How did you feel about that visit?

6. Expectations for kindergarten

   What do you think TC will learn in kindergarten?

7. Preschool

   Looking back on TC's preschool experiences, are you happy with what TC got from them? Why [not]?

8. After-school care

   Who cares for TC after school? [If an individual, get relationship; if a program, get name and description.]

   [If not answered already] **Where does the care take place?**

B. HOME LIFE

9. Household residents

   Who else lives here besides you and TC?

   What do they and TC do together? [Use activity codes.]

   How often?

Activity codes: a.   Activity play (ball, bikes, etc.)
                      b.   Watch television or videotapes
                      c.   Read books
                      d.   Play with TC's toys (blocks, cars, etc.)
                      e.   Play make-believe, dress-up
                      f.   Go shopping, eat out
                      g.   Go to museum, library, aquarium
                      h.   Go to the park
                      i.   Go to church
                      j.   Cook or make something together
                      k.   Other: LIST!!!!

List people, their ages, and their relationship to TC:	Activity codes	Frequency (each code)
_____	_____	_____
_____	_____	_____
_____	_____	_____

10. Visitors

Who visits your home on a regular basis?

What do they and TC do together? [Use activity codes.]

How often?

Activity codes: a.   Activity play (ball, bikes, etc.)
                      b.   Watch TV or videotapes
                      c.   Read books
                      d.   Play with TC's toys (blocks, cars, etc.)
                      e.   Play make-believe, dress-up
                      f.   Go shopping, eat out
                      g.   Go to museum, library, aquarium
                      h.   Go to the park
                      i.   Go to church
                      j.   Cook or make something together
                      k.   Other: LIST!!!!

(continued)

Figure AI.2.   *(continued)*

List people, their ages, and their relationship to TC:	Activity codes	Frequency (each code)
_____	_____	_____
_____	_____	_____
_____	_____	_____

11. People TC visits

Who does TC visit on a regular basis?

What do they and TC do together? [Use activity codes.]

How often?

Activity codes: a. Activity play (ball, bikes, etc.)

b. Watch television or videotapes

c. Read books

d. Play with TC's toys (blocks, cars, etc.)

e. Play make-believe, dress-up

f. Go shopping, out to eat

g. Go to museum, library, aquarium

h. Go to the park

i. Go to church

j. Cook or make something together

k. Other: LIST!!!!

List people, their ages, and their relationship to TC:	Activity codes	Frequency (each code)
_____	_____	_____
_____	_____	_____
_____	_____	_____

12a. Free half hour

Let's just say that you had a half hour AT HOME to spend with TC. What would you do?

[If PC describes a longer activity and/or one that wouldn't take place at home, clarify that you're interested in what she'd do **AT HOME** in about a half hour. The next question is about a longer activity.]

Description of half-hour activity: _____

_____

_____

_____

_____

12b. Free half day

How about if you had some free time (say, half a day) on a weekend to spend with TC. What would you do?

Description of half-day activity: _____

_____

_____

_____

_____

13. Previous evening's activities: after supper until bedtime

Think back to last night. Was it a typical evening?

[If PC says, "No, there's never a typical night," proceed by asking her to describe what TC did after supper until bedtime. If PC says "nothing," ask, "What about the night before?" You want to get her to describe a PARTICULAR evening that was fairly typical.]

Could you describe what TC did last night, after she or he ate and until she or he went to bed? [Get mealtime and bedtime. This should be a detailed response, with you doing a lot of probing. For example, if bath Is mentioned, ask what TC did while taking bath, and who was with her or him.]

(continued)

Figure AI.2.   *(continued)*

IMPORTANT: If book reading is mentioned, be sure to ask for title(s).

C.   QUESTIONS ABOUT PC

14. PC's occupation

   Last year, you were _____
   [description of PC's occupation as of HV2].

   Have there been changes? [Discuss.]

   Do you have different work plans for the future?

15. Income sources

   What are the sources of your family's income? [Get the most
   important first, then the next most important, etc. Assign 1 = most
   important, 2 = next, and so forth.]

   _____ **PC's income**

   _____ **Spouse's/partner's income**

   _____ **Welfare (PC/family)**

   _____ **Aid to Families with Dependent Children (AFDC) (child[ren])**

   _____ **Alimony**

   _____ **Child support**

   _____ **Other family members**

16. Age at birth of first child, TC

   How old were you when your first child was born?

   [If TC was not the first] **When TC was born?**

17. Thoughts about the future

   Where do you think you'll be living 5 years from now?

   What do you think you'll be doing in 5 years?

18. PC's reading habits/background

   What kinds of books do you like to read?

   Who are your favorite authors? [List all authors' names given.]

   Are there other things you like to read?

   ____ **Magazines? Which ones?** _____

   ____ **Newspapers? Which ones?** _____

   ____ **Other things?** [List.] _____

   Did your parents read to you as a child?

D. LITERACY QUESTIONS

19. **Does TC like to write?**

   _____ **No**
   _____ **Yes**

What does she or he write? [If letters] **Which ones?**

20. **Can TC write her or his own name?**

   _____ **No**
   _____ **Yes**

21. **Can TC recognize and name any letters of the alphabet?**

   _____ **No**
   _____ **Yes**

[If yes] **Which ones?**

22. **Can TC read her or his own name?**

   _____ **No**
   _____ **Yes**

23. **How high can TC count?**

(continued)

Figure AI.2. *(continued)*

---

24. **Does TC ever pretend to read books?**

    _____ **No**
    _____ **Yes**

    [If yes] **Who does she or he read to?**

25. **Has TC memorized the words to any books?**

    _____ **No**
    _____ **Yes**

    [If yes] **Which one(s)?**

26. **Can TC read any labels or signs?**

    _____ **No**
    _____ **Yes**

    [If yes] **Which one(s)?**

27. **Are there other words she or he can read?**

28. **Do you read books with TC?**

    _____ **No**
    _____ **Yes**

    When? How often? [Get time of the day, # sessions/week, and length of each session.]

29. [If yes] **What kind of books do you read?**

    _____ **Fairy tales or other old stories**
    _____ **Other, newer stories**
    _____ **True stories (for example, about people who lived in the past)**
    _____ **Science books**
    _____ **The Bible or other religious stories**

30. **Do you and TC read anything else together besides books?**

    _____ **Catalogs, newspaper ads**
    _____ **The funnies or comics**
    _____ **Magazines, newspapers**
    _____ **Cereal packages**
    _____ **Other [list]:** _____

31. **Does TC have a favorite book?**

    _____ **No**
    _____ **Yes**

    [If yes] **What is it?**

32. **Where do you get books (library, supermarket, gifts, mail order, yard sales, etc.)?**

33. **About how many children's books do you own?**

    _____ **Fewer than 10**
    _____ **Between 10 and 25**
    _____ **More than 25**

34. **Other than you, who else in the family reads books with TC?** [For each person] **How often? When?**

35. **Does TC watch *Sesame Street* on television?**

    _____ **No**
    _____ **Yes**

    [If yes] **How often? When?**

36. **Do you watch with her or him?**

    _____ **No**
    _____ **Yes, sometimes**
    _____ **Yes, always**

37. **Do you think that there are things TC is learning from watching *Sesame Street*?** [If yes] **What?**

38. **Does TC watch other educational television shows (*3-2-1 Contact, Mister Rogers,* others)? Which ones?**

    How often?

    With whom?

(continued)

Figure AI.2.   *(continued)*

39. **Do you think that there are things TC is learning from watching _____ (program named by TC)?**

40. [If yes] **Does TC watch other kinds of television shows or videos?**

    How often?

    What are her or his favorite shows or videos?

41. **Does TC like to make up rhymes?**

    [If no] **Do you think she or he knows how to make up rhymes yet?**

    [If uncertain, ask the child to think of a rhyme for the words at, mat, and sat. If necessary, reassure PC that only some children have started rhyming words at TC's age.]

E.   TC'S FUTURE

42. First grade

    Do you think TC will be ready for first grade next year? If not, why not?

43. Expectations for TC's schooling

    How many years of schooling do you think TC will attend?

44. Aspirations for TC

    What do you think TC will be when she or he grows up? Why?

Thank you so much—we're done now! Before we move on to the next thing, would you mind giving me the names and telephone numbers of two relatives or friends who would know where you are if you move in the next year or so?

CHAPTER 2—PARENTS AND CHILDREN
READING BOOKS TOGETHER

Table A2.1. Descriptive statistics for maternal book-reading variables

Variable	Home visit	Total sample	Mean	Standard deviation	Range
The Very Hungry Caterpillar (Carle, 1979)	3-year-old	83			
# of *nonimmediate*			3.77	3.25	0–14
% of *nonimmediate*			10.34	8.38	0–40
# of *immediate*			22.60	15.81	1–61
% of *immediate*			59.93	15.21	21.43–100
Total # of utterances			38.90	26.38	1–113
The Very Hungry Caterpillar	4-year-old	70			
# of *nonimmediate*			3.26	2.95	0–12
% of *nonimmediate*			10.89	9.31	0–37.50
# of *immediate*			17.87	16.17	1–87
% of *immediate*			58.22	13.27	22.73–100
Total # of utterances			31.07	26.78	1–164
The Very Hungry Caterpillar	5-year-old	68			
# of *nonimmediate*			4.09	7.78	0–59
% of *nonimmediate*			13.79	11.89	0–50
# of *immediate*			12.97	9.30	1–36
% of *immediate*			51.01	19.23	12–92.85
Total # of utterances			27.01	20.74	2–124
What Next, Baby Bear! (Murphy, 1983)	4-year-old	70			
# of *nonimmediate*			5.27	5.47	0–26
% of *nonimmediate*			16.78	13.26	0–57.14
# of *immediate*			15.97	13.85	0–72
% of *immediate*			55.52	18.21	0–100
Total # of utterances			27.64	20.12	0–89
What Next, Baby Bear!	5-year-old	67			
# of *nonimmediate*			4.54	5.21	0–25
% of *nonimmediate*			17.49	14.46	0–50
# of *immediate*			9.73	7.29	1–37
% of *immediate*			45.73	21.86	8.33–100
Total # of utterances			23.57	16.25	1–68
Elephant (Hoffman 1945/1984)	5-year-old	69			
# of *nonimmediate*			10.36	11.44	0–57
% of *nonimmediate*			17.86	10.72	0–47.11
# of *immediate*			20.03	14.16	0–71
% of *immediate*			43.56	16.65	0–83.33
Total # of utterances			50.11	38.30	2–187

Table A2.2. Change over time in mother and child utterance types during the reading of *The Very Hungry Caterpillar* (Carle, 1979)

Utterance type	Mother			Child		
	Direction	F	p	Direction	F	p
Total number of utterances	↓	3.09	.04	—	.12	.88
Number of *immediate*	↓	5.42	.005	—	.32	.73
Percentage of *immediate*	↓	4.94	.008	—	1.71	.18
Number of *nonimmediate*	—	.31	.73	—	.52	.59
Percentage of *nonimmediate*	↑	2.71	.06	—	1.07	.34

$n = 54$ dyads.
$df = 2$.
↓ = decrease in talk.
↑ = increase in talk.
— = no change.

Table A2.3. Change over time in the mother and child utterance types during the reading of *What Next, Baby Bear!* (Murphy, 1983)

Utterance type	Mother			Child		
	Direction	F	p	Direction	F	p
Total number of utterances	↓	5.53	.02	—	.01	.91
Number of *immediate*	↓	9.44	.002	—	1.23	.27
Percentage of *immediate*	↓	2.90	.09	↓	5.47	.02
Number of *nonimmediate*	—	.64	.42	—	.04	.83
Percentage of *nonimmediate*	—	.00	.96	↑	3.24	.07

$n = 54$ dyads.
$df = 1$.
↓ = decrease in talk.
↑ = increase in talk.
— = no change.

Table A2.4. Characteristics of maternal talk during book reading: Effects of time and book

Utterance type	Time			Book		
	Direction	F	p	Direction	F	p
Total number of utterances	↓	7.49	.0007	—	1.12	.29
Number of *immediate*	↓	13.09	.0001	—	2.42	.12
Percentage of *immediate*	↓	8.62	.0002	VHC > WNBB	3.69	.05
Number of *nonimmediate*	—	22.00	.80	—	2.33	.13
Percentage of *nonimmediate*	↑	4.23	.01	WNBB > VHC	11.36	.0009

$n = 54$ dyads.
↓ = decrease in talk.
↑ = increase in talk.
— = no change.
VHC, *The Very Hungry Caterpillar* (Carle, 1979).
WNBB, *What Next, Baby Bear!* (Murphy, 1983).

Table A2.5. Correlations between mothers' percentages of *immediate talk* and measures of child language and literacy in kindergarten

Task	VHC (age 3)	VHC (age 5)	WNBB (age 4)	WNBB (age 5)
Formal Definitions	−.22	−.27*	−.44***	−.38**
Superordinates	−.46****	n.s.	−.26*	−.44***
Story Comprehension	−.33**	n.s.	n.s.	−.31*
Emergent Literacy	−.28*	−.31*	n.s.	−.32**
Receptive Vocabulary	−.37**	n.s.	−.25	n.s.

n = 54 dyads.

VHC, *The Very Hungry Caterpillar* (Carle, 1979).

WNBB, *What Next, Baby Bear!* (Murphy, 1983).

n.s., not significant.

*p < .05; **p < .01; ***p < .001; ****p < .0005.

Table A2.6. Correlations between mothers' percentage of *nonimmediate talk* and measures of child language and literacy in kindergarten

Task	VHC (age 3)	VHC (age 5)	WNBB (age 5)	*Elephant* (age 5)
Narrative Production	n.s.	n.s.	.27*	.31**
Superordinates	.46****	n.s.	.27*	n.s.
Story Comprehension	.31*	.24*	n.s.	n.s.
Emergent Literacy	.35*	.31**	n.s.	n.s.
Receptive Vocabulary	.39**	n.s.	n.s.	.29**

n = 54 dyads.

VHC, *The Very Hungry Caterpillar* (Carle, 1979).

WNBB, *What Next, Baby Bear!* (Murphy, 1983).

n.s., not significant.

*p < .05; **p < .01; ***p < .001; ****p < .0005.

Table A2.7. Correlations between maternal report of *home support for literacy* and measures of child language and literacy in kindergarten

Task	Home support for literacy at 3-year-old home visit (*n* = 69)	Home support for literacy at 4-year-old home visit (*n* = 49)
Formal Definitions	.46***	.39**
Story Comprehension	.33**	.28*
Emergent Literacy	.43***	.29*
Receptive Vocabulary	.48***	.40**

*p < .05; **p < .01; ***p < .0001.

CHAPTER 3—PLAYING AT HOME:
THE TALK OF PRETEND PLAY

Table A3.1. Descriptive statistics for percentage of *pretend* and *non-pretend talk* from the play session at the 3-year-old home visit

Variable	Mean	Standard deviation	Range	Percentiles 25th	50th	75th
% of children's *pretend talk*	46.54	21.95	0–97.44	35.41	45.08	58.77
% of mothers' *pretend talk*	44.42	19.45	6.875–96.55	30.99	43.03	54.28
% of children's and mothers' *pretend talk*	45.77	19.60	6.129–96.97	32.55	44.46	55.28
% of children's *non-pretend talk*	46.24	22.40	0–100	32.81	46.76	56.21
% of mothers' *non-pretend talk*	47.21	18.67	0–92.5	38.94	47.57	61.77
% of children's and mothers' *non-pretend talk*	46.55	18.96	0–93.55	37.41	45.46	59.25

$n = 52$.

Table A3.2. Descriptive statistics for percentage of *pretend* and *non-pretend talk* from the play session at the 4-year-old home visit

Variable	Mean	Standard deviation	Range	Percentiles 25th	50th	75th
% of children's *pretend talk*	53.98	22.97	8.62–98.45	39.02	47.09	68.56
% of mothers' *pretend talk*	49.69	21.05	9.68–98.39	35.13	49.49	61.79
% of children's and mothers' *pretend talk*	51.77	21.22	9.27–98.43	37.61	53.12	64.06
% of children's *non-pretend talk*	40.04	21.93	0–91.38	27.09	37.21	53.48
% of mothers' *non-pretend talk*	40.55	18.97	0–89.25	31.69	39.00	51.23
% of children's and mothers' *non-pretend talk*	40.12	19.78	0–90.07	29.67	37.23	50.50

$n = 52$.

Table A3.3. Descriptive statistics for percentage of *pretend* and *non-pretend talk* from the play session at the 5-year-old home visit

Variable	Mean	Standard deviation	Range	Percentiles 25th	50th	75th
% of children's *pretend talk*	42.02	20.03	0–85.71	27.62	44.65	55.24
% of mothers' *pretend talk*	39.86	21.41	0–84.14	20.97	40.75	53.29
% of children's and mothers' *pretend talk*	41.43	19.28	3.947–81.73	28.48	41.47	53.44
% of children's *non-pretend talk*	48.72	17.16	14.28–93.87	38.34	46.13	57.39
% of mothers' *non-pretend talk*	50.04	19.20	14.28–96.29	38.22	48.26	62.28
% of children's and mothers' *non-pretend talk*	49.18	17.14	18.28–94.87	38.70	47.01	58.68

$n = 52$.

Table A3.4. Percentages of *pretend talk* used by the four portrait children and their mothers in the play sessions from the three home visits

Play session from	Astra	Astra's mother	Todd	Todd's mother	Casey	Casey's mother	Mariana	Mariana's mother
3-year-old home visit	41%	34%	73%	55%	22%	30%	17%	18%
4-year-old home visit	98%	98%	44%	44%	46%	31%	60%	59%
5-year-old home visit	48%	61%	39%	43%	18%	15%	20%	31%

Table A3.5. Results of repeated measures analysis of variance (ANOVA) for assessing the difference between percentages of *pretend talk* used in the play sessions at each home visit

	Difference in percentages of *pretend talk*
Mothers' *pretend talk* at three play sessions	$F(2.102) = 4.93, p = .009$
3-year-old visit vs. 4-year-old visit	n.s.
4-year-old visit vs. 5-year-old visit	$F(1.51) = 14.45, p = .0004$
3-year-old visit vs. 5-year-old visit	n.s.
Children's *pretend talk* at three play sessions	$F(2.102) = 5.70, p = .005$
3-year-old visit vs. 4-year-old visit	$F(1.51) = 4.00, p = .051$
4-year-old visit vs. 5-year-old visit	$F(1.51) = 14.00, p = .0005$
3-year-old visit vs. 5-year-old visit	n.s.
Combined mothers' and children's *pretend talk* at three play sessions	$F(2.102) = 5.34, p = .006$
3-year-old visit vs. 4-year-old visit	$F(1.51) = 3.39, p = .0714$
4-year-old visit vs. 5-year-old visit	$F(1.51) = 14.39, p = .0004$
3-year-old visit vs. 5-year-old visit	n.s.

$n = 52$.
n.s., not significant.

Table A3.6. Correlations indicating stability of mother's and children's *pretend talk* over three home visits

Mothers' *pretend talk* across three home visits

	4-year-old visit	5-year-old visit
3-year-old visit	.374 **	n.s.
4-year-old visit		.613***

Children's *pretend talk* across three home visits

	4-year-old visit	5-year-old visit
3-year-old visit	.285*	n.s.
4-year-old visit		.432**

Mothers' and children's combined *pretend talk* across three home visits

	4-year-old visit	5-year-old visit
3-year-old visit	.324*	n.s.
4-year-old visit		.532***

$n = 52$.
n.s., not significant.
$^*p < .05; ^{**}p < .01; ^{***}p < .001.$

Table A3.7. Correlations between mothers' and children's percentages of *pretend talk* in the three toy play sessions

	Children's pretend: age 3	Mothers' pretend: age 3	Combined pretend: age 3	Children's pretend: age 4	Mothers' pretend: age 4	Combined pretend: age 4	Children's pretend: age 5	Mothers' pretend: age 5	Combined pretend: age 5
Children's *pretend*: age 3	1.00								
Mothers' *pretend*: age 3	.896***	1.00							
Combined *pretend*: age 3	.947***	.987***	1.00						
Children's *pretend*: age 4	.285*	.299*	.299*	1.00					
Mothers' *pretend*: age 4	.312*	.374**	.358**	.902***	1.00				
Combined *pretend*: age 4	.307*	.341**	.324*	.969***	.972***	1.00			
Children's *pretend*: age 5	n.s.	n.s.	n.s.	.432**	.430**	.432**	1.00		
Mothers' *pretend*: age 5	n.s.	n.s.	n.s.	.531***	.613***	.583***	.852***	1.00	
Combined *pretend*: age 5	n.s.	n.s.	n.s.	.496***	.546***	.532***	.956***	.956***	1.00

$n = 52$.

n.s., not significant.

*$p < .05$; **$p < .01$; ***$p < .001$.

Table A3.8. Correlations between mothers' and children's *pretend talk* in the play sessions at each of the three home visits, and language and early literacy measures from kindergarten

Home visit	Narrative Production	Formal Definitions	Emergent Literacy	Receptive Vocabulary
3-year-old visit				
Children's *pretend talk*	n.s.	.347*	n.s.	n.s.
Mothers' *pretend talk*	n.s.	.479***	n.s.	.297*
4-year-old visit				
Children's *pretend talk*	n.s.	n.s.	.310*	n.s.
Mothers' *pretend talk*	.274*	n.s.	.324*	n.s.
5-year-old visit				
Children's *pretend talk*	n.s.	n.s.	n.s.	n.s.
Mothers' *pretend talk*	n.s.	n.s.	n.s.	n.s.

$n = 52$.

n.s., not significant.

$*p < .05$; $***p < .001$.

CHAPTER 4—EATING AND READING: LINKS BETWEEN FAMILY CONVERSATIONS WITH PRESCHOOLERS AND LATER LANGUAGE AND LITERACY

Table A4.1. Contributions to full mealtime conversations (in percentage of utterances)

Speaker	Sample size	Contributions		
		Mean	Minimum	Maximum
Mother	160	41.1	4.0	74.9
Child in study	165	33.8	3.2	62.1
Father	52	15.1	0.7	38.6
Others	—	10.0	—	—

Table A4.2. Mealtime narrative variables

Variable	Transcripts	Mean	Range
Percentage of *narrative talk* (age 3)	64	16.6	0–64.5
Percentage of *narrative talk* (age 4)	45	10.9	0–35.7
Percentage of *narrative talk* (age 5)	51	16.6	0–54.1
Number of narratives (age 3)	64	3.64	0–15
Number of narratives (age 4)	45	3.80	0–11
Number of narratives (age 5)	51	3.98	0–11
Percentage of *narrative talk* by mother (age 3)	27	40.0	0–100
Percentage of *narrative talk* by mother (age 4)	27	45.9	0–100
Percentage of *narrative talk* by child (age 3)	27	27.5	0–71.4
Percentage of *narrative talk* by child (age 4)	27	30.0	0–100

Table A4.3. Mealtime explanation variables

Variable	Transcripts	Mean	Range
Percentage of *explanatory talk* (age 3)	64	15.0	0.7–43.1
Percentage of *explanatory talk* (age 4)	45	16.3	0–51.8
Percentage of *explanatory talk* (age 5)	51	13.6	0–30.1
Number of explanations (age 3)	64	13.3	1–45
Number of explanations (age 4)	45	13.5	0–27
Number of explanations (age 5)	51	14.2	0–39
Percentage of *explanatory talk* by mother (age 3)	64	46.8	0–100
Percentage of *explanatory talk* by mother (age 4)	45	45.8	10.0–74.0
Percentage of *explanatory talk* by mother (age 5)	51	47.3	0–100
Percentage of *explanatory talk* by child (age 3)	66	28.5	0–100
Percentage of *explanatory talk* by child (age 4)	46	31.2	0–66.7
Percentage of *explanatory talk* by child (age 5)	53	28.0	0–52.3

CHAPTER 5—"YOU KNOW WHAT OXYGEN IS?": LEARNING NEW WORDS AT HOME

Table A5.1.   Rare words from toy play during 5-year-old visit

actually	delicious	matchbox	similar
aggravated	delightful	meat + eater	slime
allosaurus	description	mechanic	slowly
amen	determination	messy	someplace
anymore	dizzy	metallic	somersault
apparently	dominoes	mostly	sonar
appliance	doubly	mudhole	soothes
arch	drawer	muscles	sparkle
arches	drawers	neatly	sparkles
argue	dresser	normally	squishy
assortment	driver	notebook	stained
assume	dunes	overlooking	steadier
assure	dynamite	parallel	steady
basically	eater	participate	stegosaurus
bizarre	eaters	perfect	stickers
border	educational	perfectly	stomped
bottomless	element	plastic	strict
brachiosaurus	enormous	practicing	stumped
brontosaurus	exhibit	prank	tablecloth
brontosauruses	explosion	presume	tailgating
bronze	ferocious	probably	tartar
bumper	floppy	pronounce	teenagers
cafeteria	formula	punishment	themselves
calm	freezer	putty	though
casing	friendly	quietly	thrilled
cast	fuzzy	racer	thud
certainly	germs	racers	tonic
changers	grabby	radical	torture
chat	gypped	ramp	totally
cheater	hanger	recipe	towed
cheetahs	hardly	reckless	translucent
chores	headboard	recorder	tremor
chunk	heater	rectangle	triangle
cobra	hippopotamus	regular	turbo
community	hippopotamuses	relax	tusk
compared	hostess	reptile	tusks
concentrate	ignore	rhino	underneath
confused	imagination	rhinoceros	unless
container	intercepted	rhinoceroses	unplug
containers	interruptions	rinse	until
conversationalist	jealous	rude	usually
cooperating	juggling	ruin	vegetarian
cordless	license	sabertooth	versions
creamer	lioness	sandpile	violent
crumpets	lopsided	scrape	volcano
cubes	main	senile	wading
cucaracha	mall	session	weird
cucarachas	mammoth	shaker	whatever
decoration	maroon	shift	wisdom
definitely	mastodon	silverware	yet

Table A5.2. Descriptive statistics of *rare-word densities*

	n	Mean	Standard deviation	Range
Mothers during book reading				
The Very Hungry Caterpillar, 3-year-old home visit	82	19	8	0–46
The Very Hungry Caterpillar, 4-year-old home visit	69	20	7	0–44
What Next, Baby Bear!, 5-year-old home visit	51	11	8	0–49
Elephant, 5-year-old home visit	53	39	15	0–63
Mothers during toy play				
3-year-old home visit	83	9	8	0–48
4-year-old home visit	70	14	11	0–66
5-year-old home visit	69	12	9	0–46
Mothers during mealtimes				
3-year-old home visit	66	16	10	0–47
4-year-old home visit	46	18	11	0–63
5-year-old home visit	53	11	8	0–49
All speakers but child during mealtimes				
3-year-old home visit	66	10	10	0–68
4-year-old home visit	46	12	9	0–36
5-year-old home visit	53	26	25	0–140

All fractions have been rounded to whole numbers in order to represent complete words.

Table A5.3. Stability of mothers' *density of rare words* during book reading

	The Very Hungry Caterpillar (3-year-old home visit)	*The Very Hungry Caterpillar* (4-year-old home visit)	*What Next, Baby Bear!* (5-year-old home visit)	*Elephant* (5-year-old home visit)
The Very Hungry Caterpillar (3-year-old home visit)		.26 .0337 (69)	n.s.	n.s.
The Very Hungry Caterpillar (4-year-old home visit)			n.s.	n.s.
What Next, Baby Bear! (5-year-old home visit)	n.s.	n.s.		n.s.
Elephant (5-year-old home visit)	n.s.	n.s.	n.s.	

n.s., not significant.

Table A5.4. Stability of mothers' *density of rare words* during toy play

	4-year-old home visit	5-year-old home visit
3-year-old home visit	.45 .0001 (70)	.22 .0640 (69)
4-year-old home visit		.27 .0366 (61)

Table A5.5. Stability of mothers' *density of rare words* during mealtimes

	4-year-old home visit	5-year-old home visit
3-year-old home visit	.42 .0051 (43)	n.s.
4-year-old home visit		n.s.

n.s., not significant.

Table A5.6. Stability of *density of rare words* of all speakers but the child during mealtimes

	4-year-old home visit	5-year-old home visit
3-year-old home visit	.49 .0008 (43)	n.s.
4-year-old home visit		[.27 .1084 (37)]

Brackets indicate data that are marginally significant.
n.s., not significant.

Table A5.7. Relationships between *rare-word densities* and frequencies of informative use of rare words, and kindergarten Receptive Vocabulary scores

	n	Receptive Vocabulary scores
Rare-word densities		
Mothers during book reading *The Very Hungry Caterpillar,* 3-year-old visit	74	.36 .0014
Mothers during toy play		
3-year-old visit	74	.42 .0002
4-year-old visit	66	.33 .0060
5-year-old visit	69	.33 .0059
Mothers during mealtimes		
5-year-old visit	53	.49 .0002
All speakers but child during mealtimes		
3-year-old visit	60	.34 .0080
5-year-old visit	53	.51 .0001
Frequencies of informative use of rare words		
3-year-old visit	58	.42 .001
4-year-old visit	44	.43 .005
5-year-old visit	51	.55 .001

CHAPTER 6—HOME LANGUAGE AND LITERACY ENVIRONMENT: FINAL RESULTS

Table A6.1. Descriptive statistics of types of talk during the magnet task

	Mean	Standard deviation	Range
Percentage of *science process talk*			
Mothers	14.28	10.70	0–30
Children	12.53	10.44	0–42
Percentage of *object science talk*			
Mothers	21.78	13.62	0–61
Children	24.89	16.89	0–63
Percentage of *artistic process talk*			
Mothers	7.79	8.05	0–30
Children	14.02	17.20	0–100
Percentage of *superficial object talk*			
Mothers	54.67	22.00	0–100
Children	48.55	22.51	0–100

$n = 68$.

Table A6.2. Correlations between types of talk during the magnet task and kindergarten tasks

	Narrative Production	Picture Description	Formal Definitions	Superordinates	Story Comprehension	Emergent Litearcy	Receptive Vocabulary
Percentage of _science process talk_							
Children	.32 .0068	n.s.	.26 .0311	.25 .0421	.29 .0164	n.s.	.32 .0082
Mothers	.41 .0005	n.s.	.30 .0119	.30 .0138	.32 .0072	.24 .0510	.33 .0063
Percentage of _object science talk_							
Children	n.s.	n.s.	n.s.	n.s.	n.s.	n.s.	n.s.
Mothers	.42 .003	n.s.	n.s.	.39 .0009	n.s.	n.s.	.36 .0030
Percentage of _artistic process talk_							
Children	n.s.	n.s.	n.s.	n.s.	n.s.	n.s.	n.s.
Mothers	n.s.	n.s.	n.s.	n.s.	n.s.	n.s.	n.s.
Percentage of _superficial object talk_							
Children	n.s.	−.20 .0940	−.28 .0215	n.s.	−.27 .0246	n.s.	−.36 .0026
Mothers	−.21 .0846	n.s.	−.35 .0031	−.34 .0047	−.43 .0003	−.25 .0369	−.38 .0016

n.s., not significant.

Table A6.3. Variables making up the three overall language and literacy composites

Composite	Home visit	Variables
Extended Discourse	3-year-old	Mothers' percentage of *nonimmediate talk* in book reading (*The Very Hungry Caterpillar*) Mothers' percentage of *explanatory talk* at mealtime Mothers' percentage of *narrative talk* at mealtime Mothers' percentage of *pretend talk* during toy play
	4-year-old	Mothers' percentage of *nonimmediate talk* in book reading (*The Very Hungry Caterpillar*) Mothers' percentage of *nonimmediate talk* in book reading (*What Next, Baby Bear!*) Mothers' percentage of *explanatory talk* at mealtime Mothers' percentage of *narrative talk* at mealtime Mothers' percentage of *pretend talk* during toy play
	5-year-old	Mothers' percentage of *nonimmediate talk* in book reading (*The Very Hungry Caterpillar*) Mothers' percentage of *nonimmediate talk* in book reading (*What Next, Baby Bear!*) Mothers' percentage of *nonimmediate talk* in book reading (*Elephant*) Mothers' percentage of *explanatory talk* at mealtime Mothers' percentage of *narrative talk* at mealtime Mothers' percentage of *pretend talk* during toy play Mothers' percentage of *science process talk* during magnet play
Rare Word Density	3-year-old	Mothers' *rare-word density* during mealtime Mothers' *rare-word density* during toy play
	4-year-old	Mothers' *rare-word density* during mealtime Mothers' *rare-word density* during toy play
	5 year old	Mothers' *rare-word density* during mealtime Mothers' *rare-word density* during toy play
Home Support for Literacy	3-year-old	Mothers' reported *home support for literacy*
	4-year-old	Mothers' reported *home support for literacy*

Table A6.4. Standardized composite values for portrait families on Extended Discourse, Rare Word Density, and Home Support for Literacy

	Extended Discourse	Rare Word Density	Home Support for Literacy
Mariana	0.28	−1.05	−1.97
Casey	−1.28	0.48	1.79
Todd	0.37	0.27	0.24
Astra	0.74	−2.16	0.02

The values in this table represent standardized values for each of the composites, with a mean of 0 and a standard deviation of 1. The sample range for Extended Discourse was −1.86 to 3.02, the sample range for Rare Word Density was −2.16 to 3.11, and the sample range for Home Support for Literacy was −2.19 to 1.79.

Table A6.5. Models predicting Narrative Production: Controls

Model	Gender β (SE β)	Race β (SE β)	Mother's Education β (SE β)	Family Income at 3-year-old home visit β (SE β)	Children's Mean Length of Utterance at 3-year-old home visit β (SE β)	R^2
I	0.92 (.74)					.02
II		−0.07 (.78)				.0001
III			0.36 (.49)			.0082
IV				0.61* (.23)		.09*
V					0.77 (.58)	.03
VI	0.75 (.75)	0.24 (.78)	0.002 (.49)	0.64* (.25)	0.82 (.58)	.14⁻

⁻$p < .10$; *$p < .05$.

Table A6.6. Models predicting Narrative Production: Home environment composites with controls

Model	Extended Discourse β (SE β)	Rare Word Density β (SE β)	Home Support for Literacy β (SE β)	R^2
I	0.02* (.007)			.23*
II		0.01 (.01)		.15
III			0.22* (.08)	.23*
IV	0.01* (.007)	0.0008 (.01)	0.17* (.08)	.28**

*$p < .05$; **$p < .01$.

Table A6.7. Models predicting Emergent Literacy: Controls

Model	Gender β (SE β)	Race β (SE β)	Mother's Education β (SE β)	Family Income at 3-year-old home visit β (SE β)	Children's Mean Length of Utterance at 3-year-old home visit β (SE β)	R^2
I	−0.38 (.96)					.0023
II		−0.48 (1.003)				.0035
III			0.008 (.03)			.0000
IV				0.72* (.30)		.08*
V					1.52* (.74)	.06*
VI	−0.90 (.94)	−0.30 (.98)	−0.41 (.62)	0.85** (.31)	1.78* (.73)	.17*

*$p < .05$; **$p < .01$.

Table A6.8. Models predicting Emergent Literacy: Home environment composites with controls

Model	Extended Discourse β (SE β)	Rare Word Density β (SE β)	Home Support for Literacy β (SE β)	R^2
I	0.009 (.009)			.19
II		0.05** (.02)		.28**
III			0.25* (.11)	.24**
IV	0.000 (.009)	0.04* (.02)	0.21⁻ (.11)	.32**

⁻$p < .10$; *$p < .05$; **$p < .01$.

Table A6.9. Models predicting Receptive Vocabulary: Controls

Model	Gender β (SE β)	Race β (SE β)	Mother's Education β (SE β)	Family Income at 3-year-old home visit β (SE β)	Children's Mean Length of Utterance at 3-year-old home visit β (SE β)	R^2
I	4.87 (3.74)					.03
II		−10.5** (3.75)				.11**
III			−0.55 (2.48)			.0007
IV				2.19⁻ (1.21)		.05⁻
V					3.89 (2.96)	.03
VI	2.06 (3.70)	−9.25* (3.86)	−1.07 (2.45)	2.47* (1.22)	3.08 (2.88)	.18*

⁻$p < .10$; *$p < .05$; **$p < .01$.

Table A6.10. Models predicting Receptive Vocabulary: Home environment composites with controls

Model	Extended Discourse β (SE β)	Rare Word Density β (SE β)	Home Support for Literacy β (SE β)	R^2
I	0.07* (.03)			.23*
II		0.23*** (.06)		.34***
III			1.41*** (.40)	.32***
IV	0.02 (.03)	0.20** (.06)	1.16** (.38)	.44***

*$p < .05$; **$p < .01$; ***$p < .001$.

Table A8.1. Relationship between dramatic quality of teachers' book reading, teachers' management style, and children's involvement when children were 3 (n = 49) and 4 years old (n = 73)

	2		3		4		5		6		7		8		9	
	3 yrs.	4 yrs.	3 yrs.	4 yrs.	3 yrs.	4 yrs.	3 yrs.	4 yrs.	3 yrs.	4 yrs.	3 yrs.	4 yrs.	3 yrs.	4 yrs.	3 yrs.	4 yrs.
Dramatic quality																
1. Pitch and tone variation	.45***		.55***		.39**		.44**		.21 (n.s.)		.25⁻					
2. Highlight climax			.74***	.71***	.55***	.46***	.52***	.21 (n.s.)	.34*	.55***	.47***	.55***	.28*			
3. Character voices					.73***	.56***	.30*	.28*	.40*	.63***	.51***	.62***		-.20⁻	-.21 (n.s.)	-.31**
Management style																
4. Implicit strategies									.62***	.61***	.61***	.69***	.26⁻	-.26*		
5. Explicit strategies									.26⁻	.25*	.26⁻					
Child involvement																
6. General interest											.67***	.70***		-.21 (n.s.)		
7. Excitement														-.22 (n.s.)	-.36**	-.37**
8. Number of children																-.37**
9. Familiarity of book																

n.s., not significant.

⁻p < .10; *p < .05; **p < .01; ***p < .001.

Table A8.2.   Relationship between children's interest, teachers' reading strategies, and the content of conversations about books when children were 3 and 4 years old

	T analysis D	T vocabulary D	T org. D
3-year-olds	(*n* = 43)	(*n* = 43)	(*n* = 43)
Child excitement and involvement	n.s.	n.s.	n.s.
Teacher highlights climax	n.s.	n.s	n.s
Teacher assumes character role	n.s.	n.s.	*r* = −.46 *p* = .001
Teacher uses implicit management	n.s.	n.s.	n.s.
4-year-olds	(*n* = 66)	(*n* = 66)	(*n* = 66)
Child excitement and involvement	.32 .008	.28 .02	−.46 .0001
Teacher highlights climax	n.s	.24 .05	−.30 .01
Teacher assumes character role	.34 .005	.30 .02	−.44 .0002
Teacher uses implicit management	.32 .009	.25 .04	−.36 .003

T analysis D, teacher analysis of the text during the reading.
T vocabulary D, teacher discussion of vocabulary during the reading.
T org. D, teacher efforts to organize the group during the reading.
n.s., not significant.

CHAPTER 9—LANGUAGE OPPORTUNITIES DURING MEALTIMES IN PRESCHOOL CLASSROOMS

Note 1

Interrater reliability for the type of talk used during center-based preschool mealtimes was analyzed using Cohen's *kappa* (κ) statistic for two raters using 10% of the data. Interrater agreement was $\kappa = .87$ for the entire coding scheme and $\kappa = .76$ for *nonpresent talk*. Interrater agreement for conversational partner (i.e., whether the target child was speaking to a teacher or a child) was $\kappa = .95$. Interrater reliability for the type of mealtime setting was determined for two raters using 27% of the data and was $\kappa = .88$. These *kappas* indicate high and acceptable levels of interrater agreement.

Note 2

All statistics were performed using SPSS Version 7.0 for Microsoft Windows. A *t*-test for independent samples was performed to test whether there were differences in children's use of *nonpresent talk* based upon mealtime setting. Significant differences between the mealtime groups were found, $t(58) = 2.66$, probability (p) < .05.

Note 3

A *t*-test for independent samples was performed to determine whether there were differences among the children in each of the two mealtime groups in their talkativeness throughout the classroom day. It was not significant (n.s.), $t(58) = .25$, n.s. [*teacher stationary* (mean [*M*]= 3,217.94, standard deviation [*SD*] = 1,924.73), *teacher circulating* (*M* = 3,108.27, *SD* = 1,438.75)]. The *t*-test for independent samples that was performed to determine whether there were differences in the amount of time each group spent in mealtimes was not significant, $t(58) = .44$, n.s. [*teacher stationary* (*M* = 1,061.45, *SD* = 424.22), *teacher circulating* (*M* = 966.27, *SD* = 504.38)].

Note 4

A *t*-test for independent samples revealed that there were significant differences between the mealtime groups in the amount of time the target children spent talking during mealtimes, $t(58) = 2.71$, $p < .01$.

Note 5

A paired *t*-test was performed to test whether children engaged in more *nonpresent talk* with teachers as conversational partners than with children; this *t*-test was significant, $t(58) = 3.15$, $p < .01$ [with teachers (*M* = 44.07, *SD* = 83.69), with other children (*M* = 7.39, *SD* = 25.07)].

Note 6

Paired *t*-tests were performed to determine whether children and teachers speak and use rare words differentially across classroom settings. Paired *t*-tests rather than analyses of variance (ANOVAs) were used for all vocabulary analyses because the assumption that the covariance matrix has a constant variance was violated (Mauchly's test of sphericity). All statistical analyses were performed using SYSTAT (Systat, Inc., 1990).

Children said significantly more words overall during free play (*M* = 246.78, *SD* = 169.28) than during mealtime (*M* = 186.09, *SD* = 123.48), $t(22) = 2.39$, $p < .05$. There were no significant differences in the amount of words children used overall during mealtime and book reading (*M* = 161.65, *SD* = 150.25), $t(22) = 0.73$, n.s., and mealtime and circle time (*M* = 170.78, *SD* = 122.91), $t(22) = 0.56$, n.s. There were no significant differences in children's use of rare words during mealtime (*M* = 2.74, *SD* = 2.58) and each of the other classroom settings [book reading ($M = 2.30$, $SD = 3.34$), $t(22) = 0.51$, n.s.; free play ($M = 2.70$, $SD = 2.64$), $t(22) = 0.07$, n.s.; and circle time ($M = 3.22$, $SD = 3.90$), $t(22) = -0.45$, n.s.].

Note 7

Teachers said significantly more words during free play ($M = 1,032.91$, $SD = 426.12$), $t(22) = 5.11$, $p < .001$, and circle time ($M = 1,113.65$, $SD = 494.58$), $t(22) = 4.83$, $p < .001$, than during mealtime ($M = 646.30$, $SD = 232.08$). There were no significant differences in the amount of words teachers said during mealtime and book reading ($M = 532.83$, $SD = 326.47$), $t(22) = 1.36$, n.s. Teachers used significantly fewer rare words during mealtime ($M = 9.39$, $SD = 5.13$) than during either free play ($M = 14.09$, $SD = 7.26$), $t(22) = -2.59$, $p < .05$, or circle time ($M = 16.22$, $SD = 11.19$), $t(22) = -2.47$, $p < .05$. Teachers used significantly more rare words during mealtime than during book reading ($M - 4.83$, $SD - 5.25$), $t(22) = 3.05$, $p < .01$.

CHAPTER 10—LARGE-GROUP AND FREE-PLAY TIMES: CONVERSATIONAL SETTINGS SUPPORTING LANGUAGE AND LITERACY DEVELOPMENT

Table A10.1.   Relationships between the percentage of different content of teacher–child conversations and children's language and literacy in kindergarten (data from teacher audiotapes)

	Narrative Production	Formal Definitions	Story Comprehension	Emergent Literacy	Receptive Vocabulary
Large-group teacher talk (age 3)					
Extending (function)	−.413 .010 (38)	−.273 .098 (38)		.287 .080 (38)	−.435 .006 (38)
Explaining (function)			.345 .034 (38)		.428 .007 (38)
Group focus	.518 .0009 (38)		.308 .060 (38)		.407 .011 (38)
Teacher–child ratio				.342 .036 (38)	
Cognitive abstractions	.338 .038 (38)			.325 .047 (38)	.289 .078 (38)
Nonpresent talk	.364 .025 (38)			.303 .064 (38)	

(continued)

Table A10.1   *(continued)*

	Narrative Production	Formal Definitions	Story Comprehension	Emergent Literacy	Receptive Vocabulary
Large-group child talk (age 3)					
Extending (function)	−.384 .017 (38)		−.441 .006 (38)	−.282 .087 (38)	−.483 .002 (38)
Explaining (function)		.337 .045 (36)	.306 .062 (38)		.409 .010 (38)
Cognitive				.344 .034 (38)	
Free-play teacher talk (age 3)					
Explaining		.376 .024 (36)			
Free-play child talk (age 3)					
Explaining (function)		.337 .045 (36)			
Large-group teacher talk (age 4)					
Extending (function)	−.232 .095 (53)			−.343 .012 (53)	
Explaining (function)				.292 .034 (53)	
Group focus	.450 .001 (53)			.427 .001 (53)	
Large-group child talk (age 4)					
Extending (function)				−.288 .038 (52)	
Free-play teacher talk (age 4)					
Extending (function)	.258 .070 (50)	.306 .031 (50)	.437 .002 (50)	.297 .036 (50)	.419 .003 (50)
Explaining (function)	−.358 .011 (50)			−.272 .058 (50)	−.312 .028 (50)
Cognitive abstractions	.338 .038 (38)			.325 .047 (38)	.289 .078 (38)
Nonpresent talk	.364 .025 (38)			.303 .064 (38)	
Teacher–child ratio	−.356 .012 (49)	−.271 .060 (49)	−.316 .027 (49)	−.408 .004 (49)	−.332 .020 (49)
Free-play child talk (age 4)					
Extending (function)	.249 .085 (49)				

Table A10.2. Relationships between children's conversational experiences and language and literacy in kindergarten (data from child audiotapes)

	Narrative Production	Formal Definitions	Story Comprehension	Emergent Literacy	Receptive Vocabulary
Large group conversational partners (age 3)					
Percentage teacher		.422 .003 (47)	.453 .002 (46)	.345 .019 (46)	
Large-group content of talk (age 3)					
Percentage cognitive extending		.370 .019 (40)		.296 .067 (39)	
Percentage didactic	.319 .045 (40)				
Free-play conversational partners (age 3)					
Percentage child	.267 .076 (45)			.313 .038 (44)	.355 .017 (45)
Free-play content of talk (age 3)					
Percentage pretend	.408 .010 (39)	.302 .062 (39)		.333 .041 (38)	.449 .004 (39)
Percentage Emergent Literacy talk				.357 .028 (38)	
Percentage no talk				−.312 .039 (44)	
Large-group conversational partners (age 4)					
Percentage no talk	−.379 .002 (64)				
Large group content of talk (age 4)					
Percentage cognitive extending				.304 .020 (58)	
Percentage literacy talk				.257 .051 (58)	
Percentage nonpresent	.309 .018 (58)				.226 .018 (58)
Percentage didactic	.248 .060 (58)				
Free-play conversational partners (age 4)					
Percentage child	.258 .039 (64)			.232 .065 (64)	.232 .065 (64)

(continued)

Table A10.2 *(continued)*

	Narrative Production	Formal Definitions	Story Comprehension	Emergent Literacy	Receptive Vocabulary
Percentage teacher		−.217 .085 (64)			
Free-play content of talk (age 4)					
Percentage pretend	.267 .039 (64)				.226 .083 (60)
Large-group conversational partners (age 5)					
Percentage teacher	−.293 .019 (64)				
Large-group content of talk (age 5)					
Percentage literacy talk				.270 .041 (58)	
Free-play conversational partners (age 5)					
Percentage child		.252 .069 (53)			.248 .073 (53)
Percentage no talk				−.312 .039 (44)	
Free-play content of talk (age 5)					
Percentage pretend	.257 .078 (48)	.274 .060 (48)			
Percentage cognitive extending	.277 .057 (48)				
Percentage literacy talk					−.255 .080 (48)

Table A10.3. Patterns of teachers' vocabulary use across settings

	Total number of words	Total number of types	Number of rare words	Number of rare types
Age 3				
Free play (*n* = 44)	917.04	258.29	11.68	8.04
Large group (*n* = 44)	864.64	228.93	12.84	7.73
Book reading (*n* = 27)				
Teachers' words	455.19	158.26	6.56	4.41
Texts' words	409.41	150.15	13.22	8.22
Age 4				
Free play (*n* = 59)	1,021.58	287.15	13.88	9.15
Large group (*n* = 59)	1,028.44	269.45	14.94	7.89
Book reading (*n* = 57)				
Teachers' words	504.17	214.16	4.69	2.78
Texts' words	469.51	163.47	7.12	10.60

Table A10.4. Relationships between patterns of vocabulary use and children's language and literacy in kindergarten (data from teacher audiotapes)

	Narrative Production	Formal Definitions	Story Comprehension	Emergent Literacy	Receptive Vocabulary
Large-group teacher talk (age 3)					
Percentage of rare words				.329 .050 (36)	
Percentage of rare types				.369 .027 (36)	
Free-play teacher talk (age 3)					
Percentage of rare words				.328 .048 (37)	
Free-play child talk (age 3)					
Number of rare words		.486 .002 (37)	.320 .054 (37)	.523 .0009 (37)	
Number of rare types		.565 .003 (37)		.469 .003 (37)	.364 .027 (37)
Large-group teacher talk (age 4)					
Number of types			.247 .072 (54)		.341 .012 (54)
Number of rare words					.360 .008 (54)
Number of rare types			.238 .083 (54)		.283 .038 (54)
Percentage of rare types			.267 .051 (54)		.241 .079 (54)
Large-group child talk (age 4)					
Number of words	.274 .045 (54)			.287 .036 (54)	.232 .092 (54)
Number of types	.248 .070 (54)			.266 .052 (54)	.287 .036 (54) ·
Free-play teacher talk (age 4)					
Percentage of rare words		.242 .041 (71)		.279 .018 (71)	.224 .060 (52)
Free-play child talk (age 4)					
Number of rare words		.322 .020 (52)	.324 .019 (52)	.412 .002 (52)	
Number of rare types	.338 .014 (52)	.305 .005 (52)	.325 .019 (52)	.396 .004 (52)	.282 .043 (52)

(continued)

Table A10.4.   *(continued)*

	Narrative Production	Formal Definitions	Story Comprehension	Emergent Literacy	Receptive Vocabulary
Percentage of rare words			.312 .024 (52)		
Percentage of rare types		.234 .095 (52)	.342 .013 (52)	.278 .046 (52)	
Number of words	.362 .008 (52)	.301 .030 (52)		.378 .006 (52)	
Number of types	.358 .009 (52)	.282 .043 (52)		.362 .008 (52)	

CHAPTER 11—PUTTING THE PIECES TOGETHER: IMPACT OF PRESCHOOL ON CHILDREN'S LANGUAGE AND LITERACY DEVELOPMENT

Table A11.1.   Simple correlations between teachers' classroom language use when children were 4 years old and kindergarten assessments

	Narrative Production	Formal Definitions	Emergent Literacy	Receptive Vocabulary
Mealtimes and free-play rare-word use				
Percentage of rare words used by teachers during free play		.24* (72)	.28* (71)	.23* (72)
Percentage of rare words used by teachers during mealtime		.35** (71)		.26* (71)
Free-play strategies				
Ratio of teacher talk to child talk	.30** (75)	.25* (75)	.36** (75)	.39*** (75)
Percentage of free-play extending utterances	.25* (75)	.30** (75)	.29** (74)	.38*** (75)
Large-group teacher talk strategies				
Percentage of group focusing utterances	.39*** (75)	.20⁻ (75)	.39*** (74)	.20⁻ (71)
Percentage of teacher analysis of text during reading				.39** (62)
Percentage of teacher cognitive extending			.23* (74)	

⁻$p < .10$; *$p < .05$; **$p < .01$; ***$p < .001$.

Table A11.2. Relationships between selected effective instructional approaches and teachers' education, center characteristics, and child background factors

	Free-play % teacher rare words	Mealtime % teacher rare words	Free-play teacher–child talk[a] ratio	Free play teacher extend	Book reading text analysis	Writing area	Curriculum content	ECERS[b] language	Group focus
Teacher education	.27* (69)				.25* (70)			.39*** (72)	
% children "English adequate"			-.23** (70)		.34** (61)				-.23* (70)
Adult–child ratio			-.33** (63)						
Longer day			-.22⁻ (73)				-.23** (73)	-.34** (73)	
Family size	-.40*** (60)						-.21⁻ (82)		
Caucasian child	.31** (68)	.20⁻ (68)			.31** (70)	.21⁻ (72)	.21⁻ (72)	-.36** (72)	
Age 3 MLU[c] in toy play	.23* (66)						.24* (69)		
Mother's Education								-.23* (73)	
Family Income									

[a]Lower ratios of teacher–child talk were desirable; a negative correlation indicates that teachers spoke less relative to the amount they said to children.
[b]Early Childhood Environment Rating Scale (Harms & Clifford, 1980).
[c]MLU, mean length of utterance.

⁻p < .10; *p < .05; **p < .01; ***p < .001.

Table A11.3. Models predicting Narrative Production: Preschool environment composites, including controls

Model	Extended Teacher Discourse		Classroom Curriculum		Exposure to Rare Words		R^2
	β	$(SE\,β)$	β	$(SE\,β)$	β	$(SE\,β)$	
I	0.88*	(.33)					.23*
II			0.80**	(.29)			.24**
III					0.47	(.33)	.21*
IV	0.32	(.35)	0.58⁻	(.33)	0.39	(.32)	.29*

⁻$p < .10$; *$p < .05$; **$p < .01$.

Table A11.4. Models predicting Emergent Literacy: Preschool environment composites, including controls

Model	Extended Teacher Discourse		Classroom Curriculum		Exposure to Rare Words		R^2
	β	$(SE\,β)$	β	$(SE\,β)$	β	$(SE\,β)$	
I	1.70***	(.38)					.38***
II			0.84*	(.37)			.24**
III					1.07*	(.44)	.26**
IV	1.55***	(.41)	0.49	(.38)	0.80*	(.37)	.49***

*$p < .05$; **$p < .01$; ***$p < .001$.

Table A11.5. Models predicting Receptive Vocabulary: Preschool environment composites, including controls

Model	Extended Teacher Discourse		Classroom Curriculum		Exposure to Rare Words		R^2
	β	$(SE\,β)$	β	$(SE\,β)$	β	$(SE\,β)$	
I	7.03***	(1.46)					.41***
II			4.24**	(1.42)			.28**
III					3.81*	(1.73)	.27**
IV	5.16**	(1.62)	3.18*	(1.50)	2.84⁻	(1.48)	.49***

⁻$p < .10$; *$p < .05$; **$p < .01$; ***$p < .001$.

CHAPTER 12—PARENT INVOLVEMENT
AS A LINK BETWEEN HOME AND SCHOOL

Table A12.1. Sample means, standard deviations, and score ranges for parent involvement reports from mothers and teachers

Measure	n	Mean	Standard deviation	Range
Mother reports				
Frequency of contact with teacher (preschool)	66	7.94	8.66	0.25–20
Frequency of contact with teacher (kindergarten)	67	6.41	8.11	0.25–20
Level of responsibility (preschool)	69	3.06	2.46	1–14
Level of responsibility (kindergarten)	68	2.00	1.46	0–6
Home support for literacy at age 4	75	12.63	2.56	6–17
Teacher reports				
Frequency of contact with parents (preschool)	69	1.72	0.92	0–3
Frequency of contact with parents (kindergarten)	52	3.27	1.61	1–5
Kindergarten teacher assessment of child being read to at home	44	1.48	0.55	0–2
Kindergarten teacher assessment of parent support for children's learning	46	9.52	2.23	3–12

Table A12.2. Correlations between mothers' and teachers' reports of parent involvement

	Mother variables					Teacher variables			
	1	2	3	4	5	6	7	8	9
Mother variables									
1. Frequency of contact with teacher (preschool)	1.0								
2. Frequency of contact with teacher (kindergarten)	.43 .0005 (60)	1.0							
3. Level of responsibility (preschool)	.08 .5170 (66)	-.02 .8965 (62)	1.0						
4. Level of responsibility (kindergarten)	.21 .1042 (61)	.26 .0314 (67)	.39 .0014 (63)	1.0					
5. Home support for literacy (age 4)	.31 .0131 (65)	.19 .1268 (67)	.15 .2256 (68)	.37 .0019 (68)	1.0				
Teacher variables									
6. Frequency of contact with parent (preschool)	.52 .0001 (56)	.35 .0097 (54)	.02 .8560 (58)	.16 .2438 (55)	.24 .0609 (62)	1.0			
7. Frequency of contact with parent (kindergarten)	.03 .8434 (46)	.26 .0937 (44)	.07 .6425 (47)	.38 .0103 (45)	.09 .5529 (50)	.29 .0518 (47)	1.0		
8. Kindergarten teacher assessment of child being read to at home	.11 .5180 (40)	.48 .0030 (36)	.04 .8066 (40)	.14 .3992 (37)	.38 .0130 (42)	.29 .0725 (40)	.30 .0507 (44)	1.0	
9. Kindergarten teacher assessment of parent support for children's learning	.18 .2545 (41)	.29 .0745 (40)	.03 .8335 (41)	.32 .0426 (40)	.45 .0018 (45)	.43 .0043 (47)	.33 .0243 (46)	.57 .0001 (41)	1.0

Table A12.3. Bivariate correlations between mothers' and teachers' reports of parent involvement and children's kindergarten language and literacy outcomes

	Narrative Production	Emergent Literacy	Receptive Vocabulary
Mother reports			
Frequency of contact with teacher (preschool)	.19 .1319 (65)	.07 .5753 (65)	.12 .3614 (65)
Frequency of contact with teacher (kindergarten)	.12 .3487 (67)	.14 .2729 (67)	.30 .0125 (67)
Level of responsibility (preschool)	−.16 .1998 (67)	−.03 .7721 (67)	−.04 .7284 (67)
Level of responsibility (kindergarten)	.31 .0114 (68)	.11 .3774 (68)	.24 .0481 (68)
Home support for literacy at age 4	.29 .0122 (74)	.22 .0639 (74)	.36 .0016 (74)
Teacher reports			
Frequency of contact with parents (preschool)	.16 .2174 (62)	.11 .4202 (61)	.17 .1810 (62)
Frequency of contact with parents (kindergarten)	.25 .0760 (51)	−.02 .8852 (50)	.06 .6591 (51)
Kindergarten teacher assessment of *child being read to at home*	.36 .0177 (43)	.32 .0364 (42)	.49 .0009 (43)
Kindergarten teacher assessment of *parent support for children's learning*	.41 .0045 (46)	.32 .0296 (45)	.30 .0415 (46)

CHAPTER 13—HOMES AND SCHOOLS TOGETHER: SUPPORTING LANGUAGE AND LITERACY DEVELOPMENT

Table A13.1.   Descriptive statistics for the fourth- and seventh-grade Receptive Vocabulary and Reading Comprehension

	n	Mean	Standard deviation	Range	Interquartile range
Fourth-grade PPVT–R[a] Receptive Vocabulary (norming mean = 100)	56	101.33	15.90	66–142	91–112
Seventh-grade PPVT–R Receptive Vocabulary (norming mean = 100)	51	102.71	15.94	66–141	91–113
Fourth-grade CAT[b] Reading Comprehension (norming mean = 50)	54	47.39	24.41	2–97	25–66
Seventh-grade CAT Reading Comprehension (norming mean = 50)	51	51.82	25.45	2–98	33–73

[a]Peabody Picture Vocabulary Test–Revised (Dunn & Dunn, 1981).
[b]California Achievement Tests (CTB Macmillan/McGraw-Hill, 1992).

Table A13.2. Final models predicting Narrative Production, Emergent Literacy, and Receptive Vocabulary

	Home environment composites			Preschool environment composites			
Model	Extended Discourse β (SE β)	Rare Word Density β (SE β)	Home Support for Literacy β (SE β)	Extended Teacher Discourse β (SE β)	Classroom Curriculum β (SE β)	Exposure to Rare Words β (SE β)	R^2
Narrative Production	0.009 (.007)	−0.01 (.01)	0.06 (.09)	0.29 (.38)	0.52 (.34)	0.38 (.33)	.33*
Emergent Literacy	0.30 (.007)	0.02 (.02)	0.11 (.11)	1.29** (.44)	0.38 (.39)	0.65~ (.39)	.52***
Receptive Vocabulary	0.007 (.03)	0.13* (.06)	0.71~ (.40)	3.58* (1.67)	2.42 (1.49)	1.83 (1.47)	.56***

~$p < .10$; *$p < .05$; **$p < .01$; ***$p < .001$.

References

Abbott-Shim, M., & Lambert, R. (1997, December). *ASBI teacher rating of comply factor.* Paper presented at the quarterly meeting of the Head Start Research Consortium Steering Committee, Washington, DC.

The American Heritage Dictionary (2nd college ed.). (1982). Boston: Houghton Mifflin.

Anderson, R.C., & Freebody, P. (1981). Vocabulary knowledge. In J.T. Guthrie (Ed.), *Comprehension and teaching: Research reviews* (pp. 77–116). Newark, DE: International Reading Association.

Arnold, D.S., & Whitehurst, G.J. (1994). Accelerating language development through picture book reading: A summary of dialogic reading and its effects. In D.K. Dickinson (Ed.), *Bridges to literacy: Children, families, and schools* (pp. 103–128). Cambridge, MA: Blackwell Publishers.

Barnett, W.S. (1995). Long-term effects of early childhood programs on cognitive and school outcomes. *The Future of Children, 5*(3), 25–50.

Barnett, W.S. (2001). Preschool education for economically disadvantaged children: Effects on reading achievement and related outcomes. In S.B. Neuman & D.K. Dickinson (Eds.), *Handbook of early literacy research.* New York: Guilford Press.

Barrington, B.L., & Hendricks, B. (1989). Differentiating characteristics of high school graduates, dropouts, and nongraduates. *Journal of Educational Research, 82*(6), 309–319.

Beals, D.E. (1993). Explanations in low-income families' mealtime conversations. *Applied Psycholinguistics, 14*(4), 489–513.

Beals, D.E., & DeTemple, J.M. (1993). Home contributions to early language and literacy development. In D. Leu & C. Kinzer (Eds.), *Forty-second yearbook of the National Reading Conference* (pp. 207–215). Chicago: National Reading Conference.

Beals, D.E., & Snow, C.E. (1994). "Thunder is when the angels are upstairs bowling": Narratives and explanations at the dinner table. *Journal of Narrative and Life History, 4*(4), 331–352.

Bennett, G. (1995, October). Nights 'round the table. *Sesame Street Parents,* 40–45.

Blum-Kulka, S. (1993). "You gotta know how to tell a story": Telling, tales and tellers in American and Israeli narrative events at dinner. *Language in Society, 22*, 361–402.

Blum-Kulka, S., & Snow, C.E. (1992). Developing autonomy for tellers, tales, and telling in family narrative events. *Journal of Narrative and Life History, 2*, 187–217.

Bornstein, M.H., Haynes, O.M., O'Reilly, A.W., & Painter, K.M. (1996). Solitary and collaborative pretend play in early childhood: Sources of individual variation in the development of representational competence. *Child Development, 67*, 2910–2929.

Bowman, B., Donovan, M.S., & Burns, M.S. (Eds.). (2000). *Eager to learn: Educating our preschoolers.* Washington, DC: National Academy Press.

Brainerd, C.J. (1978). *Piaget's theory of intelligence.* Upper Saddle River, NJ: Prentice-Hall.

Bredekamp, S. (Ed.). (1987). *Developmentally appropriate practice in early childhood programs serving children from birth through age 8* (Expanded ed.). Washington, DC: National Association for the Education of Young Children.

Brizius, J.A., & Foster, S.A. (1993). *Generation to generation: Realizing the promise of family literacy.* Ypsilanti, MI: High/Scope.

Brobst, K., Boehm, A., Flecken, E., Gordon, N., Schlichting, K., & Wagenberg, L. (1993). *The relationship between book genre and parent questions during parent/child storybook reading.* Poster presented at the second annual National Head Start Conference, Washington, DC.

Bryant, D.M., Clifford, R.M., & Peisner, E.S. (1991). Best practice for beginners: Developmental appropriateness in kindergarten. *American Educational Research Journal, 28,* 783–803.

Bryant, D.M., Lau, L.B., Burchinal, M., & Sparling, J.J. (1994). Family and child correlates of Head Start children's developmental outcomes. *Early Childhood Research Quarterly, 9,* 289–309.

Bus, A., van IJzendoorn, M.H., & Pellegrini, A.D. (1995). Joint book reading makes for success in learning to read: A meta-analysis on intergenerational transmission of literacy. *Review of Educational Research, 65,* 1–21.

Carey, S. (1978). The child as a word learner. In M. Halle, J. Bresnan, & G.A. Miller (Eds.), *Linguistic theory and psychological reality* (pp. 264–293). Cambridge, MA: MIT Press.

Carey, S. (1982). Semantic development: The state of the art. In E. Wanner & L.R. Gleitman (Eds.), *Language acquisition: The state of the art* (pp. 347–389). Cambridge, England: Cambridge University Press.

Carey, S., & Bartlett, E. (1978). Acquiring a single new word. *Papers and Reports in Child Language Development, 15,* 17–29.

Carle, E. (1979). *The very hungry caterpillar.* New York: Philomel Books.

Cazden, C.B. (1988). *Classroom discourse: The language of teaching and learning.* Portsmouth, NH: Heinemann.

Chall, J.S., & Dale, E. (1995). *Readability revisited: The new Dale-Chall readability formula.* Cambridge, MA: Brookline Books.

Coleman, J.S., Campbell, E., Hobson, C., McPartland, J., Mood, A., Weinfeld, F., & York, R. (1966). *Equality of educational opportunity.* Washington, DC: U.S. Office of Education, National Center for Educational Statistics.

Comer, J.P. (1984). Home–school relationships as they affect the academic success of children. *Education and Urban Society, 16*(3), 323–337.

Cote, L.R. (1993, November). *Mealtimes in Head Start classrooms.* Poster presented at the second National Head Start Research Conference, Washington, DC.

Cote, L.R. (1995, April). *Mealtime in Head Start classrooms as an opportunity for literacy development.* Poster presented at the 22nd National Head Start Association Annual Training Conference, Washington, DC.

Cote, L.R. (1997). Mealtime in Head Start classrooms as an opportunity for literacy development. *National Head Start Association Research Quarterly, 1,* 149–155.

CTB Macmillan/McGraw-Hill. (1992). *California Achievement Tests* (CAT, 5th ed.). Monterey, CA: Macmillan/McGraw-Hill.

Cunningham, A.E., & Stanovich, K.E. (1997). Early reading acquisition and its relation to reading experience and ability 10 years later. *Developmental Psychology, 33*(6), 934–945.

DeTemple, J.M. (1999, April). *Home and school predictors of sixth grade vocabulary and reading skills of children from low-income homes.* Poster presented at the biennial meetings of the Society for Research in Child Development, Albuquerque, NM.

DeTemple, J.M., & Tabors, P.O. (2000). *Predicting maternal–child literacy functioning at early school age: Findings from an observational study of welfare mothers and their children.* Unpublished manuscript.

Delgado-Gaitan, C. (1991). Involving parents in the schools: A process of empowerment. *American Journal of Education, 100*(1), 20–46.

Densmore, A., Dickinson, D.K., & Smith, M.W. (1995, April). *The socioemotional content of teacher–child interaction in preschool settings serving low-income children.* Paper presented at the annual conference of the American Educational Research Association, San Francisco.

Dickinson, D.K. (1984). First impressions: Children's knowledge of words gained from a single exposure. *Applied Psycholinguistics, 5,* 359–373.

Dickinson, D.K. (1989). Effects of a shared reading program on a Head Start language and literacy environment. In J. Allen & J.M. Mason (Eds.), *Risk makers, risk takers, risk breakers: Reducing the risks for young literacy learners* (pp. 125–153). Portsmouth, NH: Heinemann Educational Books.

Dickinson, D.K., Cote, L.R., & Smith, M.W. (1993). Learning vocabulary in preschool: Social and discourse contexts affecting vocabulary growth. In C. Daiute (Ed.), *New directions for child development series: Vol. 61. The development of literacy through social interaction* (pp. 67–78). San Francisco: Jossey-Bass.

Dickinson, D.K., & DeTemple, J.M. (1998). Putting parents in the picture: Maternal reports of preschoolers' literacy as a predictor of early reading. *Early Childhood Research Quarterly, 13*(2), 241–261.

Dickinson, D.K., Hao, W., & He, Z. (1995). Pedagogical and classroom factors related to how teachers read to three- and four-year old children. In K.A. Hinchman, D.J. Leu, & C.K. Kinzer (Eds.), *NRC Yearbook* (pp. 212–221). Chicago: The National Reading Conference.

Dickinson, D.K., & Keebler, R. (1989). Variation in preschool teachers' styles of reading books. *Discourse Processes, 12,* 353–375.

Dickinson, D.K., Rafal, C.T., & Merianos, L. (1998, April). *The structure of teacher–child verbal interaction in preschool classrooms: Results from the Teacher-Child Verbal Interaction Profile.* Paper presented at the annual meeting of the American Educational Research Association, San Diego.

Dickinson, D.K., & Smith, M. (1991). *Descriptive coding system for verbal interactions.* Unpublished manuscript.

Dickinson, D.K., & Smith, M.W. (1994). Long-term effects of preschool teachers' book readings on low-income children's vocabulary and story comprehension. *Reading Research Quarterly, 29*(2), 104–122.

Dickinson, D.K., & Snow, C.E. (1987). Interrelationships among prereading and oral language skills in kindergartners from two social classes. *Early Childhood Research Quarterly, 2,* 1–25.

Dickinson, D.K., & Sprague, K. (2001). The nature and impact of early childhood care environments on the language and early literacy development of children from low-income families. In S.B. Neuman & D.K. Dickinson (Eds.), *Handbook of early literacy research.* New York: Guilford Press.

Dollaghan, C. (1985). Child meets word: Fast mapping in preschool children. *Journal of Speech and Hearing Research, 28,* 449–454.

Drummond, M.J. (1995). *In school at four: Hampshire's earlier admissions programme.* Hampshire County Council Education Department.

Dunn, J., & Wooding, C. (1977). Play in the home and its implications for learning. In B. Tizard & D.R. Harvey (Eds.), *The biology of play* (pp. 45–58). Philadelphia: J.B. Lippincott.

Dunn, L. (1993). Proximal and distal features of day care quality and children's development. *Early Childhood Research Quarterly, 8,* 167–192.

Dunn, L.M., & Dunn, L.M. (1981). *Peabody Picture Vocabulary Test–Revised (PPVT–R).* Circle Pines, MN: American Guidance Service.

Dunn, L.M., & Dunn, L.M. (1997). *Peabody Picture Vocabulary Test–Third Edition (PPVT–III).* Circle Pines, MN: American Guidance Service.

Edwards, P.A., Pleasants, H.M., & Franklin, S.H. (1999). *A path to follow: Learning to listen to parents.* Portsmouth, NH: Heinemann.

El'konin, D. (1966). Symbolics and its function in the play of children. *Soviet Education, 8,* 35–41.

Elley, W.B. (1989). Vocabulary acquisition from listening to stories. *Reading Research Quarterly, 24,* 174–187.

Epstein, J.L. (1983). Longitudinal effects of person–family–school interactions on student outcomes. In A.C. Kerckhoff (Ed.), *Research in sociology of education and socialization* (Vol. 4, pp. 101–127). Stamford, CT: JAI Press.

Epstein, J.L. (1986). Parents' reactions to teacher practices of parent involvement. *Elementary School Journal, 86*(3), 277–294.

Fein, G., & Fryer, M. (1995). Maternal contributions to early symbolic play. *Developmental Review, 15*(4), 367–381.

Feitelson, D., Goldstein, Z., Iraqi, J., & Share, D.L. (1993). Effects of listening to story reading on aspects of literacy acquisition in a diglossic situation. *Reading Research Quarterly, 28,* 70–79.

Feitelson, D., Kita, B., & Goldstein, Z. (1986). Effects of listening to series stories on first graders' comprehension and use of language. *Research in the Teaching of English, 20,* 339–356.

Fiese, B. (1990). Playful relationships: A contextual analysis of mother–toddler interaction and symbolic play. *Child Development, 61*(5), 1648–1656.

Frede, E.C. (1995). The role of program quality in producing early childhood benefits. *Future of Children, 5*(3), 115–132.

Galda, L., Pellegrini, A., & Cox, S. (1989). A short-term longitudinal study of preschoolers' emergent literacy. *Research in the Teaching of English, 23,* 292–309.

Gallimore, R., & Goldenberg, C. (1991). Activity settings of early literacy development: Home and school factors in children's emergent literacy. In E. Forman, N. Minick, & C.A. Stone (Eds.), *Education and mind: The integration of institutional, social and developmental processes.* Oxford, England: Oxford University Press.

Gallimore, R., Goldenberg, C.N., & Weisner, T.S. (1993). The social construction and subjective reality of activity settings: Implications for community psychology. *American Journal of Community Psychology, 21*(4), 537–559.

Garvey, C. (1990). *Play.* Cambridge, MA: Harvard University Press.

Garvey, C. (1993). Commentary. *Human Development, 36*(4), 235–240.

Göncü, A. (Ed.). (1999). *Children's engagement in the world: Sociocultural perspectives.* New York: Cambridge University Press.

Gruber, H.E., & Voneche, J.J. (1977). *The essential Piaget.* New York: Basic Books.

Haight, W.L., & Miller, P.J. (1993). *Pretending at home: Early development in a sociocultural context.* Albany: State University of New York Press.

Harms, T., & Clifford, R.M. (1980). *Early Childhood Environment Rating Scale (ECERS)*. New York: Teachers College Press.

Hart, B., & Risley, T.R. (1995). *Meaningful differences in the everyday experience of young American children*. Baltimore: Paul H. Brookes Publishing Co.

Head Start Amendments of 1998, PL 105-285, 42 U.S.C. §§ 9831 *et seq.*

Heath, S.B. (1983). *Ways with words: Language, life, and work in communities and classrooms*. New York: Cambridge University Press.

Heaviside, S., & Farris, E. (1993, September). *Public school kindergarten teachers' views on children's readiness for school* (U.S. Department of Education, Office of Educational Research and Improvement, Statistical Analysis Rep. No. NCES-93-410). Washington, DC: Fast Response Survey System (FRSS). (ERIC No. ED 364 332)

Henderson, A.T. (Ed.). (1987). *The evidence continues to grow: Parent involvement improves student achievement*. Columbia, MD: National Committee for Citizens in Education (NCCE).

Hoffman, M. (1984). *Animals in the wild: Elephant*. New York: Random House. (Original work published 1945)

Howes, C., & Smith, E.W. (1995). Relations among child care quality, teacher behavior, children's play activities, emotional security, and cognitive activity in child care. *Early Childhood Research Quarterly, 10*, 381–404.

International Reading Association and the National Association for the Education of Young Children. (1998, July). Learning to read and write: Developmentally appropriate practices for young children. A joint position statement of the International Reading Association (IRA) and the National Association for the Education of Young Children (NAEYC). *Young Children, 53*(4), 30–46.

Jastak, S., & Wilkinson, G.S. (1984). *Wide Range Achievement Test–Revised* (WRAT–R). Wilmington, DE: Jastak Associates.

Jencks, C., Smith, M., Acland, H., Bane, M.J., Cohen, D., Gintis, H., Heyns, B., & Michelson, S. (1972). *Inequality: A reassessment of family and schooling in America*. New York: Basic Books.

Jordan, G., Snow, C.E., & Porche, M.V. (2000). Project EASE: The effect of a family literacy project on kindergarten students' early literacy skills. *Reading Research Quarterly, 35*(4), 524–546.

Kane, S.R., & Furth, H.G. (1993). Children constructing social reality: A frame analysis of social pretend. *Human Development, 36*(4), 199–214.

Karweit, N. (1994). The effect of story reading on the language development of disadvantaged prekindergarten and kindergarten students. In D.K. Dickinson (Ed.), *Bridges to literacy: Children, families, and schools* (pp. 43–65). Cambridge, MA: Blackwell Publishers.

Katz, L.G., & Chard, S.C. (1989). *Engaging children's minds: The project approach*. Stamford, CT: Ablex.

Kaufman, A.S. (1983). *Kaufman Assessment Battery for Children (K-ABC)*. Circle Pines, MN: American Guidance Service.

Kavanaugh, R.D., Whittington, S., & Cerbone, M.J. (1983). Mothers' use of fantasy in speech to young children. *Journal of Child Language, 10*(1), 45–55.

Keats, E.J. (1962). *The snowy day*. New York: Viking Press.

Kontos, S.J. (1991). Child care quality, family background, and children's development. *Early Childhood Research Quarterly, 6*, 249–262.

Kontos, S., & Wilcox-Herzog, A. (1997). Influences on children's competence in early childhood classrooms. *Early Childhood Research Quarterly, 12*, 247–262.

Kracke, K. (1993). *Head Start parent involvement: Vision, opportunities, and strategies* (Report prepared for the Parent Involvement Institute). Washington, DC: U.S. Department of Education. (ERIC Document Reproduction Service No. ED 369 543)

Layzer, J.I., Goodson, B.D., & Moss, M. (1993). *Life in preschool: Vol. 1. Final report to the U.S. Department of Education.* Cambridge, MA: Abt Associates.

Lightfoot, S.L. (1978). *Worlds apart: Relationships between families and schools.* New York: Basic Books.

Linder, T.W. *Read, play, and learn! Storybook activities for young children* (Collections 1 and 2 and Teacher's Guide). Baltimore: Paul H. Brookes Publishing Co.

Lionni, L. (1987). *Nicolas, where have you been?* New York: Alfred A. Knopf.

Lloyd, D.N. (1978). Prediction of school failure from third-grade data. *Educational and Psychological Measurement, 38*(4), 1193–1200.

Lombard, A.D. (1994). *Success begins at home.* Guilford, CT: Dushkin/McGraw-Hill.

MacWhinney, B. (2000). *The CHILDES Project: Tools for analyzing talk* (3rd ed., Vols. 1 & 2). Mahwah, NJ: Lawrence Erlbaum Associates.

Madison, S., & Speaker, R. (1994, April). *The construction of literacy environments in early childhood classrooms: A spectrum of approaches.* Paper presented at the annual meeting of the American Educational Research Association, New Orleans. (ERIC Document Reproduction Service No. ED 376 970)

Martin, B., Jr. (1983). *Brown bear, brown bear, what do you see?* (E. Carle, Illus.). Austin, TX: Holt, Rinehart & Winston. (Original work published 1967).

Mason, J., & Stewart, J. (1989). *Early Childhood Diagnostic Instrument: The Comprehensive Assessment Program.* Iowa City: American Testronics.

McCartney, K. (1984). Effect of quality of day care environment on children's language development. *Developmental Psychology, 20,* 244–260.

McCartney, K., Scarr, S., Phillips, D., & Grajek, S. (1985). Day care as intervention: Comparisons of varying quality programs. *Journal of Applied Developmental Psychology, 6,* 247–260.

McCloskey, R. (1941). *Make way for ducklings.* New York: Viking Press.

McGill-Franzen, A. (1993). *Shaping the preschool agenda: Early literacy, public policy, and professional beliefs.* Albany: State University of New York Press.

McLoyd, V. (1983) The effects of the structure of play objects on the pretend play of low-income preschool children. *Child Development, 54*(3), 626–635.

Miller, P.J. (1982). *Amy, Wendy and Beth: Learning language in South Baltimore.* Austin, TX: University of Texas Press.

Murphy, J. (1983). *What next, Baby Bear!* New York: Dial Books for Young Readers.

Needleman, R., & Zuckerman, B. (1992, February). Fight illiteracy: Prescribe a book! *Contemporary Pediatrics,* 41–60.

Neuman, S.B. (1996). Children engaging in storybook reading: The influence of access to print resources, opportunity, and parental interaction. *Early Childhood Research Quarterly, 11,* 495–513.

Neuman, S.B. (1999). Books make a difference: A study of access to literacy. *Reading Research Quarterly, 34*(3), 286–311.

Neuman, S.B., & Roskos, K. (1993a). Access to print for children of poverty: Differential effects of adult mediation and literacy-enriched play settings on environmental and functional print tasks. *American Educational Research Journal, 30,* 95–122.

Neuman, S.B., & Roskos, K.A. (1993b). *Language and literacy learning in the early years: An integrated approach.* Orlando, FL: Harcourt Brace & Co.

Neuman, S.B., & Roskos, K. (1997). Literacy knowledge in practice: Contexts of participation for young writers and readers. *Reading Research Quarterly, 32*(1), 10–32.

Nord, C.W., Lennon, J., Liu, B., & Chandler, K. (1999, November). *Home literacy activities and signs of children's emerging literacy, 1993 and 1999* [On-line]. Washington, DC: U.S. Department of Education, Office of Educational Research and Improvement, National Center for Education Statistics. Available: http://nces.ed.gov/pubs2000/2000026.pdf

O'Connell, B., & Bretherton, I. (1984). Toddler's play alone and with mother: The role of maternal guidance. In I. Bretherton (Ed.), *Symbolic play: The development of social understanding* (pp. 337–368). San Diego: Academic Press.

Pajares, M.F. (1992). Teachers' beliefs and educational research: Cleaning up a messy construct. *Review of Educational Research, 62,* 307–332.

Pellegrini, A.D., & Galda, L. (1993). Ten years after: A reexamination of symbolic play and literacy research. *Reading Research Quarterly, 28,* 162–177.

Pellegrini, A.D., Galda, L., Dresden, J., & Cox, S. (1991). A longitudinal study of the predictive relations among symbolic play, linguistic verbs, and early literacy. *Research in the Teaching of English, 25,* 219–235.

Pellegrini, A.D., Perlmutter, J., Galda, L., & Brody, G. (1990). Joint reading between black Head Start children and their mothers. *Child Development, 61,* 443–453.

Peterson, C., & McCabe, A. (1983). *Developmental psycholinguistics: Three ways of looking at a child's narrative.* New York: Plenum Press.

Phillips, G., & McNaughton, S. (1990). The practice of storybook reading to preschool children in mainstream New Zealand families. *Reading Research Quarterly, 25*(3), 196–212.

Piaget, J. (1926). *The language and thought of the child.* Orlando, FL: Harcourt Brace & Co.

Piaget, J. (1962). *Play, dreams, and imitation in childhood.* New York: W.W. Norton. (Original work published 1945)

Powell, D.R. (1978). Correlates of parent–teacher communication frequency and diversity. *Journal of Educational Research, 71*(6), 333–341.

Purcell-Gates, V. (1988). Lexical and syntactic knowledge of written narrative held by well-read-to kindergartners and second graders. *Research in the Teaching of English, 22,* 128–160.

Reynolds, A.J. (1992). Comparing measures of parent involvement and their effects on academic achievement. *Early Childhood Research Quarterly, 7*(3), 441–462.

Rice, M. (1990). Preschoolers' QUIL: Quick Incidental Learning of words. In G. Conti-Ramsden & C.E. Snow (Eds.), *Children's language* (Vol. 7, pp. 171–195). Mahwah, NJ: Lawrence Erlbaum Associates.

Roskos, K. & Neuman, S.B. (2001). In S.B. Neuman & D.K. Dickinson (Eds.), *Handbook of early literacy research.* New York: Guilford Press.

Rowe, D.W. (1998). The literate potentials of book-related dramatic play. *Reading Research Quarterly, 33*(1), 10–35.

Scarborough, H.S., & Dobrich, W. (1994). On the efficacy of reading to preschoolers. *Developmental Review, 14,* 245–302.

Schickedanz, J.A., Pergantis, M.L., Kanosky, J., Blaney, A., & Ottinger, J. (1997). *Curriculum in early childhood: A resource guide for preschool and kindergarten teachers.* Needham Heights, MA: Allyn & Bacon.

Shimron, J. (1994). The making of readers: The work of Professor Dina Feitelson. In D.K. Dickinson (Ed.), *Bridges to literacy: Children, families, and schools* (pp. 80–99). Cambridge, MA: Blackwell Publishers.

Shonkoff, J.P., & Phillips, D.A. (Eds.). (2000). *From neurons to neighborhoods: The science of early childhood development*. Washington, DC: National Academy Press.

Slade, A. (1987a). A longitudinal study of maternal involvement and symbolic play during the toddler period. *Child Development, 58*(2), 367–375.

Slade, A. (1987b). Quality of attachment and early symbolic play. *Developmental Psychology, 23*(1), 78–85.

Smitherman, G. (1977). *Talkin' and testifyin': The language of Black America*. Boston: Houghton Mifflin.

Snow, C.E., Barnes, W., Chandler, J., Goodman, I., & Hemphill, L. (1991). *Unfulfilled expectations: Home and school influences on literacy*. Cambridge, MA: Harvard University Press.

Snow, C.E., Burns, M.S., & Griffin, P. (Eds.). (1998). *Preventing reading difficulties in young children*. Washington, DC: National Academy Press.

Snow, C., Cancino, H., Gonzalez, P., & Shriberg, E. (1989). Giving formal definitions. An oral language correlate of school literacy. In D. Bloome (Ed.), *Classrooms and literacy* (pp. 233–249). Stamford, CT: Ablex.

Snow, C.E., & Goldfield, B. (1983). Turn the page please: Situation-specific language acquisition. *Journal of Child Language, 10*, 551–569.

Snow, C.E., & Kurland, B.F. (1996). Sticking to the point: Talk about magnets as a context for engaging in scientific discourse. In D. Hicks (Ed.), *Discourse, learning, and schooling* (pp. 189–221). New York: Cambridge University Press.

Snow, C.E., Tabors, P.O., Nicholson, P.A., & Kurland, B.F. (1995). SHELL: Oral language and early literacy skills in kindergarten and first-grade children. *Journal of Research in Childhood Education, 10*(1), 37–48.

Stevenson, D.L., & Baker, D.P. (1987). The family–school relation and the child's school performance. *Child Development, 58*(5), 1348–1357.

Systat, Inc. (1990). SYSTAT: Statistics [Computer software]. Evanston, IL: Author.

Tamis-LeMonda, C., & Bornstein, M. (1994). Specificity in mother–toddler language play relations across the second year. *Developmental Psychology, 30*(2), 283–292.

Teale, W.H. (1984). Reading to young children: Its significance for literacy development. In H. Goelman, A.A. Oberg, & F. Smith (Eds.), *Awakening to literacy: The University of Victoria Symposium on Children's Response to a Literate Environment: Literacy before schooling* (pp. 110–122). Exeter, NH: Heinemann Educational Books.

Teale, W.H., & Sulzby, E. (1986). Introduction: Emergent literacy as a perspective for examining how young children become writers and readers. In W.H. Teale & E. Sulzby (Eds.), *Emergent literacy: Writing and reading* (pp. vii–xxv). Stamford, CT: Ablex.

Thayer, J. (1964). *Quiet on account of dinosaur* (S. Fleishman, Illus.). New York: Morrow.

Tizard, B., & Hughes, M. (1985). *Young children learning*. Cambridge, MA: Harvard University Press.

U.S. Department of Health and Human Services and U. S. Department of Education. (1995). *The JOBS evaluation: How well are they faring? AFDC families with preschool-aged children in Atlanta at the outset of the JOBS evaluation*. Washington, DC: U.S. Department of Health and Human Services, Office of the Assistant Secretary for Planning and Evaluation.

Vernon-Feagans, L. (1996). *Children's talk in communities and classrooms.* Cambridge, MA: Blackwell Publishers.

Vygotsky, L. (1978). *Mind in society: The development of higher psychological processes.* Cambridge, MA: Harvard University Press.

Walker, D., Greenwood, C., Hart, B., & Carta, J. (1994). Prediction of school outcomes based on early language production and socioeconomic factors. *Child Development, 65,* 606–621.

Walsh, K. (1997, June 2). Be sure to write!: Avoid keg parties! *U.S. News & World Report, 122*(21), 35.

Wells, G. (1985). Preschool literacy-related activities and success in school. In D.R. Olson, N. Torrance, & A. Hildyard (Eds.), *Literacy, language and learning: The nature and consequences of reading and writing* (pp. 229–255). New York: Cambridge University Press.

Whitehurst, G.J., Arnold, D.H., Epstein, J.N., Angell, A.L., Smith, M., & Fischel, J.E. (1994). A picture book reading intervention in daycare and home for children from low-income families. *Developmental Psychology, 30,* 679–689.

Whitehurst, G.J., & Lonigan, C.J. (1998). Child development and emergent literacy. *Child Development, 69*(3), 848–872.

Wilcox-Herzog, A. (1999, April). *The nature of teacher talk in early childhood classrooms and its relationship to children's play with objects and peers.* Paper presented at the biennial meetings of the Society for Research in Child Development, Albuquerque, NM.

Wilcox-Herzog, A., & Kontos, S. (1998). The nature of teacher talk in early childhood classrooms and its relationship to children's play with objects and peers. *Journal of Genetic Psychology, 159*(1), 30–44.

ZERO TO THREE: National Center for Infants, Toddlers and Families. (2000, October 4). *What grown-ups understand about child development: A National Benchmark Survey* [On-line]. Available: http://zerotothree.org/2000poll.html

Zill, N., Collins, M., West, J., & Hausken, E.G. (1995). *Approaching kindergarten: A look at preschoolers in the United States.* Washington, DC: U.S. Department of Education, Office of Educational Research and Improvement, National Center for Education Statistics, National Household Education Survey.

Zill, N., Resnick, G., & McKey, R.H. (1999, April). *What children know and can do at the end of Head Start and what it tells us about the program's performance.* Paper presented at the annual meeting of the American Education Research Association, Albuquerque, NM.

Index